The Man from Clear Lake

The Man from Clear Lake

Earth Day Founder
Senator Gaylord Nelson

Bill Christofferson

THE UNIVERSITY OF WISCONSIN PRESS

The University of Wisconsin Press
1930 Monroe Street
Madison, Wisconsin 53711

www.wisc.edu/wisconsinpress/

3 Henrietta Street
London WC2E 8LU, England

1   3   5   4   2

Printed in the United States of America

Library of Congress Cataloging-in-Publication Data
Christofferson, Bill.
The man from Clear Lake: Earth Day founder
Senator Gaylord Nelson / Bill Christofferson.
p.   cm.
Includes bibliographical references and index.
ISBN 0-299-19640-2 (alk. paper)
1. Nelson, Gaylord, 1916- .
2. Legislators—United States—Biography.
3. United States. Congress. Senate—Biography.
4. Environmentalists—United States—Biography.
5. Conservationists—United States—Biography.
6. Earth Day—History.
7. Environmentalism—United States—History—20th century.
8. Environmental protection—United States—History—20th century.
9. United States—Environmental conditions.
10. Governors—Wisconsin—Biography.   I. Title.
E748.N43C47   2004
328.73′092—dc22   2003020570

Contents

Author's Note

This is a political biography. Its subject, Gaylord Nelson, has cooperated with me, but the words, conclusions, assertions, and any errors are mine. I am not an academic and make no claim that this is a scholarly work. Its style and its reliance largely on periodicals and personal interviews as sources reflect my own background in journalism and politics.

I am indebted to many people for their counsel and encouragement. My wife, Karin, was my first reader and a true believer in the project. Our daughter, Molly, did much of the tedious early work in assembling clippings and other source materials. Later, the *Capital Times*'s charitable arm, the Evjue Foundation, made it possible, through a grant to the Robert M. La Follette Institute of Public Affairs at the University of Wisconsin, to hire a research assistant. That assistant, Thomas Ryan, examined some one thousand cubic feet of Nelson's Senate papers, which were largely unprocessed and uncatalogued at the Wisconsin Historical Society. His keen interest in the subject matter and his ability to sift through the material and find useful and important nuggets of information were invaluable. The *Milwaukee Journal Sentinel* opened its library to me, which saved enormous amounts of time and eyestrain from searching microfilm. So many Nelson friends, former staff members, and cronies shared their time, ideas, and recollections with me that I am reluctant to single out any of them.

Thanks to John Nichols and Jeff Mayers, for thoughtful advice and further encouragement when my spirits flagged, and to Karin Borgh, Bud Jordahl, and Chuck Pruitt for reading and improving the manuscript. I owe a debt to the many people, over a decade, who asked me regularly about my progress. The late George Vukelich inquired without fail, whenever he saw me, "How's the book?" What he and the others really meant was, "Where's the book?"

Finally, my deepest thanks to Gaylord and Carrie Lee Nelson, for never doubting during the long process that I *was* really writing a book, and for opening their lives and their home to me.

The Man from Clear Lake

Prologue

22 April 1970

ON A REMARKABLE SPRING DAY in 1970, environmental activism entered the mainstream of American life and politics, stirring ripples worldwide.

It was Earth Day, and the American environmental movement was forever changed. Twenty million people—10 percent of the United States population—mobilized to show their support for a clean environment. They attended marches, rallies, concerts, and teach-ins. They planted trees and picked up tons of trash. They confronted polluters and held classes on environmental issues. They signed petitions and wrote letters to politicians. They gathered in parks, on city streets, in campus auditoriums, in small towns and major cities. The weather cooperated; in most of the country, it was a clear and sunny day. The news media also cooperated and covered the event extensively.

Fifth Avenue in New York City was closed to traffic for two hours, and a photo of tens of thousands of New Yorkers strolling and jamming the temporary pedestrian mall dominated the front page of the next day's *New York Times*. An estimated one hundred thousand people took part during the day in activities at Union Square, the center for speeches and teach-ins. Mayor John Lindsay set the tone in a brief speech, saying that environmental issues might sound complicated, but it all boiled down to a simple question: "Do we want to live or die?"[1]

In Chicago, the sun seemed pale and distant on Earth Day, and the city's monitoring devices showed levels of sulfur dioxide in the

3

atmosphere above the danger point for infants and the elderly. Several thousand people attended a rally at Civic Center Plaza, where Illinois Attorney General William Scott declared that he would sue the City of Milwaukee for dumping sewage into Lake Michigan. On the front page of the *Chicago Tribune,* side-by-side photos taken during and after the rally showed an amazing sight. When the demonstrators left, "there was no post-rally litter remaining to be cleaned up," the newspaper reported.[2]

In Washington, at the Washington Monument, a crowd of ten thousand gathered to hear folk music from Pete Seeger and Phil Ochs and speeches by Senator Edmund Muskie, muckraker I. F. Stone, Chicago Seven defendant Rennie Davis, and others. Earlier, seventeen hundred people had marched to the Interior Department offices to leave symbolic puddles of oil on the doorstep, and some Connecticut Girl Scouts in canoes had pulled tires and debris from the Potomac River.[3] In Philadelphia, twenty-five thousand people heard Muskie call for "an environmental revolution" and criticize government priorities that spent "twenty times as much on Vietnam as we are to fight water pollution, and twice as much on the supersonic transport as we are to fight air pollution."[4]

Congress had adjourned so its members could go home and give Earth Day speeches. For many, it was the first time they had given an environmental speech, and they drew heavily on material from the office of Senator Gaylord Nelson, the founder of Earth Day. At least twenty-two U.S. senators participated, as did governors and local officials across the nation. The governors of New York and New Jersey signed laws creating state environmental agencies. The Massachusetts legislature passed an environmental bill of rights. President Nixon, through an aide, said he had said enough about his concern about pollution and would be watching, rather than participating in Earth Day, and hoping it would lead to an ongoing antipollution campaign. Nixon had, in fact, in his State of the Union speech three months earlier, called for a national fight against air and water pollution.[5]

There were plenty of theatrics, dramatic gestures, and attention-getting stunts. So many students in Omaha, Nebraska, wore gas masks that the supply ran out. Indian sitar music greeted the dawn over Lake Mendota at the University of Wisconsin, accompanied by "an apology to God." In San Francisco, "Environmental Vigilantes" dumped oil into a reflecting pool at Standard Oil Company offices to protest oil spills. At Boston's Logan Airport, a group of young people was arrested for blocking a corridor to protest the development of a supersonic transport. A group in Denver gave the Atomic Energy Commission an award—"Environmental Rapist of the Year."

Old automobiles were pounded, demolished, disassembled, and buried. Schoolchildren and adults alike collected trash and litter from roadsides, parks, streams, and lakes. In Ohio, students put "This Is a Polluter" stickers on autos, and at Iowa State and Syracuse Universities, students blocked autos from coming onto the campus. In Tacoma, Washington, one hundred students rode down a freeway on horseback to protest auto emissions. In Cleveland, one thousand students filled garbage trucks with trash. In Appalachia, students buried a trash-filled casket. California students cut up their oil company credit cards. In Coral Gables, Florida, a demonstrator paraded with dead fish and a dead octopus in front of a power plant.

But the real focus was the schools. The National Education Association estimated that ten million public school children took part in Earth Day programs. Earth Day organizers said two thousand colleges and ten thousand grade and high schools participated.[6]

In Clear Lake, Wisconsin, Gaylord Nelson's hometown, junior and senior high school students observed Earth Day at a school assembly with speeches, songs, and skits, then cleaned up more than 250 bags full of litter from the streets and highways in and around the village. A photo of young "demonstrators" with picket signs ran on page one of the *Clear Lake Star* the next week.[7]

Many businesses put on their best faces and joined the call for a cleaner earth. In New York, Consolidated Edison supplied the rakes and shovels that schoolchildren used to clean up Union Square and provided an electrically powered bus to take Mayor Lindsay around the city. Scott Paper, Texas Gulf Sulphur, Sun Oil, Rex Chainbelt, and other companies used the occasion to announce projects to clean up or control pollution. Continental Oil introduced four new cleaner gasolines, Alcoa ran newspaper ads touting a new antipollution process at its plants, and Republic Steel sent twenty-five company executives to speak at high schools and colleges.[8]

The business participation drew a mixed reaction. Organizers said some companies spent more money on advertising their support of Earth Day than on Earth Day itself. General Electric stockholders meeting in Minneapolis were greeted outside by a protester dressed as the Grim Reaper and later at the meeting were confronted by a student leader demanding that the company refuse war contracts and instead use its influence to channel government expenditures into protecting the environment.[9]

The nation's news media were uncertain what to make of Earth Day. *Newsweek* was bemused and somewhat dismissive, calling Earth Day "a bizarre nationwide rain dance" and the nation's "biggest street festival since the Japanese surrendered in 1945." *Time* said the day "had aspects of a secular, almost pagan holiday." The question, *Newsweek* said, was "whether the whole uprising represented a giant step forward for contaminated Earthmen or just a springtime skipalong." The event lacked the passion of antiwar and civil rights movements, *Newsweek* said, and the issues were so unfocused as to give rise to "the kind of nearly unanimous blather usually reserved for the flag." *Time* said the real question was whether the movement was a fad or could sustain the interest and commitment it would take to bring about real change. "Was it all a passing fancy?" the *New York Times* asked in a morning-after editorial, then answered its own question: "We think not. Conservation is a cause . . . whose time has come because life is running out. Man must stop pollution and conserve his resources, not merely to enhance existence but to save the race from intolerable deterioration and possible extinction."[10]

Gaylord Nelson framed the question differently. In a four-day speaking tour that took him from New England to the Midwest to the West Coast, Nelson said: "This is not just an issue of survival. Mere survival is not enough. *How* we survive is the critical issue. . . . Our goal is not just an environment of clean air, and water, and scenic beauty—while forgetting about the Appalachias and the ghettoes where our citizens live in America's worst environment. . . . Our goal is an environment of decency, quality, and mutual respect for all other human creatures and all other living creatures—an environment without ugliness, without ghettoes, without discrimination, without hunger, poverty, or war. Our goal is a decent environment in the deepest and broadest sense."[11]

A tall order, bordering on utopian. But on this first Earth Day, anything seemed possible. Nelson, after years of talking quietly, persuasively, and persistently about the environment, had unleashed a whirlwind. *Time* wondered whether Nelson was "a bit too euphoric" when he said, in his Earth Day speech in Denver: "Earth Day may be a turning point in American history. It may be the birth date of a new American ethic that rejects the frontier philosophy that the continent was put here for our plunder, and accepts the idea that even urbanized, affluent, mobile societies are interdependent with the fragile, life-sustaining systems of the air, the water, the land."[12]

But his assessment was reasonably accurate. Others who looked at Earth Day in retrospect agreed that it was a watershed event. Philip Shabecoff, a longtime *New York Times* environmental reporter, called it "the day environmentalism in the United States began to emerge as a mass social movement." *American Heritage* magazine described Earth Day as "one of the most remarkable happenings in the history of democracy. . . . American politics and public policy would never be the same again." Denis Hayes, the national coordinator for Earth Day, later called it the largest organized demonstration in the history of the world.[13]

Nelson, the visionary behind Earth Day, had spent a decade searching for a catalyst to make the environment a prominent part of the nation's political agenda. As the leading environmentalist in the U.S. Senate, Nelson had given hundreds of speeches on the issue and visited twenty-five states during the 1960s. It was clear to him that there was widespread concern about environmental pollution. Rachel Carson's *Silent Spring*, Paul Ehrlich's *The Population Bomb*, and other important and critical writing about the environment had helped raise awareness. But issues closer to home were what energized people. Even environmental politics are local. Almost everyone had a cause, a personal connection, some special project or concern, a reason to care about the environment. It wasn't all about Lake Erie dying, or the Cuyahoga River catching fire, or the Santa Barbara oil spill, or other highly publicized examples of the growing threat to the environment. It was about the local landfill leaching into wells, or the city spraying DDT, or fish dying in the river, or a myriad of other local environmental problems that became apparent during the 1960s. Nelson heard it everywhere he went. What was needed, he decided, was something dramatic, "a nationwide demonstration of concern for the environment so large it would shake the political establishment out of its lethargy and finally force this issue permanently into the political arena."[14]

That was the genius of Earth Day—tapping the wellspring of environmental concern that was bubbling just below the surface of the national consciousness. When it happened, "[i]t was truly an astonishing grassroots explosion," Nelson said. "The people cared and Earth Day became the first opportunity they ever had to . . . send a big message to the politicians—a message to tell them to wake up and do something. It worked because of the spontaneous, enthusiastic reception at the grassroots. Nothing like it had ever happened before. While our organizing on college campuses was very well done, the thousands of events in our schools and communities were self-generated at the local level."[15]

That it was Nelson who had the inspiration should have been no surprise. He had spent his life "in a career that, like a planet hooked in orbit around its star, never strayed far from a central concern over resources and the quality of the environment."[16]

Where did Nelson get his lifelong interest and dedication to the environment, which in his view became more important than issues of war and peace? By osmosis, he would say, while growing up in Clear Lake, Wisconsin.[17] That is where his story begins.

1

The Nelsons of Clear Lake

Anonymity is the enemy of civility, and produces insensitivity and callousness. The nice thing about small towns is everybody has to be civil to each other. You can't live that close without being civil. Nobody in our hometown suppressed arguing something on the merits, but it was done in a civil fashion. I think there actually tends to be more independent thinking in small towns. It helps develop individuality to be in smaller communities.

Gaylord Nelson

GAYLORD NELSON WAS a small town boy his entire life.

He achieved more than he dared imagine possible. He became a friend and confidant of some of the nation's most powerful political leaders. He won recognition as the unquestioned national leader, eloquent spokesman, and major influence on the issue closest to his heart, the environment. He mobilized millions of people and launched a new wave of environmental activism. He traveled widely to give thousands of speeches in a half-century in public life. He received high honors and prestigious awards for his work and achievements. But none of it changed, disturbed, or unsettled his inner core. He was always the boy from Clear Lake, Wisconsin, off on an adventure.

On his one hundredth birthday, Ernie Goodspeed observed, "When I came to Clear Lake eighty years ago there was a whole lot of nothing up here and there still is."[1]

Gaylord Nelson could have said the same thing. His hometown, Clear Lake, is a village in northwestern Wisconsin, about fifty miles from Saint Paul, Minnesota. Polk County, in which Clear Lake is

9

located, is a sparsely populated rural county, separated from Minnesota on the west by the Saint Croix River and sprinkled with four hundred small lakes left by the glaciers. Three small lakes—Mud Lake on the east and Big Clear Lake and Little Clear Lake on the west—bordered the village.[2]

Polk County, named for President James Polk, was formed in 1853. Its 598,400 acres were acquired by treaty from the Chippewa Indians in 1837, the year after Wisconsin became a territory. Clear Lake is in the southeastern part of the county, an area known as the Lake Country. The deep, spring-fed lake for which it is named is about a half-mile from town and is home to crappies, sunfish, bass, and a few trout.

The first settlers, mostly Scandinavians and Germans, came in 1864, when the whole region was a dense forest. There were no roads, so the settlers had to carry flour and other provisions on their backs. No village existed until 1874, when the railroad came through what was called Black Brook Crossing, where a sawmill and store with a post office were erected. Later that year, Israel Graves set up a mill near a small lake, which he named Clear Lake. The village was organized in 1877. By 1882 there was a sawmill, a stave mill, three hotels, two churches, a three-room schoolhouse, Good Templar and Odd Fellows halls, six dry goods and grocery stores, a hardware store, a furniture store, two drug stores, a meat market, two millinery shops, one shoe shop, a local newspaper, and about fifty dwellings. Five years after its founding, the village population was about seven hundred.[3]

When Gaylord Anton Nelson was born on 4 June 1916, the village was much the same. The population was 689 in the 1920 census, almost the same as forty years earlier.[4] The biggest additions to the business district were a Ford dealership and two gas stations. A creamery, established in 1906, was the largest employer and the only year-round employer of any size.

It wasn't that the village's early years had been uneventful. Clear Lake had survived several major fires, a diphtheria epidemic, and a tornado before the end of the nineteenth century. The forest was gone, having been logged before the turn of the century, like much of northern Wisconsin, stripped of its vast acreage of pines and hardwoods. What was left—endless tracts of stumps, dead branches, brush, and slashings—often burned in huge fires. Polk County fared better than much of the "cutover," the huge area of the state that had been logged out. The giant logging companies, the worst practitioners of clear-cutting, did not operate in Polk County. Smaller local mills did most of the logging, so few areas were totally cutover. The forest was largely pine, but with large stands of sugar maple, mixed with other hardwoods and some softwoods. When the county was settled, "the timber grew so tall and close together that the sun scarcely shone through, and it was dark as twilight even at noon time," recalled William Phillips, who was born in Clear Lake in 1881.[5]

Logging camps operated all winter, when it was easier to skid the logs. Oxen and horse teams hauled huge pine logs, railroad ties, and bridge pilings to Clear Lake for shipment on the railroad. When the pine was gone, woodsmen cut the maple hardwood, sawed and split it in the woods, and shipped thousands of cords of it to Minneapolis by rail. Finally, it was gone too and Polk County's lumbering days were over. By 1894, all of the land south of Clear Lake had been logged, and in a summer drought a fire raged through the pine slashings, so "it seemed that the whole country south of us was on fire," Phillips said. Besides what was cleared by natural disaster and fire, hundreds of thousands of pine stumps were dynamited to clear farmland. Dairy farming became the main industry.[6]

In 1916 Clear Lake was still very much a small rural village, with boardwalks along the gravel streets and hitching posts to tie up horses. Wagons or the few automobiles sent up huge clouds of dust, so the village watered the streets with a large tank pulled by a team of horses. There were no paved roads in the entire county, or anywhere in the northern half of Wisconsin.[7] Once the first big snowfall hit, roads were closed for the winter. Automobiles were put up on blocks until spring, and horse and sleigh became the main mode of transportation. Farmers brought their milk to the creamery by sleigh, often with their dogs running behind. Gaylord's father, a country doctor, called on his patients in a horse-drawn cutter. He usually owned at least six horses, since he might tire out three teams on a busy day. In spring, when the snow melted and the roads broke up, he used a buggy with high wheels to get through the mud holes. By late May it would be dry enough to get out the Model T, or later, his De Soto. It wasn't until 1929 that the roads were plowed and passable in winter.

When Gaylord was born the attending physician was his father, Dr. Anton Nelson, assisted by Gertrude Holmes, a grade school teacher in whose home the birth took place. That wasn't the plan. Dr. Nelson had arranged for another doctor and nurse from nearby Amery to deliver the baby, but the doctor was out of town and the nurse couldn't be located that Sunday afternoon, so Gaylord's father delivered his own son. It is likely that Gaylord's mother, Mary Bradt Nelson, a registered nurse, offered some assistance and advice herself, since she was not shy about sharing her opinions. When Gaylord's sister Janet was being born, Dr. Nelson said, "You won't be getting any chloroform or anything." Mary replied, "Who asked you?"

Gaylord joined sisters Marah Janet, age three, and Nora Margaret, eighteen months. Neither ever used her first given name; they were always known as Janet and Margaret, or Peg. His mother chose Gaylord's uncommon first name. He was named after Gaylord Smiley, the young son of a neighboring farm family when Mary Bradt was growing up in northern Wisconsin. When brother Stannard Keen Nelson was born on Gaylord's second birthday, the Nelsons had four children age five or younger. Stannard—the family called him Stan—was named for muckraker Ray Stannard Baker, a Polk County native whom Dr. Nelson admired and author of popular sketches of rural life under the pen name of David Grayson. The Nelsons' first child, a son, had died at birth in 1911.

Progressive Politics

Gaylord was born into a politically active household. Both Anton and Mary were active Progressives, deep believers in the populist, reform politics of Robert M. "Fighting Bob" La Follette that won Wisconsin national attention. La Follette, a fiery orator, became the symbol of the movement, which—in Progressive rhetoric—pitted the people against the special interests. Wisconsin Chief Justice Edward G. Ryan had described the choice in an 1873 commencement speech at the University of Wisconsin: "Which shall rule—wealth or man; which shall lead—money or intellect; who shall fill public stations—educated and patriotic free men, or the feudal serfs of corporate capital?"[8]

La Follette challenged the Republican leaders who controlled the party's candidate selection process, caucuses, and conventions, calling for direct primary elections to let the voters choose the party's nominees. He took on the powerful railroads, insisting they pay their fair share of property taxes and calling for establishment of a state commission to regulate their rates. He railed against corporate power and influence on the political system, and vowed to give government back to the people.

The power struggle took place mostly within the Republican Party, pitting the established leadership—known as the Old Guard, Regulars, or Stalwarts—against the insurgents, first known as the Half-Breeds, and later as Progressives. La Follette, a former district attorney and congressman, launched his intraparty crusade in the 1890s and, after two unsuccessful attempts to win the GOP nomination for governor, finally was elected governor in 1900. La Follette went to the U.S. Senate in 1906, but Governors James O. Davidson and Francis McGovern carried on the progressive agenda at the state level. Fourteen years of progressive rule had produced a long list of reforms and innovations—the direct primary, property tax equalization, a civil service system, lobbying regulations, a worker's compensation law, a state life insurance program, a state industrial commission, laws regulating labor by women and children, and the nation's first progressive (in another sense of the word) income tax.[9]

When Gaylord was born, Progressive dominance of Wisconsin politics had just ended. While Wisconsin's model reforms were being debated in other states and in the Congress, an internal split between La Follette and McGovern cost the Progressives the 1914 election. A Stalwart, Emanuel Philipp, won the Republican primary and the governor's race, and McGovern lost the Senate race to a Democrat. The final blow was the defeat of all ten Progressive-backed referenda questions on the statewide ballot. It was the end of the first Progressive Era in Wisconsin politics, but the Progressives and the La Follettes—Fighting Bob and his sons, Young Bob and Phil—would continue to wield power and influence intermittently for the next thirty years. In 1916, five months after Gaylord's birth, Stalwart Governor Philipp and Progressive Senator La Follette—one from each wing of the GOP—easily won their Republican primaries and were reelected in November. The struggle would continue.[10]

Gaylord's father, Anton, was a Progressive leader, often serving as the Polk County Progressive chairman. His political advice was frequently sought and well regarded. He was elected village president several times, served as president of the local bank, and was an active Mason. Gaylord's mother—everyone called her simply Mary B.—was politically active at a time when few women were, and was widely admired in the community. She served as district Progressive Party chair, president of the school board, head of the Red Cross, president of the cemetery association, and leader and activist in a variety of civic and political causes, including family planning and women's suffrage. She worked for candidates before women won the right to vote, saying, "I can't vote but I can talk." When women finally got the vote, she became the first woman jury commissioner in Polk County. The Progressives once asked her to run for the state assembly, but she said, "If you'll take care of my four children, I will." No one volunteered.[11]

"Mother was active and interested on her own, not pushed by Dad," Gaylord recalled later in a classic understatement. In a speech to the Community Club after women won the right to vote, she said: "In the Revolutionary War men had to overthrow the accepted theory of the divine right of kings. Women have had to overthrow the accepted theory of the divine right of man to rule women." It was important, she said, to teach young people the importance of voting. "This necessity still exists. If you want something you have to ask for it."[12]

In Milwaukee, where Anton and Mary met, they once heard Fighting Bob La Follette speak for five hours, winding down at 1 A.M. The railroads, among Fighting Bob's targets and enemies, offered free train tickets to medical students so they could go home and vote against La Follette—apparently believing any would-be doctor would be a conservative. Anton accepted the ticket, took the early morning train home to Thorp, and voted straight Progressive.

The Irish-Norwegians

Anton Nelson was of Norwegian descent. Mary Bradt Hogan was Norwegian and Irish, with her Irish side dominant. She was warm and outgoing, sang a lot, and was optimistic and fun loving by nature. Anton was more quiet and reserved, in the Scandinavian mode. Anton said many funny things, might allow himself a smile or twinkle in his eye, but Gaylord never heard him laugh out loud. He had fun, but didn't show his feelings, and was not one to kiss and hug or even put his arm around his wife, Janet recalled. "Dad was not a great one to show love," Stannard said. "You knew he loved you but he was not demonstrative." Janet recalled being in tears once when she tried to kiss her father and he pulled away.

When it came to expressing emotions, he was a man of few words. Eight months before their marriage, Anton addressed a postcard to "My dear Mary" in Milwaukee, told her about the weather and the telephone lines installed in Clear Lake, and signed it "with best wishes." In 1956, when he was in Chicago and Mary was at Gaylord's home in Madison, Anton wrote a postcard to say simply, "My dear Mary, I was thinking of you yesterday so much that I said to myself I should write you right away. Everything is going on fine here. Anton."[13]

Gaylord was an interesting mixture: He was both outgoing and shy. He could use his Irish charm to make friends easily, was talkative and witty, but also had the Scandinavian reticence to discuss or express his feelings or emotions. It is not an uncommon combination in Wisconsin.

Brothers Albert and Arent Bradt were the first of Gaylord Nelson's forebears to arrive in America. Born in Norway, they emigrated to Holland and later to the New World, arriving on Manhattan in 1637. The family name in Norway was Andriessen, but after they had been in America twenty-five years, for unexplained reasons they began to use the surname of Bradt.[14] Six generations of Bradts lived in New York State, until William Bradt, his wife, Mary, and most of their ten children headed west to Wisconsin in 1850. They settled in densely forested Winnebago County, in Wisconsin's Fox River Valley, to undertake the arduous task of clearing the land for farming.[15]

Their son Sheldon Elisha Bradt, Gaylord's grandfather, was fifteen when he ran off and lied about his age to join the Union Army in the Civil War. Captured by the Confederates near Atlanta, he nearly died in the notorious Millen prison camp in Georgia. Before being freed in a prisoner exchange, he lost eighty pounds and was so near death he was mistakenly put into a pile with dead soldiers awaiting burial. He was saved when a Confederate soldier noticed his eyes move and realized he was still alive.[16]

After discharge, Sheldon returned to Wisconsin and worked for a few years in a stave factory and a lumberyard. But the depression of the

1870s left him jobless, and he joined a party of pioneers who founded a colony in northern Montana. It did not turn out to be the paradise that had been advertised, and the venture did not turn out well financially, but it did give Sheldon a wealth of stories for his repertoire in later life after he returned to Waupaca County. On 23 April 1879 Sheldon Bradt, thirty-two, married Hanora (Nora) O'Brien, twenty-eight, daughter of a Waupaca County pioneer family and the first white child born in the county. They were Gaylord's maternal grandparents.[17]

Nora's parents, Felix and Mary Walsh O'Brien, and their two daughters came to Wisconsin from Prince Edward Island, off Nova Scotia in the Gulf of Saint Lawrence, in the spring of 1848. They canoed up the Wolf River from Oshkosh, sleeping under their overturned canoe at night with a fire to provide warmth and keep wolves away. Reaching Waupaca County, the O'Briens settled on eighty acres of land covered with oak and maple trees. The first settlers north of the Little Wolf River, they built a log cabin, the first permanent home in the township. The couple's third child, Hanora, was born on 23 August 1850, with a Menominee Indian woman in attendance as midwife and nurse.[18]

During the next five years, a settlement called Northport grew up a mile from the Bradt farm. Like the O'Briens, the settlers were almost exclusively Irish until 1855, when some New Englanders began to arrive. When Nora and Sheldon were married, they took over the Northport farm. Sheldon and Nora had four children. Their only daughter, Mary—Gaylord's mother—was born on 25 June 1882.

The known family history is shorter on Gaylord's paternal side. Gaylord's grandfather, Christen Nilsson, was born in Norway in 1845 and emigrated to the United States in 1866 with a friend, Mathias Peterson. Lured by offers of free land to homestead, each took possession of eighty densely forested acres in Clark County, in west central Wisconsin. They gradually cleared the land, working winters in logging camps to earn enough to live the rest of the year.[19] Peterson's nineteen-year-old niece, Gina Paulina Olson, came from Norway in 1873 to join him in Clark County. Christen married Gina in 1876. The oldest of their five children, Anton Nils Nilsson, was born on 20 February 1878. When he started school, the teacher Anglicized his surname as Nelson, and that became the family name.

The Nelsons

Gaylord's parents, Anton Nelson and Mary Bradt Hogan, met in Milwaukee, where both were training to enter the medical profession. Anton, one of nine graduates of Thorp High School in 1896, became a teacher at Thorp High a few months after graduating. He taught there several years before attending the normal school at Oshkosh. When he met Mary, he was in medical school at Marquette University, a Catholic institution in downtown Milwaukee. Mary Jeannett Bradt was one of ten graduates of Northport High School in 1898. She married a sawmill worker, Sylvester S. Hogan of Rhinelander, in December 1903, but less than six months later Hogan, age twenty-eight, died of appendicitis. Mary moved to Milwaukee and enrolled in nursing school.[20]

Anton was valedictorian of his twenty-seven-member class in the Marquette University Department of Medicine, graduating in 1907. Mary, whose classmates called her Hogan or Hogie, was the top graduate in her class at Trinity Hospital's school of nursing that same year. Dr. Nelson went to Clear Lake, bought the office of a recently deceased physician, and opened a practice. Mary remained in Milwaukee, working as a nurse while Anton established his practice. Anton and Mary were married on 10 October 1910 in Oshkosh and moved into the back of the Clear Lake building that housed Dr. Nelson's office, where they lived until Gaylord was born.

The Nelsons were, arguably, the first family of the small community. They were relatively well-off financially and people looked to them for political and civic leadership. The only other college-educated Clear Lake residents were another doctor, the school principal and teachers, the dentist, and perhaps one or two others. They lived comfortably, but not extravagantly, in a modest two-story frame house they purchased for seven hundred dollars soon after Gaylord's birth. The house was just two blocks from Dr. Nelson's Main Street office. Downstairs were a sitting room and dining room, with maple flooring, and a kitchen at the back. An open staircase led to the second floor, where the boys shared one bedroom, with Janet and Peg in the adjoining room and their parents across the hall. The house had running water but no indoor toilet until a Works Progress Administration project built a sewer system in the 1930s. Two woodstoves provided heat until a furnace was installed in about 1925. The address now is 385 First Avenue West, but when the Nelsons lived there it had no address. With 150 houses in town, everyone knew where everyone else lived, so addresses were unnecessary.

The Nelson house was filled with books and magazines. When Janet's teacher asked students to list the magazines to which their families subscribed, Janet's list was so long, with dozens of magazines, that the teacher accused her of wild exaggeration. Mary Nelson seldom turned away a traveling magazine, book, or encyclopedia salesman. The garage was filled with old copies of *Life* and *National Geographic* magazines. Reading was the main indoor pastime for all of the Nelsons, and the children all started reading at early ages. Gaylord read quite a bit of Samuel Clemens, having inherited an eight-volume set, and a lot of the fifty-two-volume Harvard Classics, which as an adult he still ranked as "the single greatest collection of writing anyplace in the world." *National Geographic*, *Lawrence of Arabia*, muckrakers, H. L. Mencken— he read it all. Gaylord's taste was always eclectic. As an adult he might read half a dozen books at once. He always ended his day with a book, even if only for a few minutes before sleeping.

Dr. Nelson was a stickler for proper grammar and language usage. Young Gaylord liked to steer the Model T and would ask his father, "Can I drive the car?" Dr. Nelson would just keep driving, finally responding, "I don't know if you're *able* to or not, but you may *try*." Or Gaylord would say, "If I'm not mistaken, it's this way," which would bring Anton's reply, "I suppose if you're not mistaken, it *must* be that way." In the army years later, when a colonel leaving the office told him, "If anyone calls I will be at the commandant's office," Gaylord couldn't resist asking, "Excuse me, Colonel, but where will you be if nobody calls?" Gaylord absorbed Dr. Nelson's love of language. As a public speaker later in life, Gaylord's enunciation was precise, and he carefully chose the right word. He sometimes agonized for hours to compose a brief but important public statement, until he was satisfied he had the exact words and phrasing to have the impact he intended.

His parents refused to define words for Gaylord; he was responsible for looking them up. One of the first gifts he could remember was a second-hand, unabridged Funk and Wagnalls dictionary. As an adult, there was always a dictionary within easy reach in Gaylord's home and office, sometimes two or three in the same room, "on the theory that if you have to get up and go look up a word, you usually don't do it." As governor and senator, he would buy cheap paperback dictionaries, rip out a few pages, put them in his pocket with his speech, and take them along to read unobtrusively at the head table during a long, boring after-dinner program. He kept one in the glove compartment of his car, "so that if you're stuck somewhere and haven't anything else to read, you can just rip out a few pages and have something good to read."

For all the intellectual stimulation at home, Gaylord was not terribly interested in school. He read a lot, but not for classes, and in grade school spent a year in an ungraded classroom for students who were not doing well. He was not lacking in intellectual capacity; he simply did not pay attention. After a year he was back in his regular classroom. "I got high marks in my six weeks exams," eighth grader Gaylord wrote his mother, who was in Madison on a trip. "My lowest mark was 82." It was mid-April, but Gaylord wrote that he, Margaret, and some friends had been swimming and stayed in twenty minutes even though it was cold. "I took the car all by myself, " wrote Gaylord, not yet fourteen. Oh, one more thing: "Dad was wondering when you are coming home."[21]

Stannard did not do well in school, because he did not apply himself, and graduated behind his own high school class, but later attended engineering school and worked in Beech Aircraft's instrument repair laboratory. In high school Gaylord and Stannard were in the same Latin class, and Gaylord complained one day that Stannard had the lowest grade in the class. His mother told Gaylord he should be thankful: "If it weren't for Stannard, *you* would have had the lowest grade." Gaylord paid more attention in high school, but did not exert himself academically, and graduated with average grades. Peggy and Janet both did well academically, but were very different. Peggy was quiet, serious, and unassuming. Janet was just the opposite, and "if she could shock somebody would go out of her way to do it," a classmate recalled.

Mealtime conversation at the Nelsons' included political talk and current events, and the children were encouraged to think for themselves. "What caused the First World War?" Dr. Nelson would ask after dinner, or, "Why did Chicago get to be such a big city?" He was sometimes unhappy that what the children had learned in school had not prepared them to handle such questions.

Both Nelson parents spent much of their lives taking care of others—Dr. Nelson in the practice of medicine and Mary Nelson in helping people in need.

The Country Doctor

Dr. Nelson worked seven days a week most of his life, seeing patients every day and always on call for emergencies. Sometimes accompanied by Gaylord, Dr. Nelson would brave snowdrifts, blizzards, and subzero temperatures in a horse-drawn cutter to deliver babies, set broken limbs with splints carved from apple crates, or perform an emergency appendectomy while young Gaylord administered the ether drip that served as the anesthetic. His office assistant was not a trained nurse, so when he was going to perform surgery, a procedure that required general anesthesia, Mary Nelson was his direct assistant. Dr. Nelson often took Gaylord along on house calls, rather than one of the other children, in the belief Gaylord might become a doctor himself. Gaylord was interested in medicine, but eventually chose law because it was the path to politics.

Probably only half of his patients paid Dr. Nelson. Money wasn't the object of his practice, and certainly was not something he would ask anyone for, which would have been unseemly in his eyes. Some patients were forced to insist on a bill, and even then he sometimes resisted. As president of the Bank of Clear Lake, he knew who could afford to pay and who couldn't, and he believed those with money would offer to pay and those without money couldn't. One patient tried to pay a bill for three years, but Dr. Nelson always avoided him and wouldn't tell him how much he owed. Finally, he said he was going to sit in the doctor's office until the bill was paid, at which point Dr. Nelson said, "Is it worth ten dollars to you?"—a fraction of what the service was worth—and the man settled up.[22] Those who did pay in the 1920s and 1930s often paid in crops, a hindquarter of beef, a chicken, some homemade sausage, or a load of wood. One person came in with a sackful of pennies to pay for the delivery of a baby.

After World War II, a collection agent from the Twin Cities suggested going after payment of tens of thousands of dollars of bills on the books, some dating back to before the Depression. Dr. Nelson wasn't interested, even though most of his patients now could afford to pay him. One former patient wrote from Indianapolis in 1956, saying, "I came to your office two or three times before we left Clear Lake in 1946, trying to find out what our bill was, but you always said you did not have it figured up. At the time we had cash on hand to pay it, but it seems to have been hard to get it again," she said, enclosing a $150 check.[23]

Dr. Nelson also served as the village's unofficial psychiatrist, counseling those in need and often helping them to get their lives back on track. The Nelsons opened their house to those in trouble, and it was not unusual to have an extra child living with the family for a time, as respite from an abusive parent or some other problem at home. Mary B. and Anton both took in strays, and she served as a surrogate mother to many Clear Lake youngsters. For their own family, they provided hospice care. One of Gaylord's earliest memories is of his Aunt Mamie, Anton's sister, a beautiful young woman, coming to live with the Nelsons while dying of diabetes. The disease was incurable when she died in 1918, three years before the discovery of insulin. Anton's father also spent his last days with the Nelsons before his death in 1929.

Open House for Hoboes

Mary B. was constantly involved in helping those in need. The Nelson house was the collection point for clothing and other items being donated to the Red Cross. Every hobo knew where the Nelsons lived, and during the Depression they would get off the train and walk straight to the Nelson house, where they knew they could do some work for a dollar, eat a meal, or get some clothing. The clothes were usually castoffs from the Red Cross, but not always. Gaylord remembered his mother giving away his first pair of zippered overshoes to someone who seemed to need them more than he did. There were two rocking chairs in the dining room, with the radio in between, and "you could come home anytime during the day and there would be some character sitting in the chair, either talking to Mother or waiting for Mother to get back," Janet said. In the depth of the Depression, it was not unusual for ten hoboes a day to pass through the house.

Clear Lake was a community where people usually knew who needed help and made certain they got it without having to ask. Dr. Nelson wasn't the only one who failed to collect his bills. During the Depression one of the local merchants, Bert Schulze, after filling an order of food or dry goods for a needy family, would tell his helper to "charge it to Schulze," meaning no one was being billed. "Charge it to Schulze" became a stock phrase in Clear Lake when refusing payment for a transaction or favor.

Despite such kindness, Polk County residents were not free from suffering during the Depression of the 1930s. Between 12 and 18 percent of Polk County's population were on relief in 1935.[24] Fred Booth recalls his grandfather, who held personal mortgages on a number of farms, foreclosing on some, and remembers people crying over the loss of their property. The radical Farm Holiday movement organized farmers to dump their milk in protest over low prices, and enough participated to close the creamery briefly in October 1933. At other times, when a family's goods were being auctioned in a foreclosure or bankruptcy, neighbors would pack the auction and buy back the items at very low prices, then return them to the family. Gaylord's sister Janet worked for the Polk County welfare department at age nineteen. Her job included interviewing people—unmarried mothers and others—to ascertain their eligibility for general relief. Decades later, she still recalled going "into homes where the man would not be in the house, he would be so embarrassed, and I would have to go through their cupboards to see what food they had in the house." She would get an authorization for a food order and set up an account for them. "I went into homes where there was no food, nothing to eat, three or four little kids, and no way of getting any," she said. After a year she lost her job because the Nelson family had enough money and county officials felt she didn't need the income as badly as others.

Anton's commitment to his medical practice left Mary B. with primary responsibility for raising the children. Anton was habitually late for dinner, and some nights didn't get home from his rounds at all. He might be up and gone in the morning before the children awoke, and not get home until they were already in bed. Gaylord had a close connection with his father because of his interest in politics, but spent long hours talking with his mother about "anything and everything," and it was Mary B. who kindled his interest in nature, plants, and wildlife. In the next generation, politics would keep Gaylord away from home much of the time, and his wife, another strong-willed, outspoken nurse, would play Mary B.'s role in nurturing the children.

2

Happy

GAYLORD'S NICKNAME, Happy, was given to him by a neighbor boy
several years older than Gaylord, who said his name "Gay Lard," which
translated into "Happy Grease."[1] That's what he called him—until
Gaylord got "big enough to hit somebody" and became just Happy. His
childhood, by his account, was more than happy—it was idyllic. While
growing up, only his parents called him Gaylord, and his mother sometimes shortened it to Gay. To everyone else in town—even the *Clear
Lake Star*, reporting on athletic events—he was Happy Nelson.

Gaylord and his friends had the run of Clear Lake, exploring everything. Gaylord and Sherman Benson, his closest sidekick, were rascals,
"like two puppies," always getting into something and causing minor
mischief—putting a heifer in the banker's house while the family was at
the movies or hiding in the bushes to embarrass young lovers saying
good night. Gaylord and Sherman were up in Clyde Jones's apple tree
one night, stealing apples, when Jones came out and turned on the light,
"so you can see better," then went back inside while the embarrassed
would-be thieves ran off. Fred Booth moved to Clear Lake as a fifth
grader and found that "when Gaylord was my friend, everybody in town
was my friend." While there were a lot of hijinks, they were never mean
or destructive. Rusty Peirson, a neighbor, said, "They weren't bad boys,
but they had a little life. They were more apt to help you than hurt you."

One hot summer day, when Gaylord was twelve, Sherman Benson's
father asked Sherman and Gaylord to take a Holstein cow, which was in
heat, to the Marquardt farm across town to be bred. Leading the big cow
on a rope, the pair set off through town to the farm. When they entered

the Marquardts' gate, they were shocked to be greeted not by Mr. Marquardt but by his daughter, Pearl, the schoolteacher. Both Gaylord and Sherman had major schoolboy crushes on her, and had discussed flipping a coin to see which one would marry her.

Now she stood on the porch and told them: "Dad is uptown, so just take the cow down to the barn, next to the bull pen." It shocked the boys that the object of their affections would know about breeding, much less talk to them about it. So Gaylord replied, "Oh, we didn't come out here for *that!*" and they marched the cow back through the village to the Benson farm. The teacher, of course, told her father, who told everyone in town. The next day, as Gaylord and Sherman walked past the barbershop, they were greeted with shouts of, "Oh, you didn't go to the Marquardt farm for *that*!" There were few secrets in Clear Lake.

It was a safe environment. A family that went on a three- or four-day trip left its doors unlocked. The local policeman was armed with only a badge, a stern look, and the moral authority that went with his position. He didn't need a uniform, since everyone knew who he was. Youngsters who got into trouble ran to him for protection. There were no parking laws to enforce, so he mostly walked the streets, tended the water tower, planted trees, and generally kept the peace. Once in a while he might be forced to lock up a drunk overnight in the town's only cell to keep him from driving. Gaylord never knew about anyone who went to prison or reform school. Everyone knew Gaylord and his gang, and no adult hesitated to administer some discipline if it seemed needed. "If you did something wrong, some neighbor would paddle your ass or correct you or call your parent," Gaylord recalled. "So you knew if your kids went out wandering around town everybody would look out for them." If you needed to find Dr. Nelson, you called "central," the village's telephone operator, who knew where he was and how to reach him. Central seemed to know where everybody was if they weren't at home, and party lines made it even more difficult to keep a secret.

Living with Nature

Young Gaylord spent much time outdoors in the woods, lakes, marshes, and farmland surrounding Clear Lake—swimming, hiking, and camping in summer, and skiing, skating, and sledding in the winter. The lakes contained fish, turtles, cattails, and muskrat houses, and migrating birds and ducks visited every spring and fall. Gaylord and his buddies got well acquainted with nature—catching snakes, trapping rabbits, snaring gophers, and trying unsuccessfully to disrupt the annual turtle migration from Big and Little Clear Lakes, at one end of Main Street, to Mud Lake, on the other. When the fifty or sixty turtles would migrate in the fall, they would go right through the village's backyards. Gaylord and a sidekick would pick them up, spin them around, face them in the opposite direction, put them behind trees or in high grass— but the turtles always knew which way to go to reach Mud Lake, where they would hibernate for the winter. Young Gaylord was intrigued.

Gaylord raised chickens and thought that might be the road to riches, based on his experience: His mother bought the chicks, and Gaylord charged the feed to her account. She would feed them when he wasn't around. When he killed a chicken he'd sell it to his mother. She would cook it, and Gaylord and the rest of the family would eat it. The business was all profit, little work, and no investment. His other profitable business was selling popcorn during concerts at the bandstand. He'd charge the popcorn, butter, and bags to his mother's account, pop the corn in her kitchen, and pocket the nickel a bag he collected. "This was my introduction to the free marketplace," he later joked.

Gaylord always had pets—a dog, pigeons, a skunk, or any other animal he could corral. When he was confined to bed at age ten with rheumatic fever, his father brought home a baby great horned owl which had been abandoned, and Gaylord watched it grow up in a house outside his bedroom window. He and Sherman Benson had a trapline for rabbits, but Mary B. made them use box traps instead of leg traps and insisted they check the traps every day. In the fall, they'd hunt squirrels and rabbits with a single shot .22 rifle. By the time Gaylord was twelve, he and a few friends would talk their parents into allowing them a camping adventure at Horseshoe Lake, twelve miles from home, with no adults. They would be the only ones on the lake, living in tents and fishing, skinny-dipping and canoeing to their hearts' content. One of the parents would drive out to check on things every night, but there was little trouble to get into, and no real danger to worry about. When the snow fell, the young people would turn out with shovels to clear off Mud Lake for skating, and after a day on the ice would gather around big bonfires made from driftwood.

Contrary to the small town life portrayed by Sinclair Lewis in *Babbitt* and *Main Street*, in which familiarity breeds conformity, in later life Nelson would argue that small town living encourages and allows individuality, while demanding civility. That small town civility stuck with him throughout his political career. No matter how sharp the debate on an issue or how strong his disagreement with a political adversary, Nelson never made it personal and never carried a grudge. He learned that from his parents. "If it was a political matter they could be quite critical of someone on issues, but you never heard them trashing anybody," he said. "I never saw my father angry, although he surely was. I am very careful about losing my temper, so I don't ever go into a rage. I always figured that's a losing game, getting mad at somebody; that takes up a lot of energy. You hurt yourself more than the object of your anger." Later, that philosophy helped him win friends on both sides of the political aisle, accomplish things he could not have achieved otherwise, and win recognition from his peers as the best-liked member of the U.S. Senate.

Enduring the Lectures

Anton and Mary Nelson had high expectations and standards for their children's behavior, but they were not tough disciplinarians. Dr. Nelson was famous among his children for his lectures. When he thought one or all of the young Nelsons needed instruction on what to do, how to do it, or the proper way to conduct themselves, he would launch into gentle, thoughtful lectures that the children thought would never end. Stannard remembered lectures lasting up to an hour. They were often about the consequences that could result from your actions and how your behavior could affect others. They were "about the way things ought to be done," but they were not moralistic.

"Forget about competing to be better than someone else," he might say in his quiet voice. "That's unimportant. People are born with different ability, physically and mentally, and if you happen to beat somebody who is intellectually or physically inferior, and was born that way, that's no achievement. You should aim to take the greatest possible advantage of the abilities you have, and if you don't do that, that's a crime. You're competing against yourself; you're competing to use your talents to the maximum possible, and that's more important than doing something to be better than somebody else, who may or may not be inferior to you."

A famous story in Nelson family lore has Stannard on the receiving end of one of his father's lectures, which went on and on. His mother was busy baking cookies in the kitchen, cutting them out, and arranging them on trays to go into the oven. In midlecture, Stannard interrupted to say, "Mother, you've got a hundred twenty cookies there." Dr. Nelson didn't say a word. He just stopped in midsentence and walked out the door.

Mary Nelson was most likely to punish one of the children for making fun of someone about religion or social standing. That was perhaps the most serious offense in her book. She would sometimes grab a willow switch and apply a few swats to make her point. Given a choice, the children would have opted for the switch over the lectures.

"There was no hand on my shoulder," Gaylord recalled. "They were never critical of anything I did. They expected you'd do what you ought to do. Whatever they did was by example."

"Their philosophy was to let us know the difference between right and wrong, but not suppress our way of life," Stannard said. "I was never restricted, but gently instructed this was right and this was wrong."

High Expectations

Their parents "had very high standards in every way," Gaylord said. "I never heard either one of them dissemble or lie. They simply did not lie. My mother would say you can tell a white lie if nobody's going to be hurt, like telling a lady who's bought a silly-looking hat that it's a beautiful hat," but that was about the limit. Gossiping or criticizing others was not tolerated either. It simply was not appropriate.

The Nelsons were not particularly religious. Mary B. had been raised a Roman Catholic and Anton a Lutheran, but Mary B. went to the Methodist church, and the children went to Methodist Sunday school. Anton did not go to church at all. Yet, Gaylord said, "Both lived by the Golden Rule far better than any religious people I knew." Gaylord and Peg were not churchgoers as adults, and Janet described herself as an atheist. Stannard converted to Catholicism after he married.

Whether it was their parents' example, Anton's lectures, Sunday school lessons, or some combination, the Nelson children, at an early age, internalized a code of behavior and a sense of remorse when they violated it. When she was nine or ten, Janet recalled, Gaylord, who was "a dreadful, dreadful tease," tormented her to the point where she lost control and bit him on the shoulder. She was devastated and felt disgraced. In her family, children didn't cause injury by hair pulling, poking with sticks, or biting. That was unacceptable behavior. She "thought about it for an hour, started dissembling, and then started being nice to Gaylord." She never committed such a transgression again.

At a Fourth of July picnic, when someone gave Gaylord a nickel and Stannard a dime, Gaylord convinced his younger brother to trade, since the nickel was bigger and therefore seemed more valuable. A short time later, when Stannard saw that Gaylord had twice as big an ice cream cone as he did, Stannard didn't say anything, but two big tears rolled down his cheeks. Stannard got over it, but Gaylord didn't. Gaylord would wake up in the night, even as an adult, feeling guilty and remorseful. The image of Stannard's tears haunted him. Finally, in 1992, Gaylord sent his brother a $500 check with a note: "I have computed the compound interest of that nickel I cheated you out of seventy years ago, plus criminal penalties, embarrassment, etc. This may get me an interview with a friend of St. Peter, which is as close as I'm likely to get." Stannard didn't cash the check; he framed it and the note and hung them on the wall in his home in Oklahoma City.

The Disciplined Doctor

Anton Nelson, tall and lean at six feet and 170 pounds, was remarkably strong and disciplined about taking care of his body. He believed both sides of a person's body should be treated equally and taught himself to use either hand, whether to write, tie a one-handed suture, or perform another task. At fifty, he could do a one-armed pull-up from a dead hang with either arm. He was a strong swimmer. To stay in shape, he practiced isometric exercises long before they were invented, training himself to be able to flex each and every muscle in his body. Gaylord was with him on a call when his Model T kicked and the crank broke his father's right arm. Dr. Nelson felt it carefully, pulled hard to make certain it was in place, went into the house to get a dishtowel for a sling, and then drove to the next patient's house, where he delivered a baby using only one arm. He was known to kill the engine of his Model T by putting his fingers on all four spark plugs at once—a trick no one else ever had the courage to try. He encouraged the Nelson children to be rugged, and they seldom wore any hats or coats, sometimes rolling in the snow in their swimming suits.

Anton was interested in virtually everything and "knew more about more things than anybody I ever met in my life," said Rusty Peirson. He could talk knowledgeably on nearly any topic, a result of his natural curiosity and wide range of reading. He was an avid gardener, always beating area farmers in the race to have the year's first ripe tomato from seed— and never telling them he did it by giving the seedlings in his homemade greenhouse a daily dose of ultraviolet light. He loved music, made his first violin himself, and played for his own enjoyment at the office, giving violin lessons on occasion. Politics, occasional hunting or fishing trips, and medical organizations took up what leisure time he had, but, Gaylord said, "95 percent of what he did was take care of people."

Hearing Young Bob

Both of his parents kindled Gaylord's interest in politics, but it was more often his father who took him to hear political speakers. Robert La Follette Jr., the son of Fighting Bob, succeeded his father in the U.S. Senate after his death in 1925. When Young Bob came to Amery in 1926, Dr. Nelson and Gaylord made the ten-mile trip in the Model T to hear him make a whistlestop speech from the back of a railroad car. Dr. Nelson held Gaylord on his shoulders so he could see over the crowd. Gaylord watched as La Follette took off his suit coat and hung it on the railing of the caboose. The coat fell and La Follette stepped on it while walking back and forth, making Gaylord, who had one Sunday suit, think, "Boy, he's going to catch hell from his mother when he gets home."

"Do you think you might like to go into politics?" Dr. Nelson asked ten-year-old Gaylord on the ride home.

"I would," Gaylord replied, "but I'm afraid by then Bob La Follette may not have left any problems for me to solve."

Thirty-two years later, in his last words to Gaylord from his deathbed, Dr. Nelson would remind his son of that conversation.

Another auto trip with his father, to a medical meeting in Eau Claire, sparked Gaylord's first attempt at environmental activism. Leaving the city of Menomonie, Gaylord was struck by the beauty of a row of huge elms arching over the highway, forming a canopy that seemed almost like a tunnel. Gaylord thought it would be wonderful for Clear Lake to do something similar on every approach to the village, with the Girl Scouts, Boy Scouts, local government, and others pitching in to plant the trees. Gaylord, age twelve or thirteen, took his idea to the Clear Lake Village Board. The board members listened politely as the Nelson lad gave his presentation, but nothing ever came of it. Unlike the way he would respond to setbacks later in his political career, he did not try again.

At Clear Lake High School, Happy Nelson was a leading athlete, growing to five feet eleven and 170 pounds by his senior year. In a high school of 140 students, he was a little above average in size but the second tallest boy on the basketball team. He was quarterback and captain of the football team, captain of the basketball team, a self-described mediocre half-miler in track, and an even worse trumpet player in the school band. Years later, when asked why he had made Richard Nixon's enemies list, he suggested that maybe Nixon had heard him play the trumpet in the Clear Lake band.

Clear Lake's most famous citizen was Burleigh Grimes, the last legal spitball pitcher in major league baseball, who pitched in three consecutive World Series during Gaylord's high school days. When he pitched for Brooklyn in the 1920 World Series, Clear Lake fans gathered at the theater, where a wire service had been installed to get the play-by-play over the telegraph line. In Gaylord's high school days, the games were carried on the radio in the school assembly hall. Grimes, known as "Old Stubblebeard" for his superstitious refusal to shave on days he pitched, won 270 games in nineteen seasons and later managed the Brooklyn Dodgers. He was elected to the Baseball Hall of Fame in 1964. Later, Grimes and Nelson would share top billing at the Clear Lake Museum.

Happy in High School

By the time Gaylord was in high school, talking pictures had revolutionized the movie industry. When he was younger there were silent movies on weekends, with piano accompaniment by a local woman. During a scene in *Les Miserables*, when chained prisoners are rowing a boat, the pianist's husband came over from his automotive garage next door to lend a hand, rolling tire chains along the wooden floor while she played.

There were plenty of dances for teenagers—at the Odd Fellows Hall and the Town Hall, barn dances with a local fiddler, and at a big pavilion seven miles from town featuring bands from Minneapolis. But no dancing was allowed in the schools, and the junior-senior prom consisted of a dinner. When they were juniors, Gaylord and two friends organized their own junior-senior dance, hired a band, and decorated the Town Hall. Gaylord dated Winnifred McClennan, "the prettiest girl in school," his junior and senior years. It was unusual for Clear Lake boys to date classmates, who "were more like sisters," Fred Booth said. It was more fashionable to date girls from nearby Amery.

High school was also when "we learned to drink together," Booth said. Three taverns opened in Clear Lake when Prohibition ended in 1933, and Booth and Gaylord could get served even though still in high school. The taverns were places to hang out, and there were not many others except the Bluebird Café, the pool hall, or the harness shop, where a group would sometimes kill time, share a bottle of wine, and "shoot the bull."

"There was a lot of heavy drinking and it started during Prohibition," when moonshine was readily available from a number of bootleggers, and there were "beer and booze joints all over the surrounding area," Erland Hanna said, "operating quite openly. It was almost socially acceptable, but you would never admit to being in one." After Prohibition, "we all drank. We didn't have much money, but you could get all you needed. It was boredom that did it."

Once in a while, the teenagers would get to the metropolis of Minneapolis–Saint Paul, on the train or by car, for a movie, the state fair, or a University of Minnesota athletic event. On one trip when they were about sixteen, Gaylord and Booth visited Washington Avenue, which then had a scandalous reputation. In one tavern, the woman bartender directed them to the back room, where they found a number of women sitting around. One grabbed Fred and got him on her lap. Another grabbed Gaylord, who yelled, "Booth, let's get the hell out of here," and they ran out of the place as if they were being attacked. "I guess this was a house of ill repute or something, but they just scared the hell out of us," Booth said. They were innocent and naïve enough that, in another Saint Paul tavern, Booth ordered a shot of liquor and, when he was served a glass of water as a chaser, drank the water first.

Gaylord didn't apply himself to his studies any more than necessary, and that was not much. He never took any schoolwork home. High school was more about maturation than learning, he recalled. His sister Janet finished high school in less than three years and had graduated before Gaylord started. If he had been motivated, Gaylord said, he probably could have taken all four years at one time.

Gaylord was one of thirty-nine graduates of Clear Lake High School in 1934, and he and Booth were chosen to be the class speakers at graduation. Gaylord had participated in forensics as an extemporaneous speaker, but something about the graduation speech intimidated him. Facing a crisis of self-confidence, he pretended he was ill and stayed home from the ceremony. Booth gave his speech on "Our Leisure Time," but Gaylord Nelson's speech on "The New Deal" went undelivered. It was probably the last time Gaylord Nelson, who became a popular, sought-after speaker, failed to rise to the occasion.

3

Into the World

GAYLORD'S ATHLETIC ABILITY ATTRACTED some interest from coaches of state teachers colleges in western Wisconsin.[1] He was invited to the normal school in Eau Claire, where he lived at the home of the football coach, Bill Zorn. There were no scholarships, but Gaylord got a meal job at a local restaurant and expected to play football and basketball. But he left after a matter of weeks, before classes really began, and went to River Falls, another normal school. Gaylord lasted only a few weeks there, too. He just didn't like either place much, he said. He may have doubted his ability, as a small town boy, to compete successfully in a bigger setting. Gaylord simply went home to Clear Lake. He was embarrassed, but his parents didn't say a word.

He spent the winter on a federal Works Progress Administration job, shoveling gravel onto a sleigh so it could be transported and dumped on a road. It helped provide the motivation Gaylord needed to clear out of Clear Lake. "I said to myself, 'This ain't the life for me,'" Gaylord recalled.

He decided he wanted to go to college in California the next fall, and his parents readily agreed. Gaylord was the third Nelson child to attend San Jose State University, where Dr. Nelson's unmarried sister, Gertrude, had retired from the faculty after a career as a voice teacher. Janet, Peg, and Gaylord all lived at her home while attending college. Janet had spent a year in San Jose, but went back to Wisconsin and completed a teaching course at River Falls. Peg went with Gaylord to San Jose, and they both lived with their aunt for a year or two, until Peg transferred to the University of Wisconsin at Madison. Gaylord lived with his aunt for three years, then with a local family his senior year, when his aunt spent a year in Seattle.

Aunt Gertie's home and sister Peg's presence helped ensure a soft landing. But California also promised adventure for Gaylord, who was "fascinated with the idea of getting to California, getting out west, a long way from home for the first time in my life." His longest trip had been perhaps two hundred miles, to spend part of a summer in Waupaca County, in central Wisconsin, with his mother's family. Now, a wide-eyed Gaylord—leaving the nickname Happy behind—got on the train to California for his first look at mountains and exotic palm, walnut, and eucalyptus trees. He claimed to have pronounced "eucalyptus" as *U-cal-a-PEE-tus* until his second semester, when he finally made some friends who set him straight.

Gaylord was admitted conditionally to San Jose State, as an out-of-state student whose grades were less than stellar. He would have to prove himself if he wanted to stay in school. "I thought, 'Wow, now I've left town and Happy Nelson's out in the West at college. I can't come home a failure a second time,'" Gaylord recalled. There was one problem: Gaylord had never studied before. Back in Clear Lake, he had never needed to. He was intelligent and well read, but didn't know the rudiments of how to study. Taking notes, cramming for exams, preparing for classes were all new to him. But he learned—"out of sheer fright," he said—that a student from a high school class of thirty-nine could compete in a college with thirty-five hundred students—five times the population of Clear Lake. "I thought, 'Here's this big school, with all these smart kids, I'm in big trouble,'" he said.

After his first quarter, before he had received his grades, Gaylord was summoned to the dean's office. Gaylord sat in the outer office, fearful and embarrassed, steeling himself to hear that he had flunked out. Instead, he heard "the best words I ever heard. 'I've been here fifteen years,' the dean said, 'and you are the first student we ever let in on condition who got almost straight A's.'" Gaylord was walking on air. He had learned an important truth: He could easily handle college. "I had run into all these sophisticated people, and I thought I would have to work very hard. But I got the measure of it—you have to do this much to do this. I got good grades all the way and graduated with distinction, but it wasn't hard," he said.

He majored in economics, minored in philosophy and physical anthropology, and got only one C in four years, in Spanish. He took his first speech course and came away thinking, "Either you can speak or you can't." Despite his case of nerves at high school graduation, Gaylord could speak. When San Jose State celebrated Founders' Day in 1960, the speaker was Gaylord Nelson, who received an honorary master of arts degree.

Campus or California politics didn't really interest Gaylord, although he didn't hesitate to argue politics when the conversation turned in that direction. He didn't take part in athletics, either, although he was encouraged to join the boxing team. He had learned boxing skills from traveling professionals who conducted camps in Clear Lake. Instead of competing, he helped in San Jose's good-sized collegiate program as an assistant who taught basics to beginning boxers. He dated but had no steady girlfriend. He did explore California, at least within two hundred miles of San Jose, visiting Yosemite, Carmel, San Francisco, and Monterey. His last recollection before leaving for law school, he told his classmates at their fiftieth reunion, was a visit to the Golden Gate International Exposition on a manmade island in San Francisco Bay. "The only part of the exhibition I specifically recall is what Sally Rand exposed" in her famous fan dance, he said—"which was quite a bit in those days."[2]

He didn't work during the school year, except for a few hours a week his last two years as a teaching assistant in the philosophy department. His parents sent a monthly allowance check. He spent summers in Clear Lake working as timekeeper and weigh master for Stokely Brothers Canning Company. At the viner station in Forest, nine miles from Clear Lake, farmers who grew peas as a cash crop would deliver wagonloads of peas for canning. Gaylord would oversee the weighing and keep time sheets for the crew of eight or nine seasonal workers.

Law, Not Medicine

Gaylord had considered becoming a doctor, like his father. But he decided that medicine would be too confining and would not allow him the time and freedom to pursue another burning interest—politics. He decided to go into law instead, since that looked like the best ticket to a political career. If that disappointed Anton Nelson, he never said so. "My parents never questioned any decision I ever made," Nelson said. After graduation from San Jose State, he went straight to the University of Wisconsin Law School in Madison in the fall of 1939, and quickly found more distractions there than he had in San Jose.

Even before school started, he attended a Young Progressives convention in Merrill, where he met two classmates who would become his closest longtime friends—Miles McMillin and John Lawton. Both would have major long-term influences on his life and career, as confidants, advisors, and social friends. McMillin would become editor of the *Capital Times*, Madison's liberal newspaper, and Lawton, an ardent outdoorsman and conservationist, became a respected Madison attorney and invited Nelson into his firm after World War II. Nelson made other longtime friends and allies in law school. Among them were Morris and Mary Rubin, who would later edit *The Progressive*, the political journal founded by Robert La Follette; John Wyngaard, who as statehouse correspondent for the *Green Bay Press-Gazette* would become the state's best known and most influential political columnist; and Aldric Revell, who as a *Capital Times* reporter and columnist would cover and boost Nelson's career.

Nelson quickly found that law school was not an insurmountable intellectual challenge. He "worked out the formula," so he didn't have to do much studying in law school at all, except read a case or two a night. Nelson had a roommate who would work for a couple of straight hours, then go out and get a beer. Nelson shortened up the regimen: "I skipped the work and just went out and had a beer." Nelson passed his courses, but usually by one percentage point higher than the lowest passing score of seventy-seven.

In his first class, on contracts, Nelson actually had studied a complicated case, but his analysis did not satisfy Professor William Herbert Page. The eccentric Page was "one of the most interesting characters in the University," the 1942 *Badger* yearbook said. "His Victorian manners, bristling sarcasm and pithy sayings make this venerable professor a teacher his students will never forget." Nelson never forgot what Page told him that day. "Pick up your books and go down to the next building," he told Nelson. "That's the music school. You might make a piccolo player, but you will never make a lawyer." Telling the story years later in a speech to law school alumni, Nelson said the same professor gave the only lecture he could recall verbatim. At the beginning of class one day, Page said: "I have a lecture that I will give you only once. The lecture is on subornation of perjury. It is this: When in the course of a trial it becomes obvious that someone has to go to jail, make sure it is your client."[3]

Wisconsin was in political turmoil when Nelson entered law school in 1939. For more than forty years it had been a one-party state, with elections decided in Republican Party primary battles between the conservative Stalwarts and the liberal Progressives. But in 1934 the Progressives had formed their own party, and the La Follette brothers led the Progressive Party ticket to victory. Phil was elected governor and Young Bob was reelected to the U.S. Senate. But after two terms and a disastrous attempt to launch a national Progressive Party, Phil lost the 1938 governor's race and gave up leadership of the party. Some, including organized labor leaders, had begun to look to the long-dormant Democratic Party as an alternative, but ten years would pass before a real Democratic revitalization began—with Nelson playing a key role.

Young Bob La Follette was up for reelection to the Senate as a Progressive in 1940, and Nelson, McMillin, and Lawton jumped in to do "shoe leather work" for La Follette. By this time Nelson had become president of the campus Young Progressives and also held an office in the Young Democrats. The Progressives were the biggest campus group, with the Young Democrats focused more on the national scene and President Franklin D. Roosevelt, who was seeking an unprecedented third term.

When Vice President Henry Wallace came to speak at a Democratic rally at the university Stock Pavilion, Nelson, Lawton, and McMillin couldn't resist a little bit of mischief. They took the Roosevelt-Wallace literature to be distributed at the event and stuffed La Follette literature inside. But the real blow to the state Democratic candidates, who shared the platform with Wallace, was the vice president's praise of Young Bob La Follette and the La Follette tradition, which President Roosevelt had asked him to deliver. The La Follettes and Progressives had been FDR allies since 1932. Wallace stopped short of endorsing La Follette, but that is how his remarks were interpreted, and the Democratic slate of candidates got up and walked out.

Nelson, Lawton, and McMillin went on the road campaigning for La Follette in the fall of 1940, with the candidate or on their own, distributing literature to voters, talking up La Follette, sticking flyers under windshield wipers on cars parked at a county fair. It truly was shoe leather work. That did not leave much time for law school. At the end of the first quarter, Nelson didn't even take exams in some of his classes and wound up short on credits. To make it up, Nelson signed up for a heavy load the next quarter, knowing it exceeded the maximum allowed without special permission from the dean. Soon, he was summoned to see Dean Lloyd Garrison, a distinguished liberal scholar who had served on the National Labor Relations Board before heading the law school.

"You are barely passing your courses," the dean said. "How do you possibly think you can take more credits and pass them?"

"I can just as successfully not study twenty credits as I can not study fifteen," Nelson said. The dean agreed to let him try, and Nelson passed them all, barely, as usual. Years later, Garrison told Nelson that was "the best legal argument you ever made." Nelson graduated on schedule, with eighty-six other young men and one young woman, with the University of Wisconsin Law School Class of 1942.

4

General Nelson

WHEN NELSON RECEIVED his law degree on 1 June 1942, the United States had been at war for nearly six months.[1] The Japanese attack on Pearl Harbor had come in the middle of his final year. Nelson had a low draft lottery number, but the draft board delayed his induction to allow him to finish his final semester.

Within sixty days of graduating, on 27 July 1942, he entered active duty. After basic training, Nelson was trained in medical technology, radiography, and X rays at Fitzsimmons General Hospital in Denver, Colorado, then remained there to train army X ray technicians. As a corporal, he was accepted for Officer Candidate School and commissioned as a second lieutenant on 25 August 1944. After an abbreviated officer training course, Nelson was assigned to the quartermaster corps at Indiantown Gap Military Reservation, a training facility tucked in a Pennsylvania mountain pass.

Nelson, who had known one black family in all of Polk County and few minorities at San Jose, was assigned to a segregated company with four white officers and two hundred black enlisted men. His all-black company, the 4513th Quartermaster Service Company, had the worst quarters on the base. They lived in obsolete World War I barracks with tar paper siding and coal-fired stoves that threw off so much soot "you'd wake up with your profile on the pillow," Nelson said. Black troops spent most of their time in their own area, with almost no recreational facilities for leisure time, while nearby white troops had recreation halls, sports fields, and even a swimming pool.[2]

Harold Curtis Fleming, a white southerner in a situation similar to Nelson's, said he was shocked and traumatized by the experience. "I really came as close as anyone to realizing what it was to be black in those days," Fleming said twenty years later, "because I was intimately involved in these men and their treatment and on the receiving end in a sense myself. It amounted to being a straw boss in a very ugly, discriminatory system." Fleming, who was with Nelson both in Indiantown Gap and overseas, later became involved in the civil rights movement as head of the Southern Regional Council in Atlanta.[3]

Nelson had much the same reaction. "I felt the discrimination myself, because you identify with your troops," he said. He recalled a high-ranking white officer inspecting Nelson's company and saying in front of the troops, "This is very good for a black company." Nelson felt his men had performed as well as any company would, black or white. Major E. Frederic Morrow, a black officer, was head of information and education for all black troops on the base. Morrow, who had been an NAACP official before entering the army, frequently ran afoul of army brass as an advocate for black troops and for his educational lectures to teach black history and instill racial pride. The army said his lectures went "beyond the bounds of military necessity" and threatened a court martial.[4] When Nelson invited him to come along to Washington, D.C., for a weekend, Morrow said there was no public accommodation in Washington where he and Nelson could both stay. Nelson arranged lodging at the apartment of a colonel in the medical corps, a doctor friend from Wisconsin assigned to the Pentagon. Nelson and Morrow could not eat dinner together at most places, but did share a meal and heard the Mills Brothers sing at a so-called black-and-tan club where the races mingled. It gave Nelson "some idea of the impact of segregation. Here was a man fighting for his country, but he couldn't go to dinner with me." Morrow later was an advisor on race relations to President Eisenhower and was the first black person ever to serve on a White House political staff.

It was no coincidence that one of the first measures Nelson introduced when he became a state legislator was a bill to integrate the Wisconsin National Guard.

Carrie Lee

At Indiantown Gap Nelson met an army nurse, Lieutenant Carrie Lee Dotson, destined to become his wife and partner for more than fifty years. It wasn't exactly love at first sight, although they hit if off well on a blind date arranged by one of Carrie Lee's nurse friends. Carrie Lee had a one-day pass from the infirmary, where she was recovering from pneumonia, so was not in top form. She was twenty-two, a brand new second lieutenant, fresh out of nursing school in Virginia and six weeks of basic training at Fort Meade, Maryland. Carrie Lee had been a cadet nurse at the Medical College of Virginia in Richmond, which entitled her to a uniform and a $40 monthly stipend. President Roosevelt had called for a voluntary nurse corps, and upon graduation she enlisted for the duration of the war. Her family had already suffered one loss while Carrie Lee was in nursing school. Her brother Delmar, seven years older, was a crew member on a B-17 bomber that disappeared over New Guinea on 15 September 1943. The wreckage and remains of the crew were not found until 1995.

Carrie Lee was born into poverty in Appalachia's Cumberland Mountains. She was born 29 January 1923 in Wise, in the southwestern tip of Virginia, but her "hometown" was Pound, a village about the size of Clear Lake, a few miles from the Kentucky border and about forty miles from Hazard, Kentucky. Hazard was later depicted in a 1980s television series as hillbilly heaven, but it was a cultured metropolis compared with where the Dotsons lived, in Dotson Holler. "We were not just rural. It was an 'up the creek and down from the holler' kind of existence," Carrie Lee recalled. "We were so poor we didn't have an outhouse," and she wore clothes made of flour sacks.[5] Carrie Lee was the ninth of ten children, of which eight survived beyond infancy. Her father died when she was three, leaving her mother unable to support the impoverished family and keep it together. Carrie Lee's father had been a thirty-third degree Mason, however, and the Masons operated a children's home in Richmond precisely for children in her situation. Delmar and another of her older brothers went to the home first, and at age seven Carrie Lee, with her five-year-old brother, became a ward of the Masons of Virginia.

Two Masons drove Carrie Lee, her brother, and mother to Richmond, but the next morning Carrie Lee said goodbye to her mother, knowing she would not see her until the next summer. It was a five hundred mile trip, and although the children were allowed to spend two weeks a year with their families, that depended on whether her mother could afford or arrange transportation to get the children home. Some years the only communication was by mail. The home, with two hundred children, seemed huge and intimidating to Carrie Lee, but she gradually overcame her initial shyness and thrived. She attended grade school in the home itself, then went to a public high school in nearby Highland Springs, Virginia, while still living at the home. Then, with the Masons' encouragement and financial support, she enrolled in the nursing school of the Medical College of Virginia, graduating in early 1945.

Nelson found his blind date, a lively, blue-eyed brunette, quite attractive—and quite outspoken. Carrie Lee felt shy and somewhat overwhelmed by this "gorgeous" guy from the exotic state of Wisconsin. She may have felt a little "frumpy and hillbilly," as she later recalled, but her date didn't notice. Carrie Lee, like many of the doctors and nurses she worked with, was profane and irreverent. She had a quick wit and a hilarious, sometimes ribald, sense of humor. She was a good-natured tease, as was Nelson. When she met Nelson at the officers' club, she admired his good looks, dark curly hair, and athletic build—a quick, positive first impression before he even opened his mouth. Gaylord was seven years older than Carrie Lee, but she would not have guessed it. He was a little shy himself, and did not seem much more experienced or comfortable with the dating game than Carrie Lee, who had not yet had a serious boyfriend. When he started to talk, she was fascinated. He had a wonderful sense of humor, and seemed well versed in just about every imaginable topic, including politics, which was not that interesting to her.

After a movie, Gaylord and Carrie Lee exchanged personal histories over dinner and a few rum and Cokes at the officers' club, and he put her on a bus back to her quarters at the hospital. Whether she was feeling insecure or not, Carrie Lee held her own in the conversation. When Gaylord mentioned fishing in a Clear Lake "crick," Carrie Lee corrected him in a light-hearted way. "Even in backwoods Virginia, we say 'creek,'" she said. A few days later, Carrie Lee got a phone call. "This is General Nelson," said the voice on the other end. "I've just thrown my dictionary away. I've looked up the word 'creek' and you're right. Want to join me at the officers' club?"

They saw each other once or twice a week for the next four or five weeks, mostly on the base, until Nelson shipped out for the West Coast and overseas. When he left, there were no tearful goodbyes or promises to get together in the future. It was wartime, everyone's future was uncertain, and no one was making long-range plans. Gaylord and Carrie Lee said goodbye, expecting never to see each other again. They hadn't even exchanged home addresses.

Provisions for Overseas

Nelson, just promoted to first lieutenant, traveled by troop train to Fort Lewis, Washington, to await orders overseas. At Indiantown Gap, he read in a bulletin instructing troops preparing to ship overseas that no liquor could be taken aboard the troop train or ship. "What the hell are we fighting for?" Nelson wondered. "You have to have a cause, don't you?" He called a former Clear Lake friend working as the manager of the Stokely Brothers cannery in Ladysmith, Wisconsin. Nelson asked him to buy two cases of whiskey, can it, label it as tomato juice, and ship it to him at Fort Lewis.

Liquor was not that readily available, and the canning season hadn't even started yet, but Nelson's friend rounded up what he could. There was enough to fill twenty-three number 2 cans. The twenty-fourth can, to fill the case, contained beans. Mission accomplished, he sent Nelson a coded telegram to let him know the shipment was on the way: "WE PUT A TIN ROOF ON THE OLD LOG CABIN." [6] Nelson never received the telegram. When the shipment had not arrived by the time he was ready to board ship, he told a captain who was still ashore about the scheme. "If it shows up," Nelson said, "take it aboard ship with you. Keep one case for yourself and save one for me in case we cross paths in the Pacific."

The voyage to Okinawa by troopship took seven weeks. The convoy, three or four days long, had to wait at sea until the United States won control of the air over Okinawa, so the ships wouldn't be sitting ducks for Japanese planes. They landed on 24 July 1945 at Naha, which had been almost totally destroyed in the fierce fighting for control of the island.

The United States was preparing to invade Japan, and Okinawa was to be a key staging area and supply depot for the invasion force. But there would be no invasion. The United States dropped atomic bombs on Hiroshima and Nagasaki within three weeks of Nelson's arrival on Okinawa, and the war officially ended within six weeks.

Even after the Japanese surrender, supplies were needed for the troops in the Pacific and the occupation army in Japan. Nelson was labor foreman for the supply dump, which contained all of the food on the island. Several companies, white and black, were assigned to the area, and fifteen hundred Japanese prisoners of war augmented the labor force. The supply dump was supposed to have enough food on hand to feed three hundred thousand troops for thirty days. It came in by the shipload, was unloaded onto amphibious landing craft, and then was loaded into a huge fenced-in dump four or five city blocks long. The Japanese prisoners did much of the heavy lifting—loading, stacking, and moving boxes, crates, and barrels of foodstuff. They worked under or alongside Nelson's company of black soldiers.

When a cargo ship arrived, Nelson would take an amphibious craft out to determine the cargo and plan where it should be unloaded and stored. That gave him access to the best provisions on the island—the precious items that would arrive in quantities too small to be put on the menu to feed three hundred thousand troops. Those scarce commodities, from turkey to grape juice, were used in trading for hard-to-get items, such as a generator from a nearby Seabee unit. Invariably some would get traded to the captain at the graves registration unit. That unit had the dreadful job of processing the paperwork and bodies of soldiers killed in action. As a small compensation, graves registration was the only unit to get a whiskey ration. Many of the troops didn't drink whiskey, so the captain always had a surplus and was willing to trade for some turkey, grape juice, or other treat. Graves registration and Nelson were the only ones on the island with a regular whiskey supply.

The situation improved when Nelson's captain friend from Fort Lewis showed up with a case of tomato juice cans. The Wisconsin cannery connection had come through. When Sherman Benson, Nelson's childhood friend, came over from his Seabee unit across the island on Buckner Bay, Nelson invited Benson to join him for a drink and pulled out a tomato juice can. "No thanks," Benson said. "We have tomato juice coming out our ears." Nelson made two quick cuts with his army can opener, and within seconds Benson recognized a familiar aroma. "My God, that's whiskey in there!" And so began the Clear Lake reunion on Okinawa.

Nurse Dotson, I Presume?

Another reunion soon followed. An officer who had been at Indiantown Gap with Nelson came to Nelson's bivouac area one day with news—some army nurses had landed, and one was that lieutenant Nelson had been dating back in Pennsylvania. After Nelson left for Fort Lewis, Carrie Lee had gone to Columbia, South Carolina, for combat training for the expected invasion of Japan. The war in the Pacific had already ended before the nurses shipped out, but five hundred nurses were assigned to replace those who had been on duty in the Pacific, so they could rotate home. It was an endless voyage on a hospital ship, from New York through the Panama Canal to the Pacific. The ship was delayed for repairs for two weeks in Panama, six weeks in Hawaii, and two weeks in the Saipan-Tinian area. It finally arrived at Okinawa in December, three months after leaving New York. Of the five hundred nurses aboard, one hundred were chosen by lot for duty on Okinawa. The others were to continue on to the Philippines and Japan. Carrie Lee was terribly disappointed when her name was called for Okinawa. Most of her friends were staying on the ship for more glamorous assignments, while Carrie Lee and ninety-nine others went over the side of the ship, clambered down the nets into landing craft, and hit the beach near Naha.

While Carrie Lee stood waiting to be assigned to a unit, an officer checking off names asked, "Aren't you that fat nurse who used to be in Indiantown Gap? Remember that Lieutenant Nelson? He's here, and I'll have to tell him you're here." The next night, a jeep pulled up at Carrie Lee's unit, and the officer in the vehicle told the guard, "Go in and tell Lieutenant Dotson that General Nelson is here." It was dark, and the sentry couldn't see Nelson or his rank insignia. Maybe he *was* a general, so he dutifully delivered the message to Carrie Lee. Between her combat training and the long sea voyage, that "fat" nurse who weighed 148 pounds when he last saw her had lost thirty-five pounds and was a

slim size eight. "You're skinny," Nelson shouted, somewhat disappoint-
edly.[7] They began seeing each other when they could, although there
was enough red tape to make it difficult. For example, an armed driver
was required to be in a jeep when there was a woman aboard, and three
was a crowd. But they managed to spend a fair amount of time together,
and romance blossomed.

By the time Nelson shipped out for the States on 20 March 1946
they had an understanding, although it was not clearly spelled out. This
time, they had exchanged home addresses. They had a vague plan that
when Carrie Lee returned they would meet at the Top of the Mark, the
cocktail lounge of the Mark Hopkins Hotel in San Francisco. The Top,
with a spectacular view of San Francisco Bay, was famous as a place servicemen bound for the Pacific would meet friends, wives, and sweet-
hearts for one last toast to the Golden Gate, which was supposed to ensure their safe return. Many rendezvoused there upon their return to
the United States as well. A romantic idea, but Carrie Lee came back
through the Panama Canal again, ended up on the East Coast, and went
back to Richmond, where she got a job in a clinic.

Nelson, meanwhile, arrived on 2 April 1946, was processed at Fort
Lewis, went on leave a few days later, and officially was discharged on
14 May 1946. After visiting an aunt and uncle in the Seattle area, he
returned to Clear Lake and plunged right into politics.

5

Losing with La Follette

NELSON RETURNED to Clear Lake just in time for the 1946 election campaign, a pivotal one in Wisconsin politics. The Progressive Party, which had split off from the Republicans to form a third party in 1934, had achieved some remarkable immediate success but had slipped badly and was on the brink of total collapse.

Philip La Follette had been elected governor, and his brother, Robert "Young Bob" La Follette Jr., had been reelected U.S. senator on the Progressive ticket in 1934. Phil won reelection in 1936, and Progressives had a plurality in the state senate and assembly during his two terms. But after a disastrous attempt to form a national Progressive Party, Phil lost a bid for a third term to Republican Julius Heil in 1938 by more than two to one. Young Bob was reelected senator in 1940, but it was a personal victory, as Heil was reelected and Republicans won both houses of the legislature.[1]

The last governor elected on the Progressive ticket never took office. Orland "Spike" Loomis won the 1942 election but died before his inauguration. Lieutenant Governor Walter Goodland, an eighty-year-old moderate Republican, became governor instead. Republicans held more than two-thirds of the seats in both houses of the legislature in the 1943 and 1945 sessions, while Progressive Party representation shrank to six of one hundred members in the assembly and five of thirty-three in the senate. Statewide, the party polled less than 6 percent of the vote in 1944 as Goodland won reelection. The Progressive Party was no longer a viable alternative as Young Bob La Follette pondered a 1946 reelection campaign.[2]

Amidst heavy lobbying and lots of backroom discussions, the Progressive Party held a convention on Saint Patrick's Day 1946 in the Portage armory to decide its fate. Anton Nelson had attended the party's founding convention in 1934 in Fond du Lac, and he wasn't going to miss this. Dr. Nelson, sixty-eight, drove all night from Clear Lake to Portage and chaired the Polk County delegation. The instructions to Polk County delegates reflected the sentiment of many La Follette loyalists: "First, keep to the Progressive Party; second, that failing, to go to the Democrats; and third, and most importantly, to do whatever Young Bob La Follette says."[3]

La Follette and the Progressives were torn about which way to go. The Republican Party was their original home and had dominated state politics for most of the twentieth century. But their conservative Stalwart wing, personified by party chair Thomas Coleman, a bitter enemy of La Follette, was now in control. The Democrats were a better ideological fit for the Progressives and were beginning to build a new liberal party, in alliance with organized labor in the industrial area of southeastern Wisconsin. Daniel Hoan, running as a Democrat, had won 41 percent of the vote for governor in a three-way race in 1944 and carried Milwaukee County. But the Democrats had not established themselves in rural counties or achieved any statewide success, except in Roosevelt's 1932 landslide. Some Progressives were determined to keep their own party alive and saw Young Bob La Follette as the only one who could provide the leadership to do that.[4]

The debate raged for hours. More than forty of the four hundred delegates spoke and were closely divided between rejoining the Republicans and remaining a third party, with little support for throwing in with the Democrats. Finally, party chair Glenn Roberts took the floor to say that no matter what the convention decided, he would not be able to recruit a slate of candidates for the fall election on the Progressive ticket. "This is a two-party state," Roberts said. "That's been proved. We've got to choose whether we go on the Democrat or Republican ticket. It isn't the label that counts; it's what you stand for."[5]

La Follette had hoped to speak after the convention made a clear-cut decision, rather than appearing to dictate the choice. But it became clear that many delegates were waiting for his direction, so La Follette expressed his view—the Republican Party offered the best hope for

Progressives. The Progressives were not going to be meekly absorbed into the GOP, he said. They were going to fight to take over the party, as they had in the past. "As presently bossed and controlled, the Republican Party of Wisconsin is not liberal, but we can go in and make the same fight we have made in the Progressive Party," he said. Once he made his wishes clear, delegates overwhelmingly, but reluctantly, voted to follow La Follette back into the GOP.[6] Nelson, still on Okinawa, read about the decision in the overseas edition of *Time* magazine.

La Follette's opponent in the Republican primary would be Joseph McCarthy, a conservative circuit judge from the Fox River Valley. Just back from World War II, McCarthy was running on the slogan that Wisconsin should "send a tail gunner to Congress." While still in the Marine Corps, McCarthy had waged a losing but attention-getting GOP primary campaign against Senator Alexander Wiley in 1944. This time, McCarthy had the strong support of the Republican leadership, and Coleman, obsessed with defeating La Follette, engineered a GOP convention endorsement of McCarthy and helped fund his aggressive campaign.[7]

Candidate Nelson

Nelson, age thirty and just back from overseas himself, returned to Clear Lake in May. "He is very much interested in the reelection of Robert La Follette," the *Clear Lake Star* reported, and would run for the state assembly from Polk County as a Progressive Republican, believing "he can be helpful to assure the reelection of Senator La Follette." Nelson challenged incumbent Republican Raymond Peabody, a banker and merchant who had held local office in the small town of Milltown and served as Polk County Board chairman before winning the assembly seat in 1942. Except for summers during college, Nelson had not lived in Clear Lake for eleven years, but was still widely known and well liked as "Doc" Nelson's son.[8]

Nelson ran a low-key campaign, spent little money, and raised few issues against Peabody. There was really only one issue in his mind: Did the voters support Bob La Follette and his Progressive slate or Joe McCarthy and the Stalwart slate? In his platform statement to the *Clear Lake Star* the week before the primary, Nelson devoted all of his space to why voters should support La Follette over McCarthy. Nelson used strong populist rhetoric but framed the choice simply: La Follette represented the people, McCarthy the corporate interests. Republicans should be the party of the people, not the special interests. Case closed. The Republican Party ran a huge advertisement for McCarthy, urging a vote for the "Regular Republican Ticket."[9]

La Follette, for his part, misread the Wisconsin political scene, stayed in Washington, and almost ignored the campaign until the final two weeks. Besides McCarthy, Coleman, and the Stalwarts, there were other forces at work against La Follette. The Democrats, whose invitation he had rejected, attacked him unmercifully. Most of organized labor abandoned him for the Democrats. In the final days, he unwisely endorsed an old friend and Progressive, Ralph Immell, in a three-way Republican primary for governor, alienating the incumbent, eighty-three-year-old Walter Goodland, and his supporters.[10]

The La Follette–Nelson ticket cleaned up in the Village of Clear Lake, with La Follette winning 77 to 26 and Nelson 95 to 16. In the Town of Clear Lake, Nelson won 70 to 4 and La Follette won 69 to 2. La Follette trounced McCarthy in Polk County, 1,419 votes to 838, but his coattails were not enough to elect Nelson, who lost to Peabody 1,232 to 1,045.

Statewide, McCarthy edged La Follette by 5,378 votes out of more than 440,000 cast, and went on to an easy victory in the November general election over Democrat Howard McMurray—in part because some Progressives were still stinging from McMurray's attacks on La Follette and the Democrats' role in his defeat. For the first time in forty years, a La Follette would not represent Wisconsin in the U.S. Senate.

Madison Beckons

In Nelson's case, his defeat was not entirely unwelcome. He already had decided that even if elected he would be a one-term assemblyman. His future, he had concluded, lay in Madison. That summer, his law school friend John Lawton had written Nelson to invite him to join his firm, Beggs and Lawton, in Madison. Lawton had graduated with Nelson in 1942 but a childhood case of polio kept him out of the military, so he had gotten a head start in the legal profession. He had been an assistant county prosecutor before entering private practice with Lyall Beggs, a former Dane County district attorney. Beggs had served in the state assembly since 1941 and was Progressive floor leader in the 1943 and 1945 sessions when the party's numbers had dwindled. Beggs was running for reelection as a Republican in 1946, and would win another assembly term while La Follette, Nelson, and other Progressives were losing.

Nelson's three years in law school in Madison had been stimulating. The state capital, the home of a great state university, and the center of the state's political action, Madison was a city alive with ideas. He had many friends there. Nelson, who had chosen law as a way to enter politics, could not see much of a future in Clear Lake in either law or politics. He told Lawton he would be in Madison after the election, win or lose.

Carrie Lee visited Wisconsin that summer and met the Nelsons, who liked her immediately. Janet and Stannard both noted something Gaylord may not have noticed, at least consciously: Carrie Lee Dotson was a lot like Mary Bradt Nelson. Both were outgoing, well-liked, caring women, trained as nurses, who were independent, outspoken, and strong willed. Carrie Lee's tongue was a little sharper and she used stronger language than Mary B., but both were forces to be reckoned with. When Carrie Lee returned to Richmond, her plan was to move to Madison by the end of the year. By then, Nelson would be there, too.

Nelson moved to Madison in the fall of 1946, rooming with Aldric Revell and his wife and helping Lawton with legal work for a fledgling public employee union that had been launched in Madison in the 1930s. It was called the American Federation of State, County and Municipal Employees—a big name for a small union that had little legal status. It started as a union for Wisconsin state workers, but AFSCME would grow to 1.3 million members, including public employees and health care workers, by the year 2000. Lawton was the lobbyist and lawyer for the county and municipal employee division of the union. He passed many assignments and cases on to Nelson, who brought no clients of his own to the practice.

Nelson did a lot of union work—organizing county courthouse or highway workers, negotiating with county boards or county highway committees, and handling other legal work. The organizing was easy compared with the bargaining once workers had formed a local union.

There was no law giving government workers the right to union representation and no law requiring the state, counties, or municipalities to engage in collective bargaining. Strikes by public employees were illegal. The employer held all the cards. "The best you could hope to do was to get [the employer] to listen to the story, tell them what was being paid for comparable work elsewhere, and that was about all negotiating amounted to," Nelson said. The bargaining sessions were not contentious, and Nelson said he "never had a disagreeable time. We'd have some good talks and go out and have a beer afterward, but the county board or city council had one hundred percent of the power."[11]

Although Lawton specialized in labor law, the four-lawyer firm had a broad general practice, handling estates, contracts, and a variety of legal work, and Nelson branched into other areas of the law. He was not a partner but was paid for the actual amount of work he did. During his twelve years with the firm, "I worked just hard enough at the law to feed the family and pay off the mortgage," Nelson said, but his main pursuit was always politics.[12]

In December 1946, Carrie Lee moved to Madison and immediately found a nursing job at University Hospitals. She fit easily into Nelson's social set, although she professed to have only "a very vague interest in politics." She was twenty-three but had never voted in Virginia, where there was still a poll tax, and did not know people who spent their time talking politics. "I got to Wisconsin and that's all they talked about. I had never heard of La Follette," she said. The Nelsons spent many evenings at the home of the Lawtons or McMillins, where the entertainment was cheap bourbon and political talk, and both flowed freely. The circle included James and Ruth Doyle, Horace and Marian Wilkie, labor leaders, university professors, progressive politicians. Almost always, there were journalists like John Wyngaard, Aldric Revell, *Capital Times* city editor Cedric Parker, *Union Labor News* editor Dick Huffman, and Ed Bayley of the *Milwaukee Journal.* The question of the day: What were liberals to do, after the disastrous 1946 election, which saw Progressives beaten in Republican primaries across the state?[13]

Some Dane County liberals had already started to move into the Democratic Party, which had built a strong blue-collar base in the Milwaukee area while their natural allies in the Madison area were caught up in the Progressive movement. A special election in 1947 for a Madison-area congressional seat helped convince Dane County Progressives to look to the Democratic Party. Carl Thompson, a young Stoughton lawyer, ran as a Democrat against conservative Republican Glenn Davis, and, while losing, won a stunning 49 percent of the vote.[14]

The Scandinavian Approach

Gaylord and Carrie Lee were married on 15 November 1947 at Pres House, a small chapel on the University of Wisconsin campus, with about two dozen family members and friends attending. Miles and Mary McMillin were the witnesses. Nelson had proposed, in his repressed Scandinavian way, on a walk with Carrie Lee along romantic Willow Drive on the U.W. campus. Gaylord shifted from one foot to the other, finally pulled out a ring with a small diamond in an exquisite rosette setting, and said, "Here, my mother wanted me to give this to you."

"He didn't say I love you and want to marry you, nor did he drop to his knees, but it was assumed that somewhere along the way that ring would join a band of a different sort," Carrie Lee recalled. She called it the classic Scandinavian approach: "If you think it, then the other person is supposed to know and already imagine that you said it." At a party for their fiftieth wedding anniversary, Nelson joked about the Norwegian who told his cousin, "You know, I love Amanda so much that sometimes it is all I can do to keep from telling her."[15]

After a weekend honeymoon in Chicago, the couple was back to work on Monday. Their apartment wasn't ready, so Carrie Lee returned to the nurses' residence and Nelson to the Revell basement for a short time until they could move into their first home, a five-room, $65-a-month apartment at 912 Regent Street, next door to the Italian Workmen's Club. The Nelsons lived there, in the heart of an old Italian neighborhood Madisonians called The Bush, for five years.[16]

6

Building a Party

THE MODERN DEMOCRATIC PARTY of Wisconsin was born in May 1948. At a meeting in Fond du Lac, the Democratic Organizing Committee (DOC) was formed, with James E. Doyle and Jerome Fox as cochairs. Doyle represented the "young turks" coming into the party and Fox the "old guard" Democrats, who were only in their forties and fifties themselves. Fox, Wisconsin national committee member Robert Tehan, and former Milwaukee Mayor Dan Hoan welcomed the newcomers. They did not see the "youngsters" as a threat but as the new lifeblood of the party and welcomed them into the leadership. Dane County attendees included Nelson, Ruth Doyle, Horace Wilkie, Carl Thompson, Julia Bögholt, and other ex-Progressives.[1]

Organizing was the DOC's middle name, but its first six months were devoted more to electoral politics than to grassroots organizing. The new Democrats were especially determined to make a successful debut in Dane County, home of the Progressive/Democrat intellectuals. The Republicans who held Dane County courthouse and legislative offices were from the GOP's Progressive wing. They faced a difficult choice: Should they seek reelection as Republicans or follow their Progressive friends and supporters into the Democratic Party? The answer was not easy or automatic. The Wilkie brothers, Ed and Horace, were a case in point. Ed, the Dane County district attorney, ran for reelection as a Republican. Horace joined the DOC and ran for Congress as a Democrat.

The incumbent state senator was attorney Fred Risser, the only remaining Progressive Party member of the legislature in the 1947 session.

He was midway through his four-year term in 1946 when his party dis-
banded. At the Portage convention, Risser had argued for joining the
Republicans, saying it was "unwise to ride in a sinking boat" and continue as a third party. Although La Follette lost his 1946 primary, Dane
County Progressives were reelected to county courthouse offices and to
the assembly as Republicans. But now many former Progressives, with
La Follette beaten and the GOP firmly in the hands of the conservatives, wanted no more of the Republican Party. In 1948, the DOC invited all of the incumbent ex-Progressives in Dane County to run as
Democrats. Risser and the others declined and ran for reelection as Republicans, which turned out to be a fatal mistake.[2]

The Democrats intended to run Floyd Wheeler, a Madison attorney, for state senate, but his law firm, which lobbied for the rural electric cooperatives, saw a possible conflict of interest. When Wheeler
dropped out of the race, Nelson dropped in and was unopposed for the
Democratic nomination. In entering the race, Nelson used a technique
he would rely on throughout his career—a "draft" movement. Nelson
had supporters put petitions in grocery stores, taverns, and union halls
across Dane County, urging him to run. He could claim his candidacy
responded to a groundswell of grassroots support. In reality, Nelson
said, "I looked into my looking glass and asked myself to run."[3]

Miles McMillin wrote many of Nelson's press releases, which were
published and displayed prominently by the *Capital Times*. On one occasion, the newspaper followed with a critical editorial because editor
William Evjue didn't like what Nelson had to say. Nelson complained
to McMillin. How could McMillin write an editorial criticizing Nelson
when McMillin had written the original release? "Well," McMillin explained, "the *Capital Times* attacked what *you* said. I didn't say it."[4]

Announcing in July, Nelson said, "I have become convinced that the
Democratic Party offers the only hope for building a sound progressive
people's movement in Wisconsin to redeem this state from the domina-
tion of political bosses and campaign barrels." La Follette's defeat "was
convincing proof of the futility of trying to liberalize the Republican
Party. . . . The fight to free Wisconsin from the control of big money
bossism must be made at every level of government."[5]

The *Capital Times* and the *Wisconsin State Journal*, the capital's conservative newspaper, both endorsed Risser in the Republican primary,

and he won handily. Risser and his GOP opponent combined had 25,128 votes in the primary to 5,066 for Nelson. But the *Capital Times* weighed in heavily in the general election, endorsing a straight Democratic ticket. The newspaper endorsed Nelson despite Risser's 100 percent voting record on issues the newspaper supported in its legislative score-card. It was nothing personal, Evjue told Risser. He had simply chosen the wrong party.[6]

The Democrats swept Dane County in November. Nelson defeated Risser, and three Democrats—Ruth Doyle, Jerome Blaska, and Her-mann Eisner—took office as Dane County's all-new assembly delega-tion. Democrats took all but one of the courthouse offices. Dane County gave President Harry Truman 61 percent of the vote over Thomas Dewey. Democrat Carl Thompson got 61 percent of the vote for gov-ernor in Dane County, but lost statewide to Republican Oscar Renne-bohm, who had become acting governor in 1947 when Walter Goodland died. Nelson beat Risser with 51.4 percent of the vote—a margin of 1,669 votes compared with margins of 13,933 for Thompson and 12,552 for Tru-man.[7] Nelson clearly owed his election to the Democratic landslide and enough straight-ticket voters to sweep him along into office. He also credited organized labor and the *Capital Times* for his election.

A Tiny Minority

The 1949 legislature was the first since 1935 to have no Progressive Party members in either house. Nelson was one of three Democrats in the state senate when the session started, with twenty-seven Republicans and three vacant seats. Eventually, Democrats won special elections to fill the vacancies, but by then one of the original trio, Robert Tehan, had resigned to become a federal judge. That left five Democrats. The Democrats couldn't even muster the six members that senate rules required to request a roll call vote and had to rely on the goodwill of the Republicans to provide the sixth person. In the assembly, Republi-cans ruled seventy-six to twenty-four. The 1949 legislature had four future governors among its members—Nelson and Republican Warren Knowles in the senate, and Democrat Patrick Lucey and Republican Vernon Thomson in the assembly.[8]

Statewide, the bright spot for Democrats was the surprise election of Thomas Fairchild as attorney general. The Republicans disavowed Fairchild's opponent, who was charged with public intoxication and urinating on a bank window in downtown Madison at high noon but went free on the grounds that his conduct "came within the reach of the constitutional right to free speech and expression," Nelson recalled. Democrats won two of the state's ten U.S. House seats, both in Milwaukee, and Wisconsin gave Truman its electoral votes. Democrats, with the infusion of ex-Progressives and help from Truman's upset, had made some gains.[9]

The legislature was a part-time job. The senate met on 103 days between January and early July 1949, when the state biennial budget passed, then for a two-day veto session in July. It did not meet at all in 1950, although some legislative committees and commissions continued to work. Fortunately, that left plenty of time to farm, practice law, or have another side occupation. Legislators elected in 1950 earned $2,400 a year, but Nelson earned only $1,200 until his second term, and as a Dane County resident could not collect the per diem others drew, making him the state's lowest-paid lawmaker for the 1951–52 session. With a virtual handful of Democrats in the state senate, there was little or no chance any Nelson-sponsored bills would pass. He was named to the Joint Finance Committee, a powerful panel that considered the state budget and all spending issues, but he was the only Democrat among five senators on the committee, and Republicans controlled the committee twelve to two.

Nelson had been deeply moved and outraged by his experience as a white officer commanding an all-black army unit and by the discrimination against his troops and black officers with whom he served. He introduced a bill, with his fellow Democrats as sponsors, to integrate the Wisconsin National Guard. President Truman had issued an executive order to integrate the armed forces in July 1948, and Nelson thought the National Guard should follow suit. Nelson's bill was referred to the Veterans Affairs Committee, where it stayed until the last day of the session, when it was killed. Meanwhile, the assembly Committee on Veterans and Military Affairs, chaired by Republican Vernon Thomson, introduced an identical bill. That bill, with the required Republican sponsorship, sailed through the assembly 91–0 and the senate 24–0 and was signed into law by Governor Rennebohm on 4 May 1949. "That was too good a bill for you to get the credit," one Republican legislator told Nelson with a laugh.[10]

Their minority status in the legislature thwarted the Democrats in passing legislation, but it did not dampen their zest for debate. Nelson loved to debate, and so did Melvin Laird, a Republican from central Wisconsin who had been elected in 1946 to fill the seat vacated by the death of his father. When he took office in 1947, at age twenty-four, Laird was the youngest state senator in the nation. Nelson and Laird would engage in long debates on the senate floor, although the eventual outcome of the vote would be obvious, with Laird's party firmly in control. The Laird-Nelson exchanges were often sharp, amusing, and quotable—"a good-natured colloquy"—but the reporter for the state's biggest newspaper, the *Milwaukee Journal,* usually ignored the Democrats because—no matter how good the rhetoric—they had no influence.[11]

The *Capital Times,* on the other hand, "hung on every word [Nelson] had to say," Laird said. "They would give him tremendous publicity on speeches that sometimes should have gone unnoticed," he joked years later. Nelson and Laird would debate all day in the senate, then after adjournment head for the Park Hotel to have a beer and "bat the breeze," often ending up at the Nelsons' apartment to continue the discussion and drinking on into the evening. Carrie Lee would come home from her shift at the hospital to find the two of them still going strong. It was the beginning of a lifelong friendship that would continue later in Washington, D.C., when Nelson was a U.S. senator and Laird a congressman and secretary of defense.[12]

Nelson loved to "bat the breeze" with anyone who had something interesting to say. Nelson valued a good conversation more than most things in life. Like his father, he had an inquiring mind that was stimulated by the exchange of ideas and opinions on almost any subject. Sometimes, he didn't mind switching sides to become the devil's advocate if it helped liven things up or cast a different light on the subject. But because he was in public life, conversation usually centered on current issues and politics.

Governor Rennebohm Calling

One day, after adjournment, Nelson wound up talking politics and policy with Governor Rennebohm at the bar of the Park Hotel on the Capitol Square, where legislators, lobbyists, and politicians congregated. Enjoying the conversation, Rennebohm suggested they continue it over dinner. Nelson said Carrie Lee was expecting him home; he was already late for dinner. The governor said he would handle the matter if Nelson got Carrie Lee on the line, so Nelson dialed the number and handed him the telephone.

"This is Governor Rennebohm," he said. "I'm here discussing issues with Gaylord and I've invited him to come over to the Madison Club for dinner. Does that meet with your approval?"

"Governor Rennebohm my ass!" Carrie Lee snapped. "You tell that S.O.B. to get home right now!"

"She doesn't believe me," Rennebohm said, handing Nelson the telephone.

Rennebohm was tickled, and never forgot it. For years, when he would see Carrie Lee at a reception or other official function, he would quietly greet her with, "Governor Rennebohm, my ass."

Actually, Carrie Lee said years later she "knew very well it was Governor Rennebohm. He was on the radio all the time, and I knew they had had drinks together before. I was angry and annoyed." Nelson understood why: "She had come home after working until seven o'clock and I was still up there having a drink or three."[13]

Building a Base

While enjoying the state senate as a place to debate issues and learn the mechanics of state government, Nelson turned much of his time and attention to organizing the Democratic Party. Despite its strongholds in Madison and Milwaukee, the party was weak or nonexistent in many counties. Democrats needed a grassroots base to field candidates for local offices and the legislature, and to provide the volunteers they needed to elect those candidates. The work facing the new DOC was hard and thankless. Cochair Jim Doyle said: "There are places around the state where it takes courage to be a Democrat. The few professed Democrats are like the early Christians. They feel as though they should hold their meetings in the catacombs."[14]

The DOC organizing work was done almost entirely by the Madison Democrats, with Doyle, Nelson, Thompson, and Wilkie doing much of the early work. DOC members would pool their information on a target county, but information was scarce and "the efforts were often feeble," Doyle said. "Very often, we were reduced to getting in touch with the postmasters in the county," who were federal Democratic patronage appointees. Sometimes that would produce a Democratic sympathizer who would be helpful. But "very often we would find that the postmaster was really a Republican in sheep's clothing . . . and these people might be totally unsympathetic, even antagonistic," Doyle said. Even the sympathetic postmasters were usually unwilling to get involved themselves, but might furnish the names of other possible contacts. The DOC would try to identify a county chairman—a former Progressive, a labor leader, an officer in a farm group. Then an invitation list would be assembled—*Progressive* magazine subscribers, former Progressive Party members, and other likely suspects. The DOC would mail an invitation to a meeting and sometimes put a notice in the weekly newspaper.[15]

The meeting was often a bust. Both Doyle and Thompson drove long distances to find no one at a meeting—not even the new county chairman. Nelson once drove to Eau Claire, a four-hundred-mile round trip, to speak at a party meeting and found no one there but a janitor. The county chairman had canceled the meeting but hadn't told Nelson. Even when he was running for governor in 1958, Nelson held a campaign meeting where only one couple showed up. But Nelson spent some time in town, meeting people individually, and found a number of closet Democrats who were supportive but did not want to be seen at a public meeting. The initial DOC meetings were always small, serving to identify leaders and lay the groundwork for another, larger meeting.[16]

While the men traveled the state, held meetings, gave speeches and did the glamorous part of the organizing effort—if there were such a thing—"the women in Dane County were a vital part of it all. They got out the mail; they did all the nitty gritty work," Nelson said. Years later, Doyle rued the way women had been treated in the DOC. "The men just asserted themselves, took it on themselves to be the bosses of the whole operation. . . . It was all just kind of taken for granted that the women would be doing the hard work and the men would be the ones who would be putting themselves forward. That was absolutely unconscious. . . . A striking demonstration of how pervasive and deep sexism is in our society," Doyle said in 1985. Doyle's wife, Ruth, was an exception, winning election to the assembly in 1948 and later serving as the only woman on the Dane County Board and as president of the Madison School Board. Another was Julia Bögholt, a longtime Democrat from Stoughton who, with Tehan, helped clear the path for the new, younger Dems, and who had served as vice chair of the DOC when it was first formed. The corps of women volunteers — Nelson's sister Janet, Esther Lawton, Lisa Tarkow, Esther Kaplan, Gretchen Pfankuchen, Marian Thompson, Carrie Lee Nelson, Hjordis Wolfe, Virginia Hart, and others — worked countless hours at party headquarters, some of them virtually full time. With their help, the DOC organized thirty-four of the state's seventy-two counties by August 1949, when Doyle stepped down as cochair to devote more time to his law practice.[17]

Nelson was chosen to replace Doyle at a DOC meeting in Oshkosh which drew about 250 members. As Doyle had done, Nelson split the job with Jerome Fox. Fox dealt with Washington on patronage issues and appointments, while Nelson was responsible for organizing. "The DOC has become a big-time organization," Doyle declared. "We are going to win in Wisconsin, not in the distant future, but in 1950. Our main objective is liberal governments in Washington and in Madison. Don't ever forget that when you're doing the humdrum work of organizing now."[18]

When the DOC held its first convention in Green Bay in November 1949, with Nelson presiding, seven hundred delegates from fifty units attended to adopt a party constitution drafted by Doyle, set up an administrative structure, and elect its first officers. Fox was elected chairman, Bögholt vice chair, Doyle treasurer, and Tehan, Bögholt, and Thompson as national committee members. "Our hour of victory is at hand," said Thompson, who had won 45 percent of the vote in the 1948 governor's race. "All that is necessary is for us to take off our coats and go out and go to work."[19]

It wasn't quite that easy. Democrats would not win a statewide election for eight years. The 1950 election produced little change. Walter Kohler, a Republican industrialist, defeated Thompson for governor. Republican Alexander Wiley won reelection to the U.S. Senate over Tom Fairchild, and Andy Biemiller lost his House seat, leaving Clem Zablocki as the only Democrat in the Wisconsin congressional delegation. Republicans controlled the state senate twenty-six to seven and the assembly seventy-five to twenty-four, and swept all of the state constitutional offices. In the state senate, Nelson was named Democratic floor leader for the 1951 session. He and his handful of Democratic colleagues continued their "trench warfare," introducing legislation which Republicans would bottle up in committee, providing fodder for future campaigns.[20]

With Republicans fully in charge, Nelson's legislative accomplishments were modest at best. The GOP allowed a few Nelson-backed bills to become law in the 1951 session. One, sponsored by Henry Maier and Nelson, expanded the state's equal rights law to forbid discrimination based on "creed, national origin, or ancestry" in addition to the existing prohibition on racial discrimination.[21] For the most part, Nelson's first four-year term consisted of playing the role of loyal opposition on the floor while continuing the slow, hard work of building a statewide base of support for Democrats.

7

Taking on McCarthy

POLITICAL MANEUVERING in the state capitol was a minor sideshow compared with the three-ring circus being staged nationally by Wisconsin's junior U.S. senator, Joseph McCarthy.

McCarthy attracted little national notice during the first half of his Senate term, and in Wisconsin most of the publicity he received was negative, as "his enemies investigated and criticized every facet of his life." Democrats, liberals, the *Capital Times*, and the *Milwaukee Journal* raised a series of ethical issues about McCarthy's conduct. They questioned whether he had failed to declare and pay taxes on income he made in the stock market in 1943; whether he had laundered that money to finance his 1944 campaign without reporting it; and whether he had violated judicial ethics by running a partisan campaign for the Senate while still a circuit judge. With a reelection campaign looming in 1952, McCarthy appeared vulnerable, either to a primary challenge within the GOP or to the emerging Democrats.[1]

In November 1949 McCarthy responded to his harshest critic, the *Capital Times,* with an attack on Cedric Parker, the newspaper's city editor, accusing Parker of being a Communist and the *Capital Times* of being "the red mouthpiece for the Communist Party in Wisconsin." Parker, in fact, may have been a Communist Party member at one time, before World War II. He certainly had associated with Communists and belonged to left-wing groups that included party members. There was no evidence that Parker was a party member in 1949, when he made the charge, but that did not matter to McCarthy, whose goal was to put the newspaper on the defensive. The most embarrassing "evidence" McCarthy cited was a 1941 editorial by William T. Evjue, *Capital Times* editor. It had called Parker "the Communist leader in Madison" and challenged Parker to publicly deny he was a Communist. The *Capital Times*, although left wing, had solid anti-Communist credentials and had played a major role in ridding the Wisconsin CIO of Communist influence. In fact, it was a struggle to have members of a Madison union disavow Communism that had prompted Evjue to attack Parker, who was a prominent CIO official as well as a journalist, in 1941.[2]

McCarthy's attack put his most severe critics on the defensive. More important, it brought McCarthy an enormous amount of statewide press attention, most of it favorable. It gave McCarthy a taste of the potential for publicity and political benefit from making such charges. It also illustrated that "newspapermen were more interested in his charges than his sources," a McCarthy biographer said, as no one really checked his claims, which included "questionable quotations . . . misleading innuendoes, non sequiturs, and the technique of guilt by association." The Parker case foreshadowed, and may have triggered, McCarthy's national anti-Communist crusade, which began a few months later.[3]

On 9 February 1950 McCarthy told an audience in Wheeling, West Virginia, that the State Department was "thoroughly infested with Communists" in key positions. He said he had a list—although the number of names varied—naming many "individuals who would appear to be either card carrying members or certainly loyal to the Communist Party, but who nevertheless are still helping to shape our foreign policy." The Truman administration, he charged, knew of the Communists in the government and either tolerated or abetted them.[4] A U.S. Senate committee agreed to investigate and hold hearings on the charges, and the curtain went up on McCarthy's spectacular but short-lived role in the national spotlight.

McCarthy's claims and tactics prompted several congressional investigations. The Tydings Committee, which investigated McCarthy's charges of Communists in the State Department, concluded in July 1950 that his claims were unfounded, relied on half-truths or untruths, and used "the totalitarian technique of the 'big lie' employed on a sustained basis." But McCarthy's crusade continued unabated. He made more headlines as he attacked President Truman and Defense Secretary George C. Marshall, and lashed out at those in the Truman administration, the Congress, or the media who challenged him. Another Senate subcommittee investigated McCarthy's involvement in the controversial Maryland Senate campaign of 1950, which used unfounded charges and even a doctored photograph to defeat Senator Millard Tydings, the Democrat who had chaired the first investigation into McCarthy's claims.[5]

When a third inquiry began, on whether McCarthy should be expelled from the Senate, Nelson invited the subcommittee to hold hearings in Wisconsin and hear firsthand evidence of why McCarthy was "unfit to hold public office." When that did not happen, Nelson sent off a large packet of material to the subcommittee, much of which had appeared in the Wisconsin media, with a list of Wisconsin citizens who should be asked to testify. Much of the information was unknown to Wisconsin voters when McCarthy was elected in 1946, Nelson said, and the subcommittee had "a moral responsibility" to complete its work before the coming 1952 election, when McCarthy would again be on the ballot. That did not happen either.[6]

Democrats Obsessed

While McCarthy's national profile increased, he still faced opposition in his own party at home. Governor Walter Kohler was privately critical of McCarthy's style, tactics, and conduct. Dissident Republicans and many Democrats thought Kohler would have the best chance to defeat McCarthy. While he publicly backed McCarthy, Kohler let it be known he was considering a challenge to McCarthy in the 1952 GOP primary.

McCarthy's defeat, in Doyle's words, "had become an obsession with Wisconsin Democrats." Some thought the place to beat him was in a Republican primary with Kohler. Doyle and others had quietly approached Bob La Follette Jr. to run as a Democrat and take back his seat from McCarthy, but he made it clear he would not run in either party. The list of prospective Democratic candidates included Nelson, Doyle, Thomas Fairchild, and Henry Reuss, a Milwaukee attorney who had run for mayor in 1948 and for attorney general in 1950.

The Democratic Party had a no-endorsement policy in primaries, so the candidates tried to work out their own system to avoid a costly free-for-all. Doyle bowed out first, in favor of Nelson, after an arbitration process in which Miles McMillin represented Nelson, Morris Rubin represented Doyle, and they chose Robert Lewis as the third party. The process was to decide who would be the strongest candidate, "and the answer was Gaylord," Doyle said. If he was not to be a candidate, Doyle wanted a role in defeating McCarthy, and he was elected in 1951 to chair the DOC and head the party's efforts during the 1952 campaign. Soon after, the DOC hired Patrick Lucey, former assemblyman and unsuccessful candidate for the Third Congressional District in 1950, as its first paid organizer.[7]

Reuss was still interested in running. While Nelson and Reuss supporters discussed a bloodless settlement like the Nelson-Doyle process, a poll of DOC members was set up to unite Democrats behind one candidate. Ed Mesheski, the Milwaukee County DOC chairman, had the ballot box, and "for one reason or another, nobody could get him to open it up," Nelson recalled. It didn't matter. In November 1951, Reuss, fearing the Madison wing of the DOC would dominate the results and keep him out of the race, announced his candidacy. A few days later, the DOC balloting showed Nelson the winner, followed by Fairchild, Reuss, and Doyle.[8]

Despite his poll victory, Nelson dropped out and prepared to run for reelection to the legislature. Nelson never was strongly interested in the nomination, since he would have had to give up his state senate seat to run a longshot race against McCarthy. Being mentioned helped Nelson's statewide standing and name recognition, but he did not believe a Democrat could beat McCarthy. When it appeared Reuss had pre-empted the Democratic field, Harold "Red" Newton, DOC activist and editor of the *Kenosha Labor* paper, formed a "Draft Nelson for U.S. Senate Committee," and the Madison CIO Council passed a resolution supporting Nelson. This time it was not a phony draft movement orchestrated by Nelson. He was out of the race and did nothing to encourage speculation that he might get in. Meanwhile, a committee to draft Fairchild formed in Milwaukee, organized by Mesheski, who had conducted the DOC balloting.[9]

In January 1952, at the urging of GOP leaders, Kohler gave up the idea of taking on McCarthy and announced for reelection as governor. If McCarthy were to be defeated, it would be up to the Democrats.

Many Democrats, including Nelson, felt Fairchild would be their strongest candidate. Fairchild had been elected attorney general in 1948, the only Democrat to win statewide office since FDR's 1932 landslide. He had run a losing but respectable race in 1950 against Republican U.S. Senator Alexander Wiley, getting 46.4 percent of the vote. He was from a respected political family—his father was a state supreme court justice—and his two statewide campaigns had built name recognition. But President Truman had appointed Fairchild as U.S. Attorney, which barred him from taking part in the early partisan maneuvering. That left Reuss in the driver's seat.[10]

Madison activists preferred Fairchild and continued to encourage him to run. In May, he said he had decided against it. Then, at the last minute, at the urging of Nelson and others, Fairchild said he would run, and his supporters scrambled to collect the signatures he needed to get on the ballot. Fairchild edged Reuss by 3,000 votes of 190,000 cast in the Democratic primary. He ran a general election campaign focused on McCarthy's failure to support programs to help farmers and workers—Social Security, the minimum wage, and union rights. The voters were well aware of McCarthy's anti-Communist crusade, and Fairchild mostly left that topic to others. Organized labor, a group of prominent citizens banded together as the nonpartisan Wisconsin Citizens Committee on the McCarthy Record, and other Democratic candidates all attacked McCarthy in a team effort.[11]

The Truth Squad

Nelson participated as a member of the Democratic Truth Squad, which trailed McCarthy at public appearances, challenged his statements, and raised issues about his record. Other participants included McMillin, Carl Thompson, Horace Wilkie, and DOC magazine editor Warren Sawall. Much of their ammunition came from a detailed document called *The McCarthy Record*, which had been prepared by Rubin, editor of *The Progressive*, with the help of McMillin and other journalists. The booklet was published in the summer of 1952 and circulated widely, raising questions about McCarthy's military career and war record, his personal and campaign finances, ethics, and any other damaging claims that could be substantiated. Almost none of the material was new, but it was the first time it had been assembled in one package and verified for accuracy. The *Washington Post, New York Times,* and others used it as a source, and it stood as the definitive work on McCarthy. The *Milwaukee Journal,* which had been attacked by McCarthy as a version of the Communist *Daily Worker,* aggressively examined his record and background and began doing investigative stories about McCarthy.[12]

The Truth Squad was more an irritant than a serious threat to McCarthy. Most audiences for McCarthy speeches were rabidly pro-McCarthy, and there were few undecided or independent voters to reach. Nelson's experience with a Truth Squad in La Crosse was typical. McCarthy was speaking, on a warm summer day, at a service club luncheon in a downtown hotel. The Truth Squad, outside with a cartop loudspeaker, could hear McCarthy through the open hotel windows. Nelson and William Proxmire, the Democratic candidate for governor, heckled McCarthy. After the speech, McMillin, who was in the audience, got up to ask McCarthy a question. "Get him out!" McCarthy thundered. "That's a representative of a Communist newspaper." Rotarians and Kiwanians escorted McMillin out, his question unanswered.[13]

After the meeting, a handful of McCarthy supporters came up to challenge Nelson and Proxmire, and there was some verbal jousting, but no real confrontation. That night, McCarthy was to speak at a pavilion outside of La Crosse, and Nelson and his cohorts amused themselves by putting anti-McCarthy literature under the windshield wipers of cars parked at the event, mainly for nuisance value. "You weren't converting anybody," Nelson knew. McCarthy mostly ignored the harassment.[14]

A Cakewalk

Nelson's campaign for reelection to the state senate was a cakewalk. The senior partner in his law firm, Lyall Beggs, had remained a Republican and was now Dane County Republican chairman. Beggs dropped into Nelson's office one day to say he was obligated to fill the Republican slate, "so let's agree on who it ought to be" to oppose Nelson. Beggs suggested George Solsrud, a county board member, "a nice man, respectable," but who would not spend a penny or a single day campaigning. Nelson agreed, and Beggs went off to recruit Solsrud, returning in an hour to say that Solsrud said he would be willing to run "if you'll circulate my nomination papers and agree that I don't have to go out speaking around the county or anything like that." Beggs accepted those terms. In a phrase he often used, which reflected his philosophy of life, Beggs said, "Gaylord, isn't it nice? Everything came out just the way it should, and nobody got hurt." Nelson won reelection easily.[15]

Although the entire Democratic ticket, organized labor, and other liberal allies made McCarthy their primary target, McCarthy beat Fairchild with 54 percent of the two-party vote and a margin of 140,000. But he ran well behind most of the GOP ticket, including Dwight D. Eisenhower, who received nearly 110,000 more votes than McCarthy. The Republican state constitutional officers all won with 63 percent or more of the vote and margins nearly three times as big as McCarthy's. In winning reelection over unknown Democratic assemblyman William Proxmire, Governor Kohler ran 140,000 votes ahead of McCarthy.[16] Clearly, a sizable number of Republican voters were splitting their tickets expressly to vote against McCarthy, but he interpreted his victory as a mandate to continue his anti-Communist crusade.

Jim Doyle said he spoke for "the great bulk of the anti-McCarthy voters in Wisconsin," not just the people in the Democratic Party, when he reacted to the results and greeted McCarthy's reelection with this widely quoted statement:

"To President Eisenhower: Our full and fervent support in the task of building the peace.

"To Governor Stevenson: Our eternal admiration for the most gallant and eloquent campaign in American history.

"To Governor Kohler: Our congratulations on your decisive victory.

"To Senator McCarthy: War unto the death."[17]

But much of the McCarthy drama was now being played out on the national stage, and Wisconsin Democrats, while continuing to attack him when the opportunity arose, returned to organizing and party building.

8

Getting Ready to Run

STATEWIDE SUCCESS for Democrats was several years off, but Democrat Lester Johnson won a 1953 special election for a congressional seat after the death of Progressive Merlin Hull. It was a major upset, which attracted national attention. Johnson was a former Progressive who, like Nelson, lost a Republican primary in 1946 and then turned to the Democrats. "I had to get beat . . . along with Bob La Follette, Ralph Immell, and Gaylord Nelson before I found out that there is no place for a liberal in that [Republican] party," Johnson said. The Ninth District, in west central Wisconsin, was mostly rural, and farm issues dominated the campaign, with Johnson keeping up a drumbeat of criticism of Eisenhower Agriculture Secretary Ezra Taft Benson. Nelson and many other Democrats campaigned for Johnson, who went door-to-door and farm-to-farm. Eisenhower had won the district handily in 1952, but Johnson won 57 percent of the vote.[1]

Soon after, the trademark "draft Nelson" for Congress movement began in Dane County. The meat cutters union at Oscar Mayer started the ball rolling, with a resolution in December 1953 urging Nelson to run against the incumbent Republican, Glenn Davis of Waukesha. Six days later, the Madison Federation of Labor followed suit.[2]

A Lincoln Day speech by Senator Joe McCarthy in Madison in February 1954 provided Nelson a platform. McCarthy attacked Eisenhower's foreign policy as immoral and indecent and accused the Democratic Party of treason. Two Madison radio stations offered Nelson airtime to respond. By inviting McCarthy to speak at their meeting, "the leadership of the Dane County Republicans rejects the leadership of

President Eisenhower and accepts the leadership of McCarthy," Nelson said. Eisenhower had carried Dane County while McCarthy lost it two to one to Fairchild in 1952. Nelson saw an opportunity to drive a wedge between moderate Republican voters and the party.[3]

McCarthy, Nelson said, "is working to destroy both political parties and replace them with the McCarthy party. . . . The violence of his attack on President Eisenhower was exceeded only by the violence of his assault on the Democratic Party. . . . When he accuses the Democratic Party of treason and calls for 'its removal from the political stage for all time to come' he is proposing a one-party system for this country—the same kind of system they have in Russia today, the same kind they had in Germany under Hitler and in Italy under Mussolini." McCarthy was a "witch doctor" who took money from and voted for Texas oil interests, Nelson charged. McCarthy and Congressman Glenn Davis, who had both voted for the interests of Texas oil producers, should be asked "what they are doing for Wisconsin farmers whose milk checks have been slashed," he said.[4] The Texas oil connection was soon to become a theme of Nelson's congressional campaign.

Farmers joined the draft Nelson movement, before he ended the charade and said he would run against Davis for the Second District congressional seat. Nelson based his decision, he said, on "careful and comprehensive surveys of opinion in the district," which convinced him that voters wanted a change.[5] In fact, Nelson "didn't expect to win and didn't really want to [win]." The district, which extended east from Dane County, included rural counties and heavily Republican Waukesha County, already a growing Milwaukee suburb. To Nelson it did not seem like a district that a Democrat could hold, even if he won it. But the campaign would give him more exposure and experience. The district abutted Milwaukee County, so the *Milwaukee Journal* would cover the race—and the *Journal* circulated statewide. He was already looking ahead to a 1958 campaign.[6]

For someone who didn't think he could win, Nelson ran a vigorous campaign, blasting away at Republican policies on agriculture, taxes, and the economy. Senator Estes Kefauver of Tennessee stumped for Nelson, who had been a Kefauver delegate to the 1952 Democratic National Convention. Crestwood, a cooperative housing development on Madison's West Side where the Nelsons had moved in 1953, staged a big rally and children's parade to support Nelson's candidacy. Crestwood was a hotbed of liberalism, like a small village filled with Democratic activists like John and Esther Lawton, Ervin and Helen Bruner, Esther and Louis Kaplan, and Nelson's sister, Janet, and her husband, Carl Lee. They talked politics incessantly and worked on campaigns and party organizing. "Gaylord," Carrie Lee said, "was the village prince." The Lees loaned the Nelsons some of the money to buy a small green house on Arbor Vitae Place, near the Lawtons.[7]

The Nelsons' first child, Gaylord A. Nelson Jr., was born on 10 August 1953. Like his father, the family called him Happy. Carrie Lee, now thirty, had long wanted a child, and gave up working as a nurse to devote full time to raising a family. "I did not know I was going to have a total commitment to boredom and being a housewife," she said years later. Gaylord's increasing political activity meant he was on the road, in the legislature, working at his law practice, or campaigning. Carrie Lee was often home alone with young Happy, and there was little money for entertainment or even a babysitter. It was boring and lonely at times, and it "seemed alien" to her for people to be so consumed by politics. But Gaylord never pressed her to play the traditional role of political wife. "Set your own precedents. There are no rules," he told her. During Gaylord's thirty-two years in elective office, she carved out a role that suited her. "Gaylord never ever has criticized me, never once said you cannot talk that way or behave that way," she said. She was, one friend said, "the mortar that holds that family together."[8]

The unlikely issue of offshore oil reserves became the centerpiece of Nelson's campaign. Nelson repeatedly hammered at Davis's vote for the Tidelands Oil bill, which transferred the ownership of billions of dollars worth of offshore oil deposits from the federal government to four states—Texas, Florida, Louisiana, and California. Nelson said royalties from the oil should have been divided among all of the states, which would have meant hundreds of millions of dollars for Wisconsin. Davis's campaign had taken a $500 contribution from a Texas oil millionaire in 1952, and Nelson suggested the contribution and the vote were linked. When Davis threatened a libel suit, Nelson challenged him to file, saying he would be "most happy to appear in court any time and repeat everything I have said concerning your record on Tidelands Oil."[9]

The debate raged in the district's newspapers and finally erupted when Nelson and Davis debated before a Farm Bureau group, where the main topic was the 1954 federal farm bill. At the end of his remarks,

Nelson said he wanted to raise the Tidelands issue, "which cost every farmer in this room about $350." Davis had refused his invitation to debate the issue, Nelson said, but "he's here tonight. As long as we're here together on this platform, I think it would be a shame to leave here without hashing this over." Morris Rubin, editor of *The Progressive,* set the stage with a question about Texas intervention in Wisconsin politics. "There are some questions Congressman Davis should answer about this Tidelands bill," Nelson began. "I'll answer them if they are asked," Davis said. "OK, I'll ask them," Nelson shot back, amidst laughter from the audience of 250. Nelson proceeded to rip Davis's vote and to demand an explanation. If the federal government had retained the royalties and used it to pay for education aids, Wisconsin's share would have been enough to pay for its school programs for ten to twenty years, Nelson said.[10]

"This vicious business of giving away the natural resources of this country has got to stop," Nelson shouted. "And I think that the taxpayers should let Congress know they want it stopped by defeating everyone who voted for it." Nelson sat down amid loud cheers and applause, according to McMillin's account in the *Capital Times.*[11]

The election results were predictable. Nelson carried Dane County by more than eight thousand votes, but Davis won Waukesha County by almost as much and ran up huge margins in the three rural counties in the district. The total vote was 74,460 for Davis and 63,449 for Nelson. Kohler got a scare in his reelection campaign for governor, defeating Proxmire with only 51.5 percent of the vote. Proxmire was making his second run for governor, after defeating Jim Doyle in the Democratic primary. Republicans kept their hold on all state constitutional offices and big margins in the legislature. Besides Proxmire's strong showing, the best news for the Democrats was Henry Reuss's victory for a congressional seat on Milwaukee's north side. Reuss defeated incumbent Republican Charles Kersten, a strong McCarthy supporter, to claim the seat he would hold for twenty-eight years.[12]

Setback for McCarthy

The 1954 elections were a serious setback for McCarthy, for whom it already had been a very rough year. Anti-McCarthy forces, led by a Sauk

City newspaper publisher upset about farm policy, had mounted a recall effort in the spring under the "Joe Must Go" banner. The movement was a true grassroots effort that got no financial or official organizational support from organized labor or the Democratic Party, although members of both certainly helped with the petition drive. A number of prominent Republicans, upset by McCarthy's continued attacks on President Dwight D. Eisenhower, also participated. The committee collected an impressive 300,000 signatures, but short of the 400,000-plus needed in a sixty-day time period to force a recall election. Nelson, like virtually every Democratic official, stayed out of the recall effort.[13]

Meanwhile, twenty million Americans had watched the Army-McCarthy hearings, which showed McCarthy and his tactics at their worst. McCarthy bullied, interrupted, and personally attacked witnesses, their attorneys, and even some senators on the committee. He finally crossed the line of public tolerance with an attack on the loyalty and alleged Communist connections of a young associate of the army's counsel, Joseph Welch. "Until this moment, Senator, I think I never really gauged your cruelty or your recklessness," Welch said. "Have you no sense of decency, sir, at long last? Have you left no sense of decency?" Welch asked. Spectators in the hearing room burst into applause. The conservative *Wisconsin State Journal,* which had supported McCarthy, called McCarthy's action "worse than reckless . . . worse than cruel. It was reprehensible."[14]

The Progressive magazine had updated and expanded upon the report on McCarthy's record, and published a special issue on McCarthy, which sold 185,000 copies. McCarthy's Senate colleagues, encouraged by the negative public reaction to his performance in the hearings, introduced charges of misconduct against him. McCarthy still had many supporters, especially among Wisconsin Republicans, but his battle with Eisenhower was splitting the party. After seeing some of his supporters beaten in primary races, McCarthy did not make any postprimary appearances in Wisconsin. When Democrats captured both houses of Congress in November and several strong McCarthy supporters were defeated, the Senate was emboldened to move on a censure resolution. The Senate censured him on 2 December 1954 for contempt and abuse of two congressional committees. For all practical purposes, McCarthy's days on center stage, as a man of power and influence, were over.[15]

Languishing in the Legislature

Wisconsin Republicans continued their dominance of the 1955 legislature, and the outnumbered Democrats continued to spar on issues in hopes of chipping away at the GOP majority in the next election. Sometimes they couldn't resist some partisan mischief, as when the eight Democrats in the state senate introduced a resolution commending the twenty-two U.S. Senate Republicans who had voted to censure McCarthy. That went into the legislative wastebasket, along with most other Democratic proposals. A few innocuous Nelson-sponsored bills did pass, but no significant policy changes were going to be made by a party with less than one-third of the seats.

Pat Lucey and other Democratic Party leaders urged Nelson to run again for Congress in 1956. Glenn Davis, who had held the seat for ten years, was going to oppose Senator Alexander Wiley in the Republican primary. Having run in 1954, Nelson would have a good chance of capturing an open seat, they argued. Nelson had no interest. "I wasn't taking on any losing races when my own office was up," he said. At the state convention in Superior in June, Nelson told the Democrats he definitely wasn't running for Congress, but would seek reelection to the state senate. Lucey "was pretty upset, thought I owed it to the party or some such nonsense as that," Nelson said. Nelson had represented all of Dane County, but ran now in a new district created by reapportionment, which gave him all of rural Dane County and everything outside the city of Madison. Crestwood, where the Nelsons lived, was outside of the city limits. They had moved in 1955 into a new home at 5627 Crestwood Place, designed by architect Marshall Erdman, a close friend. Parts of the $18,000 "prefabricated" home were manufactured off-site. Two of the four bedrooms were tiny, but the home adequately met the Nelsons' needs. A second child, daughter Cynthia, was born on 21 June 1956, joining three-year-old Happy. The family called her Tia.[16]

Nelson won reelection with 63 percent of the vote over Republican Hermann Eisner, a farmer and ex-Democratic assemblyman who had switched to the GOP. Democrat Horace Wilkie won the new City of Madison senate seat. Republicans carried the state in a landslide with Eisenhower at the top of the ticket. Moderate Alexander Wiley kept his U.S. Senate seat, first narrowly defeating Davis, the conservative congressman who won the GOP convention endorsement, in a bitter, hard-fought primary, and then handily defeating his Democratic challenger, state senator Henry Maier of Milwaukee. Proxmire made his third straight run for governor, losing this time to Attorney General Vernon Thomson, but winning 48 percent of the vote again, as he had done in 1954. The governorship had become competitive, but the GOP still held it and all other statewide offices and controlled the legislature two to one.[17]

The Death of McCarthy

McCarthy was not a player in the 1956 election, and Democrats were convinced he could be defeated in 1958. Nelson, Proxmire, Reuss, Maier, and Clement Zablocki were touted as potential candidates. But the jockeying for position ended on 2 May 1957 when McCarthy died of hepatitis. Events moved quickly then. With a special election looming, party leaders hoped Democrats could unite behind one candidate and avoid an expensive, divisive primary. Nelson took himself out of the race a week later. "Gaylord tried to maneuver me out of the race by telling me I could be elected governor the next year," Proxmire recalled, but Nelson's recollection was that he was already eyeing the governor's office in 1958, even if McCarthy had lived. After ten years in the state senate Nelson "knew state government inside out" and wanted to put that knowledge to use.[18]

Republicans in the legislature introduced a memorial resolution honoring McCarthy, but Democrats thought it went too far in praising him as "one of the most aggressive and courageous fighters against Communism." When a standing vote was taken on passage, four Democratic senators remained in their seats. Nelson was not in the chamber, having walked out into the adjoining parlor to avoid the vote. The resolution was "praiseworthy in a way I didn't think it should be," Nelson said, but it was an expression of condolence to McCarthy's widow, and Nelson did not want to appear petty or spiteful by voting against it. Even with a chance to vote against a resolution honoring someone many Democrats believed to be the devil himself, Nelson refused to make his disagreement personal. He got heat from some Democrats about it—"Gaylord ran," Henry Maier said—but Nelson felt that "my record on criticism of McCarthy had been clear for years. If I had to vote, I would have voted against it," he said, but he could see no reason to kick a dead man.[19]

Reuss was clearly interested in the Senate seat, and so was Proxmire, the state's best-known Democrat after three labor-intensive campaigns for governor in the previous five years. Proxmire, believing party leaders were lining up behind Reuss to keep him out, challenged Reuss to run, saying, "I, too, am seriously considering running." In deference to his colleague Zablocki, the senior member of the House delegation, Reuss told Zablocki he should consider the race. Much to Reuss's surprise, Zablocki decided to run, and that eliminated Reuss. Republicans, meanwhile, had a seven-way primary, with ex-Governor Walter Kohler, ex-Congressman Glenn Davis, and Lieutenant Governor Warren Knowles the most prominent contenders. Proxmire beat Zablocki handily with 60 percent of the vote, while Kohler won over Davis by nine thousand votes, but with only a third of the splintered Republican primary vote.[20]

Three-Time Loser Wins

Kohler had beaten Proxmire for governor in 1952 and 1954, but this time the Democrats were energized and unified while Republicans were divided and dispirited. When the GOP tagged him "a three-time loser," Proxmire responded on radio that he would take the votes of everyone who had ever lost or failed "in business, love, sports, or politics" and give the Republicans the votes of everyone who had always succeeded and won everything. Proxmire won 56 percent of the vote to become the first Democratic senator from Wisconsin in nearly twenty years, and only the third in the twentieth century. Proxmire promptly announced he would seek a full term in 1958.[21]

That made Nelson's decision an easy one. He had decided privately, even before McCarthy's death, to run for governor. After five sessions in the legislature, he had few victories to celebrate. He had learned the workings of state government, sharpened his speaking and debating skills, and made lasting friendships among legislators in both parties. He had earned a reputation as a decent, thoughtful, principled public official. Through his DOC organizing work and his campaign for Congress, he had begun to make a name for himself outside of Dane

County. He could not afford, politically or financially, to invest more time in the legislature. "I'd been in the state senate long enough; I'd learned all you could learn," he said. He expected to have to run for governor more than once. The 1958 race, a free ride since he was in midterm in the state senate, would get his name known across the state. He planned to run again in 1960 and "either win or go into full-time law practice."[22]

Although electrifying, the Proxmire victory was not a clear signal that Democrats were now competitive statewide. Proxmire, in four frenetic campaigns in six years, had raised face-to-face campaigning to a new level—one that has yet to be matched in Wisconsin politics. Seemingly inexhaustible, Proxmire would travel the state alone, often shaking thousands of hands in a day. Anywhere there was a crowd—a convention, sporting event, fish fry, parade, plant gate, rally, or fair—Proxmire was there, pumping hands, exiting as soon as he had met everyone and heading for the next stop. During his four campaigns, most voters had probably seen Proxmire or had shaken his hand. While Democrats celebrated his victory, they wondered whether it was a personal victory or a sign their party had come of age. The 1958 campaign would be the next test.

9

Nelson for Governor

THE FIRST SIGN of the Nelson for Governor candidacy, the inevitable "draft," surfaced in Janesville on 4 September 1957, when a group of Rock County Democrats called on Nelson to run. Within a week, Nelson said he was "actively considering" the race and might announce his candidacy "in a few hours or in a few days." Milwaukee Congressman Henry Reuss was also interested. Reuss had run statewide, was better known, and might make a stronger candidate, some Democrats said. Ninth Congressional District Democrats in Eau Claire passed a resolution urging both Nelson and Reuss to run. A Nelson for Governor club formed in Sheboygan, and 262 Dane County Democrats signed "Draft Nelson" petitions. Momentum, whether real or manufactured, was building.[1]

Nelson knew Reuss would be "very tough in a primary" and hoped for a clear field to the nomination. When Reuss called Nelson to say he wanted to come to see him on Friday, September 13, Nelson "figured he would be trying to talk me out of the race." Nelson quickly drafted a press release and sent it to the newspapers, saying he would make an announcement about the race on Monday, three days later. When Reuss came into Nelson's office, Nelson said, "'There isn't much to discuss. My release has already gone out.' That ended that. There was nothing to negotiate about." Although Nelson didn't know it, Reuss had decided long before that he would not run for governor, Reuss said years later. Jacob Friedrich, the state's most highly respected labor leader and Reuss's "sainted supporter" in his previous races, had called him months earlier to tell Reuss that labor liked Nelson for governor and would prefer that

Reuss not run. "OK, I hear you, don't lose any sleep over it," Reuss told Friedrich.[2] Reuss allowed the speculation to continue, as Nelson had done with the 1957 Senate race. Politicians do not mind being touted, even for offices they do not plan to seek.

On 16 September 1957, Nelson announced his candidacy at a press conference in Madison's Park Hotel, saying the Republicans had grown "fat and feeble—feeble from being too long in office, and fat from lack of activity." The GOP administrations had been "unimaginative, inefficient, and unbusinesslike," he charged, handling major problems by either ignoring them or denying their existence. He called for a return to "the philosophy and the purpose of the Wisconsin Idea as Old Bob La Follette envisioned it." State government operated under a century-old inefficient system of administration, he said, and needed streamlining and reorganizing. He offered an ambitious list of fourteen issues to be discussed in his campaign: fiscal policy, control of lobbying, problems of the aged, industrial development, executive and legislative reorganization, state employees, the state building program, mental health, higher education, public education, conservation, agriculture, and labor.[3]

He said he was "flatly opposed to a sales tax and [I] have been for many, many years," promising a comprehensive tax and fiscal plan during the campaign. He said he and Proxmire would work closely together. And he read a telegram from Reuss, pledging his "whole-hearted support" and predicting "your election will complete the two-party swing in Wisconsin."[4] State senator Henry Maier of Milwaukee, who had considered the race, also stayed out. Nelson's bold, early entry into the race had cleared the primary field.

Nelson's fourteen-month campaign began immediately. In the first month, he made at least eight speeches on a variety of issues. He criticized Eisenhower on civil rights in Madison, blasted Republicans in Racine for considering a move to a closed primary, called Governor Vernon Thomson irresponsible in Madison for signing a bill preventing construction of a civic auditorium designed by Frank Lloyd Wright. He challenged Thomson in La Crosse to join him in calling for U.S. Agriculture Secretary Ezra Taft Benson to resign, rapped the GOP in Sparta for mistreating and underpaying state employees, claimed in Darlington that Thomson falsely took credit for a new lobbying law, accused Thomson of "fiscal flim-flam" in Eau Claire, and unveiled in Baraboo a proposed million-dollar-a-year loan fund for college students.[5]

With the same energy that Proxmire shook hands, Nelson gave speeches and campaigned like a man possessed. For the first time in his life, Nelson was driven. By his count, he had made sixty-two speeches by March. By September 1958, he had traveled thirty thousand miles, made two hundred speeches, and campaigned in every corner of the state.[6]

He knew the issues, and he knew how to give a speech. He never had a prepared text; at most he might have an outline scribbled on the back of an envelope in the car, to remind him of key points he wanted to cover. He usually had a press release in his pocket, with a few paragraphs of quotations on the topic of the day. He would "validate" the press release by working those comments into his speech, but that usually was not the centerpiece. Nelson was an entertaining speaker. He chose his words carefully and spoke with precision. He had a perfect sense of timing when telling a joke, and he had a knack for spinning yarns. He could read an audience; if he detected disinterest or boredom setting in, he could shift gears or topics at a moment's notice. He was entertaining; he could be hilarious. "Nelson, whose upstate drawl makes him look and sound like a Will Rogers in a Brooks Brothers suit, had a full house . . . in stitches," a labor paper reported.[7]

Nelson also could be serious and moving. Most of his speeches were a mixture of populist political philosophy, thoughtful discussion of issues, and sharp partisan rhetoric, softened with flashes of humor. Nelson's idea of a good speech was one that "includes an interesting subject, is not too long, with a good laugh two or three times. If the audience thinks it's a good speech, that's considered a good speech."[8]

The pace was brutal. Nelson ended most days at home in Madison. He might leave early in the morning, campaign all day, and end with a speech somewhere like Eau Claire, several hours from home. Nelson would talk and doze on the way back to Madison with one of his young staffers—Jim Wimmer, John Brogan, or Joe Checota—behind the wheel, getting home well past midnight. Early the next morning, it started all over again. Near election day, a reporter described a day on the campaign trail with Nelson, who called it a "poky" day compared to most. He campaigned in Watertown, Juneau, Beaver Dam, Horicon, Mayville, West Bend, Hartford, and Slinger, shaking hands at plant gates, on main streets, and in businesses; meeting with local Democrats; and making four radio appearances. The day before he had worked twenty-one and one-half hours, leaving Madison with Brogan at 4 A.M. and going to bed in Watertown at 1:30 A.M. after campaigning in Waukesha and Milwaukee. Nelson had never worked so long and so hard in his life.[9]

At the official campaign kickoff in Clear Lake, more than five hundred people turned out in a village of seven hundred to give their hometown boy a big sendoff. Minnesota Governor Orville Freeman was the main speaker, and the Polk County Democratic organization sponsored the December event, but the crowd was bipartisan and a Clear Lake committee of three Republicans and one Democrat did most of the work. The ham dinner was prepared and served by more than one hundred women from local church groups of all denominations and political persuasions. It was a civic event, not a partisan one, for Clear Lake's favorite son.[10]

Clear Lake Humor

Nelson's Clear Lake background came to the fore in the campaign for governor. Nelson had always told Clear Lake stories about the characters, events, and life in the small town where he grew up. They were folksy stories, sometimes with a moral, but more often with a laugh. He had begun telling Clear Lake stories to enliven or lighten up debate in the state senate, and had always told them privately at parties. But it was in the governor's race that he really tapped the wellspring of stories and experiences from Clear Lake and became identified with them. It was a sure way to loosen up an audience. Sometimes people started to laugh when he introduced the Clear Lake characters—Trolle Christopherson, Scoop Shettel, Bunker Johnson, Bandy Van Ruden, and Fritter Wigand—before he even got to the story.

Trolle was a big baseball fan, he'd say, and Clear Lake friends pitched in to send him on the train to a Minneapolis Millers game. On his return, everyone was curious: How did he like the game? "I'll tell you," he said. "There was so much going on at the station [in Minneapolis] that I never did get down to see the village."[11]

In another Nelson story, Trolle got up to speak at a postelection unity dinner, planned to patch things up after a tough Polk County campaign in which the Democrats had won a rare victory. But Trolle was fiercely partisan. "For years, the Republicans have been lying and cheating and stealing elections," he declared. Then, realizing this was a unity dinner, he concluded: "But, with God's help, we beat 'em at their own game."[12]

Those stories, he admitted, were apocryphal but plausible. They could have happened in Clear Lake, and they could have happened to Trolle. "That's a good reputation to get, having a good sense of humor," Nelson knew, and at a time when most of the internal Democratic Party struggles were Madison-Milwaukee fights, "small town identification was a good credential, even in the cities." It wasn't that he cynically or deliberately adopted the small town persona, although he clearly could see its advantages. He *was* a product of Clear Lake, its attitudes, standards, and principles. He believed in Clear Lake's values and wanted to bring them to government and politics. Clear Lake was what Gaylord Nelson was all about. "Most men of public life leave the small towns of their boyhood far behind, resurrecting them only for the most contrived campaign appearances," a Washington reporter wrote. "It's different with Nelson. Clear Lake genuinely seems to provide him with roots and an identity."[13]

Part of his charm was that he was self-effacing. Nelson was often the butt of his own jokes. He would tell about meeting a friendly looking farmer in conservative, Republican Winnebago County and striking up a conversation. "Your face is familiar," Nelson said. "Don't I know you?" The farmer replied, "Young fellow, I meet so many people I can't remember them all." In a dime store in Beaver Dam, Nelson, not wearing a coat, walked up to a woman shopper who mistook him for a clerk and asked him, "What size are these socks?" "I don't know," the candidate replied. "I just stopped by to shake your hand. I'm Gaylord Nelson, the Democratic candidate for governor." "Well, for heaven's sakes," the woman said. "How did you know me?"[14]

"His greatest thrills came when he went into the towns and villages of the state," Nelson's young campaign manager, Jim Wimmer, said. "In nearly every town he was reminded of a house or a store similar to those he used to know in Clear Lake. At times, he would become unabashedly sentimental and pull out story after story about his boyhood and his hometown."[15]

Campaigning in the little town of Winneconne in central Wisconsin, Nelson visited an ancient feed mill that a reporter said "could have been the setting for a Dickens novel," with a "creaking floor and rotting beams." He couldn't resist a hometown comparison. "The one in Clear Lake is bigger, but this is more modern," Nelson said.[16]

Nelson collected stories and knew that a good one could never really be worn out. He was still telling about Trolle's unity speech forty years later.

Reporters enjoyed covering Nelson. He was amusing to travel with and made good copy for newspapers. But the reporters sometimes wondered whether those Clear Lake characters were too good to be true, their names just a little too amusing, their lines unbelievably funny. Later, when Nelson was governor, his boyhood buddy Sherman Benson came in for a visit. As a test, one of Nelson's staff members asked Benson, "How's Scoop Shettel?" Benson replied, without missing a beat, "Oh, he's fine. He's running a restaurant out in Reeve," a tiny crossroads community in Polk County. Scoop was real.[17]

On the Attack

Humor was only part of the recipe for a Nelson speech. Day after day, Nelson was on the attack against the administration of Vernon Thomson, who was seeking a second two-year term. Nelson's announcement speech had described the GOP as "fat and feeble," and he played variations on that theme in speech after speech. The Republicans were "too old and tired" after twenty years of being in power, he said in West Allis. The GOP had developed a lot of deadwood and "have been sweeping problems under the rug," he said in Farmington. "New and vigorous leadership" and "new blood" were needed because "the Republican leadership has grown old and tired on the job," he said in Fond du Lac. The GOP government has grown "fat and flabby under twenty years of one-party rule," he said in Cornell. He elaborated at a Madison dinner: The Republicans were "fat from eating too high on the hog and feeble from inactivity."[18]

No matter how he phrased it, the message was constant: Wisconsin had been a one-party state for too long. It was time for a change. In July, when he filed his nomination papers, he said: "Twenty years in power is too long for any administration. . . . Our great liberal, progressive tradition has been destroyed . . . by an administration that is unable to cope with the problems of today and blind to the problems of tomorrow. It will take a new administration with courage and vigor to solve our vast accumulation of problems."[19]

In stump speeches across the state, Nelson "expounded his views on normally dull subjects like taxation and the state budget in such an engaging manner that he captured voter interest and instilled understanding."[20] He covered a wide range of issues in the early months of the campaign—farm policy, the open primary, school integration, treatment of state employees, restrictions on lobbying, aids to local governments, a higher education loan plan, conservation policies, academic freedom for university faculty members, "shameful" new restrictions on relief, mental health, the aging, industrial development.

To the chagrin of some Democrats, Nelson renewed the criticism he had leveled at Lyndon Johnson, the Senate majority leader, during Nelson's 1954 congressional race. The party's future, Nelson believed, was as a liberal party, and Johnson and other southern Democrats in congressional leadership posts were too conservative. Johnson is "wrong on too many issues to satisfy me or you," he said at a campaign dinner. "We don't have to be satisfied with the lesser of two evils. We can demand better leadership and we can get it." Nelson said LBJ and the southern Democrats had failed to move quickly or strongly enough on civil rights, natural resources, and a foreign policy to promote peace. There had been too many compromises, he said, vowing to work in 1960 for a "thoroughly liberal platform and slate" at the national convention, whether he won the governor's race or not. Some Democrats wished Nelson would be quiet, and Democrats in the state's congressional delegation, including Proxmire, defended Johnson, but Nelson vowed to continue to speak out. [21]

Thomson, the incumbent, was a political veteran who had been speaker of the assembly, Republican floor leader in the state senate, and attorney general for six years before being elected governor in 1956. Thomson started his reelection campaign with some heavy political baggage. The 1958 campaign was waged against a backdrop of a national economic recession. Wisconsin farmers—usually reliable Republican voters—had demonstrated, in helping to elect Proxmire to the Senate in 1957, that they were fed up with Eisenhower's farm policy. The baby boom was putting added demands on the educational system and other state services without adding to the tax base or the size of the tax-paying population. There was internal strife in the GOP, and the 1958 party platform supported a state sales tax and a right-to-work law. There was plenty of ammunition. Nelson was determined to put Thomson on the defensive and keep him there.[22]

Nonetheless, Thomson was a heavy favorite. Proxmire had come close, but only one Wisconsin Democrat had been elected governor in the twentieth century, and that was due to Roosevelt's 1932 landslide. In June, after Nelson had been campaigning for nine months, the steelworkers' union commissioned a Lou Harris poll, which showed Thomson leading roughly 50–30 with 20 percent undecided. Nelson called Harris to discuss the poll. The most encouraging words the pollster could offer were, "Well, elections *have* been won from there."[23]

Democrats Smell Victory

Wisconsin Democrats, still euphoric from the Proxmire victory a year earlier, believed their day had arrived. In defeating his old nemesis, Walter Kohler Jr., in the 1957 Senate race, Proxmire had carried eighty-two of the state's one hundred assembly districts. A Waukesha County dinner in March, featuring Nelson and Proxmire, attracted an overflow crowd of five hundred who "laughed at every joke and cheered every speaker." The year before, the dinner had drawn sixty persons. Now, the crowd was so exuberant that state chair Patrick Lucey warned against overconfidence, and the priest who gave the invocation urged humility. When the band played the party anthem, "Happy Days Are Here Again," the crowd went wild, banging tables, singing along, and clapping their hands. Lucey asked for pledges of $2.50 a month for the coming campaign, and raised $1,000 in ten minutes.[24]

At the state party convention in La Crosse in June, some last-minute schedule shuffling thrust Nelson into the spotlight as the featured speaker. A rare Saturday session of the U.S. Senate kept Senators Hubert Humphrey, Joseph Clark of Pennsylvania, and Proxmire in Washington. Humphrey was to deliver the keynote speech on Friday night, and Clark was to be the banquet speaker on Saturday. Minnesota

Congressman Eugene McCarthy filled in for Humphrey on Friday, and Nelson was warned Saturday morning that he should be prepared to give the banquet speech if no big name substitute could be found for Clark.

When the opportunity came, he took full advantage of it, with a far-ranging, Republican-bashing speech that had the twelve hundred delegates applauding and howling, giving him thunderous applause and a standing ovation. Nelson critiqued both the state and national GOP administrations and found them lacking "the will, energy and vision to lead." Thoughtful citizens, he said, were worried about the faltering economy and about "our sense of values in a system symbolized by the grey flannel suit, the high paid coach, the low paid teacher, and the remarkable appendage attached to the rear of our cars called a tail fin."[25]

His speech covered a wide range of issues—foreign policy, agriculture, inflation, atomic bombs, the Tennessee Valley Authority, the recession, and Wisconsin's industrial growth and tax policies. Turning to the pressing issue of state finances, Nelson said Republicans "for twenty years have patched up a hodge-podge tax system." He drew "thunderous applause" when he called for a complete study and overhaul of the state tax system. "Nothing else at the convention has received such an enthusiastic response" as Nelson's speech, the *Milwaukee Journal* reported.[26]

The next day, delegates adopted a platform plank that echoed Nelson's demand for a comprehensive study of the tax system and its impact on different categories of taxpayers. While supporting the use of the income tax as "the principle source of state revenue," the plank did not specifically rule out a sales tax. The *Journal*, in its top headline, said the Democrats had "retreated" from their sales tax opposition, and explained the nuances in the plank. Those nuances apparently had escaped some of the delegates. Henry Maier, Democratic floor leader in the state senate and a member of the platform committee, said he did not intend to open the door to a sales tax and didn't believe a study committee would propose one. The plank appeared to follow Nelson's lead, but it actually had been written before his speech. Nelson, in calling for the study, used the phrase, "Let the chips fall where they may." The *Journal* interpreted that to mean "Nelson would not reject a sales tax if it could be levied equitably and fairly." The platform committee chairman, state senator Lynn Stalbaum, confirmed that the plank did not rule out a sales tax if a study of the tax system concluded one was needed.[27]

James Doyle, the former party chair, had failed to get the platform committee to adopt an amendment making the position clearer. His proposal said the Democrats would "maintain an open mind on all tax alternatives, testing them not by their labels or political connotations but by their actual impact in relation to the ability to pay, stability and Wisconsin's economy in competition with other states." Doyle did not specifically mention the sales tax, the *Milwaukee Sentinel* speculated, because "the very phrase is considered slightly obscene in some Democratic circles." Doyle and Stalbaum were to serve later on the tax study committee appointed by Nelson after his election as governor.[28]

Delegates also passed a strong civil rights plank calling for creation of a state Equal Opportunities Commission, and elected Vel Phillips, a thirty-four-year-old African American alderwoman from Milwaukee, as the first black woman member of the Democratic National Committee. Phillips's election was to "send a message and declare independence from the conservative Southern leadership of the [national] party," and offered as "dramatic proof of Wisconsin's liberalism" and "a blow for civil rights."[29]

Enough Problems Left?

Nelson's hour of triumph was marred by personal sorrow. Nelson's father, Anton, had accompanied him to the convention to see him speak to the Democrats as their candidate for governor. After Nelson's banquet speech, Dr. Nelson suffered a heart attack at a convention reception. When Gaylord visited his hospital bedside, Dr. Nelson reminded his son of their conversation on the ride home from Amery thirty-two years earlier, after hearing Senator Robert La Follette Jr. speak. Anton had asked Gaylord, after the 1926 speech, whether he might like to go into politics. Gaylord replied that he was afraid La Follette might have solved all of the problems by then. Now Anton, on his deathbed, said with a smile, "Well, Gaylord, do you think Bob La Follette left enough problems for you to solve?"[30]

Dr. Nelson died in the hospital two weeks later, at age eighty. Gaylord's mother had entered a nursing home near Madison in 1957, with what was diagnosed as arterial sclerosis and may have been Alzheimer's disease. She lived until mid-1960.

10

A Two-Party State

IN THE FINAL MONTHS of the campaign, Nelson honed his message. More and more, as election day neared, he focused on the state's finances and what he described as a growing fiscal crisis.

The postwar baby boom had greatly increased the demand for services, but state government had not changed to meet the growing needs. Wisconsin's constitution required a balanced budget and forbade borrowing of more than $100,000. To get around that restriction, the state had long used dummy corporations to finance its building construction programs. The corporations, not the state, did the borrowing, allowing state government to continue the illusion that it was not in debt.[1]

Nelson blew the whistle on the system, charging that the state debt had grown 400 percent, to $40 million, during Thomson's term as governor. He charged Thomson with hiding those figures to "fool the public" while he announced that the balance in the state budget account had increased by $2 million. "In a desperate attempt to avoid the day of reckoning on state finances, [Thomson] pulled the plug on debt financing. Instead of using debt financing as a supplement to pay-as-you-go financing of public buildings, the governor has borrowed for practically the whole building program," Nelson said. Thomson was adding to the state debt at the rate of $50,000 a day and paying higher interest than if the state had borrowed the money itself, he said. He accused Thomson of a "hoax" in announcing an $83 million antirecession building program for 1958 to create fifteen thousand jobs. Nelson revealed that $50 million worth of the work either had already been done the year before or would not be started until 1959.[2]

He repeatedly pressured Thomson to come out against a state sales tax, which the state Republican platform backed, but Thomson avoided the subject. "Your present noncommittal silence is bound to confuse the public because in the past you have taken a firm stand on both sides of the question," Nelson wrote to Thomson, promising to raise the issue weekly. When Thomson finally said he opposed a sales tax, Nelson asked him to say he would veto it if it passed—a pledge Thomson had made in 1956 but not in 1958. The sales tax was a major issue but a hot potato neither candidate discussed more than necessary and usually only if questioned about it. In the first six months of his campaign, Nelson gave ninety speeches without bringing up the issue, a reporter had noted. Opposition to a sales tax had been dogma for Democrats. Nelson did not want a sales tax, but wanted to keep all of his options open and to avoid making any anti-sales tax promises that might be impossible to keep.[3]

Nelson ridiculed Thomson for lagging on interstate highway construction, with federal funds available to pay 90 percent of the cost, sending a "congratulatory" telegram when Thomson opened the first seven miles of Wisconsin interstate in Waukesha County. At the rate Thomson was building the freeways—seven miles in two years—Wisconsin's interstates would be finished in 149 years, Nelson said. "Here's to the grand opening in 2107." Nelson charged Wisconsin lagged behind the rest of the country, when the highway jobs could help fight the economic recession. "Thomson has fallen asleep on the country's greatest antirecession measure," he said. Nelson based his criticism on a *Time* magazine article listing Wisconsin among the laggard states, but learned after the election from Thomson's highway commission chairman that the charge was untrue. Wisconsin appeared to lag because it officially opened long stretches of highway at one time, while other states opened a few miles at a time. "Why didn't you tell Governor Thomson?" Nelson asked. "He never asked me," said the commissioner, who, although a Thomson appointee, was not particularly fond of the governor.[4]

Nelson faulted Thomson for low school aids, forcing more of the burden onto local property taxpayers. The state paid only 21 percent of school operating costs and nothing for construction, while the school age population was booming and debt was soaring. Property taxes accounted for nearly half of the state and local revenues collected in Wisconsin—far too high a proportion, he said. Nelson promised to take a hard look at the state's entire tax system to make it fairer and more progressive.[5]

Thomson defended himself vigorously and threw some strong counterpunches, claiming that Nelson had voted for much of the building debt and programs he was criticizing; that Nelson wanted to halt urgently needed building on the state's college campuses to "close college doors on 15,000 students"; that Nelson was guilty of "corrupt campaigning" by misrepresenting and misquoting him; that Nelson had given "completely false" information on the interstate highway program; that Nelson was antihighway and had obstructed the state arterial highway program. In August, Thomson and his lieutenant governor, Warren Knowles, teamed up to attack Nelson on his charges about state debt and the building program. Thomson charged Nelson with making "deliberately false statements," and Knowles said Nelson was guilty of "deliberate falsehoods." Contrary to what Nelson had charged, Knowles said, there had been no attempt to hide or cover up any debt; it had even been mentioned in a press release on the governor's building program.[6]

In a speech two days later at a Waukesha County Democratic picnic, the *Milwaukee Journal* reported, a "new" Nelson reacted to the attacks in a fiery speech. Thomson and Knowles had told "flat, bold faced lies about the state building program," he said. "I'm sick and tired of Republicans misrepresenting Democrats, lying about the position of Democrats. They are incompetent, wasteful spendthrifts who don't know how to save the taxpayers' money." Nelson felt he had made responsible criticisms and the governor had responded by calling him names. "I intend to hold [Thomson's] feet to the fire until we make an honest man out of him on finances," Nelson shouted. "So far he has been—as he has been all through his political career—a penny ante political fibber." To that point in the campaign, the *Journal* said, Nelson had played the role of "a solid, responsible candidate who discussed the issues in a sober way." The "new" Nelson was "dedicated to slugging it out" with Thomson. The change came, it said, because Nelson felt the quiet campaign was not getting through to people and because he was upset by the sharp Republican attack over the building program, a keystone of the Nelson campaign.[7]

"Dry Rot"

In September, Nelson found a phrase that encompassed all of his complaints about the Republican administration. The problem: "dry rot."

In what he called "a major statement of campaign aims," Nelson said: "The overriding issue in Wisconsin in 1958 is the dry rot that has infested the Republican administration in Madison after twenty years in power." Dry rot, he said, explained why Thomson had borrowed so much through dummy corporations at too high an interest rate, why the state wasn't cashing in on the interstate highway program, why local school debts were rising, even why Thomson wanted to raise auto license fees while refusing to reform the state's tax structure.[8]

"The same dry rot has worked its way into every branch of the Thomson administration, at every level," Nelson said. Everyone who ever owned a boat "knows that when dry rot sets in, the only choice is to scuttle it or break it up for firewood. The same is true when dry rot infests the ship of state, and that's why the voters of Wisconsin must scuttle the dry-rot Thomson administration in November." Nelson hammered away at the theme in his speeches and in television commercials. It was an easy image for people to understand, he said. "Everybody knows that's a log that's gonna fall apart."[9]

People he met on the campaign trail told Nelson that he was narrowing the gap. But every candidate feels that to some extent and must believe it in order to get up and on the road again every morning. There was little hard evidence to suggest that Nelson's original plan, to run a hard but losing race in 1958 to build for another run in 1960, was wrong. A poll of farmers by the *Wisconsin Agriculturist* in August showed Thomson leading Nelson 43-28 among farmers surveyed. But among those most likely to vote, Thomson's lead was only 44-40. By October, Nelson had surged to almost a dead heat, with Thomson leading 48-45 among all farmers surveyed by the magazine. Proxmire had predicted a Nelson victory, but he was on the same ticket and hardly objective. Robert Moses of the Wisconsin Farmers Union predicted Nelson could get 57 or 58 percent of the vote. Carl Thompson, who had run for governor in 1948, said Nelson would win and offered seven reasons, including the plight of dairy farmers, the governor's unpopularity within his own party, and Nelson's strong campaign.[10]

A week before the election, Nelson campaigned around the clock in Milwaukee, shaking hands with more than two thousand people during his twenty-four-hour stint. He campaigned at cocktail parties, plant gates, police stations, businesses, wedding receptions, restaurants, taverns, churches, railroad depots, and anywhere else there were people to meet. He also made two television appearances and dropped by at 1 A.M. for a visit to the newsroom of the *Milwaukee Journal*. At 3 A.M., "Nelson, after taking a Benzedrine pill, was full of pep," the *Journal* reported. Proxmire would have shaken many more hands in the same time, but reporter Aldric Revell noted that "rarely, in his handshaking, did Nelson just walk away from the person he greeted. Most of the time he chatted with the individual and invariably asked whether the person knew of any former Republican who intended to switch parties this year." Many said they did. "You could feel it," Nelson said. Lots of Progressives were still in the Republican Party, but in 1958 they were moving over to the Democrats. With Proxmire's win and Nelson's strong campaign, they were beginning to believe the Democratic Party might amount to something.[11]

Election Night

Still, when Nelson left home on election night he fully expected to lose. During the ninety-minute car trip to Milwaukee, Nelson heard early returns on the radio, primarily from rural areas, in which he was running behind Proxmire. Proxmire would be winning by a big margin while Nelson would be ahead slightly or losing. In the Black River Falls area, for example, Proxmire was winning big and Nelson narrowly ahead. That was not surprising, since Proxmire was an incumbent running against a fairly weak challenger, and Nelson was the challenger trying to unseat the incumbent governor. But the returns reinforced Nelson's expectations: a loss, perhaps by a small margin, but a loss nonetheless. Others in the car—Aldric Revell (the only reporter to predict a Nelson victory in print) and Richard Reston, another *Capital Times* reporter, tried to be more optimistic. Carrie Lee had been saying for a year, when asked, that Gaylord had a fifty-fifty chance, meaning he was one of two candidates. She didn't say much during the ride.[12]

Win or lose, Nelson was satisfied that he had run a good, strong, all-out campaign and had done all he could. For more than a year, he had worked harder than he ever had in his life, driving himself day after day. He had not compromised his principles and had discussed the issues that were important to the state, if not always to the voters. The *Milwaukee Journal,* in its front-page editorial two days before the election, had high praise for the way Nelson had conducted his campaign. Rather than follow the usual practice of focusing on one or two catchy issues, Nelson "set a commendable standard of responsible campaigning," the newspaper said. "He has responsibly studied, written and spoken about a wide range of subjects that are not glamorous, are easier for the opposition to distort than for him to explain—but are *at the heart of a governor's job."* Nelson's campaign was "in marked contrast to the usual low estimate of voter intelligence," the editorial said. "He has centered his time and thought, in rare degree, on the hard subject matter that really belongs to the office of governor."[13]

At the home of a Milwaukee supporter, where the Nelsons awaited returns, campaign workers put incoming results into context, comparing them with returns from the same precincts in previous elections. By 9 P.M., some people were telling Nelson, "You've got this won." By the time Nelson got to his downtown headquarters at 757 North Plankinton Avenue an hour later, the celebration had started, with a sound truck supplying the music for happy Democrats dancing in the street. Nelson was cautious, as his lead became eleven thousand votes at 11 P.M. and he was besieged by reporters. By midnight the gap was twenty thousand votes, all outside of Milwaukee County, and his victory was clear. By 12:30 A.M. he led by fifty thousand votes. Nelson made the rounds of news outlets for interviews with the major newspapers, radio, television, and wire services to acknowledge and explain his victory.[14]

Gaylord A. Nelson, at age forty-two, had become the second Democratic governor of Wisconsin in the twentieth century and the first since the Roosevelt landslide of 1932. Nelson's margin of victory was 87,905 votes. He carried thirty-three of seventy-one counties, including the two big Democratic strongholds, Milwaukee and Dane, and received 53.7 percent of the vote. He did run behind Proxmire, as the early returns indicated, but that wasn't fatal. Proxmire rolled up 57 percent of the vote to defeat former Supreme Court Justice Roland Steinle. In Jackson County, where returns from Black River Falls had worried Nelson, Proxmire got 62 percent of the countywide vote, but Nelson got 56 percent, a good margin. Democrats also won three other statewide offices, as Philleo Nash ousted Lieutenant Governor Knowles, John Reynolds became attorney general, and Eugene Lamb won for state treasurer. Two more Democrats—Robert Kastenmeier in the Second District and Gerald Flynn in the First—won U.S. House seats, so the delegation was split 5-5. Perhaps most remarkably, Democrats took a 55-45 majority in the state assembly—a gain of twenty-two seats. Democrats also picked up two state senate seats, but the GOP still held a solid 20-13 majority. Control of state government was divided—but that was good news for Democrats, who had been shut out of the process for a quarter century. Wisconsin was truly a two-party state again.[15]

11

An Ambitious Agenda

IN THE DAYS after the election, Wisconsinites learned a lot more about their new governor and his family. Newspapers reported that the Nelsons had two lively children, five-year-old Happy (who warned a photographer that the family's home had mice) and two-year-old Tia; that Nelson's great-grandfather was one of the founders of the Republican Party; that Nelson's grandfather was a Union soldier; that Nelson loved maple syrup and well-aged cheese, sometimes combining them over waffles; and that the family pet was a standard poodle named Wags. Suddenly, almost nothing about the family's life was private. Carrie Lee was amazed at some of the "stupid personal questions that seemed so bizarre to me. . . . I had no secrets, but it seemed dumb for people to be that interested in things like me at age seven going to the children's home."[1]

The Nelsons' social life continued apace. One reporter who visited their home between the election and the time he took office described the scene at a Nelson party around midnight:

> University professors, magazine editors, politicians, lawyers and wives crammed the smoky, talk-filled living room. A Sumatran anthropology student from the university sat playing Burmese records on the Nelsons' Sears Roebuck hi-fi. Guitar in hand, one of the top political reporters in the state harmonized with a Madison banker on a sleepy, off-key rendition of "Won't You Come Home, Bill Bailey." And in the midst of the crush, scotch and water in one hand and a mentholated cigarette in the other, the new governor of Wisconsin engaged in sharp debate with a fisheries biologist.

Still fresh as morning after a long day at the capitol . . . Nelson listened, probed and bored in on the conservation man's ideas for two hours without ever sitting down. At two in the morning, with most of the guests long since gone home to bed, he switched to coffee, opened the day's second pack of Newports and continued the discussion for another hour. At 3:30 A.M. the governor bid the weary biologist a hearty good night. And at 8:30 A.M. his Ford rolled into Capitol Square to start another day of managing the governmental affairs of nearly four million people.[2]

Nelson plunged into his new role at once, meeting with top Democrats to plan strategy, holding hearings on agency budgets, hiring staff, and zeroing in on priorities to pursue when he officially became governor, with government reorganization and tax reform at the top of the agenda.

. When Nelson asked, at one of the first budget hearings, how much the state owed for construction bonding by the dummy corporations set up to skirt the state debt limit, no one could answer. The budget director said the state had no records of such debt, and the state auditor said he had no authority to ask to see the records of the quasi-public agencies. Nelson's claim that state taxpayers were saddled with hidden debt was true—but no one could even say whether his $50 million figure was accurate. "Having a large public debt is bad enough; to have such a debt and not know its size is many times worse," the *Waukesha Freeman* said. The debt aside, budget requests from state agencies for 1959–61 were $81 million more than the previous two-year budget. Nelson said he would use a "microscope" system to evaluate the requests and would break tradition by asking the legislature to review the budget annually, although he would submit a two-year budget to meet legal requirements.[3]

Inauguration Day

On 5 January 1959, Gaylord became Governor Nelson, Wisconsin's thirty-fifth governor, in inauguration ceremonies that drew several thousand happy Democrats to the swearing-in, a reception in the governor's office, a dinner so well attended the crowd was spread into two hotels, and a semiformal inaugural ball. (Nelson had exercised his first veto on plans for a more formal ball and said he would wear a business suit, not a tuxedo.) Nelson family members came from around the nation. As Governor Thomson escorted Nelson to the platform in the capitol rotunda, young Happy, sitting in the crowd with family friends, shouted, "Hi, Daddy!" The Clear Lake delegation stood and applauded loudly as Nelson appeared, and he waved to his hometown friends. A bus with twenty-three passengers had left Clear Lake at 4 A.M. for the noon ceremony, and many others drove their own vehicles. A huge banner hung from the balcony railing in the rotunda, proclaiming, "Clear Lake, Home of Gaylord A. Nelson." Some votes had been cast against Nelson in Clear Lake, a member of the delegation told a reporter, including one by a man who had never paid Nelson's father for delivering his children. In Clear Lake, there were still no secrets.[4]

Nelson wore a dark suit and kept the coat buttoned to avoid displaying a western-style black belt and silver buckle, borrowed from an uncle at the last minute after discovering he was wearing a brown belt. The new governor was colorblind.[5]

In his inaugural speech, Nelson claimed the legacy of Fighting Bob La Follette, quoting him on the need for "continual struggle" to make democracy work, and adding his own message: "Political leadership in our system must accept the responsibility to lead. It must respond swiftly and decisively to combat any form of tyranny and oppression. Affirmatively, it must help formulate the purpose, point the direction and propose the program that will translate the aspirations of our people into reality. That is easy when the cause is popular—difficult when it is not. I hope for the courage to make those hard decisions which distinguish responsible leadership from irresponsible demagoguery."[6]

He identified the cause of the problems facing state government: "an economic, industrial, and cultural revolution which has virtually engulfed us in the past twenty-five years," and which was accelerating. More students were entering public schools and higher education institutions every year. Increasing numbers of bigger, faster automobiles were making the state highways outmoded. Rapid growth of metropolitan areas and suburban sprawl was throwing local government into "confusion and conflict." More leisure time was putting pressure on parks and recreational areas. Advances in treatment of mental health problems were creating a demand for more and better facilities. There was no question, he said, that the state must meet those needs. The question was how it would pay for them.[7]

"The issue will be faced sooner or later whether we like it or not," Nelson said. "I propose that we face it now." He proposed a two-pronged approach: a thorough analysis and revision of the existing tax system, and a vigorous promotion of economic growth. In the meantime, he warned, the existing system was falling short of meeting the state's needs, and hinted at higher taxes. "To those who would neglect our schools, our colleges, our public welfare activities and institutions, our highway and conservation resources, I would say this—You spend more money on cigarettes, liquor, cosmetics and other luxuries than the total cost of your state government. If we have not completely lost our sense of values . . . the question in its proper perspective is really this—are you willing to give up a few personal luxuries in exchange for a more creative investment in our future?"[8]

He quoted Lincoln: "The dogmas of the quiet past are inadequate to the stormy present. We must think anew and act anew." Nelson said he would make proposals "in a non-partisan spirit" and asked legislators to consider them on their merits. "I would ask only two things of the citizens of Wisconsin: When you believe we are right, support us; when you believe we are wrong, oppose us; but let us all have a free and open discussion of our problems so that we can work toward an honest adjustment of our differences without sacrifice of principles. This is the key to every successful democratic society the world has known. . . . I ask no more of my political opponents than of my friends. If each of you will support our proposals as far as your conscience carries you and halt opposition at the border of mere partisanship, the gain will be great for the citizens of our state."[9]

Nelson's speech that night to Democrats at the Loraine Hotel was more blunt. After twenty minutes of his patented humor, Nelson "began to talk like a Dutch uncle, piling point upon point in a plea for more tax revenue," a Milwaukee reporter said. He again listed the state's pressing needs and warned that Wisconsin residents must be prepared to pay higher taxes to meet those needs. "I'd rather get licked next time than neglect these important responsibilities," he said to strong applause. The public would be willing to pay more if it understood the problems, he said. "If we don't sell the program to the public, Wisconsin will fall further back than it is now." The banner headline in the next day's *Capital Times:* "Nelson Warns of Tax Hike."[10]

Divided Government

The stage was set for a legislative session dominated by state finances. With Democrats in control of the assembly and Republicans holding the senate, impasse seemed likely. Nelson's was the first administration in twenty years in which control was split, making the session "ripe for partisanship."[11] That did not deter Nelson, who had kept a careful list of every campaign promise and was determined to introduce legislation to fulfill every single one, whether the bills passed or not. He thought it was an advantage that he had come straight from the legislature. He had been in the senate ten years and had good personal relationships with lawmakers in both parties. "I could go up to any single member in either house and make an argument on the merits," he said. Many of his proposals were "pretty good common sense stuff," and Republicans did not want to appear to be obstructionists on ideas that had "good popular support and good editorial support."[12]

So Nelson simply introduced a legislative program that was "the most ambitious and far-reaching since Philip La Follette's administration in the depths of the Depression."[13] By the time he left office, much of it had been passed. Nelson outlined his program in a "State of the State" speech to the legislature, in which he pledged a new progressive era and a return to La Follette's "Wisconsin Idea," tapping the University of Wisconsin to help find creative solutions to the state's pressing problems.

He outlined more than twenty proposals—state government reorganization, a new economic development commission, a long-range plan to improve northern Wisconsin highways, an antisecrecy in government law, a college loan program, state aid for public lake access, more wetland acquisition, a two dollar state park fee, billboard control, election law reform, court reorganization, changes in Conservation Commission appointments, increased worker compensation benefits, simplified annexation laws, a new center to treat emotionally disturbed children, constitutional amendments to allow the state to bond for buildings, and more. He asked for bipartisan support and said he would "regularly seek advice from members of both parties."[14]

It wasn't just rhetoric. After ten years in public office, he still expected elected officials to make decisions on the merits, based on rational arguments and what was best for the citizenry. He was not naïve about the nature of partisan politics and the posturing it often produced. But he still had faith in the political process and the desire of people in public life to do the right thing. If they disagreed about what was the right thing, or about how to accomplish it, he didn't take it personally. He respected differences of opinion, but he admired openmindedness and the willingness to consider a new idea or an opposing point of view. He was not dogmatic. He was a master at the art of political compromise. He understood that politics is often personal, that respect, civility, and friendship could go a long way toward solving problems when intellectual arguments had failed.

A long, bitter partisan struggle over tax policy dominated news coverage of the 1959 legislative session. But while that fundamental disagreement over taxes played itself out, Nelson and the divided legislature reached agreement on many other items. Nelson did much of the salesmanship and lobbying himself. He had an open door policy for legislators; any lawmaker from either party could see him immediately upon request. Nelson courted his fellow Democrats, speaking to Democratic caucuses, inviting members to the governor's residence, selling his program one-on-one, and sometimes calling in a chip owed him from his own time in the legislature. Both houses had Democratic loyalists who "would go along with me on most anything," Nelson said. "They didn't want the Democratic governor to be a failure. They were good troopers. They wanted to cooperate and even choked down some stuff they wouldn't have done for a Republican."[15]

Sometimes it took peer pressure. One assembly Democrat, Bill Ward of New Richmond, announced during a floor debate that his conscience would not allow him to vote for any sales tax. Harvey Dueholm of Polk County, perhaps the legislature's funniest speaker and storyteller, was Ward's roommate in Madison. Dueholm took the floor to respond: "My colleague says his conscience won't allow him to vote for this bill. I want to say that New Richmond would be better off, Saint Croix County would be better off, the state of Wisconsin, the United

States, and the whole world would be better off if the gentleman from Saint Croix County, when he goes to bed tonight, would keep his teeth in his mouth and put his conscience in the glass beside his bed." Ward eventually changed his mind during a weekend back in his district and voted with his fellow Democrats.[16]

Republicans played hardball on appointments, which needed senate confirmation. Early in the session, Senator Earl Leverich, a former Progressive who had remained a Republican and was a friend of Nelson's, told him the Republican caucus had decided to reject every appointment. Republicans thought Nelson was a one-term governor who would be gone in two years, and did not want to approve appointees who would still be serving after the Republicans returned to power in 1961. After Republicans twice rejected the appointment of a Milwaukee alderman, Matt Schimenz, to chair the Public Service Commission, on the grounds he was too prolabor and antisuburb, Nelson began to choose his major appointees carefully. He looked for people who would have some natural support in the GOP caucus, to make appointments "which were politically tough for them and politically profitable for me."[17]

He chose the head of the rural electric cooperative in Senator Robert Knowles's district and the wife of an Appleton newspaper editor for spots on the state college board of regents. He nominated a respected United Auto Workers official for the state welfare board; the head of the rural electric cooperatives as securities commissioner; and others who had support from Republican business people. The idea was to put the squeeze on by making it difficult for some individual senators to vote against specific appointees. The strategy worked and, once the dam cracked, most of Nelson's appointees were confirmed. The exception was David Carley, named to head the newly created Department of Resource Development, who was rejected repeatedly. Carley served anyway, because Nelson kept reappointing him and the law allowed him to serve until his appointment was rejected again or a successor was named.[18]

In the first floor session, the GOP killed proposals to revamp the Conservation Commission, expand the state building program, and strengthen civil rights enforcement. Other Nelson bills were delayed, to be killed in the fall: a constitutional amendment to legalize state borrowing, a two dollar fee for state park use, a ban on billboards on state highways, and an innovative "self-help" farm bill to allow farmers to establish their own marketing programs. Nelson portrayed the January–July session as a success, citing a box score that showed twenty-six of forty-three bills he proposed had been passed. His biggest success was passage of two bills he called "the most sweeping reorganization of state government since the days of Fighting Bob La Follette." One combined five agencies into a new Department of Administration to run day-to-day governmental operations. The other created a Department of Resource Development, consolidating economic development, marketing, and tourism promotion. Both would be more efficient and cost-effective, he said. The legislature also passed a $5 million outdoor recreation budget, which nearly doubled the previous appropriation and provided more public access to lakes and streams and expansion of state parks and state forests. It agreed to expand mental health facilities, regulate billboards on interstate highways, reorganize the state court system, and increase unemployment compensation benefits.[19]

Aldric Revell's assessment in the *Capital Times* was not as rosy. The two reorganization bills passed, he said, "only because of the intensive diplomatic work done by Nelson and concessions he made in changing portions of the bills." Republicans were intransigent on tax issues and other important bills, he wrote, so Nelson's forty-three-bill package "fared well as to quantity enacted but badly as to quality, since his withholding tax bill, building program, farm program, constitutional debt change, conservation reorganization and twelve million dollar tax package were the heart of his program and they were all rejected."[20]

A Deadlock over Taxes

The session's real battleground was taxes, and partisan lines were clearly drawn. It was obvious the state needed a new revenue source to meet the growing demands for schools, recreation, highways, and social services. Nelson and the Democrats favored a withholding tax, which he called a "pay as you go" system. The federal government and several states were already using it to collect income taxes through payroll deductions. Besides eliminating the need for taxpayers to come up with their state taxes in a lump sum at the end of the year, withholding would create a one-time $80 million windfall for state and local governments.

Nelson said the state's $24 million share would be earmarked for the state building program. Supporters said withholding also would increase tax collections from partial-year residents and others who avoided paying state income taxes. Republicans opposed withholding and believed that if taxes had to be increased they should be broadly based—which meant a sales tax. Nelson and the Democrats were on record against a sales tax, although he was becoming convinced that there eventually would be some kind of sales tax in Wisconsin, perhaps while he was governor.[21]

Nelson had promised, during the campaign, to review the entire state tax structure. He was preparing to name a blue-ribbon commission to conduct that study and recommend changes. But in the meantime the state fiscal year began on July 1, and he and the legislature needed to agree on a state budget. Nelson's solution, to avoid an impasse, was a one-year "bare bones" budget that would not require any major tax changes. He would ask the legislature to return in the fall to consider the budget for the second year of the biennium. Republicans objected that the constitution required a two-year budget. But a compromise was struck, in which the legislature approved the 1959–60 budget along the general lines Nelson proposed, and projected those figures into the second year as well. Everyone understood the second year budget would be reconsidered when the legislature returned in the fall. It was a paper solution, but it solved the immediate problem and allowed state government to function.[22]

The intensity of the tax disagreement was demonstrated at an April 1959 hearing of the legislature's Joint Finance Committee on Nelson's withholding plan. It drew the largest crowd ever to jam the assembly chambers, more than eight hundred people, including two hundred members of the Milwaukee Association of Commerce who came to voice their opposition. Nelson spoke himself and uncharacteristically "delivered a blistering attack" on the Milwaukee business representatives. He challenged them to come up with their own tax proposals or budget cuts, "so the legislature can decide between my solution and theirs—not between my solution and none at all." The critics, he said, "vigorously pursue their democratic right to condemn any positive action by others and just as vigorously reject as repugnant the idea that they share any responsibility for constructive and positive action themselves."

Nelson's "appearance was grim and his voice was hard and sometimes sarcastic" as he lashed out at the business group.[23]

The group's lobbyist said the plan would "blunt tax awareness"—make it too painless to pay taxes—and a sales tax would be a more reliable way to provide property tax relief. "To ask businessmen to solve your problems is somewhat improbable," the Wisconsin Chamber of Commerce president said. Business and labor were sharply split, with the AFL president testifying that workers were forced to borrow the money to pay their state income taxes, sometimes even from loan sharks. The committee chair banged his gavel when witnesses repeatedly strayed into the sales tax issue, which was not on the agenda.[24]

Nelson named his nineteen-member blue-ribbon tax study commission in June. Chaired by Miller Upton, president of Beloit College, the group included four businessmen, six legislators, three attorneys, two labor leaders, two farmers, an educator, and a small town mayor. Nelson asked the commission for recommendations to raise $30 to $35 million in new revenue for the current biennium. With the legislature to return in October, he asked for recommendations by 15 September. That was a tall order. A separate tax impact committee had been working on nine different taxing scenarios and collecting statistics on their impact. That committee had not finished its work, which was to be the starting point for the blue-ribbon study.[25] A completion date of 15 September was simply the first of many suggested to the blue-ribbon group, which did not make its recommendations until after the 1960 elections. That was fine with Nelson; indeed, that was what he wanted.

In the summer of 1960, when it appeared the commission might finish its work—and probably recommend a sales tax as part of its solution—Nelson spoke to Edwin Larkin, an Eau Claire attorney who chaired the Tax Burden Subcommittee of the panel. His subcommittee's study was important and should be done right, not rushed, Nelson told him. Nelson did not want the volatile issue injected into his reelection campaign, then in its final months. Larkin got the message. "Governor," he said, "I don't see any way we can get that done before the election. If there is one thing I know, it's how to run a slow horse race."[26]

While the commission began its work, the Republican senate killed Nelson's withholding plan, and Nelson began to give the first signs that he might be open to some sort of sales tax plan. Madison Mayor Ivan

Nestingen said he would ask Wisconsin Democrats, at their state convention, to reaffirm their opposition to a sales tax. *Capital Times* reporter Aldric Revell pressed Nelson on whether he would support the resolution, but he refused to answer directly. Revell asked the question three different ways, but Nelson ducked it every time. "I am aiming," he said, "to secure a total tax structure which will meet four yardsticks—that it will be equitable, stable, produce needed revenues, and encourage economic development. . . . If we permit a discussion of taxes to revolve around emotional, over-simplified, black and white answers we will never find a solution to our fiscal problems." But what about the sales tax, Revell asked. "That would be an over-simplified, black and white, emotional answer and all that nonsense. . . . I could say, like some people, I'm against the property tax, I'm against the sales tax, I'm against the income tax. Income and corporation taxes are too high, and we ought to get our money from Minnesota."[27]

William T. Evjue, *Capital Times* editor and publisher, who had supported Nelson throughout his career, took up the fight. In a rare criticism of Nelson, Evjue editorialized that the Democratic platform—which opposed a general sales tax—was "a sacred covenant" with the people. He reminded Nelson of his "continuous attack on Governor Thomson for his failure to tell people where he stood on the sales tax" in the 1958 campaign. "Perhaps former Governor Thomson will be asking where Governor Nelson stands on the sales tax in the 1960 campaign," Evjue concluded.[28]

As the November legislative session approached, Nelson announced he would veto any sales tax bill. Instead, he offered two tax packages to make up the 1960–61 budget shortfall of $29 million and asked the legislature to pass either. Both included new taxes on banks, savings and loan associations, cigarettes, and tobacco. One included a withholding tax and the other an income tax increase of three-fourths of 1 percent. Both eliminated a 20 percent income tax surcharge Republicans had adopted as a stopgap measure in previous sessions. If lawmakers acted with "a conscientious effort and a spirit of cooperation" they could finish the session in five weeks, he said.[29]

No sooner had he finished speaking than the Republicans, in caucus, decided to oppose both plans and wait until spring. They had no desire to pass a short-term bailout. If Nelson was going to propose tax increases, the Republicans wanted him to do it in the election year, as close to the campaign as possible. The predicted partisan impasse, which had not materialized during the earlier floor sessions, was now in full bloom. Republicans were in no hurry to solve the problem. If the delay caused a fiscal crisis, they would point out that the state never had that problem when the Republicans were in charge. If the Republicans recessed "out of sheer obstructionism," Nelson threatened, he would travel to every county to tell voters who was responsible. If he did, the GOP countered, they would send along a truth squad to tell the voters that Nelson and the Democrats were really to blame.[30]

With emotions and rhetoric at a high pitch, a December hearing offered "a dry run" of the 1960 political campaign. The five-hour hearing on Nelson's stopgap tax plan drew seven hundred people. Nelson said Republicans opposed the measure because they did not want to get him "off the hook" on the tax issue, but "the people of Wisconsin are on the hook, too," he warned, and would remember who offered a solution and who blocked it. Philip Kuehn, the Republican state chairman who would be the GOP candidate for governor in 1960, led the opposition. Kuehn called the withholding plan "political trickery" and said the legislature should wait for the blue-ribbon commission to finish its work. The deadlock continued.[31]

"Go Home"

On 14 January 1960, with the legislature back from a Christmas recess and the Nelsons home from watching Wisconsin's Badgers play Washington in the Rose Bowl, Nelson spoke to another joint session of the legislature. His message came in his opening line. "I am here to tell you to go home. I am here to say that there is no use in staying in session . . . because no matter what we Democrats do, the Republicans won't do anything. I am speaking bluntly about this because the situation has become hopeless, and I am speaking in this vein because the situation is the result of blind, unyielding, partisan obstructionism."[32]

Nelson's harsh words were out of character. Newspapers said the governor was "hardly controlling his anger" in his "stinging" speech. The *Milwaukee Journal* said Nelson "read the riot act" in "the roughest public scolding of a Wisconsin legislature by a chief executive in long memory." The lawmakers had it coming, the *Journal* said, calling it "a personal coup, for it was no easy matter to make many in his own party sit still for a blunt command to go home and come back in May or June." It was not Gaylord Nelson-style politics, but he saw no choice.[33]

Republicans were furious. Within eight hours the senate killed his 1960-61 budget. The state would not be in a crisis, Republicans said, if Nelson had done his job and had presented a two-year budget to begin with. That done, the legislature did go home, adjourning until May. Nelson launched his threatened speaking tour to blast GOP obstructionism, and Republicans countered with their truth squads. The blue-ribbon commission continued to study taxes at a very deliberate pace.

When the legislature returned in May, Nelson greeted it with a bombshell. "Good news," he proclaimed. Because of "unprecedented economic growth and prosperity" in 1959 the projected deficit had disappeared, and the budget could be balanced without any tax increases. He proposed one change: a reduction in the income tax surcharge, to be offset by plugging a loophole to raise new taxes on banks and savings and loans. The legislature quickly approved the surcharge reduction, but the senate killed the bank taxes and simply passed a resolution declaring the budget balanced, as required by the state constitution. And that was that. The session, the longest in state history until then, ended soon afterward. The tax issue aside, it had been quite productive, "an impressive achievement in practical bipartisan politics."[34]

Gaylord, right, and Stannard behind Dr. Nelson's office. (Wisconsin Historical Society, WHi-5895)

Gaylord, left, and Sherman Benson with Gaylord's "sled dog," Sport, in front of the Nelson home. (Wisconsin Historical Society, WHi-5898)

Clear Lake's version of Our Gang. Gaylord is fourth from left. (Wisconsin Historical Society, WHi-5902)

Doctors' Corner in Clear Lake, on a postcard. Dr. Nelson's office is at left, and Dr. L. A. Campbell's office is next door. (Wisconsin Historical Society, WHi-5899)

"Happy" Nelson, high school trumpet player, 1931. (Wisconsin Historical Society, WHi-5891)

Teenage Gaylord, Clear Lake bandstand in background. (Wisconsin Historical Society, WHi-5893)

Gaylord and his mother, Mary B. Nelson, at his college graduation from San Jose State. (Wisconsin Historical Society, WHi-5904)

Nelson's law school graduation portrait, 1942. (Wisconsin Historical Society, WHi-5896)

Lieutenants Gaylord Nelson and Carrie Lee Dotson on Okinawa. One hundred nurses on the island shared a small number of civilian dresses. (Courtesy of Gaylord and Carrie Lee Nelson)

Dr. Anton and Mary B. Nelson, 1948. (Wisconsin Historical Society, WHi-5894)

Senator Estes Kefauver campaigns for Nelson in 1954 race for Congress. (Courtesy of the *Capital Times*)

Nelson, left, files nomination papers for 1954 race for Congress with Secretary of State Fred Zimmerman, seated. Palmer Daugs, former state representative, looks on. (Courtesy of the *Capital Times*)

Nelson takes the oath of office as Wisconsin's thirty-fifth governor on 5 January 1959. (Wisconsin Historical Society, WHi-6659)

Nelson's inauguration as governor on 5 January 1959 filled the State Capitol rotunda. (Courtesy of the *Capital Times*)

Adlai Stevenson was charmed, in a 1959 visit, by the "delightful disorganization" of the Nelson household. (Courtesy of the *Capital Times*)

John F. Kennedy campaigns for president in Madison in 1960, with Governor Nelson running interference. (Courtesy of Fritz Albert)

Former President Harry Truman poses with Gaylord and Carrie Lee during a 1960 visit to speak at a dinner for Nelson. (Courtesy of Clear Lake Historical Museum)

12

Family Fights

"OF ALL FIFTY STATES in the union, Wisconsin is probably that state in which professional politicians most hate to tempt a primary," wrote Theodore H. White, who chronicled the 1960 presidential campaign. The Progressive philosophy that led Wisconsin to create the nation's first presidential primary in 1903 "has made and left Wisconsin in political terms an unorganized state, a totally unpredictable state, a state whose primaries have . . . proved the graveyard of great men's Presidential ambitions."[1]

Unpredictable Wisconsin, with its open primary and crossover voting, became the first key test of the ambitions of Senators Hubert H. Humphrey and John F. Kennedy in their quests for the Democratic presidential nomination. The April primary was their first head-on contest. It played out in the national spotlight and had long-lasting effects on the national and Wisconsin political scene. Governor Gaylord Nelson sat it out.

Kennedy, the fresh, charismatic candidate from Massachusetts, needed to show strength outside of New England. Humphrey, the unabashed liberal from neighboring Minnesota, was well known in Wisconsin, and could not afford a loss there. Wisconsin Democrats considered Humphrey "Wisconsin's third senator," and loyalty to Humphrey ran deep among party regulars. Kennedy had a number of prominent Democrats, chief among them state chairman Patrick Lucey and Attorney General John Reynolds. Both, like Kennedy, were Irish Catholics, and they suggested the official head of the Wisconsin campaign should not be, since religion was an issue. Madison Mayor Ivan Nestingen became Kennedy's state chairman; Lucey took a prominent and active, but unofficial, role.[2]

Two candidates not on the ballot, Senator Lyndon B. Johnson and former Illinois Governor Adlai Stevenson, also influenced how Wisconsin Democrats lined up. Johnson was unacceptable to most state party members. Nelson had regularly complained about LBJ's lack of liberalism as Senate majority leader, his "temporizing on the issue of civil rights," and his votes on oil and gas issues that benefited Texas at the expense of consumers. "He is wrong on too many fundamental issues to satisfy me or you," Nelson told fellow Democrats in 1958. Lucey rationalized his support for Kennedy on the grounds that no one as liberal as Humphrey could be nominated, and a Kennedy loss in Wisconsin could open the door to Johnson. Stevenson, the nominee in 1952 and 1956, had a core of supporters, and Madison was " the capital of Stevensonian strength in the country," White wrote. Stevenson's hope depended upon a deadlocked convention. To further complicate things for Wisconsin Democrats, James Doyle—another Irish Catholic—was the national chairman of Stevenson's campaign.[3]

Nelson, facing reelection himself in November, considered his choices. Humphrey was a longtime friend. "He was our senator," Nelson said. "We didn't have any representation [when McCarthy and Wiley were in the Senate], and anything we asked of Hubert he did. I owed him. If I was going to endorse anybody I owed it to him." But "why get my own supporters angry at me" with an endorsement. "They're going to vote for me, and they're working hard for someone they really believe in [for President], and that goddamn governor, who they support, is trying to beat their candidate. That's nothing but a loser."[4]

Nelson tried to discourage a showdown in Wisconsin. "The candidates might not mind making Wisconsin a bloody battleground, but that doesn't mean we have to submit," he said. He suggested that the candidates stay away and allow Senator William Proxmire to run as a favorite son candidate, sending an uncommitted delegation to the national convention. But Humphrey's campaign believed he could win Wisconsin and build momentum, and Kennedy was unwilling to give Humphrey the state uncontested. The legislature spurned Nelson's suggestion for a "beauty contest" primary, which would list all candidates but elect uncommitted delegates. The stage was set for a Badger state battle.[5]

Nelson opted for neutrality. He said he would "referee" the primary campaign to keep it fair and clean. It was an open secret among party insiders that he preferred either Stevenson or Humphrey but was "not unhappy with Kennedy." That was not good enough for some JFK supporters, who believed "there was no such thing as being neutral; if you weren't for them, you were the enemy."[6] Proxmire also was publicly neutral but worked behind the scenes for Kennedy.

A week after appointing himself the referee, Nelson called a foul on the Kennedy camp. He criticized Lucey and Nestingen for making "completely unfounded" charges that a change in the way national convention delegates were to be chosen amounted to a "vote steal." At issue was a change to dilute the influence of at-large delegates, elected statewide. Humphrey supporters pushed it through the state administrative committee, since Humphrey seemed likely to win a majority of the congressional districts but lose the statewide vote. Nelson said he actually agreed with the Kennedy people and opposed the rules change but objected to their "careless" charges.[7]

He evened things up when Humphrey charged that Kennedy's Senate voting record and positions on farm issues were similar to Richard Nixon's. Nelson was speaking in rural Vernon County when Kennedy called him to complain and asked him to blow the whistle again. He did, calling Humphrey's claim "preposterous," and said Kennedy's record was "far superior in every respect to that of Nixon." The score was even at one reprimand for each side.[8]

Referee Nelson made one more public statement; this time he blew the whistle on himself. Nelson regretted that his remarks had been taken as personal criticism of Humphrey. He did not object to comparing records, Nelson said; he objected when attacks became personal. His goal was to "prevent the campaign from becoming so bitter and destructive that it would be impossible to repair the damage" and unify the party afterward. "I have not moved from my position of neutrality, nor do I propose to do so," he declared. Nelson was silent the final two weeks of the campaign. He and Carrie Lee quietly voted for their friend Humphrey.[9]

Kennedy, cast as the more conservative Democrat, got 56 percent of the statewide vote and won six of ten congressional districts. Humphrey won the three rural, Protestant districts along the Minnesota border and the liberal Second District around Madison. The victory was not decisive enough for Kennedy to claim the nomination; it took another victory over Humphrey in largely Protestant West Virginia to launch him toward the presidency. The spirited, emotional primary left some long-lasting scars on the Wisconsin Democratic Party. The Stevenson-Humphrey wing of the party, headquartered in Madison, blamed Lucey for the outcome, and Dane County Democrats voted against him in primaries when he ran for governor in 1968 and 1970. Nelson escaped with little blame for not having helped Humphrey. His strategy had paid off, with his own reelection seven months away.[10]

There were other lasting divisions within the party from the hard-fought race. Presidential campaigns, Doyle said, "use the state and they use the people in the state," changing relationships between people who previously had been working together. The morning after the primary, he said, the presidential circus leaves town, but the state's political activists "are left to live for a long time afterward with some of the consequences."[11]

The Nelson-Lucey Split

Lucey and Nelson had been growing apart for several years. Their differences were more on style than substance, more on personalities than politics. It is difficult to identify an issue that would cause a split, but the tension between the two was very real. Their supporters elevated it to intense disagreement and dislike, mostly over internal party matters that sound petty and often are, but which provide the ammunition for the intraparty warfare Wisconsin Democrats seem to relish. Some wounds from the Nelson-Lucey skirmishes lasted for decades, longer than anyone could remember what the disagreements had been about. "A lot of it was a clash of personalities," Lucey said. "There were real differences, I think. There's no question they were personal. They weren't ideological," Proxmire said. Frank Nikolay, a state representative and Nelson ally, reflecting years later, said the explanation for the feud was simple: "It was about 'Who's boss?'"[12]

Lucey, son of a small town grocer, grew up in tiny Ferryville, on the Mississippi River in western Wisconsin. His parents were hard-core Democrats. They liked La Follette, but even when Democrats were in a tiny minority they did not cross over to vote for Progressives in Republican primaries. In 1948, when the Democratic Party came back to life, Nelson was elected to the state senate and Lucey won the state assembly seat from Crawford County. After one term he ran unsuccessfully for Congress, then was hired as executive director of the Democratic Organizing Committee, leaving to run Tom Fairchild's 1952 U.S. Senate race. He then went into real estate sales in Madison, where he eventually made his fortune, but remained politically active, running Doyle's losing primary campaign for governor against Proxmire in 1954 and working in Elliot Walstead's unsuccessful 1956 primary for the Senate. In 1957 Lucey chaired Proxmire's winning Senate campaign. Soon afterward, with Proxmire's strong backing, Lucey narrowly defeated incumbent Philleo Nash to become state party chairman in the DOC's first real intraparty struggle. The contest "aroused some hard feelings," but Nelson stayed out of it.[13]

Nelson and Lucey should have been natural allies. They shared the same political philosophy, moved in the same circles, and shared friendships with Doyle and other key Democrats. In fact, they were close for a time, with the Nelsons sometimes babysitting for the Luceys' young children. The relationship began to cool during the 1958 governor's race, when Lucey detected "a certain strangeness between the party headquarters and the Nelson campaign." Lucey said he saw little of Nelson—understandable since Nelson was campaigning twelve to sixteen hours a day all around the state. Nelson traced the coolness to a visit he paid to a major Democratic donor in Milwaukee shortly before the election, hoping for a contribution to pay for some television commercials. The supporter told him Lucey had been in the day before, raising money to pay off the party's campaign debt. "So here you have the state chairman—I'm running for governor and he's written me off and is raising money to pay the debt before the election," Nelson said. "Well, I considered that pretty outrageous . . . that was sabotaging my campaign." Lucey's recollection was that the party shifted some money to Nelson's campaign, hoping the Nelson campaign would raise enough in the final days to repay the party. When that didn't happen, the Nelson campaign agreed to let the party sponsor the inaugural dinner to recover its investment in the governor's race. "I don't think the party ever gave me any money," Nelson insisted.[14]

Dane County Democrats, especially the university academics, were unhappy with the way Lucey handled his role as chairman. When he tried to reach agreement upon candidate slates without bloody primaries, they saw him acting as a party boss trying to run a political machine. That was anathema in Wisconsin, where Fighting Bob La Follette had crusaded for an open primary system to let the people, not the bosses, pick the candidates. Lucey's public endorsement of John Reynolds for attorney general in a 1958 primary against Christ Seraphim, the Milwaukee County party chairman, irritated Nelson and others who believed Lucey, as state chairman, was obliged to be neutral.[15]

Once Nelson became governor, he and Lucey, "both assertive and strong-willed men, found that the interests of governor and party chairman did not always coincide," in the diplomatic words of the official party history. Lucey's job was to be fiercely partisan; Nelson's was to try to get legislators to rise above partisanship and pass his budget and program. Lucey described himself as the "nuts and bolts man" and the governor as the party's leader on issues. In Nelson's view, Lucey "wanted to run everything," and "if you weren't all out on his side — sort of the Kennedy concept — anybody that wasn't on their side, to knock 'em off one way or another. That was not the philosophy of anybody else prior to that." There was a "Lucey clique" or a "Pat Lucey caucus" in the party, Nelson believed. "He was not my state chairman; everybody knew that." But while the internal feud simmered, the two continued to work together in public. The pot would boil over publicly in 1961. For the moment, there was the 1960 election to win, and both turned their attention to it.[16]

13

Still the Underdogs

IT WAS A GIVEN that Nelson would run for reelection. No governor could be satisfied with a single two-year term. Nelson made it official in June 1960, a week after the legislature ended its session. He had set a lot of things in motion "which should have been done and which have been neglected in the past," he said. He wanted to be around to see them to completion. The announcement was "curiously restrained, almost matter of fact," columnist John Wyngaard wrote, and Nelson "exuded a calm confidence that he has a good case for the electorate and that he expects to win." Issues aside, Wyngaard observed, in the end the deciding factor might be Nelson's personality. "One of his long suits is that people generally like him," even Republicans who say they won't vote for him. "It is one of the priceless assets of a politician, the capacity to like people," and Nelson "has managed to keep the affectionate regard of so many persons who don't regard themselves as Democrats," he said. Confident or not, Nelson told his party's state convention that "we are still the underdogs." Yes, 1958 was a breakthrough, but the 1960 election would prove whether the Democrats had really come of age and made Wisconsin a two-party state.[1]

At their state convention, Republicans endorsed Philip Kuehn, a Milwaukee area businessman and former GOP chairman, over Jack Olson, a Wisconsin Dells tourism executive. The GOP tried hard to make its convention endorsements stick and discouraged divisive primaries, which had cost them dearly in the past. In 1956 the GOP endorsed conservative Glenn Davis over a sitting Republican U.S. senator, Alexander Wiley. That ended in defeat for Davis and the party's leadership, and Wiley was reelected. When McCarthy died in 1957 the GOP made no endorsement and Davis narrowly lost the primary to Walter Kohler, who was beaten by Proxmire in the general election. Kuehn, then the party chairman, blamed Kohler's loss on "fratricidal bickering." Kuehn's convention endorsement in 1960 cleared his way to oppose Nelson, with no primary, as Olson accepted the convention's decision.[2]

To give Kuehn room to maneuver on the tax issue, the Republican platform did not specifically call for a sales tax but spoke in general terms about the need for "modern tax reform which will be equitable." The Democratic platform opposed a general sales tax "for whatever purpose and in whatever form." That put Nelson in an uncomfortable position while he awaited the recommendations of his blue-ribbon commission, likely to include some kind of sales tax. He assured the delegates that "I will recommend nothing that is not in accord with liberal Democratic principles and with our time honored tradition of basing taxation on the ability to pay." The sales tax became a major issue, but not until the final weeks of the campaign.[3]

Nelson attended the Democratic National Convention in Los Angeles, but was not a delegate since he had been neutral in the primary. He remained neutral at the convention, where Kennedy appeared to be the likely nominee but did not have it locked up. Lucey and others had promoted Nelson to be keynote speaker, and he had actively campaigned for the spot, sending out a recording of some of his speeches. The nod eventually went to Senator Frank Church of Idaho. Nelson was chosen, however, to narrate and appear in the party's campaign film, which was shown at the convention and broadcast on national television.[4]

Now, talk circulated that Nelson was on the short list of people being considered by Kennedy as vice presidential candidates. A few weeks earlier, told he was in contention, his reaction was, "What? A guy from Polk County?" The truth was that he was not interested; he was running for governor. His comments upon arriving in Los Angeles made that clear. If Kennedy won the nomination and consulted him, Nelson would recommend his friend Hubert Humphrey for the second spot. If Stevenson were the nominee, Nelson would work for Kennedy to join the ticket.[5]

After winning the nomination, Kennedy asked Nelson to his suite to tell him that he had chosen Lyndon Johnson as his running mate.

Kennedy said he was worried that Proxmire, a sharp critic of Johnson, would denounce his decision. In a 1959 Senate floor speech, Proxmire had sharply attacked LBJ's iron-fisted control of the Senate and called for giving party caucuses a greater voice on policy. When Proxmire looked for help in his battle against the all-powerful majority leader, he found himself without an army. Nelson had also been critical of Johnson, but assured Kennedy that both he and Proxmire would be team players and support the ticket.[6]

Kennedy told Nelson he had chosen Johnson because House Speaker Sam Rayburn, another Texan, had told him it was important. "If I hadn't, could you imagine what my presidency would be like, with Rayburn the speaker and Johnson the majority leader and both of them mad at me?" Kennedy asked. That explanation didn't ring true to Nelson, who thought the decision was a smart political choice to bring Texas into the Democratic column. He believed Kennedy "thought it was necessary to convince a northern liberal he had done this for important, practical political reasons." Returning to Madison, Nelson said he could "live with the Democratic ticket" but would have counseled against Johnson's selection "had I been asked," ending rumors that Nelson had been consulted on the choice.[7]

The "First Family"

Back home, the Nelsons tried to take a week's family vacation at a cottage in Three Lakes in northern Wisconsin, but a crisis cut it short after two days. Gaylord, Carrie Lee, six-year-old Happy, and four-year-old Tia had gotten only to Waushara County when a state trooper pulled over the black sedan with license plate number 1. When he called his office from a service station, Nelson learned that threatened violence at a strikebound Racine plant, J. I. Case, needed his attention. He spent most of the next day on the telephone, and a day later he headed home, to try to convince both sides to resume negotiations. Nelson did keep his promise to take Happy fishing and helped the young angler land a twenty-seven-inch muskie, just under the limit.[8]

The family had begun to adjust to life in the thirty-four-room executive residence on Lake Mendota. The Nelsons were still amused that they had moved from their Democratic enclave on Madison's West Side to the small, wealthy suburb of Maple Bluff, where their neighbors were mostly Republicans of the country club set. Carrie Lee was equally at home chatting with neighborhood youngsters or playing hostess to Jacqueline Kennedy or Eleanor Roosevelt, both of whom visited the mansion in 1960. Sometimes she played the role of southern belle for the amusement of friends, putting on long gloves and her accent to imitate some of the society women.[9]

Although a staff and full-time childcare came with the residence, the Nelsons did their best to be themselves. The menu was simple but tasty, featuring Carrie Lee's recipes, Gaylord's own salad dressing, and Chinese meals with recipes from Carl Lee, a native of China married to Gaylord's sister Janet. Adlai Stevenson was delighted with a ground beef and macaroni casserole Carrie Lee prepared for a buffet dinner when he was an overnight guest. At 4 A.M., Tia woke her parents and demanded, "Where is that man? I forgot to kiss him good night." Off she ran to Stevenson's room to give him a loud smack. Saying goodbye the next day, Stevenson told Carrie Lee, "You have the most beautifully disorganized household I have ever seen in my life."[10]

Carrie Lee found the house too big and impersonal. "Living here is part of a job," she said. She worked hard at combining a normal family life with official entertaining and keeping up with social and political friends. With an au pair to help with the children, she took time to quietly volunteer once or twice a week at a state mental health facility. There she offered severely retarded adolescents some personal attention, taking them for walks, washing and setting their hair, even inviting a few to a tea party at the governor's mansion. She reluctantly tolerated Gaylord's absence during the campaign and the demands on his time as governor. But she drew the line at campaigning herself and appeared on the campaign trail only when absolutely necessary. She had "no driving interest in politics," she told a reporter. She had not really understood when she met Gaylord how serious his interest was.[11]

A Tougher Nelson

Nelson hit the 1960 campaign trail hard, but it was nothing like his year-long, breakneck pace of the previous race. No underdog now, he was the incumbent, favored to win. Nelson still presented himself as the small town boy from Clear Lake. He had served a year and a half as governor but still hadn't worn formal clothes and planned never to do so. He had never worn a hat in his life until the previous winter, when at Carrie Lee's suggestion he bought a fedora. He still liked nothing better than stimulating conversation with friends over a few drinks. Political columnists still said his warm personality, sense of humor, and friendliness were among his key assets. But he wasn't quite as happy-go-lucky as he had been before becoming governor. The job was taking a toll.

In his battles with the legislature, observers had detected a tougher side to Nelson, who would "turn a fighting face to his constituents," used harsh language to criticize business groups that opposed him, and was even willing to tell his many friends in the legislature to go home since they were wasting taxpayers' time and money. Republican opposition, Wyngaard mused, had changed the formerly easy-going Nelson into "a more combative, assertive and resolute party leader." Nelson was growing "balder, grayer and leaner by the month," another reporter observed. "More important, he is tougher in his mind." Those who wondered if Nelson was too easy-going for the governor's job found him a "strong, hard-working governor" and "tireless campaigner" whose outlook had been matured by the office and "more inclined to drive himself and those around him."[12]

Nelson, now forty-four, had been graying back from his temples for at least ten years, so it was difficult to attribute that to the cares of being governor. Always in good physical condition, he was playing cutthroat badminton at the YMCA to keep in shape. In a campaign or on the badminton court, he was competitive. He did not like to lose. "Gaylord plays a really dirty game" of badminton, a friend said admiringly. In 1960 he wanted a big victory, a mandate to take to the 1961 legislature when the battle over tax policy resumed. He had another plan up his sleeve— one that would begin to establish his credentials as a leading conservationist and environmentalist. But first he needed to be reelected.[13]

The campaign never reached the intensity of the 1958 race. Nelson told one editorial board there were no state issues in the 1960 campaign, and one political scientist said, "The policy debate at the state level must be labeled vapid." Kuehn, the Republican candidate, was on the attack but mostly resorted to generalities: The Democrats were fiscally irresponsible, big spenders. Nelson's budget was the biggest in state history by 25 percent, and Wisconsin income tax rates were among the highest in the country. Another Nelson term would mean more spending, higher taxes, more government regulation, a bigger bureaucracy. It would be a "gross calamity" if the Democratic platform ever were enacted.[14]

For the first time in Wisconsin history, the candidates for governor met in a debate. The September debate, sponsored by the Milwaukee Public Affairs Forum, was broadcast statewide on radio from the Milwaukee Eagles Club and aired live on several television stations. It was surprisingly mild. The two candidates were not only polite to one another; they nearly passed like ships in the night, without ever mentioning what was billed as the chief issue in the campaign—the sales tax. In what the *Capital Times*'s William Evjue later lampooned as an "Alphonse and Gaston" routine where excessive politeness stood in the way of action, neither candidate brought up the sales tax during the hourlong broadcast. They sparred gently on general issues. The predominantly Republican audience cheered Kuehn loudly, prompting a jibe from Nelson: "I notice that you brought your campaign workers with you. I have mine out going door to door tonight."[15]

After the broadcast ended, the audience of six hundred had a chance to ask questions. Someone asked: "Are you convinced that Wisconsin can fulfill its fiscal needs without relying on a general sales tax?" Nelson said yes, if the state had enough economic growth. Kuehn said he opposed a sales tax unless it replaced some existing taxes like the income tax surcharge and reduced property taxes. Under those circumstances, Kuehn said, "I would accept a reasonable sales tax program." And that was that. In response to another question, Nelson backed a withholding tax and said most states, even with Republican governors, had such a system. Kuehn said he opposed it because it means collecting three years' taxes in two years, and that making taxes "painless" would hide the real cost of state government.[16]

The Democrats were increasingly confident, and on a four-day campaign swing by Nelson in mid-October through the Republican Fox Valley, Nelson said he had never seen such enthusiasm and energy on the part of Democrats. Turnout for Democratic events in most communities was several times what it had been in 1958, although the numbers were still small. In Shawano, two people had attended a Nelson breakfast in 1958; two years later more than twenty turned out to meet him. That was certainly an increase, but the 1960 population of the city was sixty-one hundred and the county population was thirty-two thousand. But based on the four-day visit, the *Capital Times*'s Revell, the only reporter to predict Nelson's 1958 victory in print, made "an educated guess" that Nelson, who had won by 87,905 votes the last time, would "far surpass" that and win by 110,000 votes or more.[17]

Six days before election day, Kuehn issued a position paper which came close to saying a sales tax was inevitable. "The time for demagoguery, vacillation, and delay is over," Kuehn declared, accusing Nelson of hiding behind his study commission and playing politics with the issue. "I am not afraid, as is the present governor, of doing that which is right and that which is necessary. I am not afraid to say publicly that which I admit privately," he said. Again he said the sales tax would replace other taxes, not be added to them. The position paper, which broke little or no new ground, got short notice in the press, except for the *Capital Times*, which gave it a banner headline: "Kuehn Urges '61 Sales Tax."[18]

The *Wisconsin Agriculturist* reported Nelson leading Kuehn 52 to 34 percent in a poll of farmers, while Nixon held a three-point lead over Kennedy. An Associated Press analysis called Nelson a "smashing favorite" to become the first Democrat since the 1890s to win reelection. A poll by a Milwaukee public opinion firm the week before the election had Nelson leading by 20 percent. Pat Lucey predicted a 100,000-vote Democratic majority in Milwaukee County and a landslide for the state ticket. Democrats sensed another big victory in the making. While his advisors dreamed of the biggest victory in Wisconsin history—receiving more than a million votes, a 400,000-vote margin of victory, winning both houses of the legislature, and running ahead of Kennedy—a confident Nelson eased off on the throttle a bit in the final weeks.[19]

"What the Hell Happened?"

On election night in Milwaukee, the early returns were a shock. Kennedy was losing Wisconsin, and Nelson appeared to be in trouble. Nelson said he did not want to hear the blow-by-blow of the early returns, which had caused such anxiety in 1958. "I don't want to hear anything until something significant comes in," he said. After the polls closed, he and Carrie Lee took time to visit an old friend, *Milwaukee Journal* reporter and critic Richard S. Davis, in a Milwaukee hospital. Then they holed up in a suite in the Hotel Wisconsin, awaiting returns being re-layed by Ed Bayley, Nelson's chief of staff, who was stationed at the *Milwaukee Journal* newsroom. Nelson was running ahead of Kennedy almost everywhere, and Bayley felt Kennedy was dragging down Nelson's vote. At 10:15, when all Milwaukee County votes were in and Kennedy's margin was slimmer than expected, Nelson asked Bayley, "Does your projection show we're licked?" Bayley said he didn't know. An hour later, Kennedy called Nelson from Hyannisport, Massachusetts, to wish him luck, and to ask Nelson what had happened in Wisconsin. "I guess my political antenna is out of whack," Nelson replied. When Robert Kennedy phoned Lucey to ask, "What the hell happened in Wisconsin?" Lucey "was at a loss for an answer." Nelson held on to a slim lead, and finally about 1 A.M. it began to widen and he could relax. He would be reelected.[20]

There was little else to celebrate. Nelson's margin of victory was smaller than in 1958, as he received 51.6 percent of the vote. The presidential returns were a reverse image of the governor's race, as Richard Nixon carried the state by nearly 65,000 votes and a winning percentage of 51.8, drawing 4,307 more votes than Nelson. John Reynolds squeaked through to reelection as attorney general, but Republican Warren Knowles won back the lieutenant governor's office, the GOP's Dena Smith became state treasurer, and Republicans took the First District congressional seat. The worst news for Nelson was that the Republicans had gained ten seats in the assembly, reversing the fifty-five to forty-five advantage the Democrats had held in the 1959 session. The GOP maintained its twenty to thirteen majority in the state senate. For the first time in state history, Wisconsin voters had chosen a governor of one party and given control of both houses of the legislature to the opposition.[21]

The *Capital Times* quickly sounded the death knell for Nelson's programs. All of his aspirations to rekindle the Wisconsin Idea had been crushed, the paper said, predicting the session would be "one of frustration for Nelson. He will have to tone down his legislation or see his bills killed without mercy," Revell wrote in a postmortem. Nelson was unbowed. "I consider it my responsibility and my duty to propose the best program I know and to fight for it," he said. He said he would be nonpartisan in judging Republican legislation, asking Republicans to do the same for him. Clearly, some "restraint, cooperation and statesmanship" would be required if the government were not to come to a standstill. Republicans did not have the required two-thirds majority to override a veto in either house. Neither party could operate without the other.[22]

After putting down a persistent rumor that he would join the Kennedy cabinet, perhaps as secretary of agriculture—an idea he thought ridiculous—Nelson turned his attention to preparing a budget and legislative package. Tax policy would be the defining issue of the 1961 session, but Nelson kept his vow to offer a strong legislative program. In "a fighting inaugural address," Nelson pledged to meet the state's problems with "the surging spirit of a militant progressivism." If necessary, he said, he would recommend tax increases to pay for essential state services, because "to fail to perform them is to commit slow, certain suicide." He said the public was not aware of all of the pressures facing state government, or the costs involved. "The only way to satisfy those who demand tax cuts is to reduce services—to keep our children home from school, to let our highways deteriorate, to strangle our rivers in pollution, to harden our hearts to the mentally ill, to shut our eyes to the decay of our cities, to doom our elderly to a life of poverty and despair," he said. He was not willing to do that or duck the issues, Nelson said, telling Republicans, "We cannot afford two years of stalemate."[23]

Two weeks later, he laid out forty proposals in his "State of the State" speech. His "to do" list ranged from major items like reapportionment to minutiae like creating uniform accident reporting. Most of Nelson's proposals that had been killed in the last session were back—a constitutional amendment to permit state borrowing, his farm marketing bill, billboard regulation, and a million dollar student loan fund. Noting the unprecedented split in control of the government, he called for "restraint" and "a spirit of good will. . . . The voters of Wisconsin have elected a bipartisan government and we must make it work," he said.[24]

14

The Conservation Governor

NELSON HELD BACK one major proposal from his wide-ranging 1961 "State of the State" speech so that it could be showcased and considered separately, on its own merits. It was an ambitious, visionary program to expand the state's recreational land holdings, at a time when a growing population and new mobility by automobile were putting increasing pressure on scarce public lands. Its adoption put Wisconsin in the forefront of conservation programs in the nation. It was to make Nelson "the Conservation Governor," stamp him indelibly as an environmentalist, and make him a national leader on the issue.[1]

Its official name was the Outdoor Recreation Act Program (later modified to Action instead of Act), but in Wisconsin it has always been called ORAP, and pronounced *ORE-app*. On its face, it was simple: a ten-year, $50 million program to acquire land for recreation and conservation purposes, paid for by a cigarette tax of one cent per package. But its underpinnings and inner workings represented an upheaval in the way Wisconsin handled conservation issues, and the huge scope of the program made preserving recreational land a high priority for the state.

Nelson had hatched the basic idea—that he wanted to expand and accelerate land acquisition—during his first term as governor. He had a lifelong interest in the environment, but had been stymied for ten years as a minority member of the legislature. As a first term governor he had modest success, expanding the outdoor recreation budget, increasing public lake and stream access, and acquiring Blue Mounds State Park, but failed to win approval of a two dollar state park admission sticker to raise revenue for park system expansion. He had warned then that "our

state parks and forest recreation areas have been neglected for too long,"
with park attendance growing twenty times as fast as park expenditures.
One problem, he said, was that Wisconsin favored the traditionally
male sports of fishing and hunting, while doing little for parks used by
families.[2] Family recreation was the major factor in the booming park
usage, as Illinois families headed for Wisconsin and families in southern Wisconsin headed up north for weekend or vacation getaways. A
University of Wisconsin study estimated that 25 percent of all Chicago
area residents took at least one overnight trip to Wisconsin in 1959.[3]

If Wisconsin residents doubted there was a problem, the Fourth of
July weekend of 1960 convinced them. Every state park was jammed beyond capacity, and people were turned away. Southern Wisconsin parks,
hardest hit with a huge influx of Chicagoans, were so overcrowded they
experienced health and sanitation problems. The crush and resulting
mess dramatized what state officials already knew—recreation usage was
skyrocketing, while available land and facilities were static. The number
of camper days in Kettle Moraine Forest jumped 85 percent from 1957 to
1959, and many public hunting and fishing areas had similar reports. In
five years, camper use increased 500 percent at Big Foot Beach, near the
Illinois border, and 400 percent at Terry Andrae State Park on Lake
Michigan. Nelson toured ten crowded parks in August 1960 and declared that the state should "double and redouble" facilities and land acquisition, before new interstate highways worsened the problem. The
need to expand recreational facilities was undisputed, but the state's financial crisis—and traditional, bureaucratic decision making—stood in
the way.[4]

During his first term, Nelson had tried unsuccessfully to change the
operation of the Conservation Commission and Conservation Department and make them more responsive to the governor. In his 1958 campaign Nelson had charged the Conservation Commission was being run
by a group of Republican appointees as if the state were running "a rich
man's rod and gun club." He said he would eliminate the commission
and give control of conservation policy to the professionals in the Conservation Department. The policy-making commission was designed to
insulate the agency from political interference. But Republicans had
controlled the statehouse so long that all six commissioners had been
appointed by Republican governors and were neither independent nor

nonpartisan. "Our entire conservation program is mired down in politics," Nelson said.[5]

When he became governor, Nelson proposed a surprisingly modest "reorganization" plan to allow him to replace the six incumbent commissioners with people nominated by a nonpartisan citizen advisory body. He described it as a way to take politics out of conservation policy; opponents called it a power grab to give Nelson immediate control of the commission. Nelson's plan was killed by the Republican legislature. It was mid-1961 before Nelson appointees finally constituted a majority on the commission.

Meanwhile, Nelson had moved in his first term to realign long-range planning for conservation. His reorganization plan, which won legislative approval, created a new Department of Resource Development (DRD), combining functions formerly spread across many agencies. It was described as an economic development agency, but its responsibilities were broadly defined. The new DRD was to "inventory Wisconsin's resources, analyze their strengths and needs, and develop comprehensive plans for future state development." Although not emphasized, the mandate included natural resource planning; the DRD was in the conservation and recreation business, too. Nelson, a strong proponent of planning, stumped the state to urge creation of regional planning commissions, which later made some significant contributions to state resource, conservation, and recreation planning.[6]

Now, as his second term began, Nelson was ready to move on ORAP. To plan it, he chose David Carley, director of the new DRD; Harold "Bud" Jordahl Jr., a professional natural resource manager with the Conservation Department who became the DRD's resource specialist; William Fairfield, Nelson's press secretary; and James Wimmer, his executive assistant. Jordahl took the lead in putting the program together.[7]

The first step was to ask the Conservation Department's director, Lester Voigt, for his wish list—"If you had millions of dollars to spend, what would be your priorities all over this state? They produced a hell of a long list," Nelson said. It included acquisitions and capital improvements totaling $42.7 million. That list and others from the Conservation Department became the nucleus of the ORAP proposal. It included projects of some type in nearly every county—and every legislative district—in the state. That would be key to selling the program to the public and to the legislature.[8]

Jordahl refined the idea, adding the use of "conservation easements" to stretch the budget and protect natural areas and scenic beauty without purchasing the land. He proposed matching federal money for flood-control dams to create twenty small lakes in southwestern Wisconsin, the only part of the state without an abundance of lakes. The plan included tourist information centers on the borders, youth conservation camps, aid to expand urban recreation space, and a study of the potential of recreation and tourism in the Lake Superior region. A cynic could say there was something for everyone, rural or urban, in all regions of the state, in order to generate support. The projects were solid on the merits, but their geographic distribution gave everyone a reason to support ORAP.[9]

The proposal took shape quickly and quietly, for the most part. Columnist John Wyngaard had gotten wind of a "crash conservation plan" being prepared by the governor and described the forthcoming program as "closer to [Nelson's] heart than any other major policy program he had evolved thus far."[10] His source, from all indications, was the governor himself. Despite that small leak, Nelson's announcement of ORAP took the government and the public by surprise. It was more ambitious and comprehensive than anyone could expect.

"The choice we are faced with, quite simply, is now or never," Nelson told the legislature on 15 March in what was billed as a resource development message. "Wisconsin's entire recreational future will continue to be undercut, month by month, unless we start immediately on a program of wise and prudent investment in our outdoor assets, enhanced for future generations by careful planning and multiple use concepts." He laid out the urgent need for a program—the increasing pressure on recreational land and facilities, fueled by the growing population and "massive urban expansion" in southeastern Wisconsin and the Chicago metropolitan area. Land acquisition was more urgent than development, he said. "First priority should be given to securing for the public these vital assets which are fast disappearing," he said, calling for expanding a number of state parks, fish and wildlife habitat, and state forests. "If you adopt this program, whatever else you do this session, you will leave a permanent mark in history as the Conservation Legislature," he said.[11]

Selling ORAP

The proposal was front-page news across Wisconsin. Fairfield began a steady stream of press releases, localized to highlight proposed development and acquisition in each county, and illustrated by maps. Editorial support was strong. In northern Wisconsin, a Vilas County weekly editor reported, response was almost universally positive. "We have come up with no one who disagrees completely, regardless of party affiliation," he wrote. Response "ranged from sincere interest and cautious agreement to hopeful enthusiasm exceeding anything we have ever heard to a new state 'tax and spend' program."[12]

When a draft of the actual ORAP legislation was completed in April, the first opposition surfaced. Not surprisingly, it came from the Conservation Commission and the Conservation Department. Their biggest objection was Nelson's plan to create a new state recreation committee to recommend how to spend ORAP funds. That committee would take power from the Conservation Commission, and the commission wanted it eliminated. It also wanted the cigarette tax revenue to go right into the conservation fund instead of a special ORAP fund, and wanted money for administrative staff and overhead to run the program. Nelson, fearing the new revenue would be drained to maintain or expand existing bureaucracy, had called for the money to be spent mostly for land acquisition, with some designated for development, and a tiny amount for administration. If the governor would not agree to the changes, the Conservation Commission said, it would ask the legislature to make them.[13]

In the meantime, Nelson's proposal was gaining momentum, as the publicity campaign continued and Nelson, Carley, Jordahl, and others stumped the state to sell it. In every appearance, they told local residents and newspapers of all the specific plans for their area. Speaking in tiny Cassville, on the Mississippi River, Nelson offered a long list of specific benefits for the region—purchase of scenic easements along the river, two tourist information stations on the Iowa-Wisconsin border, creation of twenty-five to thirty new lakes in the area, several thousand acres of fish management projects, ten thousand acres of wildlife or game management projects, development of Wildcat Mountain State Park, and improvements at three more state parks in the area. That was typical of presentations being made in nearly every county in the state.[14]

Editorial support was strong, backing Nelson's plan as "one of the finest things to come out of the statehouse in many a year." Attorney General John Reynolds said it would be "the greatest plan that any state has ever passed," and proclaimed that "Kennedy, Nelson, and conservation" were the three things that would foster the growth of the Wisconsin Democratic Party. Three hundred hunters and fishermen, delegates to the Wisconsin Conservation Congress, gave Nelson a standing ovation as they unanimously endorsed the plan. ORAP "might turn out to be the most fruitful thing politically [Nelson] has devised in his career," Wyngaard wrote.[15]

Mail to the governor's office ran strongly in favor of the plan, but there were some naysayers. Why should hunters and fishermen have "the recreation financed at the expense of the taxpayer?" one Stevens Point man wrote. His hobbies were bowling, photography, and spectator sports, he told Nelson. "How soon may I expect the state to provide me with a bowling ball and shoes, film for my camera, and free passes to all basketball, football, and baseball games?" Nelson replied that not only sportsmen would benefit but the entire population, including birdwatchers, amateur photographers, and picnickers.[16]

A public hearing on ORAP before the legislature's conservation committees generated more support than anything else Nelson had ever proposed. "The opinion of the North is unanimously in favor of this program for resource development," a Vilas County Chamber of Commerce spokesman said. Local governments, sportsmen's clubs, conservation groups, civic organizations, and farm groups all testified in support of the plan. Nelson called it "a now or never situation," with the state losing its natural resources "not by the inch and the ounce, but by the square mile and the ton."[17]

The only real opposition—aside from the tobacco industry—came from Door County, the state's "Cape Cod," on the tip of the Green Bay peninsula in Lake Michigan. Door County did not want another state park; it wanted to develop the area, add to the tax base, and create jobs. The county believed private resort owners, not the state, should meet the growing need for recreation. An amendment, tailored to apply only to Door County and requiring county board approval for any new state parks, was attached to the bill and that opposition disappeared.[18]

A redrafted bill took care of other objections and attracted more support. The most significant change added $100,000 per biennium for capital improvements in county forests. Representative Paul Alfonsi, chairman of the assembly Conservation Committee, asked for the change, which helped cement his support. Alfonsi, who represented three sparsely populated, tourism-dominated counties in the far north, was instrumental in winning assembly passage of the bill. A competing amendment, incorporating all of the Conservation Commission's objections and shifting power back to the commission, was introduced. With Republican majorities in both houses, it could have passed, in theory. But Alfonsi and senator Clifford "Tiny" Krueger, a former Progressive who chaired the senate Conservation Committee, were persuaded to support Nelson's version. When the Republican cochairman of the Joint Finance Committee tried to hold ORAP hostage until Nelson agreed to a Republican sales tax bill, Alfonsi personally made the motion to pull the bill from committee for floor action. Alfonsi served as floor manager for the bill, which cleared the lower house on a vote of 87 to 6 in Nelson's "greatest political triumph of his career" with easy passage "in a house securely controlled by members of the rival Republican party." Wyngaard forecast "an early vote of concurrence" in the senate.[19]

But the Republican senate leadership plotted to kill the bill, or at least hijack it. Senator Earl Leverich, Nelson's pipeline to the GOP caucus, told him the Republicans thought the bill was too popular to give him credit. The bill was "popular as hell," Nelson knew, and several Republican mavericks, led by Krueger, intended to vote for it. But a Republican head count showed that a motion to table the bill would result in a tie vote, allowing Lieutenant Governor Warren Knowles, a Republican, to cast the deciding vote to table. Technically, they wouldn't be voting to kill the bill, so the vote could be defensible. Republicans then could rewrite the bill and introduce a similar proposal, for which they could take the credit. They had used that technique in the legislature for years, as with Nelson's bill to integrate the Wisconsin National Guard.[20]

Republicans offered "a fistful of amendments" to Nelson's bill, which state senator Robert Knowles called "the most ingenious pork barrel bill ever drafted. There's something in it for almost everybody." The key vote was on tabling the bill. The Democratic floor leader, senator William Moser, said, "The only problem with this bill is that Governor Gaylord Nelson introduced it. The only purpose for the delay is for the Republican party to draft a new proposal and take the credit."[21]

Ace in the Hole

But Nelson and company were one step ahead this time. Leo O'Brien, Republican senator from the Green Bay area, was neither a maverick nor an independent thinker. An insurance salesman and public relations man with no real political ambitions, he was a reliable vote who "rarely strayed from the regular Republican fold." The leadership took his vote for granted, but in this important instance that was a mistake. A Republican businessman with close ties to O'Brien had become impressed with Nelson, whom he had heard about *ad infinitum* from his friends John J. Brogan and his son, John. The Brogans were long-time Democrats from Green Bay, and young John had worked in Nelson's campaign for governor. Through the Brogans, the businessman also came to know key Nelson staffers Bill Fairfield, press secretary, and Ed Bayley, chief of staff. One weekend in 1959, at the Brogans' Door County cottage, the Republican made an offer. "If you ever need a vote in the state senate, let me know." It was a one-time offer, to be used only in a real emergency. With the impending defeat of ORAP, Nelson and Fairfield decided the emergency was at hand. Fairfield, through Brogan, reached the businessman and told him the situation. The governor needed the vote in the state senate the next morning. The Republican, who was largely responsible for the election of O'Brien to the senate, agreed to ask O'Brien for his vote.[22]

O'Brien didn't attend the senate Republican caucus the next morning, idly walking around the empty senate chamber while his colleagues caucused. He wanted to avoid making a commitment on the bill. His absence didn't cause any alarm among the GOP leadership; O'Brien was a safe vote. But when the roll call vote to table ORAP was called, O'Brien voted no. Republican leaders, thinking he had voted mistakenly, huddled with him to try to get him to change his vote. But O'Brien held firm. It was no mistake, he said, repeating his instructions: "No on all amendments, yes on final passage." The tabling motion and a series of amendments all failed on identical 17 to 15 votes, with O'Brien casting the deciding vote every time. On final passage, the vote was 26 to 5 as "ten Republicans jumped on the bandwagon."[23]

Nelson signed the ORAP bill into law on 28 August 1961. It was "perhaps the most important single act by a Wisconsin legislature in the last quarter century," Nelson said, guaranteeing that the 1961 legislature would be remembered for "the foresight shown in assuring our children and grandchildren of the outdoor resources with which our state is so richly blessed." Wisconsin's innovative program quickly drew national attention, was praised and promoted by Interior Secretary Stewart Udall, and was used as a model by other states. Udall called it "the boldest conservation step ever taken on a state level in the history of the United States." Wyngaard wondered about the "relative ease of the achievement" and why no one had thought of it before. "If one of Governor Nelson's predecessors in statehouse control has shown such enterprise and imagination, Nelson might now continue to be a relatively obscure state legislator."[24]

For ORAP was much more than a pork barrel, laundry list of projects and land acquisitions, even though that had helped sell the program. It marked a fundamental change in the way the state viewed and used its natural resources. It involved the state in conservation, recreation, and tourism to a greater extent than ever before. It expanded the boundaries of conservation programs beyond hunting and fishing and broadened the constituency for such programs beyond the so-called red shirts—outdoorsmen—to encompass family recreation, camping, picnicking, swimming, hiking, and boating. It recognized that some wild and scenic areas should be preserved and left undeveloped, in their natural state. It broadened the tax base for conservation programs, which had relied mainly on fees from licenses and permits. In concert with new requirements for natural resource planning insisted upon by Nelson, the legislation laid the groundwork for a huge expansion of state-owned recreation land. In the words of one scholar, it marked "a watershed moment in the rise of Wisconsin environmentalism. It influenced the direction of both state and national policy-making, injecting one of the first 'modern' environmental issues into the political milieu, . . . challenged the status quo in Wisconsin's conservation community and established Gaylord Nelson as a national environmental leader."[25]

The first year after it was enacted, the state spent $3 million to acquire more than 36,000 acres of land. The program, Nelson said, "has already proved it will leave a deep and lasting imprint on the future of our state."[26] In its first ten years, the ORAP program spent $40 million on state parks, forests, fish and game management, youth conservation camps, and other recreation and conservation projects. It acquired more than seven hundred miles of stream shoreline. In addition, ORAP leveraged federal money to spend more than $30 million to purchase 300,000 acres of land.[27]

When the original ten-year program was ending in 1969, Governor Warren Knowles, with Nelson's strong support, won approval of the legislature and a statewide referendum to extend the program to 1981 as ORAP-200. The new program expanded its scope to clean up water pollution and broadened the tax base to include general state revenues and bonds. It provided, through bonding, $56 million for recreation and conservation and $144 million for local water treatment plants. By 1981, when ORAP-200 expired, the two ORAP programs combined had acquired more than 450,000 acres and spent $93 million in state and matching federal funds.[28] ORAP-200, in turn, was succeeded by the Knowles-Nelson Stewardship Program, which in the year 2000 was allocating $46 million annually to conserve and protect wildlife habitat, sensitive lands, and recreational opportunities.

15

The Great Tax Debate

THE LONG-ANTICIPATED AND INEVITABLE CLASH over a sales
tax came in the 1961 legislative session and dominated the state's political debate for a year.

Nelson's blue ribbon tax study commission finally made its report in
December 1960, conveniently finishing its work a month after his reelection. Its major conclusion was obvious: Fundamental changes in
state tax policy would be required to respond to the increasing demands
and pressure on state resources. The commission recommended small
increases in income tax rates, a withholding system, a 2 percent sales tax
that excluded food, repeal of the personal property tax, and other
changes to make the system more equitable and close loopholes. Much
of the new revenue, it said, should go to property tax relief. Nelson had
no immediate public reaction. He would consider the report and make
his recommendations to the legislature as part of his budget, he said.
Republicans said they would withhold judgment until then.[1]

When Nelson presented his tax package, it did not include a sales
tax, but he left the door open. Although he had never advocated a sales
tax, Nelson said, "I do not view it with the intransigent and dogmatic
opposition with which many in my own party do. I can conceive of future fiscal crises in which the clear choice of progressive-minded officials might lie on the side of a sales tax" if the only alternative were to
cut vital services. "But we in Wisconsin are not at the point where such
a choice is necessary," he declared.[2]

Instead, he proposed a 1 percent increase in income tax rates, a withholding tax, a reduction in the income tax surcharge, a franchise tax on banks and savings and loans, and an excise tax on tobacco. His "surprise solution" included no taxes at all on 1961 income below $10,000 and proposed a variety of new deductions to benefit "everyone from working wives to homeless ministers." The package would raise an additional $83 million over the two-year budget cycle. Nelson's plan went to the legislature's Joint Finance Committee in mid-February for long, torturous consideration, amendment, and eventual death. A compromise tax bill would not be passed until Christmas.[3]

While bottling up the tax bill, the legislature did pass a state budget that gave Nelson much of what he wanted—but not without a fight. When the finance committee made some major cuts, reducing Nelson's proposed campus building program and cutting faculty pay raises in half, Nelson went on the offensive. The session was "the most fruitless and least productive" he had ever seen, Nelson said. His attack on the "do nothing" legislature got the Republicans' attention and helped win passage in June of a budget he could live with.[4]

That avoided a budget impasse, but the legislature had not passed a tax bill to raise the additional $60 million needed to balance the two-year budget. Republicans were split on the sales tax and ended up introducing a package without enough votes to pass it, despite sizable GOP majorities in both houses. It included a 3 percent sales tax but also had a withholding plan and other inducements for Nelson to sign it. But after a "runaway" Republican state convention ignored GOP legislators and took a hard-line stand for a sales tax and against withholding, assembly Speaker David Blanchard changed course. Blanchard, one of six Republicans who had drafted the bill, surprised his colleagues by calling for elimination of both the withholding plan and a sales tax credit designed to soften the impact on lower income taxpayers. Blanchard's changes set up a showdown with the governor. "The water is really muddied now," the *Milwaukee Journal* said after the convention vote. "There can be no absolute victory on this issue for either party."[5]

Republicans managed to pass a bill in August with a 3 percent general sales tax and without the withholding plan and other Nelson proposals. Predictably, Nelson vetoed it. He called for compromise by "thoughtful and responsible leaders of both parties" to resolve the issue. Republicans reacted strongly, saying Nelson was guilty of a lack of courage, a lack of leadership, "economic irresponsibility," and "political bigotry," among other things, and had made it clear that "tax revision in 1961 is dead." The legislature adjourned, and Nelson pledged that before it reconvened on 30 October he would work with both parties to find a compromise to head off the looming state fiscal crisis.[6]

Nelson's problems were not only with the Republicans. He was beginning to move toward some type of sales tax as part of a compromise, but many Democrats had made opposition to a sales tax an article of faith since the DOC formed in 1949. Nelson warned lawmakers meeting on a compromise plan that "there are Democrats who want to campaign in 1962 on the sole issue of defeating the sales tax, and who would be satisfied with the expedience of a tax increase to balance the budget, even though this would leave the 1963 legislature facing another large deficit, requiring another increase in taxes."[7] Nelson wanted a responsible, long-term solution to the state's problems. While seeking to win over some Republicans on withholding and other issues, he also needed to find some Democrats who could live with a sales taxes.

Feuding with Lucey

To further complicate matters, Nelson's differences with party chair Patrick Lucey, never a secret among Democrats, worsened and spilled over into public view. A number of Wisconsin Democrats had joined the Kennedy administration, including Robert Lewis, Nelson's agricultural advisor, who went to the Department of Agriculture, and Ed Bayley, Nelson's executive assistant, who took a high level post in the new Peace Corps. Philleo Nash, Nelson's former lieutenant governor, was Kennedy's commissioner of Indian Affairs. But federal patronage was channeled through Lucey, Kennedy's main man in Wisconsin, and federal appointments were being made without consulting Nelson. Some Democrats complained about Lucey taking sides in every intraparty contest and charged he was too preoccupied with national issues and wasn't paying enough attention to passing the party's legislative agenda or electing Democratic legislators.

Lucey had told Nelson, when he became governor, that he would leave the chairmanship if Nelson wanted to replace him. Nelson decided the time had come. "There was a lot of stuff going on within the party that I wasn't happy with, and I asked him to get out [in June 1961] and he wouldn't do it," Nelson said. So, with Lucey running for an unprecedented third term as chairman, Nelson fielded his own candidate, state representative Frank Nikolay. In the past, Nelson had rejected suggestions that he "seize the reins of power and become the unchallenged leader of his party," so his decision marked a change in strategy. Lucey was "at the peak of his power and influence," and a fierce struggle was expected. But a month before the state convention, Nikolay's National Guard unit was ordered to active duty in response to tensions with the Soviet Union over Berlin. Nelson then invited Lucey to work out a peaceful agreement on "party policy, direction, organization and issues." If they could agree, Nelson said, he and his supporters would not field another candidate.[8]

Nelson-Lucey meetings often included Attorney General John Reynolds, a Lucey ally, and a Nelson second, often Ed Bayley. The meetings, typically at the Simon House restaurant and bar near the capitol, "were prickly to begin with" with tension lessening a bit after the first martini, but "sometimes they would flare up and say really cutting things. It was hard to keep them civil very long," Bayley said. This time, after a tense meeting, Nelson and Lucey issued a joint statement saying they had "engaged in an extensive discussion of the various issues that gave rise to this contest for state chairman." They declared party peace and unity, "confident that all factions can be reunited and that we can forget past differences" to concentrate on party building and the 1962 campaign.[9] But it was a fragile truce, and Nelson-Lucey skirmishes continued throughout their careers.

The Democratic Party appeared likely to give Nelson another headache at its mid-October state convention. Most party regulars still opposed any sales tax. Nelson had vetoed the sales tax bill, but was working on a compromise that clearly could include some version of a sales tax. Ten days before the convention, when Nelson met with a bipartisan group of legislators to begin work on a compromise, the GOP asked Nelson point blank whether he would sign any bill that included a general sales tax. He didn't say yes or no; he said he would have to see the whole package. "I knew we were going to pass a bill and it had to have a sales tax," he said later, but he was not ready to give that away without more negotiating.[10]

Divided Democrats

A showdown with rabid anti-sales tax Democrats at the convention seemed inevitable. On Saturday afternoon, as the delegates adopted their "Statement of Principle," ex-party chair Jim Doyle was "subjected to prolonged boos and jeers" when he proposed support of the 2 percent sales tax recommended by the blue-ribbon panel on which he had served. The stage was set for Nelson's Saturday night speech, which he had labored on for a full day, "writing and revising and contriving a paragraph that would get public notice." Nelson spoke of the responsibility of governing, of the need to sometimes compromise to solve a pressing problem. He was not the governor of the Democratic Party, he said. He was the governor of the entire state of Wisconsin. As one reporter wrote, Nelson said "[h]is responsibilities as governor transcend party lines. . . . He has an obligation to act in the interest of the entire state. . . . He would go above party politics . . . without being tied down by political slogans, traditions, or obstructionism." He would fulfill his obligations and do what was necessary to end the state's financial crisis.[11]

Then came the line he had struggled with, the one that crystallized his position in a way he hoped would attract attention and get a positive response, even from those who disagreed with him: "The Democratic Party does not stand or fall with me. You can get other candidates and other leaders. But I stand or fall with my conscience. It's easier for you to get another candidate than it is for me to get another conscience."[12]

The response was generally enthusiastic. Some Democrats said it was about time someone gave that practical speech to the party, and mail to the governor's office praised his stand. Others thought it was courageous but politically risky. One state senator called Nelson "a dead hero" politically, and another said, "Maybe he's a statesman, but he's sure not a politician." The next day, the number of delegates steadily dwindled as debate over resolutions dragged on. The diehards, representing 10 percent of the total who attended the convention, passed a "no confidence" vote on Nelson and Democratic legislators for their attempts to work out a compromise on the tax issue.[13] Nelson discounted its significance, but it was an early warning of the campaign to come a year later, when the Democratic candidate for governor would run on a pledge to repeal the sales tax passed during Nelson's term.

A week after the convention Nelson offered his compromise tax plan. It included what he called "an excise tax on luxuries." Everyone else called it a sales tax. It called for a 3 percent tax on nine categories of purchases—entertainment and sports admissions, cosmetics, alcohol and tobacco, sports equipment, new furniture and household appliances, automobiles, overnight lodging, restaurant meals, and radio, television, and musical equipment. The proposal did not violate the Democratic platform, Nelson insisted. The platform opposed a general sales tax. This was something else—a selective tax on specified items "not necessary for life or health, and which the consumer can always postpone buying." It did not include food, clothing, medicine, or other necessities. The bill also increased income tax rates .5 percent, cut property taxes on manufacturers' and merchants' stock in half, and established a withholding system.[14]

Nelson called for "a coalition of responsible legislators in both our parties" to band together to pass it. "Sometimes," he told the legislature, "in politics as in other pursuits, it becomes necessary to speak bluntly to your best friends. Sometimes, you must tell them they are wrong. I'm telling my friends in the Democratic Party, my friends among the independents, and my labor friends—you are wrong when you oppose the compromise tax plan—you are tragically wrong. Your opposition to this plan is not based on fact—it is based on fiction." John Wyngaard praised Nelson for standing up to "the tycoons of organized labor" who had announced their opposition even before his speech, "something that no other current politician could probably have done." His message, in essence, was that liberals must recognize "that when they demand more government benefits for everybody, the tax collector must collect from more people." Nelson "probably crossed a line in his own political position" in trying to bridge the huge liberal-conservative split on tax policy, he said.[15]

Opponents claimed the $50 million to be raised from sales taxes made the system more regressive. Nelson said the reverse was true. The $50 million would go to reduce property taxes, an even more regressive form of taxation. "When you took reduction of property taxes in, the total impact on the tax structure was neutral," Nelson said. "But a lot of people were just emotionally anti-sales tax, period. Democrats had run against it as unfair to the poor. I remember talking with Ivan Nestingen and asking him, 'If I could show you the overall impact would be absolutely neutral on progressivity, would you support it?' And he got red in the face and angry and said no."[16]

A five-hour public hearing on the bill produced little support. Only five people testified in favor, including Nelson and his tax commissioner, John Gronouski. Twenty-five others, representing business, labor, and the Democratic Party, opposed it. Much of the opposition was predictable. Bankers opposed a new bank tax, truckers opposed the business tax, the restaurant industry opposed the tax on meals, motels opposed the tax on accommodations, the bowling industry opposed the tax on bowling, and automobile dealers wanted a general sales tax, not a selective one.[17]

As the assembly vote neared, Nelson urged legislators to have the "courage to recede from a previous position and accept a compromise" rather than taking "the easy way out" and opposing it. "On the overriding issue of this legislative session, the issue of basic tax revision, the hour of decision has arrived," Nelson said in a letter to lawmakers. "It has taken us many years and monumental efforts to reach this point. It has required massive studies, almost endless debates and—finally—dedicated efforts to achieve an honorable compromise on the differences between our two political parties." The assembly killed the bill on a 55 to 41 vote, with twenty-two Democrats among those opposing it.[18]

"We either compromise or we invite fiscal chaos," Nelson said in a conciliatory speech to the legislature, asking it to reconsider. Disagreement over tax policy was healthy, he said, and everyone had fought hard for his own position. "Now, however, it is clear that each of us cannot have his own way," he said, and it was time for compromise. Nelson said he believed "each and every one has come here with the intention to do what he believes best for our state. . . . Good intentions are not always adequate. Good judgment, too, is important. I believe good intent and good judgment now indicate that this issue should be as abruptly concluded as possible." The next day, ten Democrats changed their votes and the assembly passed the compromise bill. But the senate killed the bill a week before Christmas. The *Wisconsin State Journal* banner headline suggested the impasse could result in a 90 percent income tax surcharge.[19] Legislators seemed on the brink of giving up on any tax revision and finding a temporary, distasteful solution. Which party would get the blame in the 1962 elections was uncertain, but there was no question the issue would dominate the next campaign. It was a high-risk strategy for both parties.

Tavern Diplomacy

Nelson solved the problem, as he did many others, in a personal conversation over a few drinks. He ran into state senator Robert Knowles on the Capitol Square, and the two sat down at the nearby Wagon Wheel tavern. Nelson and Knowles were friends from their days of serving together in the senate. Knowles's brother Warren, who also had served with Nelson, was now lieutenant governor and presided in the senate. Robert was an influential and respected member of the GOP senate caucus. "Let's both write down the absolute minimum necessities we need on both sides" to get a bill passed, Knowles said. "What can you sell to your caucus, and what can I sell to mine?" They discussed the issue for an hour and agreed on a proposal both could live with. They went back to their respective caucuses the next day and got agreement. "We resolved the whole damn thing over a bottle of beer in a tavern," Nelson said.[20]

The resulting bill, passed by both houses of the legislature on 22 December, imposed the 3 percent sales tax on the nine categories Nelson had proposed. It increased income tax rates 1 percent, eliminated the income tax surcharge, and created state withholding with 65 percent forgiveness on 1961 income taxes. The bill, the first major change in Wisconsin tax law since 1911, was rushed to the governor's desk in typewritten form, which the legislature authorized so it could be signed and published before January 1. In signing it on 28 December, Nelson said his main objection was the legislature's refusal to enact a bank tax he had proposed.[21]

"Every citizen of Wisconsin can find objections to one or another feature of this one hundred page act," he said. "I object to certain provisions myself. But on balance, I think that all of us will agree that this . . . represents a massive improvement in Wisconsin's tax structure, offering deep and lasting benefits for our entire state."[22] The issue was resolved, but far from dead. It would play a prominent role in the 1962 political campaign, now just months away.

The session had been "tailor-made for partisanship," but despite the partisan split on taxes, the 1961 GOP legislature had adopted several important parts of Nelson's program. Besides the centerpiece of his legislative program—the $50 million ORAP plan—his successes included creation of a $5 million student loan fund, a state commission on aging, a voluntary agriculture marketing plan, and a package of highway safety improvements. The state's share of school costs increased from 20 to 25 percent, providing $65 million in property tax relief over the biennium. Voters approved a constitutional amendment, which he supported, to allow merchants' and manufacturers' inventories and livestock to be taxed differently from other property, such as real estate, which enabled $30 million in property tax relief in the 1961–63 budget.[23]

Nelson struck another blow for natural resource conservation, using a politically risky veto to put down what became known as the "county forest crop revolt." Under a program started in the 1920s, the state supported the creation and preservation of county forests and paid state aid to local governments that put land into the "forest crop" program. Unhappy with the financial arrangements, with two million acres in county forests, local governments won passage of a bill in 1961 that would have virtually ended the program by allowing counties to sell the forest land for private development. Despite the potential political fallout from the twenty-seven affected counties, Nelson vetoed the bill. The senate overrode him twenty-five to four but the override fell three votes short in the assembly. Bud Jordahl, Nelson's advisor on natural resource issues, called it his "most courageous veto as governor." It saved the program and millions of acres of county forests. Nelson named a task force to rewrite the law, and the resulting legislation, enacted in 1963, made the county forest system permanent. That change, Jordahl believed, was a greater achievement than ORAP, although ORAP was "much more sexy." The new law allowed counties to sell forest land if it could be justified as "higher and better use," but it also required that more than economics be considered in making that judgment.[24]

There were defeats as well. One was the failure to give the state Human Rights Commission the power to act against housing discrimination. The issue was dramatized by a state capitol demonstration and sit-in organized by the National Association for the Advancement of Colored People. Participants included Nelson's sister Janet Lee. When someone pointed out Janet's participation to Nelson and suggested she should quit that, Nelson replied, "I don't tell her anything."[25]

Overall, the two sessions under Nelson's administration were "the most impressive of any in roughly a half century, accomplished with little fanfare amidst the turmoil of partisan brawling." A state historian said: "How successfully this process of negotiation and compromise worked depended in large measure on the personality and skills of the governor." He credited Nelson as "an experienced infighter from his days in the state senate, a strong party leader when it came to persuading Democratic legislators to accept compromise settlements, and a skilled negotiator in working with the opposition party."[26]

16

On to the Senate

THE GENERAL ASSUMPTION WAS that Nelson would run for the United States Senate in 1962 against Republican Alexander Wiley. In fact, Nelson had made that decision halfway through his second term as governor. "I had achieved practically everything that I could achieve [as governor]. I figured that I could get reelected easier than I could beat Wiley, but two years wouldn't add much to what I could achieve. There was nothing major I wanted to get done in the four years that I didn't get done. So it was either take on Wiley, lose, and go back and practice law, or win and go to the Senate," Nelson said.[1]

Wiley was a formidable opponent. An attorney, businessman, and farm owner, he began his political career in Chippewa Falls, in northwestern Wisconsin, as a district attorney. In 1936 he was the Republican candidate for governor, losing badly to Progressive Philip La Follette in a three-way race. But the tide turned in 1938, Republicans swept every statewide office, and Wiley became a United States Senator. He had been reelected three times, the last time in 1956 when the Republicans had tried to dump him, endorsing conservative Glenn Davis. But Wiley, benefiting from a sympathetic backlash, beat Davis in the GOP primary and easily defeated Democrat Henry Maier, a state senator, in the general election. In 1960 Maier was elected mayor of Milwaukee.

With twenty-four years in office, Wiley was the senior Republican in the Senate and the ranking member of the Foreign Relations, Judiciary, and Aeronautics and Space Science Committees. He had a moderate, if undistinguished, record in the Senate, was well known, and had few enemies. His biggest handicap was that he was seventy-eight years

old. Nelson would be forty-six at the time of the election. As the youth-
ful new President John F. Kennedy said, a dramatic change was taking
place, with a new generation, born in the twentieth century, picking up
the torch. Nelson would never raise the age issue, but he did not need to.

"The two men are as far apart in personality as it is possible to reach
in politics," Aldric Revell wrote in handicapping the race for the *Capital Times*. "Nelson is young, vigorous, imaginative and courageous"
while Wiley was "aging, a master of mediocrity, and a fence straddler of
historic proportions." To avoid debates, Revell said, Wiley should consider a tour of overseas military bases during the campaign and let voters remember him in his younger days. Wiley, "a glad-hander type and
no orator," would be no match for Nelson on the stump, he said. "It is
questionable whether Wiley is fully aware of what is going on in Washington, even though he has been there twenty-four years." Still, it
would be an uphill fight to beat Wiley, who was like a comfortable old
shoe, "an overstuffed armchair in a modern living room."[2] Revell's analysis made readers smile, but in the end Wiley's campaign strategy was
much as he suggested.

Nelson announced on 12 March 1962 that he would not run for reelection, clearing the way for Attorney General John Reynolds, who
was anxious to launch a campaign. There were several reasons, Nelson
said, but elaborated on one. "Four years of constant traveling around the
state, with most weekends away from home, is as much an imposition
on my wife and kids [as] I can expect them to bear." A third child, Jeffrey, had joined the family in May 1961, shocking some people to think
the Nelsons could actually be having sex in the governor's mansion,
Carrie Lee joked. To Carrie Lee, the Senate promised a more regular
and predictable family life, outside of the mansion and the fishbowl in
which a governor and his family inevitably live.[3]

Nelson entered the Senate race in late May, speaking of the need for
"the vigor and the courage and the imagination" to meet challenges.
The only word he dropped from Revell's litany was "young" and he
didn't need to say that. He invited Wiley to join him in a "public forum"
to discuss the issues, but the two never appeared together. Nelson's
campaign kickoff dinner in the Clear Lake High School gymnasium attracted several hundred people and raised $2,000. It was a love fest with
old friends. "It's kind of hard to give a talk in your home town," Nelson

said. "I shot out too many windows around town with my BB gun to pose as a guy with an unblemished record."[4]

The five-dollar dinner contrasted with the Democratic Party's Jefferson-Jackson dinner a month earlier, when Lucey had raised the ticket price to $100 and persuaded President Kennedy to speak. Nelson stayed out of a party dispute about the high price, and the Milwaukee dinner raised $100,000 for the national party and the $180,000 for Wisconsin Democrats. It stirred the bad blood between Nelson and Lucey, when Lucey, as party chair, decided he would introduce the president. Nelson believed protocol and tradition demanded that the governor introduce the president, but Lucey, long a Kennedy insider, did it himself. A minor flap? Perhaps, but nearly forty years later both Nelson and Lucey recalled it vividly and both insisted they had been right back in 1962.

Political dinners continued to give Lucey and Nelson heartburn. A few months after the Kennedy dinner, when Nelson was honored at a testimonial, Lucey was irked at not being seated at the speakers' table and had left by the time he was introduced. In 1967, when Senator Robert Kennedy spoke at a dinner for Nelson's Senate reelection, Lucey and his wife walked out when they discovered they were not seated at the Kennedy table. "Every Nelson dinner I've gone to, I've suffered some insult or other," Lucey complained.[5]

Three Cents for Gaylord

The shadow of the sales tax compromise fell heavily over the campaign. Reynolds was running for governor on a pledge to repeal the selective sales tax signed into law by Nelson. Reynolds wanted to make his race with Philip Kuehn, who was running again, a referendum on the sales tax. The governor's staff carefully pointed out that Nelson had vetoed a general sales tax but had to accept the selective sales tax, insisted upon by the Republicans, to prevent a financial crisis. The fine points were lost on the average voters, however.

Throughout the state, clerks, cashiers, and retailers, after adding up the bill, would say, "and three cents for Gaylord" as they added on the sales tax. "It was just knocking the hell out of me," Nelson discovered on a trip with Louis Hanson to Farm Progress Days, a huge agricultural exhibition outside of Chippewa Falls. Heading north, when they stopped for a beer, the bartender, collecting for the beer said, "Three cents for Gaylord." Nelson "reached right into his hand and said, 'Thank you very much, I'm Gaylord.'" The bartender said, "That's just a joke around here." "Yeah, the joke's on me," Nelson replied. The embarrassed bartender bought the next two rounds of beer.[6]

When the Democratic platform committee endorsed repeal of the sales tax, some Nelson loyalists saw it as a double-cross by Reynolds, Lucey, and tax commissioner John Gronouski, who wrote the plank. With the state Democratic convention looming, Nelson said he could support the call for sales tax repeal—but with a catch. "State government can be financed and property tax relief granted through reliance on the income tax," he said, but that would mean an income tax increase, which should be acknowledged in the platform as well. "Let's not promise $50 million in tax relief unless we tell them where we can raise the money," he said at the convention. "We cannot promise the public the moon with a lot of hot air."[7]

The convention crowd in Sheboygan fell silent when Nelson, in his keynote speech, defended his record and then said, dramatically: "What I am going to say to you I have never said before in my fourteen years in public office. I am saying it now because it is a fact and you should know it. Make no mistake about it: The one person in our ticket in serious political trouble is I." Supporters were telling him they were having trouble getting signatures on Nelson nomination papers because people said Nelson had let them down. The "three cents for Gaylord" campaign "has succeeded beyond the dreams of any Madison Avenue huckster," he said. That was particularly disheartening because "I took the only honorable and reasonable course open to me," Nelson said. "It was the best bill I could get through the Republican legislature."[8]

Then he changed his tone. "I have taken some lickings in my lifetime, and I expect to take a few more before I quit politics. But I will tell you one thing right now—I do not intend to take a licking for the wrong reasons. You will hear from me in this campaign from one end of the state to the other. The record will be set straight honestly, fairly, and forcefully. If I can't win on my record, I don't want to win at all." Delegates responded enthusiastically, and passed a resolution praising his tax stand, brushing aside objections that it contradicted a platform plank calling for repeal of the sales tax, which also passed.[9]

Nelson was not just crying wolf. He had seen a Louis Harris poll, taken in the Tenth Congressional District in northern Wisconsin, showing him losing to Wiley by a big margin. Nelson had carried the district with 56 percent of the vote for governor two years earlier, and needed to do well there to have a chance at the Senate. Nelson decided to tell delegates the truth—he was in trouble. He personally wrote a new speech the day of the convention. Some suggested he did it because he was still unhappy about the 1960 election, in which he narrowly won reelection after being considered a shoo-in. One staffer had predicted he might win in 1960 by the biggest margin in history. He wanted Democrats to understand he had a tough race ahead, could take nothing for granted, and needed their help.[10]

Nelson vs. Wiley

The campaign played out much as Revell had predicted. Nelson focused his criticism of Wiley on four main issues: Wiley's vote against Medicare, his opposition to a strong bill regulating the drug industry proposed by Senator Estes Kefauver, his votes to slash public housing programs, and his support for a bill that would end all farm price supports in six years. Late in the campaign, Kefauver came to Wisconsin to blast Wiley's role as "protector of the big [drug] companies" Kefauver was trying to regulate. Wiley "tried to impede my investigation and cut the legislation to ribbons," he said.[11]

Nelson also stressed his record as governor, highlighting the Outdoor Recreation Action Program, his $5 million student loan fund, reorganization of state government, and creation of a commission on aging. More than forty of his proposals were adopted by the Republican legislature, Nelson said, distributing an eight-page list of accomplishments that included no mention of sales tax or withholding taxes. Wiley's record during the same four years, Nelson said, was 101 bills introduced, none passed. Nelson repeatedly challenged Wiley to debate, finally debating an empty chair, which brought howls of protest from Wiley. Wiley said he had been "working day and night" in Washington, where the Senate was in session, while Nelson was traveling the state at taxpayers' expense, leaving "an empty governor's chair" in Madison.[12]

Wiley mostly stayed in Washington. When he did come to Wisconsin, it confirmed that his long-distance campaign was the best strategy. His strong suit—his image as a friendly, affable, likable older gentleman—suffered damage every time he came home. He had become irascible. Campaigning in Milwaukee, Wiley called Nelson a "nitwit" when a reporter asked about Nelson's criticisms of his votes on the drug bill. Wiley didn't confine his outbursts to his opponent. When a *Milwaukee Journal* reporter, William Bechtel, asked Wiley how he could reconcile his vote against Medicare with a letter he was circulating saying he supported the program, Wiley said he had a right to change his mind. Then he exploded, saying, "Keep your damned nose out of my business and I'll keep my nose out of yours." When Bechtel tried to ask a question later on another subject, Wiley said, "Keep your mouth shut." The story ran statewide. Two weeks later, Wiley blew up at another *Journal* reporter who asked him about Medicare, saying "I wish you would learn to mind your own business and not try to mix me up on Social Security." Afterward, he apologized and said he had mistaken the reporter for Bechtel.[13]

The *Janesville Gazette,* a Republican newspaper, said in an editorial headlined "Unfortunate Visit" that Wiley "was doing little good for himself or his party," citing his "unnecessary rudeness" and concluding that "it would not seem too much if he were to speak some down-to-earth words once in six years when he asks for re-election." The *Racine Journal Times* said Wiley was "destroying his own image," which had been that of "a dignified, jovial, elderly politician grown to some degree of statesmanship," but concluded that voters must wonder "if Wiley is not just a garrulous old man who is beginning to lose his usefulness as a legislator."[14]

By contrast, Nelson was the Kennedy-style candidate—young, vigorous, idealistic, liberal—a representative of the new generation of political leaders. President Kennedy announced his support for Nelson early, but some national columnists wrote that the White House was "satisfied" with Wiley, who supported Kennedy's trade liberalization policies and generally went along on foreign policy issues. Perhaps there was a residue of bad feeling from the 1960 primary, when Nelson was not a Kennedy man. Whatever the reason, the Kennedy administration was not particularly helpful to Nelson, although Kennedy did write a letter a week before the election offering his "wholehearted support" to Nelson.[15]

Missiles in Cuba

The president planned to campaign for Nelson in October, but the Cuban missile crisis prevented it. Tension had been mounting since Fidel Castro's rise to power in 1959, his embracement of socialism, and the failed CIA-backed invasion of the Bay of Pigs in 1961. The United States began a full trade embargo against Cuba in February 1962, and some pressed for military action as reports of troop buildups and Soviet-supplied aircraft, weapons, and missiles became public. The Soviet Union warned in September that an American attack on Cuba could provoke a nuclear war. On 3 October 1962, Congress passed a resolution declaring the United States was determined to prevent "by whatever means may be necessary, including the use of arms, the Marxist-Leninist regime in Cuba from extending, by force or threat of force, its aggressive or subversive activities to any part of this hemisphere."

Attorney General Robert Kennedy came to Wisconsin on 7 October 1962—two weeks before the crisis—to campaign and attend a Green Bay Packers football game with Nelson and Reynolds. When he asked Nelson to assess the administration's handling of the Cuban situation, Nelson said public opinion was ahead of the president, and suggested the president impose a "belligerent blockade," which would be honored by U.S. allies and put more economic pressure on Castro. Kennedy said that would not work because "the Russians would challenge it and there would be a serious international problem. What we should do," he told Nelson, "is just send over the bombers and it would be all over in twenty minutes, long before the Russians could react." When the crisis erupted two weeks later, the attorney general supported a blockade rather than an attack. "I could not accept the idea that the United States would rain bombs on Cuba, killing thousands and thousands of civilians in a surprise attack," Kennedy wrote in his book about the crisis. Nelson said James Reston, the respected *New York Times* reporter, told him several years later that Robert Kennedy had also told him before the crisis that he favored bombing.[16]

President Kennedy got as far as Chicago's O'Hare Field on 20 October, to be greeted by Nelson and other Wisconsin Democrats who were to join him on the last leg of the trip to Milwaukee, but he returned to Washington instead to deal with the developing crisis. The cover story was that he had a cold and was not feeling well. "He isn't ill at all; he looks in perfect shape," Nelson thought. "Something big is happening."[17] In fact, Kennedy had learned four days earlier there were Soviet nuclear missiles in Cuba, and he was returning to Washington to meet with advisors and plan a course of action. Two days later, he announced the naval blockade of Cuba. Reconnaissance photos showed Soviet missiles ready for launch, and Soviet cargo ships, with submarine escorts, were steaming toward Cuba. The two superpowers faced off, and the world watched anxiously. Nuclear war seemed a very real possibility.

Wiley, as senior Republican on the Foreign Relations Committee, was summoned to Washington for a briefing, with an air force plane dispatched to pick him up in Milwaukee. That would bolster his prestige as an important player on foreign policy. "Wiley can wrap himself in the mantle of bipartisan statesmanship," the *Capital Times* Washington correspondent wrote. "He can let the citizens of Wisconsin know he is here at the young President's elbow, guarding the diplomatic ramparts," although he would actually do and contribute little. More importantly, the crisis would keep Wiley out of Wisconsin and off the campaign trail, and "since he has been his own worst enemy up to now, this is the best thing that could have happened to him," Ivan Kaye said. It allowed a number of well-known Republican "Minutemen" to go on the road in Wiley's place. Wiley backers said the crisis vindicated Wiley's often-criticized contention that the only campaign issues were "war and peace, containing communism, and maintaining the free enterprise system."[18]

Nelson got his own briefing from the State Department in Chicago on 25 October, with about one hundred Midwest senators, House members, and governors. The situation was tense, with Soviet ships holding their positions outside the blockade line while Ambassador Adlai Stevenson confronted the Soviets at the United Nations. The next day, Soviet Premier Nikita Khrushchev said the Soviets would remove their missiles if the United States guaranteed it would not invade Cuba. With a private agreement that the United States also would remove its missiles from Turkey, Khrushchev said on 28 October that the missiles in Cuba would be dismantled, having "looked down the gun barrel of nuclear war" and concluded that "the course was suicidal," as Kennedy advisor Ted Sorensen put it.[19]

The crisis was over, but Wiley remained in Washington. Nelson urged Wiley to return. Wiley was called to Washington to be briefed, not to give advice, Nelson said. "I can't think under what pretense he will remain there now. It is becoming increasingly obvious all over the state that Senator Wiley is not prepared to debate or discuss the major issues that face the nation. His outbursts every time he is questioned clearly indicate his lack of preparation to discuss them," Nelson said. When a reporter asked Wiley about Nelson's claim that Wiley was hiding in Washington, where he wasn't needed, Wiley blew up again. "Nelson is a stupid person, and that is the definition of a nitwit," he said. "I am not fearful about anything. I am a whole Viking and he is only half a Viking." Wiley was of full Norwegian ancestry and could speak the language, while Nelson was only half Norwegian and could not speak it, he said, as if that had some relevance.[20]

Wiley was in Washington for nine days, finally returning to Wisconsin on 1 November, five days before the election. In his first appearance, at a GOP luncheon in Milwaukee, he was talking about the Cuban crisis and, indirectly, of criticism of him, when he became emotionally choked up, took out a handkerchief, said, "I guess I better sit down," and ended his speech. He spent the final weekend campaigning in small towns, making some safe public appearances to shake hands and be photographed, but making little news.[21]

Low Expectations

Conventional wisdom gave the Republicans the advantage in the 1962 race. Kuehn was expected to defeat Reynolds, who was running mainly on a sales tax repeal platform. Most pundits gave Nelson a chance but thought he would run a close but losing race to Wiley, whom people would reelect mostly out of habit. There were almost no reliable public polls. A Louis Harris poll in late August showed Wiley and Nelson in a dead heat and Kuehn leading Reynolds 44–40. An October survey by the *Wisconsin Agriculturist,* published the weekend before the election, gave Wiley a 59–40 lead among farmers.

There was no long wait for Nelson on this election night. Within an hour after the polls closed, it was clear that Nelson would become a U.S. senator. Nelson, at a small dinner with Carrie Lee and their closest political friends in Madison—Jim and Ruth Doyle, Esther and Louis Kaplan, Morris and Mary Rubin, Thomas and Eleanor Fairchild—decided at 10:15 P.M. it was safe to fly to Milwaukee and claim victory. By the time he landed, his Milwaukee campaign manager, William Korbel, told him he had a forty-thousand vote lead. In the end, Nelson carried twenty-nine counties, rolled up a margin of sixty-eight thousand votes, and won 52.7 percent of the two-way vote. For the first time in history, Wisconsin would have two popularly elected Democrats in the United States Senate. The governor's race was the tightest in the twentieth century, with Reynolds winning by twelve thousand votes out of 1.2 million cast. Republicans swept the four other constitutional offices, controlled both houses of the legislature, and held six of ten House seats.[22]

Nelson's victory could not be ascribed to a single cause. Clearly, his record on conservation helped him pry away some traditionally Republican votes in the north, where he ran well. Hindsight, after he had established himself nationally as an environmentalist, suggested that his environmental credentials were the key to his election, but there is no compelling evidence to support that theory. Wiley's age and irascibility, contrasted with Nelson's youth and vigor, certainly made an impression on voters. The voters "preferred an effective and hard-working young man, even with some reservations about his political orientation, to a venerable but garrulous old one whose boasts did not always square with the proofs of his service," Wyngaard wrote.[23] But the determining factor, as likely as not, was Nelson's personality—his outgoing warmth, charm, friendliness, and sense of humor. It was difficult to dislike Nelson. That, as much as anything, had propelled him to the Senate. Yes, the Wisconsin Democratic Party had come of age, won its third straight governor's race and elected a second U.S. senator. But Nelson's victory was as much a personal triumph as a sign of the party's maturity. He was headed for Washington as Wisconsin's most powerful, and most popular, Democrat.

17

The First Shall Be Last

Vice President Lyndon B. Johnson swore in Nelson as a United States senator on 8 January 1963. Eleven other new senators also took the oath, but all had been sworn in earlier in private ceremonies. Nelson had served his full term as governor and attended John Reynolds's inauguration before flying to Washington. Alexander Wiley had rejected any suggestion he resign early to give Nelson a boost in seniority, and Nelson would not resign early to turn the state over to Republican Lieutenant Governor Warren Knowles, even for a short time.[1]

So Nelson, after four years as Wisconsin's number one citizen, began his Senate career dead last in seniority—number one hundred on the list. That meant waiting until ninety-nine others chose their offices. He would be the lowest ranking member, in either party, on any committees. He was truly a backbencher, sitting in the back row of the Senate between Joseph Clark of Pennsylvania and Eugene McCarthy of Minnesota. Nelson was a legislator again, but this time his party was in the majority in both houses and held the presidency—a far cry from the days when there were not enough Democrats in the state senate to force a roll call vote.

In an interview with the *Christian Science Monitor,* Nelson made his own agenda clear: "I think the most crucial domestic issue facing America, both on the national level, and facing state governments, is the conservation of our natural resources. . . . We only have in this country now, in my judgment, another ten years in which to preserve a significant amount of the outdoor resources that we have. They're being destroyed carelessly and criminally throughout the nation by the pollution of our waters, the drainage of wetlands, the rapid growth of our cities eating up land all around them. . . . Therefore I think the federal government and the state governments must make a massive acquisition of these capital assets now." Wisconsin's $50 million ORAP program was probably the best acquisition plan in the country, but was still "inadequate to meet the problem" in Wisconsin, he said.[2]

One of his first official acts as senator was to sign on as a cosponsor of a bill to create a youth conservation corps. Ten days later he joined five other Democrats in sponsoring a bill to increase the amount of federal money available to cities for the purchase of park and recreation land. But mostly he was playing the role expected, if not demanded, of a freshman senator—he was seen but not heard. In his first month, his office issued only three press releases, all on minor matters. Nelson turned down invitations to appear on television programs and make speeches in Florida and Illinois.[3]

He also declined most social invitations as his family, which had preceded Nelson to Washington, settled into a rented house in northwest Washington. The departure from Wisconsin was "kind of wrenching" for Carrie Lee. Unlike many of Nelson's Senate colleagues, the Nelsons had little money. He drove a battered 1954 Mercury to the Capitol, and there was little extra in the family budget for entertainment. With Jeffrey still a toddler, Happy and Tia, aged nine and six, starting a new school, and Nelson "totally immersed in being the new senator," Carrie Lee had her hands full. In February, the family moved again, to a new four-bedroom Dutch colonial they bought in Chevy Chase, Maryland, for $40,000.[4]

One early invitation they did accept was for dinner at the home of their old friends Hubert and Muriel Humphrey. Having misplaced the invitation, the Nelsons were uncertain about the time but showed up promptly at 6 P.M.—to be met at the door by Muriel Humphrey in a kimono and hair curlers. They were two hours early. Dinner parties might begin at six in Madison, but not in Washington. Within a few years, as Carrie Lee learned to juggle Nelson's schedule and family obligations, the Nelsons would become known as the hosts of some of the most entertaining dinner parties in the capital. But it first took some adjustment after four years as the center of attention in the Madison political and social scene. Nelson, known everywhere in Wisconsin, was "taken aback by his new anonymity." At a dinner party he introduced himself to broadcaster Edward R. Murrow, who clearly did not recognize his name and moved on down the line with no further conversation.[5]

Being governor was "the toughest political job there is," Nelson told an interviewer, but as a senator, "it's a tougher job to have your voice heard." There were different ways to make your voice heard, and political observers in Wisconsin watched to see which Nelson would choose. He did not seem likely to sit quietly in the back row for long.[6] Wisconsin's senior senator, William Proxmire, had chosen the outsider's role, directly challenging majority leader Lyndon Johnson's leadership in speeches on the Senate floor, later opposing several key Kennedy initiatives and appointments. He was a conservative penny-pincher on federal spending, but insisted he was still a liberal. After five years in office, he had become a lone wolf who got a lot of press coverage but had little influence in the Democratic caucus or the Senate. Wisconsin had always loved mavericks, and Proxmire's image played well with the voters during his long career. But it did not make him effective in the Senate, where party discipline trumps independence.

Gaylord and Prox

Except for their politics, and the fact that both were sons of physicians, Nelson and Proxmire were very different people. Proxmire, reared in the wealthy suburb of Lake Forest, Illinois, earned degrees from Yale and Harvard, married a Rockefeller, and decided he wanted a political career — as a Democrat. He moved to Madison in 1949 for a short-lived stint as a *Capital Times* reporter, won an assembly seat in 1950, and started running statewide two years later. He had chosen Wisconsin as a state that might be open to an outsider, and the fledgling DOC was open to all comers. There were few places where one could be the party's nominee for governor three years after moving into the state. Proxmire was intense, serious, focused, driven, named "most energetic and biggest grind" in prep school. When he was determined to improve his golf game, he once played ninety holes in a day. Proxmire was a health fanatic whose daily regimen included enormous amounts of exercise and a Spartan, nonalcoholic diet.[7]

Nelson, the small town boy who did the bare minimum in school, would rather "bat the breeze" than make a formal speech. He was passionate about politics and ambitious in his career, but no one had ever accused him of being a grind. He said more than once that if he had to campaign like Proxmire, spending every available minute shaking someone's hand, he would not run. Nelson was softer around the edges— friendlier, more approachable, more charming, more likely to be socializing than studying, and far more likely than Proxmire to eat heartily and have a drink in his hand. An athlete as a young man, he stayed in shape, using the barbells and punching bag in the Senate gym. He was strong enough to rip a three-inch thick telephone book in half, and was a master of one-armed pushups. "He puts matchsticks between his knuckles, then bends down and picks them out with his teeth," a gym employee said. But physical fitness was not his religion, as it seemed to be Proxmire's.[8]

At a party at the Nelsons', Proxmire said he did two hundred pushups every morning and, when Nelson challenged his claim, dropped to the floor to prove it. "Oh, I thought you meant one-armed pushups," Nelson said after watching Proxmire do a few. "Anybody can do them with two arms." Nelson demonstrated what he meant and Proxmire, who had never tried the technique before, could not do a single one, much to his chagrin and the amusement of onlookers. Despite the contrasts in their approach to life and politics, Nelson and Proxmire were friends, campaigned for one another, and managed a cooperative and peaceful coexistence in the Senate. But they were never close; their differences were too great.[9]

Fitting In

Hubert Humphrey had shown it was possible to be an outspoken northern liberal and still survive in a Senate dominated by conservative southern Democrats. Humphrey, "without sacrifice of principle or purpose, made his way in the political situation as it was and prospered accordingly," John Wyngaard noted. Humphrey got a chilly reception when he arrived in the Senate as an unabashed civil rights crusader, but after "a few years in purgatory" won over his early critics with a combination of sharp intellect, good humor, and outgoing personality.[10] Nelson seemed a good candidate to do likewise.

He had the good sense to spend his first month absorbing the atmosphere, learning rules and procedures, and reading extensively on issues. But it would not take him long to figure out the Senate's inner workings and, with his sense of humor and affability, to win himself a spot in the Senate's inner circle. If the Senate were a club, Nelson was going to be an active, influential member. He never sought or held a leadership position, but didn't need one to have an impact. The friendships he built and the respect he won from his colleagues of all political persuasions served him better in moving his agenda than any partisan leadership post could have.

Nelson did take one bold and somewhat risky stand in a closed-door Democratic caucus just a week after being sworn in. He was the only freshman to vote for a futile challenge to his party's leadership, a proposal to limit the power of the Senate Democratic Steering Committee, which was dominated by southern conservatives. There was nothing for Nelson to gain, and potentially a lot to lose, but it was a vote on principle — the first of many he would cast during eighteen years in the Senate. Nelson wanted to make an impact, but made it clear he would not sell his soul to do it. "I have always voted independently," Nelson said at the end of his first term. "I believe that my party is the best party, but it isn't perfect. I have voted with the administration about seventy-five percent of the time, which is about five percent more agreement than I have with my wife."[11]

His transgression did not prevent Nelson from getting a spot on the Interior Committee, his first choice, as well as Public Works, which he also had requested. Public Works was considered more powerful, but Interior had the issues Nelson cared about the most, and provided a platform on environmental issues. The southern-run Steering Committee, which Nelson had challenged, made the assignments. The committee was not as forgiving with Proxmire, who had campaigned hard for an open seat on the Finance Committee despite his opposition to Kennedy's tax cut. That seat went to a freshman, Abraham Ribicoff of Connecticut.[12]

Nelson waited two and one-half months to make his maiden speech in the Senate, taking the floor or 25 March to speak in support of a bill by Senator Maurine Neuberger of Oregon to ban phosphate detergents. Nelson, a cosponsor, cast the issue in much broader terms than cleaning up detergents. "Unless this nation girds for battle immediately," he said, "its people are not going to have clean water to drink, clean air to breathe, decent soil in which to grow their food, and a green outdoors in which to live a few decades from now." Calling the bill just one step toward a program to save the nation's natural resources, he said, "We need this . . . just as desperately as we need the defense against atomic missiles."[13] Four senators, a few tourists, and a handful of reporters were in the chambers for his speech. He also made his first insertion into the *Congressional Record,* an eight-page report, prepared by his staff, on "The Threat to the Public from Detergent Pollution." It was an issue he would spearhead for years.

In staking out an early claim as an environmental leader in Congress, Nelson had little competition. There were only a half dozen senators who could qualify, on the basis of their knowledge, experience, and interest, as what Nelson would consider "broad-gauge environmentalists" or conservationists, the term then in use. Edmund Muskie of Maine led the list, which included Henry "Scoop" Jackson of Washington, Frank Church of Idaho, Clinton Anderson of New Mexico, Lee Metcalf of Montana, and Humphrey of Minnesota. But most were preoccupied with other issues and other major committees—Jackson with Armed Services, Muskie with Public Works, Anderson with Aeronautics and Space, and the others with their own agendas or assignments. The Interior Committees in both houses were dominated by westerners, whose home state interests at times ran contrary to good national policy on issues like public land management, water and grazing rights, mining, and reclamation projects. Nelson joined Interior as the only member from east of the Mississippi River.[14]

In the House, Chairman Wayne Aspinall of Colorado ran the Interior Committee with an iron fist. He was crusty, tough, knowledgeable, and had no time or patience for those who had not done their homework and didn't know an issue as well as he did. He believed members should mark up bills and work out differences in conference committees themselves, and had disdain for those who relied on staffers for information or advice. Aspinall had little regard for the Senate. When John F. Kennedy, beginning to prepare for a presidential race, asked Aspinall in 1957 for advice on conservation issues, Kennedy mentioned a bill he had supported in the previous session. "Yes," Aspinall told him, "it was passed through the Senate just like you pass a lot of projects through the Senate. You don't understand what's involved and you just go ahead and pass them, and then let the members of the House work them out." Many a conservation bill sailed through the Senate only to run aground on the shoals of Aspinall's committee. Conservation legislation wasn't passed until he had passed on it. "Guys like Aspinall *were* the outdoor movement," Congressman Henry Reuss said. "Of course they were wrong on everything, but nobody crossed them."[15]

"Most Congressmen know little about conservation and care little," *Field and Stream* magazine reported in 1968. "They are content to go along with the crowd, to vote the party line, to follow the piecemeal course charted by the leadership." All of them favored conservation in the abstract, the article said, but "when the chips are down many are apt to cast their votes with the special interests."[16]

Nelson was different. The environment was his priority, and his mission was to make it the nation's priority. He had his work cut out for him.

18

Enlisting the President

NELSON WENT to the U.S. Senate with a clear and ambitious objective: to make environmental issues a part of the nation's political agenda. It took only seven years—an eye-blink in congressional time—to achieve and surpass that goal. Earth Day, which Nelson founded and nurtured, was the defining moment in the modern environmental movement. On Earth Day in 1970 environmental politics were forever changed, and the environment became a permanent part of the national political debate.

When it happened, it seemed to blossom overnight. While there was an element of luck and timing—being in the right place at the right time with the Earth Day idea—it was also a tribute to Nelson's single-mindedness and persistence. The question of how to advance the environmental agenda was on his mind every day.

Two weeks after his election in 1962, Senator-elect Nelson went to Washington to lobby for committee assignments, look for a house, meet with Senate friends, and begin his transition to senator. That was all duly reported in the Wisconsin press. He also met quietly with Attorney General Robert F. Kennedy, the president's top political advisor. Nelson's proposal: a national tour by President Kennedy, with a series of speeches on conservation issues. Nelson "told [Robert Kennedy] we needed to get the issue onto the national political agenda, and until we did so we weren't going to do anything serious about this issue." Nelson argued that the issue was good politics, and he brought some persuasive evidence along—a huge scrapbook filled with clippings about Wisconsin's Outdoor Recreation Act Program (ORAP). The issue had made front-page news, generated strong editorial and grassroots support across the state, and helped Nelson to win the Senate seat. Kennedy said he would discuss the tour with the president.[1]

Nelson had begun lobbying President Kennedy on the issue when he spoke in Milwaukee in the spring of 1962 at the Democratic Party's Jefferson-Jackson dinner. While riding from the airport to the hotel, Kennedy said many issues had gotten too complex for the public to really understand them. Except for Medicare, he said, there were few issues that were simple to explain. Nelson suggested there was another "significant, important, appealing issue" that was easily understood — conservation of natural resources. The issue, Nelson said, affected people in all walks of life, with nearly everyone having some interest, if for different reasons. Nelson urged Kennedy to make conservation a major issue. The president responded that "maybe it was important, but since he had been born and raised in the city he hadn't really given much thought to that matter."[2]

Once in the Senate, Nelson continued his campaign to get Kennedy to embrace the issue. At lunch with White House staffer Lee White, he "pounded me on the head, explaining how we were missing the greatest damn bet ever for politicians," White said. When that didn't bring visible results, Nelson explained the idea to Mike Manatos, a White House liaison with the Senate. A Manatos memo to Larry O'Brien, another Kennedy staffer, said that the response to ORAP in Wisconsin had been "so overwhelming that [Nelson] thinks the President could have 'fantastic' results, and I am inclined to agree." A presidential trip "should be strictly non-partisan (but in effect it would be partisan) and would be aimed at the millions who have no party label but vote for an individual because he is 'for' something in which they are interested," Manatos said.[3]

In May 1963, meeting with leaders of twelve national conservation groups, the president said he was planning a fall tour of conservation areas — the first national presidential tour ever devoted exclusively to conservation. Nelson hailed the trip as "the most encouraging break in behalf of the preservation of our natural resources in modern times," which could "turn the national spotlight on the serious crisis facing our lakes and rivers, our forests and parks and hunting grounds." Nelson, with his old friend and political ally Louis Hanson, Patrick Lucey's successor as Wisconsin Democratic chairman, visited the White House in July. Kennedy revealed he was planning a five-day tour, probably in September, and invited Nelson to accompany him for part of the trip. Nelson encouraged the president to visit Wisconsin.[4]

The president had asked Nelson earlier, in a one-paragraph note, for a memo to suggest new initiatives in the field of conservation— and "any suggestions that you might have to amplify our program."[5] Nelson's five-page letter to the president on 29 August 1963 focused on persuading him of the urgency of the issue and suggested the case he should make to the public:

> The question is how to maximize the effect—how to hit the issue hard enough to leave a permanent impression after the headlines have faded away—how to shake people, organizations and legislators hard enough to gain strong support for a comprehensive national, state and local long-range plan for our resources. . . .
>
> Though the public is dimly aware that all around them, here and there, outdoor assets are disappearing, they really don't see the awful dimension of the catastrophe. The real failure has been in political leadership. This is a political issue to be settled at the political level, but strangely politicians seldom talk about it.[6]

The president, Nelson said, should tell the public that "there is no domestic issue more important to America in the long-run than the conservation and proper use of our natural resources, including fresh water, clean air, tillable soil, forests, wilderness, habitat for wildlife, minerals and recreational assets."[7]

America was destroying its natural assets faster than any civilization in history, despite fifty years of warnings from conservationists, Nelson wrote. The destruction was accelerating greatly and the population increasing. Time was running out. The president should say he was making the trip because it was "America's last chance" to preserve its resources. "Americans in all walks of life are interested in natural resources," and interest in the issue "cuts across political party lines, economic classes and geographical barriers," he told the president.[8]

"Members of this vast interest group include all people in one way or another, from ladies with a flower box in the window to the deer hunters with high-powered rifles; the boaters, who range from kids with flat-bottomed scows to the wealthy yachtsmen; family campers; bird watchers; skin-divers; wilderness crusaders; farmers; soil conservation-ists; fishermen; insect collectors; foresters, and just plain Sunday driv-ers." A vast army stood ready to be mobilized on the conservation issue, Nelson assured the president. Many already belonged to special interest groups with some connection to conservation. The people were ready to move on the issue. They simply needed a leader—and who better than an energetic young president to lead the charge, while also helping him-self politically.[9]

Nelson enclosed nine pages of quotations for possible use in Kennedy's speeches, ranging from Henry David Thoreau ("What is the use of a house if you haven't got a tolerable planet to put it on?") to Wal-lace Stegner ("We simply need that wild country available to us, even if we never do more than drive to the edge and look in. For it can be a means of reassuring ourselves of our sanity as creatures, a part of the geography of hope"). The biggest collection was from Nancy Newhall, author of a poetic text that accompanied photographs by Ansel Adams and others in a Sierra Club book, *This Is the American Earth*.

When plans for the trip were announced, Nelson was disappointed that Wisconsin was not on the itinerary, although neighboring Minne-sota was.[10] Nelson and Hubert Humphrey had written the president to ask him to visit northern Wisconsin and Minnesota and Michigan's Upper Peninsula to see areas with outstanding recreation potential. Nelson especially wanted Kennedy to see the Apostle Islands, an archi-pelago of twenty-two small islands off the southern shore of Lake Superior. The islands had been suggested as a national park in 1930, and Nelson had asked as governor for a federal-state study of the feasibility of making the Apostles a national lakeshore. Interior Secretary Stewart Udall had ordered a study of the area, and Nelson planned to introduce a bill designating it as a national recreation area. A Kennedy visit could accelerate the process.

Tension Gets Attention

President Kennedy did visit the Apostle Islands, but it was another Wisconsin-related issue, poorly handled by the White House, that pre-cipitated the addition to the president's itinerary. The trip to Wisconsin became a way to win back Nelson's favor.

Early in September, Ralph Dungan of the White House appointments office called Nelson to ask his opinion of John Gronouski, Wisconsin's tax commissioner. Nelson and Gronouski had a stormy history. Nelson had appointed Gronouski as tax commissioner and had relied on his help to research and sell a solution to Wisconsin's budget crisis. The package that eventually passed included the controversial sales tax that had threatened to end Nelson's political career. But in 1962, when Nelson ran for the Senate and John Reynolds ran for governor on a "repeal the sales tax" platform, Gronouski stumped for his friend Reynolds and denounced the sales tax, despite his role in proposing, passing, and administering it. Nelson was furious, regarding Gronouski's activity as "deception and worse, treason," his top aide said. Gronouski had tried to straddle the split between Nelson and Lucey but backed Kennedy in the 1960 primary and, when the split with Nelson came, ended up solidly in Lucey's camp. Lucey still had more White House access and influence than anyone else in Wisconsin.[11]

Now the White House was asking about Gronouski, and Nelson was candid. They did not get along personally, and his attack on the sales tax "irritated the hell out of me," Nelson told Dungan. But, he added, Gronouski was bright, able, and hard-working and would be loyal to the president. Dungan said he was not seeking a recommendation about a particular job, just checking on Gronouski for future reference. A few days later, Mike Manatos called Nelson at home on Sunday to tell him Gronouski would be appointed the next day as postmaster general. Nelson exploded. "I told them they could take that appointment and go jump in the lake," he said, although newspaper reports said he "uttered an epithet that must have startled Manatos." It did not help that Representative Clement Zablocki, at a picnic on Milwaukee's Polish south side, proudly and prematurely announced Gronouski's appointment on Sunday afternoon. Gronouski was to be the first cabinet member in history of Polish descent.[12]

Nelson went to a party that night at the home of Edwin Bayley, his former aide, who had become director of information for the Agency for International Development. Several reporters were at Bayley's party when Nelson recounted his conversation with Manatos and repeated his displeasure. By Monday morning, network news stories were reporting that Nelson opposed Gronouski's appointment—and Nelson

was invited to the White House. He assured Kennedy he had no intentions of opposing the appointment, although he was unhappy about
how it had been handled. The meeting ostensibly was to discuss the
upcoming conservation tour, and Kennedy said Wisconsin should be
included, because the trip had been Nelson's idea. A smiling Nelson
emerged from the meeting and told his administrative assistant, William Bechtel, the president was going to the Apostle Islands. A few
hours later, the White House officially announced Gronouski's appointment. Within twenty-four hours, the White House gave Nelson
the go-ahead to announce Kennedy's visit to Wisconsin.[13]

President Kennedy left Washington on 24 September 1963 for a five-
day, eleven-state conservation tour. Because the Senate voted that
morning to ratify a nuclear test ban treaty, takeoff was delayed to allow
a vote by the four senators who accompanied the president on the first
leg of the trip. Joseph Clark of Pennsylvania, Hubert Humphrey and
Eugene McCarthy of Minnesota, and Nelson flew with the president
by helicopter from the White House to Andrews Air Force Base, where
they boarded *Air Force One*. The plane was filled with more than fifty
reporters from the national press corps and crews from all three television networks. "This is it," Nelson said to himself excitedly. "Now this
is going to be on the national political agenda." In his words, "That
turned out to be a little naïve."[14]

"I assumed if the President did a tour and said this was an important
issue the press would believe him, but there weren't any reporters who
understood the issue, and no environmental reporters anywhere in the
country," Nelson recalled. The national press was just not that interested
in conservation. "Every place we went, the press peppered the president
with questions on foreign policy. They didn't really care what he had to
say about the environment. Because I had been paying a lot of attention
to this issue for years, it was an upfront issue for me; it wasn't with them
or their editors. They seemed bored with the whole thing, really."[15]

The president's conservation speeches did not engage the public the
way Nelson had hoped. Kennedy never issued the dramatic warning
Nelson had suggested—that the country was headed for disaster if it
continued to degrade the environment. Nelson's impression was that
Kennedy's staff did not understand the issue themselves and saw the
trip as a political opportunity; as a result, Kennedy gave short shrift to

conservation in most of his speeches. In fact, the president spoke about conservation almost everywhere he went, but often strayed into other issues—and whenever he strayed, those issues dominated the stories and headlines.

The first stop was Milford, Pennsylvania, to dedicate the home of Gifford Pinchot, first chief of the U.S. Forest Service. Then it was on to Wisconsin. The president boarded a helicopter in Duluth, Minnesota, with Nelson, Governor Reynolds, Interior Secretary Udall, and Secretary of Agriculture Orville Freeman aboard, for a flyover of the Apostle Islands. A looming thunderstorm diverted all but one of seven press helicopters, but the president's chopper continued for an abbreviated look at the islands. Martin Hanson, a conservationist, prime supporter of the Apostles project, friend of Nelson, and brother of Wisconsin Democratic chairman Louis Hanson, acted as guide and sat next to the president to tell him about the Apostles. As Hanson was explaining the islands were nesting grounds for bald eagles, two of the huge birds took off from a marsh area and gave Kennedy a good look. But what really seemed to make an impression, Hanson said, was the large number of sailboats he saw in the area. "His eyes lit up. Here was the Massachusetts sailor seeing some of the best sailing water around." Kennedy said the white sandy beaches and curving shoreline of the islands reminded him of Cape Cod.[16]

His speech to a crowd of ten thousand when the chopper set down at the Ashland, Wisconsin, airport was totally on the conservation theme Nelson had suggested, drawing heavily on a speech draft from Bechtel, Nelson's aide. Crediting Nelson with suggesting the trip, Kennedy declared that Nelson "has a strong conviction, as I do, that every day that goes by that we do not make a real national effort to preserve our national conservation resources, is a day wasted."[17]

"What we are doing here today—concentrating the attention of the country on this great natural resource—must be repeated all over the country," Kennedy said. He pledged support for preserving natural resources and recreation areas, mentioned the Apostle Islands and adjacent Bad River area by name, but "carefully did not pledge himself to the Apostle Islands project." Northern Wisconsin faced special economic problems because of the decline of ore and timber industries, he said, which the federal government could help with area redevelopment programs, conservation programs, rural area development programs, and increased fisheries research.[18]

He mentioned Wisconsin's "magnificent outdoor recreation facilities," saying: "If properly developed, recreational activities and new national parks, forests and recreational areas here can provide enjoyment for many millions of people for many years to come. Certainly if we are to provide the stewardship which future generations have a right to expect, we must set aside substantial areas for the day when our population is much larger and our people will travel with greater ease." The government would try to save natural resources "from Massachusetts to Hawaii," he said.[19]

The stop lasted only twenty minutes, but, as Kennedy pointed out, he had said a lot more than the only other president to visit Ashland, Calvin Coolidge, who spent several weeks fishing there in 1928 and never said a word publicly.

That night, in Duluth, Kennedy spoke strongly of the need for conservation and against waste of natural resources. But he also called for passage of his proposed $11 billion tax cut, up for a House vote, and pledged federal help to redevelop the depressed region encompassing Minnesota, Michigan, and northern Wisconsin. The redevelopment and tax cut proposals dominated the coverage and headlines. Kennedy ended the first day of his "conservation" tour "with a plea for support of virtually his entire domestic program." It was "a perfectly dreadful speech, one of the worst reporters could remember," said Sander Vanocur of NBC News. "He rambled all over the lot, touching all bases, including conservation. Not once during his speech was he interrupted by applause."[20]

Playing to the Crowd

As he headed west, natural resources provided the backdrop for the president's speeches, but the content zigzagged between conservation and other concerns. In Grand Forks, North Dakota, Kennedy was to discuss rural electrification, but deleted a strong defense of the Rural Electrification Administration from his speech. He delivered a rambling speech on the need for "parity of opportunity" to improve the living standards of rural residents, the importance of government service, and the nation's global obligations. At the University of Wyoming in Laramie, Kennedy "bore down heavily on the conservation theme." He declared, "Our primary task now is to increase our understanding of the natural environment to the point where we can enjoy it without defacing it, use its bounty without permanently detracting from its value and above all maintain a living, evolving balance between man's actions and nature's reactions."[21]

In Billings, Montana, he "departed completely from the keynote of his advance text" and launched into an emotional foreign policy speech, defending the nuclear test ban treaty and delivering "an anti-isolationism sermon." The crowd of seventy-five hundred applauded and cheered early in his speech when he talked about the test ban treaty, passed the day before. Kennedy, reading the crowd, shifted gears and "started to develop the peace theme, his right forefinger stabbed the air, and the strident tone of the campaign returned to his voice," Vanocur said. He got an enthusiastic response. In contrast, he had spoken for a half hour in Duluth without ever being interrupted by applause, and was interrupted only once by applause in Grand Forks. Before Billings, the president's speeches and the crowd's reaction seemed "lackadaisical," the *New York Times* reported. "Although declared the nation's number one conservationist by Orville Freeman, Mr. Kennedy did not display, in remarks on that issue, the fire and enthusiasm that often mark his public addresses." The *Wall Street Journal,* noting Kennedy's shift of focus as the trip went on, concluded that "he was rather bored with the whole subject of conservation" and found he was getting a better audience response when he discussed broad foreign and domestic policy issues. "When he switched to the supposedly sure-fire 'Western issues' of dams and electricity and national parks, his audiences just couldn't have cared less," the newspaper reported.[22]

The *Washington Post* was kinder, in an analysis which acknowledged that Kennedy "has not shaken off his campaign habit of giving essentially the same, disjointed speech at every stop." A presidential visit made such a strong political and media impact wherever he stopped that "one perhaps does not even need to take into account the quality of the President's speeches, which was not notably high on this trip, or the audience response to them," the *Post* said charitably. What Kennedy discovered, Vanocur said, was that people in the West wanted to hear him discuss "cosmic issues" of peace and war, the economy, or education, and were "really not very much interested in hearing him talk about conservation. He welcomed that discovery. It fit the mood he was in." Reporters welcomed the shift in emphasis as well, since it helped them to compete for space with other breaking news stories. Peter Lisagor of the *Chicago Daily News* did his best to liven up his story, saying the president was "wandering through the West like a strolling repertory player, "alternating the roles of an airborne Paul Bunyan with Smokey the Bear."[23]

In Great Falls, Montana, the president almost entirely ignored his text on natural resources and instead talked about the need to build a strong domestic economy that could support U.S. foreign policy efforts. In Hanford, Washington, he said a new atomic generator he was dedicating would help keep the United States ahead of the Russians. In conservative Salt Lake City, Utah, he returned to foreign affairs and sharply criticized some of the positions taken by Senator Barry Goldwater of Arizona, who was emerging as his likely opponent for the presidency in 1964. The ultraconservative policies, such as opposing the test ban treaty and breaking off relations with the Soviet Union, Kennedy said, "would lead the nation into a dangerous world of retreat—not of strength," would be "fatal to our national security" and "invite a communist expansion." The Associated Press said flatly: "This was the most important speech Mr. Kennedy has made in his 10,000-mile western tour." The large crowd at the Mormon Tabernacle responded with a tremendous ovation.[24]

The conservation message was somewhat garbled on the fourth day as well. He did some pork barrel politics at Astoria, Oregon, announcing plans to reopen a former naval air station as a training and rescue facility. In Tacoma, Washington, he told a crowd of twenty-five thousand that his trip had been "an inspiring journey" and he had "been impressed by the power potential, the reclamation and irrigation possibilities and the timber resources of a series of federal projects." He praised the outdoors as a haven to escape modern day tensions, and spent the night in a forest cabin in Lassen Volcanic National Park in California.[25]

On the tour's final day, he returned to the theme of preserving resources, dedicating the Whiskeytown, California, dam and reservoir and warning that the U.S. population could reach 350 million by the year 2000. "What will they do? What kind of a country will they find?" he asked, saying the present generation had an obligation to "make it possible for them to see green grass." Those remarks were eclipsed in many news accounts, however, by another prediction Kennedy dropped into his speech—that people in the year 2000 would have more leisure time because the forty-hour workweek would be reduced by automation. That offhand remark was the lead paragraph and headline in the press coverage. The trip ended on an upbeat note in Las Vegas, where he told cheering Nevadans he would support making the Lake Mead–Hoover Dam area a national park as well as bringing water from Lake Mead to Las Vegas and preserving the Lake Tahoe shoreline.[26]

Assessing the Trip

By White House standards, the trip had been a success. It had given the president a platform, with many popular recreation sites as a backdrop, to talk about the nonpartisan issue of conserving natural resources. Politically, it had put him in eleven states, only three of which had supported him for president in 1960. And it had allowed him to begin to draw the distinction between himself and Goldwater. In its weekly review of the news, the *New York Times* headlined the item on the trip "'64 Warm-Up." "During the first two days (of the trip)," it said, "the President gave what reporters felt was a lackluster performance as he droned through speeches on conservation and related matters, his mind and heart seemingly elsewhere." But he "sounded and acted like himself when he turned to foreign policy and Goldwater."[27]

Kennedy said the trip helped educate him about the conservation issue. "I do not think that these trips do very much for people who come and listen," he said in Tacoma, "but I can tell you that they are the best educational three or four days for anyone who holds high office." Yet it was not at all clear that Kennedy had really absorbed what the conservation issue was all about. He assured his audiences repeatedly that he did not just want to "preserve . . . hoard . . . protect" natural resources. He also wanted to tap them to boost the nation's economy. "In looking at nature," he said, "I have been impressed really more by man. Everything that I have seen was given to us by nature, but man did something about it." Developing the nation's resources would help strengthen the U.S.

economy, he said. Dedicating the huge Whiskeytown dam in California, he talked of how the Grand Coulee Dam had paid for itself and brought development, including atomic reactors, to the Northwest. "Every time we bet on the future of this country we win," he said. The president and Interior Secretary Udall believed, the *Post* said, that "America' s resources are so vast and the ingenuity of scientists is so great that they can be developed even faster than they have been."[28] That was a far cry from a call for wilderness preservation.

The *Times* editorialized that Kennedy had seemed "more interested in conservation of the Democratic Party than in the conservation of America's natural resources." Kennedy and Udall had supported some excellent legislation, the newspaper said, but what was needed was "the strong follow-through only the President can provide. He created the opportunity to do so on this very trip, but that opportunity was almost completely ignored."[29]

From Nelson's perspective, the trip was a failure. It had gotten the president solidly on record as promoting conservation of natural resources and perhaps exposed him to the potential political benefit of espousing the cause. It had given him a firsthand look at the Apostle Islands. But it had not dominated the news the way Nelson had hoped, nor had it awakened the nation. "It didn't do what I had hoped for. But it was the germ of the idea that ultimately became Earth Day . . . finding some event that would be big enough to bring this issue to the attention of the political establishment. His trip didn't do that."[30]

His hopes for vaulting the environment to the top of the national agenda dashed—at least temporarily—Nelson returned to working on the issue one step at a time.

19

Joining the Club

IN A PROFESSION known for producing strange bedfellows, Nelson broke new ground in building friendships and alliances with senators across the political spectrum. Nelson's small town warmth and humor, coupled with Carrie Lee's hospitality, irreverence, and innate skills at putting together an interesting mix of people at a party, soon broke through the barriers that had kept many new members out of the Senate mainstream. Nelson quickly won acceptance and established himself as a popular and respected member of the Senate club. It was not a calculated effort. The Nelsons just liked people.

"Gaylord was intrigued by other politicians," said Senator George McGovern of South Dakota. "Some he didn't like very well, but there were very few that he walked away from. He was interested in finding out what made people tick, what was their background, how did they come to the Senate, what do they do when they're not on the Senate floor, what drives them. I used to see him sitting in the Senate sometimes—some fellow would be making a speech and Gaylord would be studying the guy, not so much listening to what he was saying but trying to figure out what makes this guy function the way he does."[1]

Nelson usually ate lunch in the private dining room reserved for senators, where a small group of Republicans sat at one table and Democrats at another in an adjoining room. There was no better place to get acquainted with old-timers like Allen Ellender of Louisiana, Richard Russell of Georgia, Harry Byrd of Virginia, Sam Ervin of North Carolina, or James Eastland and John Stennis of Mississippi—Dixiecrats whose long seniority gave them a tremendous amount of power. "I enjoyed the people with a historical view of what went on in the Senate. They were mostly southerners; they had been there forever," Nelson said."You could learn an awful lot talking to them."[2]

Russell, a thirty-year Senate veteran, was the most respected southerner and probably the most influential senator besides the majority and minority leaders. "No southerner wanted to vote on the other side from him," Nelson said. "He would bring ten or twelve or fourteen people automatically with him" on any issue. Nelson also chatted up the Republican table, dropping a quip, a joke, or an observation to Everett Dirksen of Illinois, John Tower of Texas, or others. "All the Republicans I knew were friendly, I would joke with them," Nelson said. Nelson "penetrated the Republican aisle about as completely as anyone I knew," Walter Mondale said. "He was liked very, very much by a lot of Republicans." It wasn't a calculated campaign to win friends and influence people. It was just Gaylord being Gaylord. By his third term, his colleagues rated him as the most popular and best-liked member of the Senate.[3]

"He would come up to people in the cloakroom or the dining room and listen to stories from senators he didn't agree with on anything—Eastland, Long, Stennis, and others," McGovern said. "He got real joy out of listening to their stories and backgrounds. It was a great political asset, and it sort of endeared him to people. Here's a guy who isn't all that enamored of the dignified ways of the Senate. You could see him sitting around a restaurant or bar in Clear Lake telling those stories. He became a real person rather than just another vote to be counted. People saw him as a human being and that increased his legislative effectiveness. He could go to a committee chairman and say, 'Look, I'd appreciate your help.' He was rather effective at moving things he was interested in. He wasn't a master of the Senate rules, but he knew enough about the cloakroom and the dining room and the back rooms so that he was quite at home with the Senate process."[4]

"There was just great affection for Gaylord. He was unpretentious, had a wonderful sense of humor in good taste. He felt issues deeply, but at no time did he ever get nasty," Senator Thomas Eagleton of Missouri said. "On the Democratic side, if someone was on the fence, a close vote with no strong feelings, Gaylord would get more than his fair share."[5]

"It's a human institution," Nelson said. "If you like someone, and what they want doesn't affect you or doesn't offend your conscience, you do it." Political differences should not be personal, Nelson always believed, but "there were people who, if they proposed something, it automatically had a lot of opposition. To function effectively, you have to get along with the people who are there." In a political body there will always be disagreements. "Some people dislike people who don't agree with them. But I never personalized it. If you're mad and you carry a grudge, it hurts you more than the person you hold the grudge against. They may not even know about it," he said.[6]

Friendship with Russell Long

One key friendship that blossomed early in Nelson's Senate career was with Russell Long. It seemed an unlikely matchup. Long was a scion of the political dynasty that had dominated Louisiana politics for much of the twentieth century. His father was "the Kingfish," Huey Long, who had served as governor and U.S. senator. His mother, Rose, had filled out Huey's Senate term after his assassination in 1935. Uncle Earl Long had been governor. Three other relatives had served in the House. Russell Long, a senator since 1948, disagreed with Nelson on virtually every major issue of the day—civil rights, the nuclear test ban treaty, foreign aid, federal aid to education, and a host of others. But Long was a gentleman, a raconteur with a great sense of humor and an endless supply of stories, an engaging, interesting person. He had inherited a streak of Huey's economic populism that endeared him to liberals like Paul Douglas of Illinois. Long, a staunch segregationist, and Hubert Humphrey, the impassioned civil rights advocate, had been friends since their days as debate partners at Louisiana State University.[7]

Long and Nelson hit it off immediately, swapping tales of Baton Rouge and the bayous for those of Clear Lake. Long enjoyed the Nelsons' company, and they became close social friends. "We'd have him out to the house, or he'd take us to dinner. He was lots of fun, and smarter than hell," Nelson said. When Nelson was going to drive him to dinner in his 1954 Mercury, Long was bewildered. "What is this, a campaign car?" he asked. No, Nelson explained, he couldn't afford to own two good cars and the other was at home. "Pull in here," Long said, indicating a Chevrolet dealership, "I'll get you a car. You're a senator; you can't be driving around in a car like this." Nelson just kept driving.[8]

Although influence was not his motive for befriending Long, the relationship moved Nelson onto the fast track in the Senate. As Nelson began his second session in Congress in 1965, he joined Paul Douglas and a handful of other liberals in voting for Long as Democratic whip, the number two leadership post. Long's main opponent, John Pastore of Rhode Island, was closer to Nelson philosophically, but Nelson thought Long would do the best job of rounding up Democratic votes. Soon afterward, Nelson was named to the Labor and Public Welfare Committee, considered a plum because it handled more domestic issues than any other committee, including education and the War on Poverty. Nelson retained his Interior seat but gave up Public Works. He also got a seat on the Select Committee on Small Business.[9]

Later that year, when Long became Finance Committee chairman, he tapped Nelson—ahead of more senior members—to replace him as chairman of the Small Business Monopoly Subcommittee. Nelson used the post to launch a high profile, ten-year investigation of the drug industry, for which Long had laid the groundwork. Nelson supported Long for whip again in 1969, when he lost the post to Edward Kennedy of Massachusetts. Nelson drew some fire at home in liberal Madison for that vote, but explained that he had promised Long his vote six weeks before Kennedy entered the race. The election of Kennedy, a leading presidential candidate for 1972, was "in the best interest of the party," Nelson said in a letter to Wisconsin editors, but he "could not in good conscience go back on my word."[10]

Long also was instrumental in helping Nelson get a seat on the Finance Committee in 1971. Nelson and Lloyd Bentsen of Texas both were seeking the seat, to be filled by a vote of the Senate Democratic Steering Committee. Nelson won by a single vote, from James Eastland of Mississippi. Nelson thought Eastland would never support him because Nelson opposed the oil depletion allowance, but he asked, Eastland said "yup," and Nelson won the seat.[11]

During night sessions, a handful of senators would sometimes go to Eastland's beautifully furnished hideaway office in the Capitol. The group, a mixture of liberal and conservative Democrats, might include Ernest "Fritz" Hollings of South Carolina, Byrd, Nelson, Eagleton, Mondale, and Eastland. "Eastland liked it because we could get in some good debates and arguments," Eagleton said. "We all called him Mister Chairman; he was also president pro tem of the Senate."[12]

Nelson was not averse to having "a drink or three," as he would put it, and used liquor as a social lubricant. He drank virtually every day of his adult life, but never admitted to a hangover the morning after or let it interfere with his responsibilities. The hideaway sessions might convene when senators were waiting for the final vote of the day. "Drinks were the signal for conversation time and the end of the business day," a Nelson aide said. "It was always his private time, with business finished and no professional responsibilities. He disapproved of senators who would drink in the hideaways and then go down and give a speech."[13]

That was not uncommon in the Senate of the 1960s, and Long was sometimes one of the offenders. "Often, a hard day's work was rewarded with two or three strong scotch and waters with several colleagues in somebody's Capitol office," Long's biographer said. "Daily powwows over cocktails in numerous Capitol Hill hideaways were legendary. They were an accepted part of Washington life." When Nelson got enough seniority to have one of the fifty hideaway offices himself, he often invited several colleagues, including the senator handling that day's major bill, to his Spartan fourth floor den for "incredible, unvarnished discussions" that included some humor and teasing, but also rigorous questioning and inquiry.[14]

Nelson could get along without going along. He made friends and allies on the strength of his personality, while holding firm to his liberal positions and ideals. He was uncompromising on his core beliefs and not afraid to stand all alone, as he did on at least one major vote. He was not a pushover. When a union president wrote what he considered an "arrogant" and threatening letter demanding his vote on an issue, Nelson replied that if the union chief had delivered it personally, "you would have gotten a punch on your nose for your insolence." The Wisconsin Athletic Commission issued Nelson a boxing license. "Nelson manages to make everyone like him without sacrificing his principles," said Paul Douglas of Illinois, succinctly identifying the key to Nelson's success. "I don't think he had an enemy in the Senate," Congressman Robert Kastenmeier said.[15]

Rewards of Friendship

Personal relationships paid dividends and often trumped political and philosophical differences in the Senate.

During the filibuster over the 1964 civil rights bill, Nelson was eating in the private dining room with Richard Russell, a main opponent of the bill. "If the people in Minnesota and Georgia knew what I did for Hubert Humphrey in his last campaign, they'd probably throw us both out," Russell said. Russell, whose own reelection was a sure thing, had sent a sizable contribution back to the Democratic Senate Campaign Committee and "asked them to give it to Hubert instead," he told Nelson. "Why did he do it? It was pretty clear to me," Nelson said, "that Russell had a high regard for the integrity and performance of Hubert Humphrey as a member of the institution."[16]

When President Richard Nixon wanted to appoint Glenn Davis, a conservative congressman, to a federal judgeship in Wisconsin, Nelson short-circuited the process. Nelson's opposition had been reported in the press, but he wanted to avoid using his senatorial veto to kill the nomination. Davis supporters hoped Nelson might not block the nomination but simply vote against it. In a Senate cloakroom conversation with Eastland, the Judiciary Committee chairman, Nelson told him the Davis nomination would have strong opposition from blacks, Jews, organized labor, the bar association, and others. Eastland, a conservative who opposed civil rights laws and integration, replied, "Gaylord, you're telling me all the reasons I ought to be *for* him. Gaylord, what do *you* want?" Nelson said he did not want the Justice Department and the White House even to nominate Davis or send his name to the committee. Eastland said, "Awright," "stuck his cigar back in his mouth, and walked back onto the floor," Nelson recalled. That was the end of the Davis nomination. He was never nominated and eventually withdrew his name from contention.[17]

When American Motors, the Wisconsin-based automaker, was in desperate financial straits in 1967, company representatives came to Long, the Finance chairman, to discuss a change in the tax law. The existing law allowed the company to carry losses forward for five years; American Motors wanted a change to allow its losses to be carried backward five years as well, instead of the current three-year limit. It would mean millions of dollars to the company and perhaps save the business, the state's largest employer. The company wanted Proxmire to introduce the bill, but Long told them, "If you want to pass that legislation, you'd better have Senator Nelson introduce it." Nelson did introduce it and the bill passed, with Long's support. It amounted to a $20 million tax refund for American Motors.[18]

When Nelson's reelection campaign began the next year, a lawyer who was helping raise money for Nelson asked a contact at American Motors to sell some tickets for a Nelson fund-raising dinner. The American Motors person called back to say he had not been able to sell a single ticket. When Long heard that, he called Nelson, who was in Wisconsin campaigning. Long was "absolutely outraged," Nelson said. "If you approve of it, I will get you some substantial contributions by tomorrow afternoon," Long told Nelson. Nelson said he did not want the money, but he hoped American Motors employees knew what he had done to save the company and their jobs. A year later, after Nelson had been reelected, American Motors came to him again, asking help in getting an extension on the deadline to meet new air pollution standards. Nelson helped get the extension, saving them a huge penalty.[19]

Even as an outspoken critic of the Vietnam War, when passions ran hot, Nelson maintained relationships with those on the other side. When Senator John Stennis, Armed Services Committee chairman and leading war hawk, invited Nelson for a weekend of dove hunting with friends in the Virginia countryside, Nelson's administrative assistant, Bill Cherkasky, said, "Senator, you'd better make sure you aren't the dove in this hunt."[20] President Johnson sent a one hundred dollar bill, via Hubert Humphrey, to a 1968 Nelson fundraiser. "If he'd been smart enough to write a check, I would never have cashed it," Nelson said. "He never got angry with me for opposing him on the war in Vietnam, like he did with some others."[21]

Dinner at the Nelsons'

The Nelsons didn't burst onto the Washington social scene overnight, but once they found their footing, they began to invite an eclectic guest list for lively dinner parties that became an institution. Carrie Lee was mostly homebound with three young children for the first year or two. Nelson was immersed in his new job and spending much time in Wisconsin. To Carrie Lee, it seemed he was gone as much as when he was governor, and she was left to "run this kind of single parent household" without the help she had as Wisconsin's first lady. But she gradually realized she could occasionally get a sitter and make arrangements to accept invitations that were too exciting to pass up.[22]

It was difficult to juggle plans around Nelson's Senate schedule, so Carrie Lee began to invite people to their home for dinner. They began with Wisconsin friends and acquaintances. But the guest list soon grew to include members of Congress from both parties, journalists, lobbyists, diplomats, Capitol staffers—anyone interesting enough to contribute to the scene and strong enough to hold their own.

In Washington, as in Madison, the Nelsons always had personal friendships with journalists, and no eyebrows were raised at such fraternizing. The guest list ranged, at times, from television commentators like John Chancellor and Sander Vanocur to national newspaper people like Drew Pearson, David Broder, Clayton Fritchey, Alan Otten, and Joseph Alsop. Wisconsin journalists like Jack Kole and Frank Aukofer of the *Milwaukee Journal* bureau were frequent guests. "The symbiosis between journalists and politicians was all over the place," said Joe Miller, a political operative and longtime Nelson friend. Marian Burros, food editor of the *Washington Star,* and later the *Washington Post* and *New York Times,* belonged to a gourmet cooking club with the Nelsons and several other couples, including the Swedish ambassador, Wilhelm Wachtmeister, and his wife, Ulla.[23]

The parties were much like those the Nelsons were known for in Madison, with an interesting mix of outspoken people exchanging stories and opinions over drinks and dinner. "We didn't belong to the country club. I was willing to do simple cooking and buy jug wine," Carrie Lee said. Her "good old home cooking" started with cookbooks, but she was always experimenting and improving recipes. "Everybody realized it was going to be very casual, low key, anything goes in conversation," Carrie Lee said. "You teach your friends to leave their seriousness at the door, put on a sense of humor hat, come in and have a good time. Those who want to go home early. We haven't had a lot of people go home early. It was easy to say we had a good time at the Nelsons' so people would say that sounds like fun, let's go."[24]

The conversation was often contentious, loud, and hot, with Nelson frequently kindling it and fanning the flames. What was the point of having a roomful of smart, opinionated people—like Senators John Culver, Edmund Muskie, or Daniel Moynihan—if you couldn't get a little conflict going? "It gets pretty fierce," Carrie Lee acknowledged.[25]

Nelson might demand, loudly, of a guest, "'Where the hell did you ever come up with a stupid idea like that?' They'd yell right back. This was not a formal organization or group, you just let 'er go," said Bernie Koteen, a Nelson friend. "He could hit lots of decibels, and get lots of decibels in return, but never with rancor. Gaylord often tests people to see how much pressure they take. They'd bounce back, and if they didn't bounce back Gaylord didn't like it so much, it wasn't fun. It was mostly to keep things stimulated."[26]

"Without a doubt they gave the most interesting parties," said Eagleton. "Watergate was on the agenda in the Nixon years, and some of us would even switch sides in order to keep the momentum going. It was always a lot of fun. I don't think the Nelsons ever gave a dull party."[27]

Popular folk singer Theodore Bikel, a friend of the Nelsons, sang an impromptu concert for guests at a dinner party before President Johnson's 1965 inauguration. The guest list included Wisconsinites and Washingtonians alike—Senators Frank Church and Russell Long, University of Wisconsin President Fred Harrington, *Capital Times* editor Miles McMillin, NBC television commentator Sander Vanocur, Democratic National Committee member David Carley and state chair Louis Hanson, the president of Pabst Brewing in Milwaukee, a U.W. professor, a member of the U.W. Board of Regents, the national news editor of the *Washington Post,* and others, including the Nelson children, Happy, eleven, Tia, eight, and Jeffrey, three. The party "was anything but formal," and Carrie Lee, who wore a gingham apron over her dress for most of the evening, had prepared the buffet dinner herself—chicken breasts on rice with a mushroom-almond sauce, baked ham, salad, rolls, and petit fours.[28] The party was typical of those the Nelsons would host once or twice a month for the next thirty-five years, although the guest list was usually smaller, ranging from six to twenty, and guests at the inaugural party were probably better behaved than the Nelson norm.

Part of the recipe for success was Carrie Lee's judgment about who would mix well. "I was pretty selective," she said. "Over the years, we invited lots of people we really care a lot about that we wouldn't see otherwise. I very carefully decide who I think will blend with each other." That referred more to seating arrangements than the invitation list. The Nelsons never wanted a homogenized crowd. Nelson was known to dance the twist with advice columnist Ann Landers or to give a facial massage to Dolly Saxbe, wife of an Ohio Senator, in the middle of the cocktail party. The word was, "If you're invited to the Nelsons, you'd better go."[29]

The Nelsons were gregarious and much more comfortable entertaining in their own home, where Carrie Lee was queen of the kitchen and dining room while Gaylord presided over the cocktail hour and raised provocative issues. The wide social circle with its vortex at the Nelson home clearly benefited Nelson politically, although that was not the main motivation. It was "a remarkable adjunct to his career," Joe Miller said. "It was and it wasn't calculated. But there is no question they knew what they were doing."[30] The best evidence that it was primarily social is that the Nelsons continued to play host to the same sort of dinner parties twenty years after Nelson had left the Senate.

The Nelsons generally made it a point not to use their parties as a way to court people who might be helpful politically; this was fun, not business. There was one exception. Nelson went out of his way to reach out and befriend Wayne Aspinall, who chaired the House Interior Committee and had life and death authority over environmental legislation. "He was not someone you would seek out to socialize with," Nelson said. "He was smart, tough, and no one would slip something by him. He had kind of a contempt for the Senate." Nelson recognized his importance early on and invited the Aspinalls to dinner, along with Senators Hubert Humphrey and Albert Gore Sr. and their wives. When they learned, during cocktails, that it was Julia Aspinall's birthday, Carrie Lee—prepared for any social emergency—got a small birthday cake she kept in the freezer, found a bottle of champagne in the refrigerator, and toasted the event. Nelson continued to work on establishing a personal connection with Aspinall, which paid off handsomely as Nelson pushed his environmental agenda in future sessions.[31]

20

Defending the Constitution

THE MCCARTHY ERA and McCarthyism did not end with Senator Joseph McCarthy's death in 1957. The anti-Communist furor ignited by McCarthy continued well into the 1960s, and some of the abuses and invasions of privacy lingered even longer. Nelson, an outspoken civil libertarian, was unwavering in his commitment to protect the rights to free speech, privacy, and other core freedoms, even when it put him at political risk.

The House Un-American Activities Committee, known as HUAC, had targeted Hollywood writers in the 1940s and Alger Hiss and other governmental officials in the 1950s. As the 1960s began, it was looking for Communist influence on college campuses. The committee conducted widely publicized hearings and investigations, with leftist professors on the firing line. A growing number of people were calling for HUAC to be abolished because of abuses of the rights of witnesses, whose lives and careers often were ruined by the publicity surrounding their appearance or by their refusal to testify. The committee's conservative supporters responded with a film, *Operation Abolition*, purporting to show Communist influence behind a campus protest against 1960 HUAC hearings in San Francisco. The film itself became the center of controversy, with HUAC opponents claiming it was distorted and doctored facts.

Nelson came to the Senate as an outspoken opponent of HUAC and its tactics, after a run-in with the committee as governor. Esther Kaplan, Nelson's personal secretary in the governor's office, had been listed in a full-page advertisement in the *Washington Post*, calling for HUAC's abolition. Eight other Wisconsinites, mostly professors and clergy, also were listed, but Kaplan's connection to Nelson made her the public target. Kaplan was not just Nelson's secretary. She and her husband, Louis, who became director of University of Wisconsin Libraries, were close personal friends and political allies of Nelson, part of a small inner circle. Kaplan was chagrined; as a longtime American Civil Liberties Union member, she had agreed to allow her name to be used in the campaign against HUAC but did not know about the newspaper ad. When a reporter called her about it, Kaplan learned that Eleanor Roosevelt also was listed and said she was "honored to be in the same company as Eleanor Roosevelt." Nelson "was not happy," she said, but rose to her defense.[1]

HUAC's chairman, Representative Francis Walter, a Pennsylvania Democrat, said Kaplan and other signers were following the Communist Party line or in the "strange company" of such people. "When they attacked Esther, I attacked them, right back," Nelson said. "I said I was upset with her because she didn't ask me to sign it first. She was on my staff, a good citizen, a good Democrat, and I couldn't let HUAC get away with that kind of smear campaign."[2]

The attack, Nelson said, "reinforces the arguments of those who advocate abolition of the committee. The critics of this committee are right. It should be abolished." HUAC had violated constitutional rights, he said, undermining "the very freedoms that most sharply distinguish our democracy from the Communist system." The committee, he said, "has persecuted individuals on the basis of their beliefs and their associations; it has robbed them of dignity, held them up to public ridicule and forced upon them social ostracism or loss of livelihood. A free society should not tolerate" such abuses. He urged Wisconsin members of Congress to vote to abolish HUAC, "when the occasion arises."[3]

When HUAC's appropriation came up in the House a month later, Congressman Robert Kastenmeier of Madison was the only Wisconsin member to vote against it. Members of both parties gave HUAC chairman Walter a standing ovation and voted 412 to 6 to fund his committee. Three Wisconsin Democrats—Clement Zablocki, Henry Reuss, and Lester Johnson—voted with the majority. Zablocki said the decision to continue the committee had been made before Nelson's request, and only the appropriation was at issue. Nelson should mind his own business and stick to state issues, Zablocki told a reporter. Reuss said he

Defending the Constitution • 199

supported continuing the committee but "strongly disapproved" of the tactics of some of its members "in questioning the patriotism of almost anyone who ventures to criticize it." Johnson said his constituents supported the committee and added, "We have to do everything we can to stop Communism."[4]

In Madison, Republicans on the assembly Judiciary Committee introduced a resolution commending HUAC and saying the committee had been attacked by "known Communist agents and well-meaning but misinformed citizens who frequently endorse any 'cause' that has been represented to be 'idealistic,' 'noble,' or 'democratic.'" After failing to soften it with amendments, three Democrats joined in an eleven-to-one committee vote for passage. The committee had warmed up for the debate by watching *Operation Abolition*. Democrat William Ward said he voted yes because "I'm going to be branded a Communist if I vote against this." The only Democrat to vote no, Frank Nikolay, said, "There are a dozen letters on my desk calling me a traitor and a subversive." Republican Kyle Kenyon said gravely that he would vouch for Ward's loyalty. "He's not a Communist." He did not offer the same testimonial for Nikolay or the other Democrats. The resolution passed both houses by large margins and did not require the governor's signature.[5]

A few months later Nelson took his argument into the lions' den, telling the state American Legion convention that his opposition to HUAC was tied to his defense of the rights of minorities, "one of the reasons we went to war in 1941." Too many people, "in our zeal to protect our country from our cold war enemy . . . are willing to close off those very individual freedoms which have made our country great and strong." The next day, by unanimous voice vote, the twenty-one hundred delegates adopted a resolution supporting HUAC. It said "numerous known Communists and fellow travelers, organizations and individuals sympathetic to the Red menace are constantly discrediting the committee and calling for its abolition." It did not mention Nelson.[6]

On the last weekend of the 1962 Senate campaign, a Republican press release tried to link Nelson and Paul Corbin, a Wisconsin Democrat who had been grilled by HUAC about his loyalty and alleged Communist ties. Lieutenant Governor Warren Knowles attacked Nelson as the only one of fifty governors to oppose HUAC. "While Senator Wiley has been voting to shore up our defenses at home and abroad, his opponent, Governor Nelson, has advocated the abolishment of HUAC, our first line of defense against Communism at home," Knowles said.[7] It had little or no impact on the race.

As a senator opposing a ground war in Vietnam, Nelson was invited in early 1965 to speak at a lecture series entitled "The Peace Race," sponsored by the Berkeley, California, Board of Education. When the board sent Nelson a loyalty oath, swearing he was not a member of the Communist Party, Nelson refused to sign. California law required the oath of anyone receiving public funds, and Nelson was to receive a $300 speaking fee. He was prepared to speak for free rather than sign the oath, but the school board found a loophole, withdrew its request, and apologized to Nelson. In his speech, he said he found the request "offensive to my own conscience" and "an insult to the people of Wisconsin who have elected me to represent them." He was stunned, he said, by some of the mail he received from constituents afterwards, berating him for his refusal to sign. He had sworn his loyalty when taking the oath of office and would do so if asked by Congress or the Wisconsin Legislature, he said, "But I will not accept the superior claim to patriotism of some other state or some self-righteous organization or some neighborhood bully. My loyalty is to the nation and to the principle for which it stands, and I will not sacrifice those principles under a threat of having my reputation smeared."[8]

The Red Patrol did not exist only in the House of Representatives. In the Senate, Thomas Dodd, a Connecticut Democrat, chaired the Internal Securities Subcommittee, which engaged in much the same type of Communist-hunting as HUAC. In June 1966, Dodd's committee issued a report calling the University of Wisconsin a hotbed of communism, based largely on the secret testimony of Robert Siegrist, a conservative radio commentator sponsored, the *Capital Times* said, by "Milwaukee industrialists whose politics are of the McCarthy-Birch stripe." Nelson blasted the "preposterous" report, calling it so "spectacularly inept" it would have no impact, "except to amuse people who know something about the University of Wisconsin, about the ways of students, and about the real Communist problem."[9]

As examples, Nelson offered two of the twenty people cited in the report. One, William Gorham Rice, a distinguished law professor and

Nelson friend, "is as well-known for his two-fisted opposition to communism as he is for his unrelenting devotion to civil liberties," Nelson said. The report said Rice had signed a petition criticizing HUAC and opposed the U.S. policy in Vietnam, and suggested he was "somehow involved in communist attempts to subvert American youth," Nelson said. Also cited was a Madison radio announcer and commentator on WIBA, a station owned by the *Capital Times,* who had interviewed Communists on his program and had attacked Siegrist. The report used his on-air name, Papa Hambone. Nelson knew him as George Vukelich, a friend and outdoor writer who had written the script for an Apostle Islands promotional film. If his crime was to interview Communists, Nelson said, "[o]ne wonders why NBC and CBS were not cited for filming Soviet delegates at the United Nations." In the cases of Rice and Hambone, Nelson said, "not a single charge is made of any form of activity which could possibly be classified as 'un-American.'"[10]

Earth Day under Surveillance

In April 1971, Senator Edmund Muskie released an FBI memo revealing that the agency had monitored 1970 Earth Day activities. The next day, Nelson proposed a bill creating a commission to study the full range of domestic surveillance and intelligence activities and make recommendations to protect constitutional rights. "If the FBI has nothing better to do than conduct surveillance on the kind of citizen events that Earth Day represents, then the FBI has gone far beyond the limits that are tolerable in a free society. The all-pervasive intrusions of this secret police force into the activities of American citizens poses a threat to liberty itself," Nelson said.[11]

Fifty FBI field offices reported on fifty-seven Earth Day events in 1970, and in three cases "activities on the part of subversive elements were reported," an internal memo in Nelson's FBI file said. Of particular interest was the Washington, D.C., rally, where speakers included Muskie, muckraking left-wing journalist I. F. Stone, and antiwar activist Rennie Davis. Stone, the memo said, "had been identified as a Communist Party, USA member in the 1930s" and "consistently espoused the interests of the Communist Party front groups." Davis, a leader in Students for a Democratic Society in the 1960s, was a member of the Chicago Seven and was tried for conspiracy for their role in organizing protests at the 1968 Democratic convention. A third participant, whose name was blacked out when the file was released at Nelson's request in 1999, was described as saying he "considered himself a communist although he was not a Communist Party member," and had been arrested during the Chicago convention protests. Stone and Davis "spoke against pollution, the Vietnam War and the Nixon Administration," the memo said. Davis's speech included obscene comments, "called for tearing down the capitalistic structure and for support of Black Panther Party (BPP) leader Bobby Seale," who was facing a murder charge in the death of another BPP member, the report said. People with "subversive backgrounds" also were active in Earth Day events in Salt Lake City and Tempe, Arizona, it said, without identifying them.[12]

"FBI coverage of Earth Day activities was aimed strictly at identifying involvement of subversive or violence-prone elements," the memo said, triggered in part by "prior expression of White House interest in learning the extent of radical participation in the ecology movement." Nelson's FBI file also included a memo written in November 1962, after his election to the Senate, summarizing material on Nelson in the bureau's files. As governor, he had sent a message read at a 1960 University of Wisconsin Student Senate rally "in favor of civil rights in general and the southern Negro students in particular." A 1961 article in the *Worker*, the Communist Party newspaper, said Nelson had called for an end to HUAC. "An informant advised in August 1962" that the Communist Party preferred Nelson to Wiley in the Senate race and, though its influence was limited in Wisconsin, was trying to "influence some trends in the Democratic Party."[13]

Nelson said he was "astonished that the FBI could conceivably dream up any legitimate excuse for conducting surveillance" of Earth Day. If that fell under the FBI's jurisdiction, "no political activity in the nation is beyond their reach, including the annual meetings of the chamber of commerce and the manufacturers association," Nelson said. Noting that thousands of schools, 150 members of Congress, and 100 representatives of the Nixon administration were among the Earth Day participants, Nelson asked: "By what constitutional or statutory authority do these events come within the jurisdiction of the federal government for surveillance?"[14] For all the indignation it engendered, the disclosure did not lead to passage of Nelson's bill, which died in committee.

"A Strict Constructionist"

When President Nixon nominated William Rehnquist for the Supreme Court in 1971, Nelson opposed confirmation primarily because of Rehnquist's record on civil liberties. As an assistant attorney general, Rehnquist had put government expediency ahead of the Bill of Rights, Nelson said. Rehnquist had defended and supported warrantless wiretaps, preventive detention of suspects without trial, no-knock entry into private property, mass arrests, use of illegally obtained evidence against an accused, and widespread surveillance of people not engaged in illegal activity. Rehnquist, a Wisconsin native, was "an able lawyer, a man both of deeply held convictions and personal integrity," Nelson said, but that was not enough. "On the question of the guarantee of individual rights in the first ten amendments to the Constitution, I am a strict constructionist," Nelson said in a Senate speech. "The Bill of Rights was specifically adopted to protect individual liberties against oppression and the excesses of governmental power. Mr. Rehnquist's interpretations of these guarantees are at such variance with my own that I am unable to support his nomination."[15] Nelson and others also raised questions about Rehnquist's opposition to civil rights, but he was confirmed in 1972 and became chief justice in 1986.

The nation had declared war on drugs in 1970, and Congress enacted a comprehensive antidrug law that included a no-knock provision, allowing federal drug agents, with a search warrant, to forcibly enter a suspect's home without identifying themselves first. Nelson and Senator Sam Ervin of North Carolina opposed the provision in 1970, when it was enacted in what Ervin called "a period of hysteria" over rising crime rates. Amid reports of dozens of "mistaken, violent and often illegal police raids," Nelson and Ervin teamed up in 1974 to win passage of an amendment repealing the no-knock authority. "The no-knock provisions are unnecessary, dangerous and unconstitutional," Nelson said.[16]

The Watergate hearings chaired by Ervin had exposed abuses of wiretapping, with the Nixon White House and its "plumbers" trying to trace leaks of information by ordering "national security" wiretaps on staff members, government officials, reporters, and private citizens. Most were done by the FBI, but some by the White House's own "internal security" unit. In some cases it involved burglary to install a tap or bug. As the disclosures continued, public opinion ran heavily against wiretapping and surveillance. The fact that the 1972 Watergate burglary itself was conducted to install electronic bugs at the Democratic National Committee offices added to the public uneasiness about government spying and snooping into their private lives. Ervin wanted Nelson on the Watergate committee, but Nelson, up for reelection in 1974, ducked the assignment as "a dumb political move" and had no regrets. "The committee did its job and I wouldn't have added much," he said.[17]

A month after Nixon resigned in 1974, Nelson was distressed to read in a newspaper story that tape recordings from the Oval Office, which had played a key role in Nixon's downfall, were going to be turned over to Nixon for his use or disposal. After Nixon's pardon by President Gerald Ford, the General Services Administration had signed an agreement to that effect. The deal drew considerable criticism, but there was uncertainty about whether anything could be done about it. "It seemed to raise legal and constitutional issues of the first order," Nelson said.[18] At stake was control of not only 880 tapes but millions of documents, which Nixon could have destroyed after five years.

The solution came from a young lawyer on Nelson's staff, Lewis Paper, who offered what Nelson called "a simple but ingenious proposal that would avoid the legal quagmire and allow the government to take custody of the Nixon tapes." His idea, which Nelson and Ervin introduced as a bill, was to have Congress rescind the GSA agreement, seize the tapes and records, and let the courts decide ownership of the material. If the courts ruled that Nixon owned the tapes, the government was seizing them under its eminent domain powers and would compensate him. If the ruling said that the government owned them, that would be the end of the matter. The bill became law on 19 December 1974 and Nixon challenged it, but a federal appeals court and the Supreme Court upheld it, without ruling on ownership of the material. In 2000, the government reached a settlement agreement to pay Nixon's estate $18 million for the materials. In 1978 Congress enacted the Nelson-sponsored presidential records bill to ensure that the papers of all future presidents are the property of the American public.[19]

Watergate's Legacy of Reform

The excesses of Watergate caused widespread distrust and suspicion of the political process and elected officials. Reports of serious financial abuse in Nixon's 1972 presidential campaign led Congress in 1974 to reform campaign finance laws, set limits on contributions, and establish the Federal Election Commission to enforce the law. In early 1977, when a congressional pay raise drew a public outcry, Congress tied its raise to adoption of a code of ethics, to shore up public confidence in the institution. "It is absurd that the Senate has to demean itself by enacting a code of conduct," Senate majority leader Robert Byrd of West Virginia said. "But in a climate of public distrust it is a necessity." Byrd named Nelson to chair the committee drafting a new ethics code, causing Nelson to joke that it was Byrd's way of getting even for Nelson's failure to support him in the race for majority leader. Actually, he was chosen as someone whose own conduct and ethics were above reproach and who "was able through wit and compromise to defuse many of the sharp controversies."[20] While passage of some sort of code was inevitable, it took all of Nelson's skills to pass a comprehensive, meaningful code.

As a state senator, Nelson had pressed for a ban on favors from lobbyists. "A mooching legislator is totally unable to consistently vote his own convictions," Nelson said. "When you try to mix thick steaks and potent martinis with lawmaking the public interest is bound to suffer." Nelson made it a practice to pay his own way, which served him well in a minor but highly publicized incident in 1953. Nelson and several other legislators had lunch with Norris Maloney, a lobbyist for the rural electric cooperatives. Nelson, who ordered a $1.25 hot pork sandwich, left early and didn't want to embarrass his freeloading colleagues by putting money on the table. He wrote a check when he got back to the office and enclosed a note, telling Maloney his policy was not to accept anything from lobbyists, whether friends or foes. That would have been a private transaction if Maloney's secretary had not mistakenly filed a report, intended for Maloney's board members, with the secretary of state as part of Maloney's lobbying report. It named the legislators Maloney had entertained at lunch. To the newspapers, it looked like a clear case of hypocrisy—Nelson pressing for tougher rules while taking a free lunch from a lobbyist. But he produced his cancelled check and Maloney verified that Nelson had paid his own tab. "This streak of honesty was not discernible in other legislators," the *Capital Times*'s editor observed.[21]

Nelson conducted himself that way throughout his career. "There were no sleazy deals. He was consistent and predictable on questions of legislative morality. There were no ethical lapses," said Sherman Stock, who ran Nelson's Milwaukee office during his entire eighteen years in the Senate. "I never had to apologize for being on his staff."[22]

Disclosure was a key element of the ethics code Nelson guided through the Senate. It required disclosure of all sources of income, investments, assets, debts, and gifts worth more than one hundred dollars. It banned gifts worth more than one hundred dollars from lobbyists and special interests. It prohibited senators from joining corporate boards, banned junkets by lame duck senators, and ended office "slush fund" accounts. Those were the relatively noncontroversial provisions, which also applied to senior aides and spouses of senators. It was modeled largely on a House proposal by Wisconsin Congressman David Obey, who chaired the House ethics panel.

A limit on outside earnings, however, sparked strong opposition in the Senate and was at the heart of a sharp three-day debate, pitting Nelson against his friend and fellow liberal Edmund Muskie of Maine. Muskie was outraged at a provision which limited senators to $8,625 a year—15 percent of their $57,500 annual salary—from speeches, articles, or other earned income. The limit had been $25,000 a year in speaking fees. Muskie, among those who earned the most for speeches, argued that it was unfair to limit his income while there were no limits on "unearned" income from investments. Muskie owned no stocks or bonds, he said. He had purposely chosen the lecture circuit as a way to supplement his salary while avoiding conflicts of interest, and had a thirty-year, scandal-free public career to back up his arguments. Nelson had not enriched himself in public office either. He had voluntarily disclosed his personal net worth for years, and in 1978 it was $142,912. He had received as much as $27,354—the most in the Senate—for speeches and articles in 1970, the year of Earth Day, donated $10,550 to Earth Day and the Nature Conservancy, and reported a net of $15,469 after expenses. But that was a short-lived phenomenon. He reported no honoraria in 1973 and $2,000 in 1974. His net worth in 1980, his last year in office, was $147,354.[23]

Nelson and Muskie were longtime political allies, had campaigned for each other, worked together on environmental legislation, and were personal friends. "There is no man in this institution for whom I have a higher respect," Nelson said. But the debate was long, hot, and sometimes personal.[24] "You're throwing us to the wolves," Muskie said. "The Senator [Nelson] is putting a cap on my income, and he doesn't give a damn what the consequences may be for my family." Muskie was emotional and "frequently appeared to lose his temper . . . Nelson displayed the folksy but urgent manner of a small-town physician prescribing an unpleasant regimen," the *New York Times* reported. Nelson chided Muskie for complaining that the Senate was becoming "a rich man's club" and "shedding hot tears flooding the place" after voting against the $13,000 pay raise to $57,500, which would help senators in modest circumstances. Muskie had a "great capacity for making a bad cause sound like a religious crusade" but was merely asking for "the right to earn more outside income. There's no principle involved." When Muskie argued that the code would punish everyone, even those innocent of any conflicts of interest, Nelson responded that his concern was public perception. "We have just one capital asset, the very fragile cloak of public confidence," Nelson said. When it is frayed by perceived conflicts, "there is nothing left. . . . [G]overning becomes impossible."[25]

After what Nelson called "the best debate I've been in on the Senate floor," the Senate overwhelmingly rejected Muskie amendments to either eliminate the earnings cap or impose it on all income, then passed the code on a vote of eighty-six to nine. "This code is a milestone," Nelson said, eschewing personal credit and saying that the abuses of Watergate gave the main impetus for adopting the code. He also predicted, correctly, that he and Muskie would continue their friendship despite any harsh words spoken in the heat of debate, recalling "one hell of a big fight" the two had over the Vietnam War during a 1965 dinner party at the home of Ambassador W. Averell Harriman. "It didn't affect our friendship at all," he said.[26]

21

Saving the Appalachian Trail

HE LIVED eight hundred miles away from the Appalachian Trail and had never been on the trail in his life. But when he learned, in a chance encounter at a cocktail party, that the trail was in danger, Nelson became its champion.

Nelson was still in his freshman year in the Senate when Dr. Cecil Cullander approached him at the party to tell him about the plight of the trail. As the twenty-one-hundred-mile foot trail snaked its way through fourteen states, from Georgia to Maine, slightly more than one-third of it ran across federal lands. The vast majority was on private property, remaining open only at the goodwill of the landowners. As land was sold or passed on to the next generation, increasing numbers of people were closing off sections of the trail that crossed their lands. Development of scenic parkways also was eating away at the trail. If the trend continued, Cullander told Nelson, in another generation the trail would no longer exist, except as a series of shorter segments, perhaps with no access in between. Hikers had always walked alongside highways in some areas because there was no access to the private lands, but the situation was worsening. One twenty-five-mile stretch near Shenandoah National Park in Virginia ran entirely along a public highway. The southern end of the trail itself had been moved twenty miles north, to Springer Mountain, Georgia, because of development.[1]

Nelson wasted no time. The next day, he had his staff begin work on a bill to save the Appalachian Trail. Nelson considered the trail "a rare gem, one of our environmental treasures," like Yosemite or Yellowstone National Parks. He had never seen it, but "didn't have to be on it to know it was good," he said later. He was intrigued by the fact that volunteers who used it maintained the trail, that it had a constituency. Nelson thought political support would not be hard to line up, since the trail was popular in fourteen states. He did not expect a lot of resistance. "I don't think there was any opposition to the concept. I think it had powerful emotional support," Nelson said later. "It just took introducing a bill and spending some time pushing it at the hearings."[2]

That begged the question: If the trail really was so popular, why had none of the twenty-eight senators from states along the trail introduced legislation? One answer was that the best place to get action was from a seat on the western-dominated Senate Interior Committee, which had jurisdiction. Nelson, the freshman, was the only member of the committee from east of the Mississippi River. But Nelson also had a keen interest in natural resource and environmental issues. As the Appalachian Trail issue demonstrated, it clearly was not a parochial interest.

The Appalachian Trail was the brainchild of Benton MacKaye, a New Englander, forester, regional planner, conservationist, and visionary who was one of the eight founders of the Wilderness Society. In an article in 1921, MacKaye proposed the trail as the link connecting a series of overnight shelters, camps, small communally owned communities, and farm camps. That grandiose scheme, which he described as "a project in housing and community architecture," never materialized. The trail was another matter. The beginnings of the trail already existed in the 1920s, and more than two hundred miles of trail had been built in Vermont and New Hampshire. MacKaye envisioned the trail being built and maintained by local or state groups. He identified some of the potential problems getting permission to use private property and rights-of-way but said "these matters could easily be adjusted." He acknowledged that he had proposed "no scheme . . . for organizing or financing this project," and both needed some attention and work.[3]

During the next fifteen years, the trail became a reality. Under the coordination of the Appalachian Trail Conference, a coalition of hiking clubs formed in 1925, the trail grew steadily. Volunteers, sometimes with help from the federal Civilian Conservation Corps, cleared, built, and hacked out one segment after another. By 1937 the trail was completed. Now it was time to answer the question posed by Arthur Perkins, a lawyer and MacKaye friend who helped ramrod the construction: "When we get the trail, Ben, what are we going to do with it?" In other words, how could it be protected? A 1938 agreement by the National Forest Service and Park Service guaranteed protection of the 875 miles of trail on federal lands. Most of the states along the trail also acted to protect the trail on state-owned lands. But, as MacKaye said in his article, "difficulties might arise over the use of private property" and those difficulties remained unresolved.[4]

Nelson introduced his bill to protect the Appalachian Trail on 20 May 1964, warning that unless Congress acted, "the day will soon come when large parts of the Appalachian Trail, except those passing through national parks, will be destroyed." With opportunities for outdoor exercise on the decline, losing the trail would be tragic, he said. The bill authorized federal acquisition of land or easements along the trail's route. Nelson offered a philosophical argument, similar to that espoused by supporters of the National Wilderness Act, then pending in Congress. "The mental and spiritual well-being of the people may depend upon sufficient places to retreat for contemplation, to commune with nature." With increasing pressure on recreation areas from a growing and increasingly mobile population, scenic and wilderness areas were at a premium, Nelson said. "Parks and recreation areas are only part of the answer. The most important recreation of all is the kind people find in their everyday life. What this means is an environment—an outdoor environment—an Appalachian Trail."[5]

The bill did not pass, but Nelson reintroduced it at the start of the next session, with senators from many of the Appalachian Trail states as cosponsors. He followed it in October 1965 with a second bill to establish a nationwide system of hiking trails, including the Appalachian Trail. At that point, Nelson was surprised to pick up a powerful ally—President Lyndon Johnson. Nelson suspected the Department of the Interior was dragging its feet on making its report to the Senate Interior Committee on his hiking trails bill, but he could not imagine why. "It became clear after several calls to the Interior Department that I was getting the run-around," Nelson recalled. He kept pestering Dr. Edward C. Crafts, head of the Bureau of Outdoor Recreation, who finally confessed: The president liked Nelson's idea, but he wanted credit for it. The president's 1965 message on natural beauty expressed his support for a system of trails in and near cities for biking, hiking, and horseback riding. "In the back country," Johnson said, "we need to copy the great Appalachian Trail in all parts of America."[6]

Nelson, less concerned about credit than results, readily agreed to put the president out front. He enlisted Senator Henry Jackson, the Washington Democrat who chaired the Interior Committee, to sponsor the bill and give it an extra push. On 1 April 1966, Nelson and Jackson introduced President Johnson's national hiking trails bill, to protect the Appalachian Trail and earmark nine other trails for study as possible future national scenic trails. The legislation, Nelson said, would be "a benchmark in the history of wise outdoor recreation development in this nation." Hiking trails, he said, "represent perhaps the most economical form of public investment in outdoor recreation. There ought to be a place to hike within an hour's reach of every American."[7] That bill died in the Senate Interior Committee.

The bill that finally passed in the next session, signed by President Johnson on 2 October 1968, permanently preserved the Appalachian Trail and established the Pacific Crest Trail on the West Coast as national scenic trails, and identified fourteen other trails for study and possible inclusion in the system. Acquisition moved at a snail's pace until 1978, when $90 million was appropriated to acquire private land along the Appalachian Trail. Gradually, in fits and starts, the protection Nelson envisioned took place.[8] The Appalachian Trail Conference reported that less than twenty-five miles of the 2,144-mile trail remained in private ownership by the year 2001, while an estimated three to four million people hiked a portion of the trail each year.

The national trails system expanded by the end of the century to eight scenic trails and nine historic trails. The two trails designated in 1978—the Appalachian, administered by the National Park Service, and Pacific Crest, with oversight by the National Forest Service—were the only ones near completion two decades later. The Park Service is responsible for twelve of the seventeen trails in the system, the Forest Service for four, and the Bureau of Land Management for one. The system also recognized a number of existing recreation trails, which include nature trails, river routes, and historic tours, mostly managed by local or state governments.

Wisconsin's Scenic Trails

One of the fourteen scenic trails designated for study in the 1968 bill was the North Country Trail, which winds more than four thousand miles across seven states, including northern Wisconsin. It runs from the Adirondacks on the New York–Vermont border to the prairies of North Dakota, where it joins the route of the Lewis and Clark National Historic Trail. Double the length of the Appalachian Trail, it was designated a national scenic trail in 1980. Twenty years later, about seventeen hundred miles of the trail had been completed. It will eventually be the nation's longest trail.

Wisconsin also has the Ice Age Trail, which zigzags for a thousand miles along a glacial divide, with moraines marking the edge of activity by glaciers ten thousand years ago. Raymond Zillmer, a Milwaukee lawyer, avid walker, and mountaineer, had the idea in the 1950s for a national park that followed the moraines. "We spend millions to go fast; let's spend a little to go slow," said Zillmer, who founded the nonprofit Ice Age Park and Trail Foundation in 1958. Zillmer enlisted Congressman Henry Reuss of Milwaukee, who worked with the National Park Service to develop plans for an Ice Age Scientific Reserve. The forty-two-thousand-acre reserve would be a joint federal-state project with units and interpretive centers linked by a trail. The House passed Reuss's bill late in September 1964, in the closing days of the session, and Nelson was able to win Senate passage within a week, just before adjournment.[9] Congress designated the Ice Age Trail as a national scenic trail in 1980. Volunteers had been working on trail segments for fifteen years. As on the Appalachian Trail, several thousand volunteers build, maintain, and support the trail. About six hundred miles of the trail were open for use in 2001.

22

The Hard Detergent Battle

WHEN YOUR IDENTITY is wrapped up with a place called Clear
Lake, it is logical that water quality would be one of your priorities. Nelson, thinking both locally and globally, fought relentlessly against water
pollution. He was the first major public figure to speak out on pollution
of the Great Lakes and to propose a cleanup plan, as part of a comprehensive clean water agenda that also sought to protect the oceans.

Nelson's first speech in the Senate was on the need to clean up water
pollution from detergents. It was an issue he had already raised as governor and one that he would continue to champion during his Senate
career. In retrospect, it seems obvious that the mountains of foam on
the nation's rivers and lakes were signs of a problem. The foam, primarily from dish and laundry detergents used in homes, businesses, and
commercial laundries, was sometimes five to ten feet high, floating
down the rivers and over the dams. Clearly, that could not be good for
the water, could it? During the 1950s, almost no one asked that question. In the 1960s, when Nelson and others began to ask, the detergent
industry denied it was doing any harm and even claimed the suds were
beneficial. Nelson believed otherwise and was determined to clean
up the detergent industry no matter how long it took. The detergent
manufacturers—giant corporations like Procter and Gamble, Colgate-
Palmolive, and Lever Brothers—were a powerful, well-entrenched
interest group with considerable influence in the Congress. They resisted regulation every step of the way.

Synthetic detergents, developed about the time of World War II,
quickly became part of American life, with no real thought about

damage they might do. In the late 1950s it was discovered that the new detergents contained ingredients that resisted the bacteria in sewage treatment systems, intended to break them down into harmless byproducts. In what has since become a common term, they were not biodegradable. The main culprit was alkyl benzene sulfonate (ABS), a wetting agent. It passed right through septic systems or municipal treatment plants and into lakes, streams, groundwater, and wells, producing the foam.

As governor, Nelson learned from state agencies that nearly one-third of the shallow wells in Wisconsin were contaminated by detergents. He ordered a study, which turned up evidence of pollution of underground water in sixty-four of the state's seventy-two counties. "My mother got her dishes clean without the aid of detergents," Nelson said in a 1962 speech to the Wisconsin Conservation Congress. "We need legislation protecting our waters, and we sorely need legislation against harmful detergents." As he was preparing to leave the governor's office, Nelson called on conservation groups to support a state law banning detergents that would not decompose. One of the ingredients, ABS, "is practically immune to destruction by biological means," Nelson said, and pollution from detergents was "seeping into our water supplies everywhere, reducing efficiency of our sewage treatment facilities, causing unsightly foaming on streams, and even appearing in fresh water supplies in some places." He pointed to phosphates as the detergent ingredient causing algae to bloom on the state's lakes and called for Wisconsin to join Germany, which already had enacted a phosphate ban. The algae were a sign that eutrophication, a natural aging process in lakes, was being greatly speeded up by the flood of phosphorus, a nutrient that encouraged the growth.[1]

In his first year in the Senate, Nelson cosponsored a bill to ban detergents that did not decompose and told a Senate subcommittee that new scientific breakthroughs would allow the industry to switch to biodegradable products by the 30 June 1965 deadline in the bill. The industry said the foam was not a pollutant but merely an aesthetic issue and might actually serve a useful purpose as a visual marker or tracer for other sources of pollution. It claimed that the ban would stand in the way of scientific progress and cost hundreds of millions of dollars, and that it would be impossible to meet the deadline. Having made those arguments, the Soap and Detergent Association did an about-face just three weeks after the Senate bill was introduced. At a legislative hearing in Madison, where a similar state bill was pending, the industry said it would voluntarily change over to a new, nonpolluting detergent by 31 December 1965. Later the industry said it would make the change by 30 June 1965 — the "impossible" date in the original federal bill. Despite that assurance, Wisconsin went ahead and became the first state in the nation to ban so-called "hard" detergents containing ABS after 31 December 1965.[2]

A change in composition of the detergents eliminated most of the foam, but it did not stop the flow of phosphates into the nation's water. Nelson, not satisfied with the industry's voluntary pledge, continued to push for enforceable standards and government testing. While pleased by the switch from "hard" to "soft" detergents, Nelson said, "I have still seen nothing to guarantee that the public interest is any more certain to be protected than it was two years ago." Nelson introduced an updated bill in 1965 and continued to refine it in subsequent sessions, to achieve what he called a "first time safe" principle of testing products for environmental and health hazards before they went on the market. His three-point detergent plan called for a limit and eventual ban on phosphates; establishment of test protocols, standards, and regulations; and an intense federal effort to develop safe, nonpolluting substitutes for phosphates. The bills received several public hearings and considerable public attention, but the industry was always able to block passage.[3]

But as lakes and rivers declined and died from eutrophication, with algae choking off oxygen, which killed other plants and fish, the public began to demand action. By the late 1960s, nearly ten thousand lakes had been affected, and Lake Erie, the worst example, was said to have aged fifteen thousand years in the previous fifty. There was a general belief that "the nation's lakes and streams were getting more polluted every day, and phosphate detergents were the primary reason" and "a growing public consensus that in order to save lakes (like Lake Erie), phosphates must be banned from detergents."[4]

By 1970 there was more evidence linking phosphates to pollution. A congressional study recommended removing phosphates from detergents. A study of eutrophication in the lower Great Lakes, conducted by the International Joint Commission, recommended replacing phosphates in detergents by 1972, as well as improved sewage treatment and a reduction in agricultural fertilizer runoff, the other biggest source of phosphate pollution. The Council on Environmental Quality (CEQ) chimed in with similar recommendations. Detergent makers began to announce plans to reduce the phosphate content of their products. Then came a new problem: The most likely substitute for phosphates, called NTA (nitrilotriacetic acid), had not been adequately tested and was a suspected carcinogen. The industry quit using NTA and switched formulas again. The new ingredients had their own hazards, containing caustic agents that could irritate or damage the eyes, nose, and throat and that were especially dangerous to children.[5]

Meanwhile, the Federal Trade Commission (FTC) refused to require detergent makers to label their products to list all ingredients and disclose that phosphates contributed to water pollution and were unnecessary in soft water. The Nixon Administration's witnesses urged the FTC to delay action pending further study on the safety of phosphate substitutes. "If the right hand washes the left hand in this administration, it apparently does not do so with detergents," Nelson said, citing a letter from the Environmental Protection Agency (EPA) supporting labeling of detergents. The administration's position "is seeking to postpone efforts to cut back on the use of phosphates and is reducing the industry's incentive to eliminate them entirely," the *Minneapolis Tribune* said. "Raising the specter of untested phosphate substitutes in an effort to block a sensible warning to housewives about excess household detergent use is a scare tactic," the *Milwaukee Journal* said."[6]

An About-Face

Several months later, the administration did a shocking about-face on the phosphate issue. In a joint news conference on 15 September 1971, the surgeon general, EPA, and CEQ suggested that consumers return to using phosphate detergents, which were less harmful to health than caustic substitutes. Local communities should reconsider efforts to ban phosphate detergents, they said, urging the FTC not to implement the labeling rules either. "A capitulation to soap and detergent-makers," complained Congressman Henry Reuss. The administration's position "followed closely the line of reasoning advanced by leading elements in the soap and detergent lobby," the *New York Times* said. The action "may have delighted the detergent industry," the *Washington Post* said "but it has only confused the women and men who load the wash." The industry's fingerprints were easily detected. The president of Procter and Gamble, the nation's number one detergent maker, chaired the Detergent Sub-Council of the National Industrial Pollution Control Council. President Nixon created the council in 1970 to "reassure the corporate community regarding impending waves of environmental regulation, and allow direct communication between businessmen and both the CEQ and the President." The press conference took place at the request of the Detergent Sub-Council.[7]

The EPA also said it would support construction of waste treatment plants to eliminate most of the phosphates. "Now, there is no argument about the need to remove nutrients from waste water at the treatment stage," Nelson said. "What is arguable is that this has never been viewed by anyone other than the soap and detergent industry as a substitute for the removal of phosphates from detergents." To be effective, the program also required removal of phosphates from detergents and controls on farm runoff, he said. It would also take a real commitment of federal dollars — $1.5 billion just to save the Great Lakes, he said.[8]

While detergent makers advertised that the surgeon general recommended phosphate detergents, another round of congressional hearings produced a report calling for a reduction in phosphorus content to 8.7 percent immediately, and to 2.2 percent by the end of 1972. Now the industry *wanted* to be regulated, if regulation meant the 8.7 percent limit and a federal law that preempted stronger state and local laws. But that didn't happen, and many states and local governments adopted their own laws on detergents, despite legal challenges from the industry.[9]

Nelson mounted his last campaign against phosphates in 1977, when he won Senate passage of a virtual ban on phosphates in laundry detergents sold in the eight states in the Great Lakes basin. "Tens of millions of Americans depend on the Great Lakes for drinking water and recreation," Nelson said, and five years of research had shown that even the most advanced treatment plants were unable to eliminate phosphate pollution. This time Nelson had the EPA on his side. The agency's Chicago office had released a study that found deterioration in open waters of Lake Michigan south of Milwaukee, with phosphates identified as the cause. With EPA's endorsement, the Senate passed Nelson's amendment to an omnibus clean water bill. That provision drew heavy fire from the industry, and even with EPA support it did not survive. A Senate-House conference committee dropped it from the bill.[10]

Ultimately, state and local regulation, improvements in the treatment and removal of phosphorus from sewage, and the development of more alternatives to phosphate detergents all combined to reduce phosphate pollution. In the mid-1990s, after many states had passed phosphate detergent bans, the industry voluntarily quit manufacturing household laundry detergents with phosphates.[11] While Nelson's efforts did not produce federal legislation, they increased public awareness, spurred other states and local governments to follow Wisconsin's lead and act on their own, and kept the pressure on manufacturers to clean up their act and find alternatives to phosphates.

23

The Great Society

CIVIL RIGHTS had not yet emerged as a burning issue in Wisconsin at the time of Nelson's 1962 Senate campaign. The lunch counter sit-ins, Freedom Rides, marches, and racial clashes in the South "occurred in places far from Wisconsin, where conditions were presumably much worse for blacks," a state historian wrote. The civil rights movement in Wisconsin took shape more slowly than in many other states. The black population was growing but concentrated in a few cities, notably Milwaukee, where blacks made up 8 percent of the city's population in 1960.[1]

A classic northern liberal, Nelson was an outspoken advocate and a certain vote for civil rights legislation. In his first months in office, he signed on as a cosponsor of five civil rights bills, including measures to guarantee access to public schools and public accommodations. The movement, meanwhile, was marching toward center stage in the spring of 1963. In May the use of fire hoses and police dogs in Birmingham, Alabama, against peaceful demonstrators horrified many Americans who watched the scenes on television. In June, after Alabama Governor George Wallace "stood in the schoolhouse door" to personally block two black students from entering the University of Alabama, President John F. Kennedy placed Alabama's National Guard under federal authority and ordered it to force admission of the students. In a televised address, Kennedy declared that the nation was facing "a moral crisis as a country and as a people." A week later, he sent Congress "the most comprehensive and far-reaching civil rights bill ever proposed," and Nelson signed on as a cosponsor.[2]

As the bill, facing the threat of a southern filibuster, languished in the Senate, civil rights supporters organized a March on Washington, and gathered 250,000 strong on the Mall on 28 August 1963. Members of Nelson's staff joined in the march, and Nelson was on the platform at the Lincoln Memorial when Dr. Martin Luther King Jr. delivered his impassioned "I have a dream" speech. The march solidified the movement but changed few votes in the Congress. While a majority of people in the country favored a civil rights bill, a white backlash was said to be building, with even some supporters saying Kennedy was moving too fast.

Nelson, who sat between Edward and Robert Kennedy on the Senate Labor and Welfare Committee, was on the Senate floor on 22 November 1963 when President Kennedy was assassinated in Dallas. Nelson walked into the Marble Room just off the floor, a private lounge where senators could relax and read their home state newspapers. Quentin Burdick of North Dakota was standing at the wire service "ticker tape" machine. "Look, the president's been shot," Burdick said, showing Nelson a bulletin. Edward Kennedy was presiding in the Senate, and Nelson started onto the floor to tell him the news and take over the chair, but "someone else had just told him and Teddy was getting up and left the Senate."[3]

In his first address to the Congress as president, Lyndon B. Johnson resolved to make passage of the civil rights bill a monument to Kennedy's memory. Nelson called for action before Christmas. "The American system, humiliated by the events in Dallas, is now on trial before the world," Nelson said. "If we really believe in that system, we should show the world how well it can work." He called for immediate action on "the crucial and urgent matters which have been studied and debated so long already."[4]

Passage did not come until the next summer, after heated, divisive debate and evidence that Wisconsin was not immune to white backlash. George Wallace, an ardent segregationist, entered Wisconsin's presidential primary, running as a Democrat against Governor John Reynolds, a "favorite son" candidate running in place of President Johnson. The House passed the civil rights bill in February, and Wallace made it a major issue in the April primary. Two weeks before the primary, Nelson sent Wisconsin newspapers a detailed analysis of Wallace's record in Alabama, charging Wallace had seized control of public schools by force of arms, headed Alabama toward a police state, denied the right to vote, and caused a breakdown of law and order. The world would be watching, he said, to see whether Wisconsin voters would "rally round the banner of a racist."[5]

In what was perceived as a referendum on civil rights, Wallace won 34 percent of the Democratic primary vote. His surprisingly strong showing was aided by a low voter turnout and by crossover votes of Republicans who voted in the Democratic primary, since there was no contest on the GOP ballot. Wallace's appeal was broader than the civil rights issue, as he campaigned against welfare, government giveaways, and "pointy-headed" liberal intellectuals who thought they knew more than the average person. "We didn't have anyone else to vote for, and yet we wished to express our displeasure to the do-gooders who are so long on theories but so short on practical good sense," one Wallace voter wrote Nelson.[6]

A Lutheran pastor in Luxemburg, Wisconsin, insisted he did not support segregation but feared the bill would "deprive state rights and give the federal government the greatest power in the history of this nation." He was one of many who wrote Nelson in opposition to the bill. "This Bill is not one for so-called Negro 'rights,' but a plan to get control of this nation first for 'Socialism' and then 'Communism,'" a Milwaukee woman wrote. "Don't waste too much time trying to win the Negro vote," said a man in Jackson, Wisconsin. "For every Negro vote you pick up you are likely to lose the votes of two or three whites." Taking rights from one person and giving them to another would "effect a revolution, not a reformation," an Appleton voter said. "I am not against the colored people or fair employment or fair voting rights; but I am against the way you are trying to achieve it," another Appleton writer, a chiropractor, wrote Nelson.[7]

Nelson patiently answered them all. When a Milwaukee man claimed "pressure from a minority group" was responsible for his support of the bill, Nelson responded strongly. "The thousands of letters I have received on this issue have reflected just the opposite—that it is those who are against the bill who are organized into a tightly knit pressure group, while those in favor of this legislation represent all parts of our nation, all religions and races, both political parties and all age groups," he wrote. He suggested the man may have been the target of "racist propaganda" initiated in the Deep South and spread by the chamber of commerce, some real estate firms, newspaper editors, public schoolteachers, and "even one of our Congressmen."[8] Nelson enclosed a packet of material and urged him to study the bill. The congressman was William Van Pelt of Fond du Lac, the only member of the Wisconsin delegation to oppose the bill when it passed the House in February. The real test was the Senate, where southern filibusters had killed civil rights legislation in the past. But this time the Senate voted to cut off debate, and on 19 June 1964 passed the most important civil rights legislation in the nation's history by a vote of 73–27. President Johnson signed it into law on 2 July 1964.

Nelson changed his opinion of Johnson, whom he had criticized when running for governor in 1958. As a senator, Johnson's lukewarm civil rights stands and support for Texas oil interests made him unacceptable to many northern liberals. But Nelson got acquainted with him as vice president and "came to consider [him] very good" after he became president and was "strong on civil rights and poverty questions. He made a record as president that he couldn't stand on running for re-election as a Texas senator," Nelson said. "He changed when he became a national figure, or maybe he did what his instinct always was. That wasn't the guy I saw from a distance as a young candidate for governor" in 1958. Presiding in the Senate as vice president, Johnson called Nelson up to his desk and told him, in the personal and earthy terms he preferred, why it was important to pass the civil rights bill. "I have a fine black couple that works for me," Johnson said. "She's got a master's degree and he's got a bachelor's degree. When they get in their car and head for Texas, as soon as they hit the South there's no bathroom they can use. This fine, educated lady has to go up in a cornfield to pee. We've got to put an end to that."[9]

In March 1965, after Alabama state troopers and sheriff's officers used tear gas and clubs against six hundred peaceful marchers in Selma, Johnson sent a voting rights bill to Congress. Nelson expressed "100 percent support" for the bill. "The shame of Selma is a stain on America's record," he said. In Wisconsin's presidential primary Wallace "spoke in words of honey," Nelson said, but now "the record is clear for all to see." Nelson reminded the people of Wisconsin that a year earlier he had warned that the "shortcuts" offered by Wallace—"the brutal enforcement of arbitrary decrees by guns and dogs and hoses; the knock

on the door in the night; the bombs exploding on a Sunday morning—
are a primrose path to national suicide."[10] The Voting Rights Act of
1965, which became law in August, prohibited literacy tests and poll
taxes and empowered the federal government to oversee voter registration and elections in problem areas.

The next week the Watts section of Los Angeles erupted in six days
of rioting, looting and burning. Over the next three years the civil rights
struggle was waged against a backdrop of racial tension and disorder
that flared in most of the nation's large cities and, as Johnson warned,
made reform more difficult. Milwaukee was no longer immune to racial
unrest, and two years of peaceful demonstrations aimed at school de-
segregation and open housing had increased tension. On 30 July 1967 it
boiled over in a major, two-day riot in Milwaukee's inner city, resulting
in four deaths and fifteen hundred arrests. Soon afterward, a series of
daily open housing marches led by James Groppi, a Catholic priest who
had marched at Selma, kept the city on edge. "We are kidding ourselves
if we think that Father Groppi is the problem," Nelson wrote to a constituent who complained about the marches. "If he were transferred, we
would still have thousands of citizens with inadequate educations, low
incomes, poor housing, and poor job opportunities. These are conditions which must be corrected."[11]

In April 1968, after Dr. Martin Luther King Jr. was assassinated in
Memphis, racial violence flared in 125 American cities, but Milwaukee
staged a peaceful memorial service attended by 7,000 and "a generally
orderly march through the inner city and downtown areas by 15,000
persons, both black and white." The next week, Congress passed a civil
rights bill banning housing discrimination and containing strong anti-
riot provisions. The bill also gave federal protection to civil rights workers, as Nelson had proposed. Milwaukee passed an open housing ordi-
nance soon afterward, marking "the end of the militant civil rights
movement in Milwaukee."[12] Nationally, the focus shifted to equal
rights for women, the elderly, the physically disabled, and others.

The War on Poverty

When President Johnson declared "unconditional war on poverty" in
his 1964 State of the Union speech, Nelson said, "I am enlisting to serve
in that war for the duration."[13]

Nelson had begun to focus on poverty soon after his arrival in the Senate. In a widely reprinted speech, "The Face of America's Poor," Nelson said the "invisible poor" made up one-fourth of the population—senior citizens, farmers, migrant workers, unskilled and unorganized workers, residents of depressed areas, and people with handicaps or other problems such as alcoholism. Unorganized and discouraged, with no one to speak for them, these poor citizens were excluded not only from the good life but from many government programs, Nelson said. "If we consign a fourth of our people to a life of poverty in the midst of our own prosperity, we corrode democracy," Nelson said. "And we confess that in solving the greatest problem of all—the maintenance of the dignity of our fellow men—we have not triumphed at all. We have failed."[14]

Nelson not only enlisted in the war on poverty but also offered a program he said would "enable the President to win that war." Nelson called for a $10 billion, ten-year fight against poverty, paid for by a cigarette tax increase of five cents per pack. "This is a tax which will do no harm whatsoever," Nelson declared. "And this is a program which will be of incalculable benefit to America forevermore." The plan was patterned after his successful outdoor recreation program as governor, which raised cigarette taxes to expand recreation lands. But, while generating some favorable reaction, the federal plan ran into a wall of opposition from tobacco state legislators and Nelson never introduced it in bill form.[15]

Two other Nelson proposals to combat poverty and unemployment—Operation Mainstream and the Teacher Corps—got warmer receptions and became law in 1965.

Nelson proposed in 1964 that the federal government put unemployed, unskilled workers to work on conservation and recreation projects. The program would stop the waste of natural resources while it reduced the ranks of the unemployed, he said. To demonstrate the need and potential for such a program, Nelson's office surveyed more than two thousand state and local officials, asking them to describe projects they could undertake with such a program. They suggested enough projects to provide 425,000 man-years of work. The price tag was $1 billion, equal to the total outlay of the Johnson war on poverty. Nelson refined the idea to apply specifically to chronically unemployed poor adults, primarily in rural areas, and scaled back the spending.[16]

What became known as the Nelson Amendment was passed by Congress and became law in 1965 for the second year of the Johnson antipoverty program. Dubbed Operation Mainstream, it made federal grants to state and local governments and to nonprofit groups. One of the first to use the program was the Farmers Union, which launched a program it called Green Thumb in five states, putting four hundred men to work doing landscaping and conservation work along state highways, planting trees, building parks and rest areas, and rebuilding historic sites. The initial appropriation was much smaller than the $150 million Nelson sought, but in the program's first year $13.4 million went to agencies that put fourteen thousand adults to work. Thirty-five years later, Green Thumb had grown to be the nation's leading provider of community service training and employment opportunities for both older and disadvantaged workers.[17]

The Teacher Corps was such a good idea it was appropriated by the president. Nelson proposed a national teacher corps, to send recent college graduates into poverty-stricken school districts, in February 1965. "The Peace Corps is an extraordinary success overseas because of the practical idealism of America's young people," Nelson said. "I propose to use that same idealism on our most pressing domestic crisis—education in our depressed neighborhoods." The idea was to team young teacher-trainees with experienced teachers, give them three months of intensive training, and send them into schools in the nation's slums. Edward Kennedy, who had a bill to get retired teachers back into schools, asked to become the cosponsor of the Teacher Corps. Later in his career, to Nelson's dismay, Kennedy claimed authorship.[18]

President Johnson adopted the idea in a speech to the National Education Association, neglecting to mention Nelson and Kennedy. The senators had discussed the bill with the White House in hopes of heading off opposition, but never imagined Johnson would champion the plan. He later credited them with the idea, but Nelson was less concerned about credit than getting it passed. The proposal easily passed the Senate as part of the Higher Education Act of 1965 and survived a challenge in the House to become law in November 1965. But as a small program that did not yet have a constituency, it faced an uphill struggle. The bill authorized spending $100 million in the first two years, but the House refused to appropriate any money. Fear of federal control of the schools, the program's impact on a teacher shortage, and other concerns fueled opposition. The program did finally get a small $9.5 million appropriation to begin training in the summer of 1966, but the number of participants was greatly reduced. The program had to fight for its life every step of the way in its first two years, but by 1968 had proved itself and won enough local support to win additional funding. Even at its peak, the Teacher Corps never received more than $37.5 million a year, but "arguably did more to improve the education of low-income children than its Great Society cousin, Title I, which has provided billions of dollars in general aid to low-income schools," an education writer said in 2000, when presidential candidate Al Gore proposed a similar plan. The corps shifted in the 1970s to retraining teachers to teach in poverty-stricken areas and ran until 1981. During that time, it trained more than twenty-five thousand teachers.[19]

As the war in Vietnam began to compete with the war on poverty for federal dollars, Nelson was outraged by suggestions that Congress would end its campaign against poverty. "I think it is time we stood up and said we are not going to ignore poverty, we are not going to ignore urban decay, we are not going to go back on our civil rights pledges or give up fighting air and water pollution, because if we do these problems will overwhelm us," he said in what was described as a "blistering speech" to a conference on rural poverty. "We cannot turn back," he said. "If we are hoodwinked into retreating at this crucial moment in the fight, we will pay dearly for it in the years to come in terms of wasted manpower and squandered resources, as well as . . . human suffering and injustice." If America turned its back on domestic problems, it would "move from the Great Society to the Puny Society," he said.[20]

When Richard Nixon became president in 1969, some expected him to shut down the Office of Economic Opportunity (OEO), the federal antipoverty agency, of which he had been sharply critical. Nelson, the new chairman of the Senate Subcommittee on Manpower, Employment and Poverty, was among key congressional leaders who served notice that Congress wanted a voice in any decisions on the poverty program. Nixon relented, and a two-year, Nelson-sponsored OEO extension became law in 1969. But Nelson and the Nixon administration sparred for the next several years over antipoverty programs, as Nixon shifted programs from OEO to other agencies—Job Corps to the

Department of Labor, Head Start to Health, Education and Welfare, VISTA to a new agency—and finally tried to dismantle OEO.[21]

In 1973 Nixon attempted to close down OEO and end funding for community action agencies administratively by simply not funding the programs. Nelson introduced a "sense of the Congress" resolution to keep OEO alive, but it was a federal court decision that finally kept OEO in business, saying Nixon's action violated congressional intent. In Congress the debate was more on where to house poverty programs than on whether to continue them. Nelson argued strongly for a separate agency, to give the poor their own voice in the government. Nelson's bill, to rename OEO the Community Services Administration (CSA), was signed into law in the fall of 1974 by the new president, Gerald Ford.[22] The CSA was legislated out of existence in 1981 and the functions were transferred to the Department of Health and Human Services, after the Reagan landslide swept Nelson and a number of other key Senate liberals out of office.

In his final month in office, Nixon quietly signed a Nelson bill creating a permanent, independent Legal Services Corporation to provide legal aid to the poor. Nixon had tried to rein in the program, which began under OEO, restrict its activities, and bring it under tighter control, but Nelson's bill did the opposite. The administration reluctantly came to support the bill, and Nelson's old friend Melvin Laird, a domestic policy advisor to Nixon, helped round up Republican votes to end a filibuster. It was a major victory for Nelson and liberal Republican Jacob Javits of New York, who cosponsored both the Legal Services and OEO extension bills.[23]

Nelson and Javits also teamed up in a four-year struggle between the Congress and the White House over manpower programs, policies, and public sector jobs. In late 1970 Nixon successfully vetoed a Nelson manpower-training bill, objecting to the public service jobs in the program. The measure, the Nelson-O'Hara bill, was "a comprehensive, well-conceived and tightly-framed piece of legislation" designed to "take hundreds of thousands of people permanently off the relief rolls" by training them and placing them in jobs. In 1971, as an economic recession continued, Nelson won passage of the Emergency Employment Act, providing $2.25 billion to create up to 150,000 public service jobs for the unemployed. The Nixon administration initially opposed the bill, which was "a watered-down version of the Nelson-O'Hara bill," but came around to support it, and Nixon signed it into law in July 1971.[24]

The prolonged tug-of-war over manpower policies ended in 1973 with a compromise that produced the Comprehensive Employment and Training Act (CETA), setting the course for federal jobs programs for the next decade. The Nelson-Javits bill, as signed, consolidated federal manpower programs and decentralized their operation. It included special revenue sharing proposed by Nixon but also included the public sector jobs he objected to. CETA provided block grants to state and local governments to support public and private job training and such youth programs as the Job Corps and Summer Youth Employment. In 1982 Congress replaced CETA, which was expiring, with the Job Training Partnership Act. The new law gave the states more control over how they distributed vocational training funds and ended federal funding for public service employment programs.[25]

Nelson files nomination papers with Secretary of State Robert Zimmerman for the 1962
Senate race. (Courtesy of the *Capital Times*)

The Nelson family Christmas card, 1962. The children, from left: Happy, Jeffrey, and Tia. (Courtesy of Gaylord and Carrie Lee Nelson)

Facing top: Green Bay Packers football game on 7 October 1962, a month before the election and two weeks before the Cuban missile crisis, drew a quartet of Democrats. From left: Senate candidate Nelson, gubernatorial candidate John Reynolds, Attorney General Robert Kennedy, and congressional candidate Owen Monfils. (Wisconsin Historical Society, WHi-5906)

Facing bottom: Interior Secretary Stewart Udall, Congressman Robert Kastenmeier, Nelson, and Democratic state chairman Patrick Lucey during an October 1962 visit by Udall to Madison. (David Sandell photo, courtesy of the *Capital Times*)

Nelson portrait, 1962 Senate campaign. (Courtesy of the *Capital Times*)

President Kennedy visits the Apostle Islands in September 1963, flanked by Governor John Reynolds, left, and Nelson. Behind the president, from left, are Secretary of Interior Stewart Udall, Secretary of Agriculture Orville Freeman, and tour guide Martin Hanson. (Courtesy of *Duluth News Tribune*)

Nelson wades on a sandy Apostle Islands beach. (Courtesy of Frank Wallick)

Facing bottom: Hubert Humphrey, center, "Wisconsin's third senator," was vice president-elect in January 1965 when William Proxmire, left, was sworn in for a new Senate term, escorted by Nelson, right. (Courtesy of the *Capital Times*)

Nelson gazes at his beloved Apostle Islands. (Courtesy of Frank Wallick)

Campaign portrait, 1968 (Courtesy of Fritz Albert)

The Nelson family on stage at an event during the 1968 Senate reelection campaign. (David Sandell photo, courtesy of the *Capital Times*)

Nelson with Senate majority leader Mike Mansfield. (Courtesy of Fritz Albert)

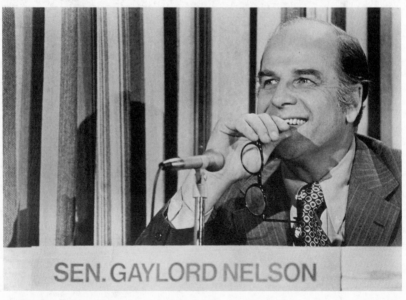

Nelson chairing a Senate hearing. (Courtesy of the *Capital Times*)

24

Islands and Rivers

NELSON WAS NOT a parochial politician. He took an expansive view on most issues, especially the environment. Even the two Wisconsin projects closest to his heart—preservation of the Apostle Islands and protection of the Saint Croix River—fit nicely into a broader Nelson agenda for the nation. But both also had a special personal and emotional pull for Nelson, who had been introduced to Lake Superior's Apostles as a child, and who grew up within twenty-five miles of the scenic Saint Croix. As surely as Earth Day is Nelson's national legacy, the Apostles and the Saint Croix are his legacies to Wisconsin from his Senate years.

The Apostles, near the western tip of Lake Superior, comprise a scenic archipelago of twenty-two wooded islands. Their white sand beaches, sea caves, dramatic sandstone cliffs, and sculpted shorelines, carved over millions of years by wind, water, and glaciers, inspire poetic descriptions. So does the great inland sea, Superior itself, Longfellow's Gitche Gumee, the "shining Big-Sea-Water" of *The Song of Hiawatha*.

"Words aren't adequate to describe the feeling one has standing on that ancient shore, sensing the whole history of the earth unreel in the rocks, the cold waters, the fog of even a summer morning. One gains an impression, then, of the forces that created man—the same forces that could just as easily sweep him away," Nelson wrote of Lake Superior.[1]

Bringing the Apostle Islands under federal protection took Nelson and his allies nine years, but the idea of making the Apostles a national park had surfaced long before. With the local economy in sharp decline even before the Great Depression, the nearby communities of Ashland

and Bayfield believed a national park would bring tourists and jobs. Congress ordered a study of the area in 1930, but the National Park Service report was negative, largely because the islands, like most of northern Wisconsin, had been heavily logged. There was continuing local interest but little action until the 1950s, when the postwar recreation boom reopened the discussion.[2]

Nelson broached the idea in 1961, in a discussion with Louis and Martin Hanson at their lodge on Beaverdam Lake, near Mellen in Ashland County, nearly surrounded by the Chequamegon National Forest. It was the beginning of a long personal and political association with the brothers, who had invited Nelson to Mellen to explain his Outdoor Recreation Act Program (ORAP) at a public dinner at the local rod and gun club. Nelson, accompanied by David Carley and Bud Jordahl, two of ORAP's designers, was stumping the state for his plan, to use a cigarette tax to expand the state's parks and recreation system.[3]

The discussion turned to whether the federal government might create a national park or lakeshore to preserve the Kakagon–Bad River sloughs. Nelson and Jordahl had discussed the sloughs while putting together the ORAP package, which included the acquisition of twenty thousand acres of land and several access points to lakes in the south shore region of Lake Superior. Federal studies had highlighted the sloughs as being of potential national significance, the only viable marsh on the Great Lakes. The Outdoor Recreation Resources Review Commission, created by President Dwight D. Eisenhower to study future recreational needs, and a "fourth shore" study by the National Park Service had identified some Apostle Islands areas as deserving protection and said the Kakagon–Bad River marshes should get further study.[4]

The slough was on the Bad River Indian Reservation, home to a band of Ojibwa (Chippewa) Indians who had been resettled from the Apostles to the south shore of Lake Superior in the 1850s. Another group, the Red Cliff band, was assigned to reservation land on the nearby Bayfield peninsula. The Bad River tribe approached the Hansons to discuss federal recognition of the slough, and in May 1962 the tribal council passed a resolution urging a federal-state study on establishing a "national shoreline recreational area" on the reservation. Nelson took the idea to Washington on 22 May 1962, meeting with Interior Secretary Stewart Udall, Indian Affairs Commissioner Philleo

Nash, and Bureau of Recreation Director Edward Crafts. Nelson cited the Interior Department's study in 1959, which said the sloughs and marshes had "some of the greatest wildlife potential, particularly in terms of waterfowl, that remain unprotected on the Great Lakes." Udall directed Crafts to undertake a study of the area. The proposal included twenty thousand acres in a seventeen-mile strip on the lakeshore, but not the Apostles.[5]

That proposal was a far cry from the Apostle Islands National Lakeshore established eight years later. The effort, Jordahl said, "involved the presidential administrations of Kennedy, Johnson and Nixon, re-sulted in twelve bills and bill drafts being written and rewritten . . . produced thousands of pages of congressional testimony and hearings records," and involved countless citizens, public officials, and state and federal agencies.[6]

Crafts came to Wisconsin in June 1962 to tour the area, suggesting that a broader package, including the Apostles and Bayfield peninsula as well as the sloughs, would be more attractive. Nelson ordered a state study, and media coverage was widespread and mostly positive. But there were hurdles to overcome. The state Conservation Department, a bureaucracy Nelson had been fighting to tame, opposed the idea. The department, which already had three of the islands in a state forest, sug-gested the state create its own recreation area. Later, as the proposal took shape, property owners, county governments, and the Indian tribes all would weigh in with objections or outright opposition.[7]

Supporters organized a grassroots campaign. A committee of prom-inent citizens, chaired by Dr. B. C. Prentice, a physician friend of the Hansons, played an important role, over a long period, in encouraging citizens and business groups to write letters, testify at hearings, and demonstrate their support for the project. Their ability to sustain that organization and enthusiasm over an eight-year period, despite delays, setbacks, and fierce opposition from some quarters, was remarkable.

Before Nelson left the governor's office he created a "people's lobby" on conservation issues to bring together a wide array of conservation-minded organizations under one umbrella to push a common agenda. Udall was the keynote speaker at a conference in October 1962, a few weeks before Nelson's election to the Senate. It drew an overflow crowd of people who were encouraged and energized to find common cause on issues they cared deeply about. Udall praised Nelson's ORAP plan and seconded Nelson's call to set aside more land for recreation and fish and wildlife habitat. In mid-December the group—officially the Wisconsin Council for Resource Development and Conservation—held its first steering committee meeting, and Nelson offered a far-reaching agenda, starting with a state ban on phosphate detergents. The group would offer significant support to the lakeshore plan—Martin Hanson was its secretary—and became an influential lobbying force on conservation issues in the legislature. It was also an important political base for Nelson.[8]

President Kennedy flew over the Apostle Islands in September 1963 during a national conservation tour (chapter 18). Udall accompanied him and got his first look at the area. The president carefully stopped short of an endorsement of the project but did say that "Lake Superior, the Apostle Islands, and the Bad River area are all unique. They are worth improving for the benefit of sportsmen and tourists. . . . These islands are part of our American heritage. . . . In fact, the entire northern Great Lakes area . . . is a central and significant part of the fresh water assets of this country, and we must act to preserve these assets." Endorsement or not, his words and the resulting publicity raised the status of the Apostles idea. As Nelson put it, "[O]f course [Kennedy's remarks] would be noticed by the park service and everybody else."[9]

Jordahl, a key player in formulating Nelson's ORAP program, was Mr. Inside on the Apostle Islands project. He moved from the state Department of Resource Development to the federal Interior Department in the spring of 1963. As regional coordinator for the western Great Lakes region, he helped develop a workable proposal. As the lakeshore idea moved along, Jordahl served on the Upper Great Lakes Regional Commission, where he was involved in the planning and political process. Finally, he served on the Wisconsin Natural Resources Board in the 1970s and was its chair when the state transferred its land in the lakeshore to the federal government.[10]

As the proposal went through a series of drafts and redrafts, the campaign to create the lakeshore continued. The editor of *Wisconsin Tales and Trails* magazine, Howard Mead, devoted a section of the summer 1964 issue to the Apostles, with color photos, text, maps, and commentary which was reprinted and widely distributed by supporters. Martin Hanson, whose talents included wildlife photography, collaborated with

Madison filmmaker A. Stuart Hanisch on a film about the Apostles. With footage of the area's scenic beauty and wildlife and a moving, poetic script written by George Vukelich and read by radio commentator Edward P. Morgan, it gained a wide audience in Wisconsin and in Washington, D.C. It "stole the show" from Nelson and Udall at its premiere in April 1964, at a Madison Press Club luncheon.[11]

There were dozens of issues, large and small, to be resolved before the Interior Department and Nelson were ready to make a proposal. The area would be a recreation area, not a national park or a wilderness area. Park or wilderness designation would exclude or restrict hunting, trapping, commercial fishing, and wild rice gathering, raising issues for both the tribes and sportsmen who used the sloughs. It excluded Madeline Island, the biggest and most developed of the Apostles, on which a state park was established in 1962. It included tribal lands but gave each tribe the option of leasing or selling lands to Interior, or exchanging the lands for other suitable land within the reservation boundary. It would be a federal project, not a joint federal-state venture. Private property owners could either retain the right to use their land within the lakeshore for the rest of their lives, or have a twenty-five-year right to use it, which could be transferred to others.[12]

The bill Nelson introduced on 7 September 1965 proposed creating a 57,500-acre national lakeshore to include all but one of the twenty-two Apostle Islands, thirty miles of Bayfield County shoreline, and the Bad River–Kakagon slough, described as a 10,000-acre wild rice marsh interlaced by two rivers. Nelson called it "the greatest recreational project ever proposed for Wisconsin." Its price tag was $11 million.[13]

The proposal was introduced with the support of the National Park Service, but it did not yet have Interior Department backing, and no hearings were held during the Eighty-ninth Congress. Nelson was disappointed when President Johnson, in his 1966 "natural heritage message" to Congress, urged creation of eight new parks and recreation areas but merely called for more studies and planning on the Apostles. Nelson reintroduced his bill in January 1967, and this time the president's conservation message asked Congress to establish the Apostle Islands National Lakeshore, "to add a superb string of islands to our national seashore system." The Senate passed the bill in August 1967 and sent it to the House—where Congressman Wayne Aspinall ruled.[14]

Aspinall, Interior Committee chair, had his own system of operation. He was thorough, deliberate, and methodical. He would not be
rushed. The Senate sent him a lot of bills, but they waited their turn
until he decided they were ripe for House action. In the case of the
Apostles, that would not be until 1970. Soon after the Senate passed the
1967 Apostles bill, Aspinall's committee closed down for new business.
Nelson had befriended and courted Aspinall to try to clear the way, but
Aspinall cut no corners, even for the president. When Nelson's administrative assistant, William Bechtel, asked for help from the White
House in speeding up action, a memo from the deputy director of the
Bureau of the Budget said that was unlikely. "The President wrote
Chairman Aspinall to try to get some House Committee action on
the Redwoods National Park bill, which has a higher priority than
the Apostle Islands, but without success. We doubt that the President
would want to spend the kind of capital which would be necessary to
get the Apostle Islands bill moving," the Budget Bureau said.[15] The bill
stayed in Aspinall's committee.

Nelson introduced the bill for a third time in 1969, uncertain of its
fate with a new president, Richard Nixon, and a new Interior secretary,
Walter Hickel. President Johnson had included the Apostles in his final
budget message before leaving office, but that did not guarantee anything. Nelson had strongly criticized Hickel's appointment, accusing
him of "a lackadaisical concern" over environmental problems and lacking the "background, depth of understanding or . . . commitment to the
issue of conservation," and voted against confirming Hickel. But Hickel's Interior Department supported Nelson's bill, and the Senate again
passed it in June, despite signals from the administration that there
might be no money available for new parks or recreation areas. Aspinall
held no House hearings on new parks until 1970, when the administration relented.[16]

There had been another important change in the political climate
since the bill's first consideration in 1965. The lakeshore area Indian
tribes had been prime movers and supporters of the bill then. But the
militant "red power" movement, with Native Americans demanding the
right to self-determination and seeking redress for past injustices, had
sprung up nationally in the late 1960s. Private landowners, who opposed the lakeshore, helped fuel and encourage the tribal opposition.

The Bad River and Red Cliff bands now wanted no part of the project. They did not want their lands included, they said, and testified in opposition to the entire project. They mounted a national campaign, with tribes from many other states weighing in to oppose the lakeshore as another land grab of tribal holdings. They even objected to including any land which had previously been part of the reservation, but which had been sold to nontribal owners, because the tribes might someday reacquire the lands. They confronted Nelson at his Earth Day speeches in Madison and Milwaukee, where he patiently explained that his bill would not take any Indian land unless the tribes petitioned to be included. But the details of the bill were often lost in the rhetoric. The uproar threatened the entire bill. At one point, Interior representatives said the lakeshore was not viable without the tribal lands, causing Nelson to explode. The Indian lands were not essential to the project, he declared. "[I]f the Interior Department cannot support a project like this, you had better transfer the conservation responsibilities of this country somewhere else. . . . [If] you want to wash it down the drain and get rid of the only collection of islands of this kind in the United States, you just continue this procedure," Nelson angrily told a park service representative at a hearing.[17]

"If you get this bill to the floor with the Indians of the United States against it, you are not going to pass it," Aspinall said at a House subcommittee hearing in June 1970. He was "not afraid to confront the issues and principles involved. We have never taken a step backward on that, but we have also never walked into a fire that we knew would consume all of us." Finally, with Nelson's support, Aspinall's committee amended the bill to exclude all tribal lands. Hickel backed the new version, the House and Senate quickly passed it, and President Nixon signed it into law on 26 September 1970. The final version included twenty of the twenty-two islands (another was added in 1986), 39,500 acres, and eleven miles of Lake Superior shoreline, but no tribal lands and no Kakagon slough, which had spurred the project in the first place.[18]

Nelson continued to monitor, nurture, and support the lakeshore during its development. When he heard that the owner of one of the small islands, not yet acquired by the government, was cutting the island's trees, Nelson "stalked fellow Interior Committee members on the Senate floor and in their offices until he had enough signatures to authorize immediate government purchase of the island." Nelson, "more than any other individual, provided the essential continuity and the tenacity to see the proposal through," Jordahl said. "If I wasn't on the Interior Committee, we probably wouldn't have passed either the Apostle Islands bill or the St. Croix bill because it just requires too much daily, monthly, yearly persistent pushing," Nelson said. It also helped that Congressman Robert Kastenmeier, a Nelson friend and ally from Wisconsin, was on the House Interior Committee and worked tirelessly with Aspinall to produce the final compromise bill.[19]

Saving the Saint Croix

A losing battle over construction of a power plant on the Saint Croix River became the impetus to save the last clean river near a major metropolitan area in the entire Midwest. Nelson played a leading role in the losing fight to stop the power plant and in the successful struggle to protect the river.

The Saint Croix begins in northwestern Wisconsin, forms about one-third of the Minnesota-Wisconsin border, then joins the Mississippi River southeast of Saint Paul, at Prescott, Wisconsin. In its nineteenth century heyday, it was an important industrial river, carrying billions of board feet of logs from the north woods to the sawmills at Stillwater, Minnesota, and beyond. Even then, the river's scenic beauty and wildlife attracted tourists, hunters, boaters, canoeists, and fishermen. Minnesota and Wisconsin established interstate parks by the turn of the century at the dalles of the river, with its waterfalls, rocky cliffs, and stone formations, which separated the upper and lower sections of the river. By 1964, when the power plant issue arose, residents of the nearby Minneapolis–Saint Paul metropolitan area—a half-hour's drive away—heavily used the Saint Croix for recreation, especially the lower river, below Stillwater, where it widened into Lake Saint Croix, a haven for boaters.[20]

Northern States Power (NSP) announced plans in May 1964 to build a giant coal-fired power plant on the river, south of Stillwater. Opponents on both sides of the river formed the Save the Saint Croix Committee and began a publicity campaign and petition drive, attracting national attention and editorial support. Nelson, a member of the

Senate Public Works Subcommittee on Air and Water Pollution, held hearings in Stillwater in December 1964, inviting Sigurd Olson, the noted conservationist and nature writer, to testify. "This is a national issue," declared Olson, a Minnesotan who had guided canoe trips on the river. But the federal government had no jurisdiction, and the decision was up to the state of Minnesota. A state-federal task force, formed to study the issue, did cause NSP to modify its plans somewhat.[21]

The Minnesota Conservation and Water Pollution Control Commissions, which would decide whether to issue the plant's permits, held a joint hearing in January 1965. "Call the roll of the great American rivers of the past, and you will have a list of the pollution problems of today," Nelson told the commissioners. He called the roll himself: the Androscoggin in Maine, the Connecticut, Hudson, Delaware, Ohio, Mississippi, Missouri, and Minnesota Rivers. "The story in each case is the same; they died for their country," he said. "They died in the name of economic development." The fight over conservation issues "has been unequal—eloquent spokesmen preaching lofty conservation generalities on the one hand pitted against a sincere, well-organized group on the other speaking the magic words of economic growth," he said.[22]

The dispute had convinced him, Nelson said, that federal action was needed to preserve the river, and he was drafting a bill to make the entire Saint Croix and its tributary, the Namekagon, national scenic waterways. He introduced the bill two weeks later, with Senator Walter F. Mondale of Minnesota as a cosponsor. Mondale had just been appointed to finish the term of Hubert Humphrey, the new vice president. "One of first things Gaylord and I did was introduce the Saint Croix bill, which is a wonderment even today, a beautiful bill," Mondale said. "I used to kid him because I found out most of the opponents of the bill lived on my side of the river. . . . Gaylord had a way of getting me to do tough things . . . the Saint Croix bill looks easy now," he said thirty years later, "but at the time I took a lot of rackin'. . . . Gaylord was a big influence in getting me into these damned disputes and I'd get all ripped. Now I look back and I'm proud of every one of them. I tell young politicians, 'Do something you think you'll be proud of. Don't trivialize your life.'"[23]

Nelson had some other familiar allies in the struggle. Jordahl was a Bureau of Land Management representative on a federal task force which studied the viability of the Saint Croix and Namekagon as wild rivers. Later, as the Interior Department's regional coordinator for the Midwest, he was able to keep the proposal on track, jousting with the Army Corps of Engineers, calming local residents, and running interference with competing governmental agencies. In the House, Kastenmeier played a key role and kept the pressure on.[24]

By the time the power plant won approval from Minnesota authorities in May 1965, the Nelson-Mondale bill had won the endorsement of the Department of the Interior and was headed for Senate passage. It called for the upper Saint Croix and the Namekagon to be designated as wild rivers, and the lower Saint Croix as a scenic, recreational river. Together, they would form the Saint Croix National Scenic Riverway. The Saint Croix plan was in the spirit of a national wild rivers bill proposed by the Johnson administration, but expanded it to include tamer, scenic waterways. Nelson wanted the Saint Croix bill considered separately, since it was farther along and the climate seemed right for passage. Stuck at O'Hare airport in Chicago with Wayne Aspinall, Nelson asked his advice. "Better send your bill alone," Aspinall said. "The other one isn't going to pass this year." As it turned out, neither was Nelson's bill. Mondale discovered widespread concern, opposition, and hostility from property owners in the Stillwater area who feared the federal government would condemn and take their land. The bill relied heavily on scenic easements and zoning, rather than condemnation and purchase of property, but questions remained. The House took no action on the Nelson-Mondale bill.[25]

Nelson and Mondale introduced another bill in early 1967. This time, they agreed to fold their proposal into a comprehensive wild and scenic rivers bill, which cleared the Senate on a unanimous vote but again got stuck in the Aspinall committee logjam. Aspinall had called the wild rivers plan "the craziest idea I ever heard of" when President Johnson first discussed it in his 1965 State of the Union address. He was not anxious to act, and even less anxious to spend money to acquire land and easements. While Aspinall delayed, the Army Corps of Engineers, which had suggested for years that the upper river needed flood control management, sought money to plan for a 120-foot dam on the upper Saint Croix, which would flood seventy-five thousand acres and create a forty-mile-long reservoir. The corps asked for a delay in a wild river designation while a study proceeded; their plans and wild river status were incompatible. With Nelson, Mondale, and William Proxmire all opposed, the money for the study was cut, and conservationists won a major victory over the dam-building corps. Meanwhile, Northern States Power had offered at no cost a "perpetual easement" on more than seventy miles of river frontage the utility owned on the upper Saint Croix. The company, whose development plans had started the movement to save the river, was now willing to give up its development rights to help bring it to a close. Eventually, NSP donated twenty-five thousand acres of land along the upper Saint Croix to the federal government and the states of Minnesota and Wisconsin. One final compromise removed the lower section of the Saint Croix from the bill, calling for further study. Aspinall finally scheduled the bill for a vote in committee, where it passed in June 1968. The House passed it 265 to 7 on 12 September 1968. The Senate agreed two weeks later.[26]

President Johnson signed the bill into law on 2 October in a ceremony at which he also signed Nelson's national hiking and scenic trails bill. The final bill included one hundred miles of the Saint Croix, eighty-five miles of the Namekagon, and twenty-four miles of the Wolf River in Menominee County. Three of the nine rivers designated were in Wisconsin, and $12 million of the $16 million authorized by the bill from the Land and Water Conservation Fund was for those three rivers. Wisconsin was the only state east of the Mississippi River to have any rivers included. Fittingly, Jordahl was at the ceremony to represent Nelson, who was in Wisconsin getting ready to take Interior Secretary Stewart Udall on a raft ride down the Wolf River rapids. Nelson had earlier worked out a state-federal joint venture to buy fifty-nine miles of the Wolf and its tributaries in Langlade County, in addition to protecting the Menominee tribe's river lands.[27]

The Udall-Nelson tour was a two-day campaign swing for Nelson's reelection. Udall praised Nelson at every stop, but the biggest endorsement came at a Green Bay dinner. Legendary Packers coach Vince Lombardi called Nelson "the nation's number one conservationist," and said, "I would vote for him if he were a Republican or Democrat." Lombardi was "making what could be described as his first political appearance," the Associated Press said. Nelson ally David Carley had helped Lombardi make a substantial amount of money in the development business, and encouraged Lombardi to speak up for Nelson. Udall's second day included a boat trip on the Saint Croix and a testimonial banquet in Baldwin, where Nelson's fifth grade teacher in Clear Lake said she "kept an eye on every vote" Nelson made.[28]

The lower Saint Croix, dropped from the initial bill because of costs and park service opposition, went through a long, torturous legislative process. It finally won congressional approval in late 1974, and President Gerald Ford signed the bill in January 1975. It added the lower fifty-two miles of wider, slower, and deeper river from the Saint Croix Falls dam to the Mississippi. The National Park Service, Minnesota, and Wisconsin jointly manage the lower Saint Croix, which is heavily used as a recreational area. Reflecting on the struggle years later, Mondale said, "If it hadn't been for that bill, you'd have had high rises and honky tonks on both sides of that river. It would look like a lot of other rivers that have been exploited. Instead, within twenty-five miles you have three million people who can go there" and enjoy it.[29]

25

Protecting Consumers

THE CONSUMER MOVEMENT was just beginning to find its footing when Nelson went to the Senate. Nelson quickly moved to the forefront of efforts to protect buyers from price gouging and unsafe or inferior products. As a first term senator, he waded into consumer protection issues that challenged the practices of two major and powerful industries, automobile and pharmaceutical. His work on tire and auto safety brought relatively quick legislative action, propelled in part by the automakers' overreaction to consumer advocate and gadfly Ralph Nader, who became a Nelson ally. Nelson's hearings on the drug industry stretched over a decade, attracted widespread attention, and produced a number of significant, hard-won reforms in drug testing, marketing, and pricing.

Nelson's first foray into consumer issues was prompted by a constituent, a Milwaukee engineer who in 1963 wrote "a convincing letter" claiming that many tires being sold, even on new automobiles, were inadequate and incapable of safely carrying even normal loads. Some preliminary investigation confirmed the engineer's claims, and in May 1964 Nelson called for the Commerce Department to investigate tire safety and recommend standards for tires. "We know that bald, worn, overloaded, or shoddily made tires cause accidents," Nelson testified at a Federal Trade Commission hearing. 'We know that safe tires can save our lives. Unfortunately, however, we have no standards for judging how safe and durable a tire is." Witnesses told the FTC that many new cars were equipped with inadequate tires, tire sizes and ratings were meaningless and unintelligible, and drivers had virtually no way to choose the right tires.[1]

Nelson introduced a bill in April 1965 to require safety standards and a grading and labeling system for tires. The automobile industry voluntarily agreed to some Nelson demands, including equipping some 1966 models with larger, heavier tires. After holding hearings on Nelson's bill, the Commerce Committee chairman, Warren Magnuson of Washington, introduced a committee version of the bill with himself as the sponsor. Nelson, who may have been irritated but seldom complained about seeing his ideas hijacked by colleagues, continued to work on the issue. The provisions became part of the broader auto safety bill passed in 1966, which Nelson played a major role in shaping and passing.

Another Nelson bill in early 1965 broke new ground, proposing seventeen safety features for new cars that Nelson said could cut auto fatalities in half. They included shoulder harnesses, collapsible steering wheels, padded dashboards, safety door latches, and safety glass. Many were available as optional equipment at an added cost. The federal government required those features in new cars it purchased for its own use, but not in all vehicles manufactured. A law was needed because the industry believed "safety doesn't sell cars," Nelson said, and "it is the stylist who reigns supreme . . . not the safety and engineering experts." The industry said safety devices added to costs but not to sales because consumers were not interested. "We have never felt it would be a good idea to force customers to accept anything they would not use," a spokesman said. Nelson had some personal experience with that. When he was governor, Wisconsin had passed the nation's first law requiring new cars to have seatbelts. Nelson had a seatbelt in the state car he had driven for four months but had never used it. When a newspaper wanted a photo of the governor putting on his belt, as part of a "wear your seatbelt" campaign, the photographer and reporter had to lift the seat out in order to find the belt.[2]

Unsafe at Any Speed

The climate for auto safety changed dramatically in November 1965, with the publication of Nader's book *Unsafe at Any Speed: The Designed-in Dangers of the American Automobile*. While focused on the Corvair, with a faulty rear suspension system that could cause rollovers, the book charged that the industry knowingly produced and marketed cars with engineering and design deficiencies. Nader's claims got some media attention and interest from a Senate committee. But it was General Motors, the Corvair's manufacturer, that made Nader's crusade a cause célèbre. Press reports that private detectives were shadowing Nader and trying to dig up damaging information to discredit him caused a furor. Nelson demanded a Justice Department investigation to see who was responsible for "this filthy business." When GM admitted it had hired the detectives, Nelson condemned it as "a carefully planned, well-financed scheme whose purpose could only be intimidation or smear." Two weeks later, GM's president took responsibility and apologized before a Senate subcommittee. The incident made auto safety a major national concern and made Nader's book a bestseller. Nader became Nelson's ally on auto safety and other consumer issues over the next several years.[3]

America's highway safety program was a failure, Nelson said in a speech to the National Safety Council in early 1966. "We are doing just enough to ease our conscience. We have set up a lot of organizations. We issue stirring little messages. . . . Then we go out and kill another forty-nine thousand people for 1965, the year of the greatest safety program in history," he said. In some cases the program was simply weak and ineffective, but in others it was "a deliberate premeditated fraud upon the American people." Anyone who dared to question the auto industry "will be informed by a team of industry experts who know everything and reveal nothing that you are absolutely wrong."[4]

But, after the issue heated up, the National Traffic and Motor Vehicle Safety Act that became law in 1966 contained most elements of the three auto safety bills Nelson had introduced. It required standards and labeling for tires, minimum safety standards for all cars, and research into safer car design. Nelson, invited to the bill signing by President Johnson, noted that his bills had been denounced and scoffed at two years earlier, but the final package had passed without a dissenting vote in either house. Nelson continued to blast the tire industry, which resisted and blocked the development of standards. In 1967 he asked manufacturers for information on standards used in recalling defective tires, then—after most refused to answer—authored an amendment requiring manufacturers to recall defective tires.[5] In 2000, when Ford and

Firestone recalled millions of radial tires linked to accidents that caused more than one hundred deaths, it was widely noted that federal standards had not changed since 1968.

The tire industry responded by organizing a drive in 1969 aimed at combating and discrediting Nelson and Nader. The eighteen major tire manufacturers who belonged to the Rubber Manufacturers Association formed a new, well-financed Tire Industry Safety Council. The talk at the industry meeting where the idea was hatched "wasn't so much about how to make tires safer but about how to stuff gravel in the mouths of consumer advocates who call for safer tires," columnist Jack Anderson wrote. A secret memo said Nelson and Nader "can be expected to harass the industry until and unless we can make it uncomfortable to do so." The memo suggested attacking Nelson for insulting the union workers who make tires, and "nudging [Nelson] into the politically ticklish area of state motor vehicle inspections." The way the industry saw it, "When Nader was not pursuing the industry, he was feeding information to Nelson. A hit on one would damage the other, the reasoning went," wrote the author of a book on Nader. More than three hundred thousand tires had been recalled in the previous three years, Nelson noted, but tire makers relied on "image-making and public relations despite the fact that tires continue to fail and the American public still lacks confidence in vehicle tires."[6] If the campaign was designed to muzzle Nelson, it was a colossal failure. Nelson continued to press for requiring manufacturers to recall and repair or replace defective tires and other safety-related defects. In 1973 his bill authorizing the Department of Transportation to order vehicles to be recalled for safety reasons, and requiring manufacturers to pay for repairs, was passed and signed into law.

Probing the Drug Industry

Nelson banged the gavel to open his first hearing as chair of the Senate's Monopoly Subcommittee on 15 May 1967. By the time he wrapped up his extensive hearings on the drug industry ten years later, Nelson had brought about significant changes in the way drugs were prescribed, priced, and promoted. His hearings heightened public awareness, saved consumers and taxpayers billions of dollars, and saved countless lives.

He was not able, however, to overcome the opposition of the powerful $3-billion-a-year pharmaceutical industry to win passage of many of the tough reform bills he introduced.

Estes Kefauver, as chair of a Senate Judiciary subcommittee, had held hearings and won passage in 1962 of amendments to the Food and Drug Act requiring drug manufacturers to prove the safety and effectiveness of their products to the FDA before marketing them. Although his hearings had focused on pricing, the amendments were on safety, and passed largely in response to reports of serious birth defects caused by the use of thalidomide during pregnancy by women in Europe. The Kefauver-Harris drug amendments also gave the FDA jurisdiction to regulate advertising of prescription drugs. Kefauver died in 1963 after a heart attack on the Senate floor.

Nelson became chairman of the Monopoly Subcommittee in June 1966, when his friend Russell Long, about to become Finance Committee chairman, stepped aside and helped Nelson get the post, even though he was not in line by seniority. Nelson wanted the job mainly to tackle the drug issue, which also was a priority for Long. In a Senate speech, Long had charged drug companies with participating in an international cartel to fix prices of antibiotics at "identical, grossly inflated, and unconscionably high prices." Nelson, in an April 1967 speech announcing his planned hearings, said the American public was being "dramatically shortchanged" on prescription drugs, often paying twenty times as much as could be justified. "They are being charged exorbitant prices for drugs which they desperately need. . . . They do not know that drugs which are just as pure and just as potent are available at a fraction of the cost." For example, he said, one firm offered a blood pressure medication to the Defense Department for sixty cents but sold the same drug under a trade name to pharmacists for $39.50.[7]

Nelson began his hearings with a bang. The first day produced testimony that an American drug firm was charging U.S. consumers twice as much as the rest of the world paid for the antipsychotic drug Thorazine. The next day, witnesses produced a survey showing that some cities buying drugs for public hospitals were paying up to forty times as much as other communities for the same drug. A Cornell University doctor and pharmacology professor testified that some drugs had as many as thirty "phony" (brand) names, making "all kinds of serious as well as ludicrous mistakes possible." Another witness said drug firms were spending $3,000 to $4,000 per year per doctor to advertise brand name drugs and persuade doctors to prescribe them. That could represent "a real and present danger to the doctor's independence and to the patient's welfare," he said.[8]

The drug industry fought back. Manufacturers criticized Nelson's hearings as one-sided, sending film clips to Wisconsin television stations and canned editorials to newspapers to complain. In fact, Nelson had invited the drug firms to testify and wanted to get them in front of him, on the record. When he took over the subcommittee, Nelson inherited a staff member, economist Benjamin Gordon, who did the research, lined up witnesses, and helped Nelson orchestrate the hearings. The subcommittee was largely a two-man show on the drug issue, with little participation from other members. The style of the hearings was deliberately confrontational—"black hats and white hats, who's a villain and who isn't a villain," Gordon recalled. Nelson had the advantage of reading prepared testimony of witnesses before the hearings, and Gordon sometimes suggested questions. But "after a short while [Nelson] was so knowledgeable in this subject that even if he didn't have any questions he just knew what the hell it was all about, and he had complete command," Gordon said. "I've never come across anyone with as thorough a command like he had." If the "black hats" wanted to testify, Nelson was glad to accommodate them and more than prepared to match wits on a complicated subject.[9]

Nelson backed down from no one. When the American Medical Association passed a resolution against requiring doctors to prescribe generic drugs, Nelson pointed out that 48 percent of the AMA's income came from drug company advertising in its professional journal. "One might wonder about the [AMA's] independent judgment," he said. He challenged a drug company president about why one customer paid sixty times as much as another for the same medication. When *Reader's Digest* magazine ran an eight-page advertising section promoting brand name drugs, paid for by the Pharmaceutical Manufacturers Association but made to look like regular articles, Nelson complained to the post office, which found it violated federal law.[10]

Spotlight on Chloromycetin

The hearings spotlighted the widespread and inappropriate use of a powerful antibiotic, Chloromycetin, which had been shown fifteen years earlier to have serious, and sometimes fatal, side effects. Testimony showed the drug, heavily promoted by its manufacturer, Parke-Davis, was being prescribed in four million cases a year, including treatment of such minor ailments as colds, sore throats, flu, and acne. Witnesses said its use should have been limited to special cases, to treat diseases like typhoid fever and Rocky Mountain spotted fever, where other drugs were not effective. They estimated that at least 90 percent of the prescriptions written for Chloromycetin were inappropriate. It had been known since 1952 that the drug could cause aplastic anemia, a disease that destroys the body's ability to produce blood, resulting in a painful death. A later study estimated the drug could be fatal to one of every twenty thousand patients using it. With forty million Americans believed to have taken the drug, that would translate to two thousand deaths. Parke-Davis continued to advertise the drug, its salesmen continued to promote it, and doctors continued to prescribe it despite the evidence and warnings. A Food and Drug Administration commissioner, James Goddard, said warnings from the FDA and AMA had not penetrated to physicians. Nelson himself, while visiting San Diego, was given a prescription for Chloromycetin to treat a sty in his eye, but tore it up and used an old-fashioned hot pack instead.[11]

When a Parke-Davis official, Leslie M. Lueck, appeared before his subcommittee, Nelson compared advertisements for Chloromycetin in American medical journals with those in a British publication. The U.S. ad contained a warning required by the FDA of possible fatal side effects, but the British ad did not. Lueck and the counsel for the Pharmaceutical Manufacturers Association, Lloyd Cutler, said the company's ads met all legal requirements for the countries in which they were published. That set Nelson off. He told Cutler:

I have not questioned whether or not it met their requirements. I have assumed that. There is a very serious moral question involved that ought to be brought up. It sure shocks me. What the witness says is we will meet the standards of the country where the drug is sold. That means, of course, there is not a single under-developed country in the world that has any defense against the exploitation of their people for profit by an American corporation who does not warn them of the serious, mighty serious, possibly fatal consequences here. So you mean to testify that your company will stand on the proposition that we will send drugs to Tanganyika, we will send to Latin American countries, we will send drugs to all the undeveloped countries in the world and since they do not have any standards, we will fool them all we can and make a great big profit and never tell the doctors that there is a risk of serious blood dyscrasias. Is that what you are telling the committee?[12]

Cutler protested that Nelson was "indicting every drug company in Great Britain and the United States." Nelson responded, "Any company, drug company or any other kind of company that would do that, I would be pleased to indict on moral grounds. . . . I would think that you would not sleep at night, frankly, you or any drug company that would do that."[13]

Nelson reviewed advertising for Chloromycetin, including an ad from 1956, four years after the dangers of the drug were known. It showed two smiling children, saying, "They never make faces at . . . Chloromycetin," and explaining, "Children really like the taste of this custard flavored preparation. And it slips soothingly down the sorest throat." It did say, in smaller print, that the drug was potent and should not be used indiscriminately for minor infections, but the promotional copy called it a "pleasant-tasting broad spectrum antibiotic preparation for pediatric use" and said mothers appreciated the fact it did not need to be refrigerated. The committee heard testimony from three men whose children had died from blood disorders after using Chloromycetin. They described the gruesome deaths, with their children's bodies covered with bleeding ulcers and later gangrene. "I might just as well have taken a gun and shot him," a California doctor said of his ten-year-old son, to whom he gave Chloromycetin for a urinary infection. "I know of no more torturous death, especially in children," said another doctor, whose five-year-old daughter died after taking the drug. A newspaper publisher told of his nineteen-year-old daughter's "intense suffering beyond description." Others across the country who had lost relatives to the drug wrote Nelson to tell their stories.[14]

The FDA told Nelson's committee in February 1968 that it would take additional steps to discourage improper use of Chloromycetin, including a mailing to every physician in the nation to warn of the hazards associated with it. The FDA also revised the warning label and ordered more disclosure of the hazards in advertising. Nelson said he was not certain that would be enough, suggesting the label say "dangerous drug" at the top, that 90 to 99 percent of the people using the drug should not be, and that "great tragedies" were resulting. "It should warn the doctor not to use it without making some careful investigation. You ought to hit them in the teeth with it—hard," Nelson told Goddard. Goddard said he was "at my wits' end" about what more the FDA could do. "There has never been a drug that has received the attention that chloramphenicol [the generic name] has in the form of editorials, news articles, tight language in the package circular, what is allowed in the ads and everything else," Goddard said.[15]

The combination of the hearings, the widespread publicity they generated, and the new FDA efforts paid off. Five months later, Nelson reported production of Chloromycetin had declined by nearly 80 percent from the previous year. Nelson was pleased that "as a direct consequence" of his hearings "thousands of people have been saved untold agony, and there is no way of knowing how many lives have been spared." But he called it "scandalous" that it took congressional hearings, rather than efforts by the FDA, medical profession, or drug industry to reduce usage of the drug, and singled out the AMA for failing to inform doctors of the danger while accepting misleading advertising to promote the drug.[16]

There were other victories in the first year of the hearings. Two major retail drugstore chains took steps to encourage doctors and patients to use generic drugs. Prices for a tranquilizer, resperine, were cut 70 percent by one drug company and 33 percent by another. One company cut the price of an arthritis drug, prednisone, by 40 percent, and a competitor followed by cutting its price by 80 percent.

Nelson plowed ahead, moving on to investigate the role of drug salesmen, or "detail men," in pushing brand name drugs. Testimony revealed many physicians relied heavily on the representations and assurances made by the detail men, who were trained in sales techniques and often were the doctors' principal source of information on side effects, application, and safety of new drugs.[17]

A Health, Education and Welfare Task Force on Prescription Drugs backed up Nelson's conclusions. In a September 1968 report, the task force said drug makers were making exorbitant profits, grossly overstating the differences between generic and brand name drugs, and wasting research money to duplicate existing drugs. Doctors relied too much on advertising and promotion, and drug salesmen could not be relied upon for objective information, it said. The *Washington Post* called the report "a serious indictment of the American drug industry." The *New York Times* called for an end to the system that charged ill people high prices for brand name prescriptions while selling the same drug for much less to hospitals and government agencies.[18]

Drug manufacturers were reported to be working to defeat Nelson in his 1968 reelection campaign. A Republican Senate campaign staff member said doctors and drug industry representatives were interested in contributing to Nelson's opponent, state senator Jerris Leonard. That prompted howls of outrage. "The drug industry would rather take this money out of the pockets of the American poor and the sick and the elderly and pour it into an attempt to defeat Sen. Nelson than to make the obvious reforms which are needed within the industry," Senator Wayne Morse of Oregon said. The reports were probably overblown, although the drug industry was waging a campaign against Nelson. A Madison doctor sent Nelson a contribution of twenty-two dollars, a dollar for every time a drug salesman attacked Nelson, "by innuendo or by direct statement," during their calls on him during August 1968. It would have been more, the doctor said, but he had been gone fourteen days during August. When Nelson rolled up 62 percent of the vote to win reelection, a frustrated Leonard, who had called Nelson's drug hearings "a political gimmick," acknowledged his problem in opposing Nelson. "No one is for higher drug prices. Everyone is for conservation, and no one wants to ride on unsafe tires," Leonard said in his concession. Nelson resumed his hearings within a month after the election.[19]

Questioning the Pill

The hazards and possible side effects of birth control pills—the Pill for short—put Nelson's hearings back on the nation's front pages in early 1970 and ignited debate about the Pill's safety. Specialists testified on studies linking birth control pills to a wide range of disorders, including heart trouble, liver damage, strokes, diabetes, and breast, cervical, and uterine cancer. The Pill had come into use in the 1960s, and an estimated eight and one-half million American women were "on the Pill" in 1970. Defenders of oral contraceptives said there was no clear evidence linking the pills to cancer or other diseases, and that the Pill was less dangerous to women than being pregnant. "One cigarette is three times as dangerous to life as one pill," a Harvard Medical School physician testified. "The Pill is safe." Others said aspirin—or playing football— was more dangerous than the Pill. Robert Finch, secretary of Health, Education and Welfare, said there was no clear-cut evidence that birth control pills were harmful, although they might cause problems for a small percentage of women who used them. Finch said he hoped the "scare talk" would not make women stop using oral contraceptives, the best method of birth control. But, as *Newsweek* noted, "Most of the headlines were scary—more frightening, indeed than any balanced perspective of informed medical opinion would justify." A Gallup poll done for the magazine found 18 percent of American women taking birth control pills had stopped, with 23 percent more saying they were considering stopping. The biggest single reason for stopping was alarm caused by Nelson's hearings.[20]

Population control advocate Paul Ehrlich, Nelson's friend and ally on environmental issues, said the scare from the hearings could be responsible for one hundred thousand new births to women who quit taking the Pill. "We are just beginning to see the first of the pregnancies of women who panicked in January, stopped their pills, and did not seek or use another means of birth control," Dr. Elizabeth Cornell of Columbia University testified a month later. A woman with a population control group said one hundred thousand unwanted "Nelson babies" would be born in 1970 alone. That claim had a special irony since Nelson himself was a strong proponent of population control. Dr. Cornell said that claims about side effects were unproven. The testimony, she said, was "like a bikini—what has been uncovered has been interesting but what has been left concealed is vital."[21]

Nelson insisted that his primary concern was whether women were getting the information they needed, in a form they could understand it, so they could make their own informed decisions about whether to take the Pill. He said it was difficult for a woman to sort through the technical data available. "But she probably ought to know about five or six things, such as leg pains, to look out for so she can know to see her doctor," he said. The *Newsweek* poll found that "a startling two-thirds of pill-taking women say they have never been told about possible hazards by their physicians." The hearings, Nelson said, were simply giving women information they should have had long before. "What is troublesome is that these hearings are being attacked on the grounds that the people are being told something," Nelson said.[22]

Nelson claimed vindication when the FDA took the unprecedented step in March 1970 of ordering makers of birth control pills to include in every package of pills a leaflet warning of possible dangers. "I have come to the conclusion that the information being supplied to the patient . . . is insufficient," FDA commissioner James Edwards told the committee. The seven-hundred-word leaflet, in clear language, warned of blood clotting and said women with breast cancer, liver diseases, or other ailments should not take the pill. It said the hormones in the Pill were known to cause cancer in animals, but there was no proof they caused it in humans. It urged women to call their doctors if they experienced any unusual changes in their health. It was all Nelson could have asked or expected, and the decision came less than two months after his first hearing on the Pill—lightning-fast speed for the federal bureaucracy. Although the requirement put more information into the hands of women, eighteen months later the number of American women taking oral contraceptives was estimated by one drug company at ten million— more than at the time of the hearings. Many women decided it was safer, or better, to take the pills than to be pregnant.[23]

Oral contraceptives became safer over the next decades, with greatly reduced dosages of the hormones estrogen and progestin. The risks of blood clots, heart attacks, and stroke decreased correspondingly for healthy, nonsmoking women, but the FDA continued to warn women with certain medical conditions, such as a history of blood clots or breast or endometrial cancer, against taking the pill. In 2000, forty years after the pill became available, it was the most popular form of birth control in the United States.[24]

"A Dandy Drug"

Nelson's hearings continued until 1977, exposing exorbitant prices and profits, misleading advertising, drug industry abuses, and the gullibility of American consumers. He had fun with what he called "a dandy drug" called Vivarin, advertised as a stimulant and sold over the counter. Nelson read an advertisement in which a woman said she had been "dull, tired, and drowsy" when her husband came home from work, but after taking the drug she was "a more exciting woman" and had rekindled her relationship with her husband, who sent flowers to his "new wife." Nelson asked, "What's in that drug?" An FDA official said a Vivarin tablet contained caffeine equal to a half cup of coffee, plus a little sugar. "I know a lot of people who drink more coffee than that, and it does not do all that," Nelson said. He heard testimony that many painkillers did not work better than, or even as well as, aspirin, which sold for a fraction of the cost. He blamed drug advertising for creating a nation of "pill-poppers" and said his father, Dr. Anton Nelson, had his own prescription for the common cold—"soup and booze." His father, Nelson recalled, was always cautious about prescribing medicine and would say that "if you get a cold and go to the doctor, you'll get well in a week, and if you stay home and don't go to the doctor, you'll get well in seven days." Nelson said many diet drugs were "sheer quackery," often little more than placebos, questioned whether nonprescription tranquilizers and sleep aids did more harm than good, and warned against the abuse of amphetamines prescribed to aid in weight loss.[25]

In late 1973, the Department of Health, Education and Welfare (HEW) announced that it would dramatically change the way it paid for prescriptions under Medicare and Medicaid, limiting payments to the lowest cost at which the drug was available. In most cases, that meant paying the price for the generic drug rather than the brand name. With HEW spending on prescriptions totaling $1.5 billion a year, savings were estimated at $28 to $60 million in the first fiscal year. The *Washington Post* credited Nelson for the new policy. The HEW announcement was not made to Nelson's subcommittee, however, but before a health subcommittee chaired by Edward Kennedy, who had begun his own hearings on much the same topics Nelson had covered. Nelson's staff fumed. Nelson's drug reform bills were referred to Kennedy's subcommittee, on which Nelson served. Kennedy sat on most of Nelson's legislation, later introducing his own bill, with many of its provisions taken from earlier Nelson proposals. "Kennedy just stole that. Just stole it," one observer said, prompting an uncharacteristic blowup by Nelson in a meeting with Kennedy, which left both senators "quite angry."[26]

Nelson himself had prescribed some strong medicine on drug issues. At various times, he proposed sweeping reforms to establish a national drug testing and evaluation center; require HEW to preapprove drug advertising; create a federal drug directory to list all drugs, including generic names, side effects, and costs; outlaw the use of trade names on prescription drugs; ban salesmen from giving free samples to doctors; and end all prescription drug advertising, including ads in medical journals. The industry considered Nelson its sworn enemy. Pharmaceutical manufacturers were more effective in defending themselves in Congress than in the news media. Few substantive changes ever passed the Congress. What new regulations did result came largely from administrative action by federal agencies. When Nelson ended his hearings on the drug industry in 1977, his subcommittee had held 135 days of testimony on drugs alone. It was one of the three longest series of hearings in Senate history.

26

The Great Lakes

THE GREAT LAKES, the largest fresh surface water system in the world, are the most visible symbol and indicator of what is happening to America's water. The five lakes span 750 miles from east to west, cover 94,000 square miles, and contain about one-fifth of the earth's fresh surface water and 90 percent of the U.S. supply. If their water were spread evenly across the forty-eight contiguous states, it would be more than nine feet deep. More than one-tenth of U.S. residents and one-fourth of Canada's population live in the Great Lakes basin, and more than 250 cities rely on the lakes for their water supply.[1] The fact that both Lake Superior and Lake Michigan border Wisconsin gave Nelson added standing as the leading voice for cleaning up Great Lakes pollution.

"A dull, gray tide of pollution is moving through our Great Lakes, following the path of human progress," he said in early 1965 speeches to the State Bar of Wisconsin and the National Wildlife Federation. The lakes had been becoming more polluted every year for fifty years, he said, "but we paid little attention because we thought these lakes were so vast that even Americans could not destroy them." In fact, he said, lakes are more likely to be permanently ruined than rivers, which can flush themselves over time. For all of its vast size, the Great Lakes eco-system is fragile. "Once it seemed we could only destroy the water in our rivers, but now we are organized, and mechanized, and automated, and now we are embarked on a systematic campaign to destroy the greatest source of fresh water on the face of the earth—the Great Lakes themselves," Nelson said.[2]

The evidence was widespread when Nelson sounded the alarm.

"The southern tip of Lake Michigan is turning into a cesspool," he said, with steel plants, oil refineries, sewage systems, and ships pouring human waste, industrial acids, and iron slag into the lake, causing pollution on the lake bottom that is "practically irreversible," a federal study found. Fish, gulls, and loons were dying by the thousands, beaches were closed, and the pollution was spreading.[3]

"If we want an example of where we are going, we need only look at Lake Erie," he said. The dumping ground for sewage from five major cities, it received, among other things, 2.5 million tons of silt a year. "Some people think it will eventually just fill up," Nelson said. "But before it does, life will cease to exist in its waters." Testing showed high concentrations of chlorides, calcium, sodium, potassium, and sulfate compounds. "It is no longer simply water. It is a disgusting, disgraceful chemical tank." The previous summer, one-fourth of the lake—twenty-six hundred square miles—was without enough oxygen to support life. "Can you conceive of a human failure more enormous than the systematic destruction of a magnificent fresh water lake such as Lake Erie?" he asked.[4]

Nelson's speeches were not all gloom and doom. But there was a litany of problems: "We have destroyed our rivers. . . . We have plundered our forests. . . . We are strip mining our mountains. . . . We are overpopulating and overdeveloping our public parks. . . . We are bulldozing away most of the green spots and open spaces in our cities. . . . We are pushing heavy industry into the last sanctums of natural beauty. . . . We are blighting the landscape with junkyards. . . . We are damming our trout streams, filling in our swamps, cutting down our trees, poisoning our birds and suffocating our fish." Yet, there was hope, he said. "I think we now have the greatest opportunity in recent history for a major breakthrough in conservation. . . . [I]t is entirely possible that we will blow this chance. And if we do, we may never have another like it."[5]

Hope sprang from the Eighty-eighth Congress, Nelson's first session, hailed as the "Conservation Congress" for its passage of landmark legislation—the Wilderness Act, the Land and Water Conservation Fund, and the Clean Air Act of 1963. President Lyndon Johnson highlighted conservation in his 1965 State of the Union speech, declaring that "the next decade should be a conservation milestone," and subsequently proposing an agenda that included pollution controls, park acquisition, and beautification programs. The LBJ agenda borrowed some Nelson programs like scenic easements and wild and scenic river protection, but Nelson did not object, declaring that "popular demand for wise conservation policy has finally found a national voice." The nation and the news media seemed to be awakening to the issue, Nelson said. "I welcome these heartening developments," he told the State Bar. "They are long overdue—and are of priceless value. They give us a new chance to save our land. But I want to warn you that it may be our last chance."[6]

Nelson soon introduced a bill to clean up pollution from ships and port facilities, requiring ships and large pleasure boats to install sewage storage or treatment facilities. The bill was simply the first step in an all-out attack on pollution, he said. But even that brought "a national boating organization down on my neck," he said, because the bill might require boaters to install better toilets. "They're all for fighting pollution, understand—the other guy's pollution. But leave us alone." A large part of the problem with fighting pollution, he said, was that the nation had "a vast network of special interest conservation. We have lost our broad vision of the public interest, and we have fallen to quarreling over little pieces of it." Some parts of Nelson's bill were passed as part of the Clean Water Restoration Act of 1966. In the next session, the Senate passed several parts of his bill as part of a comprehensive water pollution bill, but it died in the House. Nelson's major provisions finally became law in the Water Quality Improvement Act of 1970. He then began a push to control waste dumping in oceans and the Great Lakes, which was incorporated into a broader Marine Protection, Research and Sanctuaries Act passed in October 1972.[7]

Nelson had warned, in speeches and a series of articles he authored for the *Milwaukee Journal,* that the price tag on a comprehensive pollution cleanup effort would be huge. His estimates ranged from $50 to $100 billion over fifteen to twenty-five years. That was a lot of money, he acknowledged, but "we are a rich nation" spending nearly $50 billion a year on national defense, $50 billion on interstate highway development, $5 billion on the space program, several billion on agriculture, and a billion on Appalachia's economy. The nation made those investments because it believed they were in its vital interest. "Is there anything really more vital in the long view of history," he asked, "than the proper protection and conservation of our fresh water lakes, rivers, and streams, our wilderness, the soils and forests, the air we breathe, the bugs and birds and animals and the habitat in which they live? I think not."[8]

Nelson announced his sweeping antipollution package—the most comprehensive set of water pollution bills ever introduced in Congress—in February 1966. "They will revolutionize America's approach to water pollution. They will involve considerable costs. They will undoubtedly be controversial. But they are also inescapable," he said. "My judgment tells me that the people of America are ready at long last for this kind of legislation." Recapping "the grim facts" about the state of the nation's water, he quoted an unnamed New York woman: "We Americans are standing ankle deep in sewage, shooting rockets to the moon." The problem had been clearly documented, Nelson said; the question was what to do about it. "Surely, we cannot build a great society while standing ankle deep in sewage."[9]

Among the "revolutionary concepts" in Nelson's package of six bills was a proposal for the federal government to pay 90 percent of the cost of local sewage treatment facilities, which could cost billions of dollars a year. "Cleaning up the waters of America is even more important than the building of the interstate highway system," which was built with the same funding formula, Nelson said. At the time, the federal government was paying 30 to 40 percent of the cost of treatment plants. Many communities did not even apply for the money, Nelson said, because they could not afford the other 60 to 70 percent. The interstate highway funding came, columnist Drew Pearson noted, because of "pressure from the oil, gas, tire, auto, and Teamster lobbies. . . . As a result, the nation is crossed and counter-crossed by new highways. But there are no powerful lobbies working against pollution." Nelson's package also included a carrot-and-stick approach to help industries build their own treatment plants, with federal grants and loans to cover up to 50 percent of the costs, while strengthening federal enforcement and increasing penalties for industries that continued polluting the water.[10]

Nelson knew that his multi-billion-dollar programs would be a hard sell because of sharply escalating costs of American involvement in the Vietnam War, which he opposed. Compared with Nelson's vision, President Johnson's conservation program for 1966 was a drop in the bucket—a river cleanup proposal to cost $50 million the first year and $7 to $10 billion over ten years. Nelson praised Johnson's program as "the best any president has ever done," but said it fell far short of what was needed. "I admire his courage in proposing much stronger enforcement procedures," Nelson said, but "we cannot purify our lakes and streams with a court order. We must actually build the physical plants necessary to remove sewage and industrial waste." As with many Nelson environmental proposals, progress was slow and incremental. Nelson's 90 percent funding bill went nowhere in that session, and he lost on an amendment to provide even 50 percent funding. Congress did authorize a 30 percent federal share, with incentives that could increase it 55 percent in some circumstances, but the grants for treatment plants were a paltry $3.5 billion over six years, a small fraction of Nelson's plan.[11]

It was only in the post–Earth Day era that Congress passed the Clean Water Act of 1972, the first comprehensive law to address water pollution problems. The bill had a three-year cost of $25 billion, including $18 billion for grants to states to underwrite 75 percent of the costs of new treatment plants. The bill set a goal of eliminating all polluting discharges into the nation's waterways by 1985. It spent three times as much as President Richard Nixon wanted, so he vetoed it. Both houses of Congress had passed it unanimously and easily overrode his veto, although Nixon impounded some of the money and delayed its release, slowing the effort. Between 1972 and 1990 the nation spent nearly $150 billion on sewage treatment facilities, roughly equivalent to Nelson's projection in 1965.[12]

Persistence Pays Off

Many shared the credit on most major environmental issues. Senator Edmund Muskie of Maine, chairman of a key subcommittee, was the main sponsor of the Clean Water Act, Clean Air Act, and many environmental bills that included parts of Nelson's program. In one area, however, Nelson's persistence was virtually the only reason that a joint federal-state effort began to clean up the Great Lakes. He singlehandedly pushed the issue for more than a year and a half, in the face of strong resistance from Wisconsin Governor Warren P. Knowles.

Nelson wrote the governors of Minnesota, Michigan, and Wisconsin in March 1966 to call for convening federal-interstate conferences on Great Lakes pollution. Reports of mounting pollution in Green Bay, the Milwaukee area, and the Duluth-Superior area made it clear one state could not solve the problem by itself, he said. A federal team of more than twenty-five experts would survey and document Wisconsin water problems if such a conference were called, Nelson said. Governor Knowles rejected the idea, suggesting that the three states meet on their own. Inviting federal participation could bring federal enforcement and cleanup orders, he feared. Not so, Nelson said, if the conference were limited to Wisconsin and federal representatives. The conference could bring court orders and enforcement action under federal pollution laws, but only for interstate pollution.[13]

After two months of impasse, Nelson went on the attack, saying Knowles was "playing with dynamite" and jeopardizing Lake Michigan cleanup. He released a letter from a federal official in Chicago saying Wisconsin had refused to provide data on industrial waste going into the Lake Michigan basin. A state official explained there was a "gentlemen's agreement" with the paper mills not to give pollution data to the federal government or make it public. "There is a strong cover-up here which needs to be explored and exposed," the *Capital Times* said. "It is an example of how the state's hands have been tied in the anti-pollution program. It helps to explain why our streams, rivers and lakes have become open sewers." Nelson continued to push and prod Knowles, writing Interior Secretary Stewart Udall to confirm that a team of federal experts was ready to help, and criticizing Knowles at a House subcommittee hearing in Milwaukee. "We are losing the war against pollution in Wisconsin," Nelson testified.[14]

After six months, Nelson gave up on Knowles and asked Udall to call the conference on his own. The federal government had that authority where pollution was clearly an interstate problem, as Nelson had told Udall several times. When Udall took no action either, Nelson fired off another letter in March 1967 to Great Lakes governors, expanding the list to include Illinois.[15]

When six more months passed with no action, Nelson lost his patience. He "exploded in anger" at a conference of a Great Lakes task force and Great Lakes senators in Washington, decrying the apparent lack of concern over pollution in the lakes. He singled out the Great Lakes Commission, with representatives of eight states, for its failure to support his call for a federal-state conference. "I can't get the governors of these states to suggest a conference. . . . They're afraid of the industries and municipalities that might be hurt and groups like yours should be yelling their heads off," Nelson told the director of the commission. "I need help, because this is a rapidly deteriorating, horrible situation." If evidence were needed, a seventy-five-mile oil slick had just been discovered on Lake Michigan, and Chicago area beaches were threatened. Lake Erie was dead and Lake Michigan dying, Nelson said, asking rhetorically if the Midwest was going to be "stupid" enough to let Lake Superior die as well.[16]

Governor Otto Kerner of Illinois, the only Democrat among the four, finally requested a conference on Lake Michigan, and Udall ordered it to be held in Chicago on 31 January 1968 with representatives of Wisconsin, Illinois, Indiana, and Michigan. Three months later, Udall approved a cleanup program which Nelson said would "eliminate most phosphate chemicals, reduce both municipal and industrial pollution, and bring pollution from ships, pesticides, nuclear power plants and dredging operations under control."[17]

Nelson did not stop there. He asked Udall to call a similar conference on Lake Superior. "Each and every day, sixty thousand tons of pulverized mine wastes are poured into the lake, along with municipal and shipboard wastes," Nelson said. Udall was reluctant to act because Minnesota Congressman John Blatnik, a Democrat and chairman of the House Public Works Committee, would object. A prime target of Nelson's was Silver Bay, a taconite plant operated by Reserve Mining Company in Blatnik's district. The plant was dumping taconite tailings into Lake Superior, the source of drinking water for many communities in Minnesota and Wisconsin. Facing pollution controls, the company would most likely threaten to close the operation, and perhaps even do so, threatening thousands of jobs.[18]

Nelson urged Udall several times to act but "had just about given up." In the final days of the Johnson administration, as Udall prepared to leave his cabinet post to a Nixon appointee, Nelson made one last effort. "I had to tell him an outright lie—which I was happy to do, since it was for a good purpose," Nelson said. He told Udall that a former Nelson staff member in Wisconsin had told him that Knowles was about to call for a federal-state conference, as soon as the new Republican administration took over in a few days. "Now, Stewart, Governor Knowles hasn't been on our side on this issue," Nelson said. "It would be a great tragedy to allow Governor Knowles to get credit for saving one of the three greatest bodies of fresh water in the world, when you could get the credit and save one of the greatest lakes on the planet. He's going to do this momentarily. I think you ought to pre-empt him." Udall picked up the telephone and told an assistant to draft an order for a Lake Superior conference immediately. He issued the call in his last two days on the job. "If he had waited three days, Nixon never would have done it," Nelson said. The conference initiated a battle over the Silver Bay taconite plant that went on for years, in and out of court, finally resulting in 1977 in approval of a tailings storage basin seven miles away from the lake and controls on air pollution. Nelson called it "the most productive and defensible 'white lie' I ever told."[19]

"It is my firm belief that . . . Senator Nelson's sustained attack on Great Lakes pollution, his dramatizing of the 'burning' of Ohio rivers soaked with oil waste, and his description of once beautiful Lake Erie as a 'disgusting chemical tank' . . . led to the . . . interstate pollution conferences on Lakes Erie, Michigan and Superior, which led to enforceable orders to clean up the Great Lakes, with impressive results," said William Bechtel, a longtime Nelson staff director who later served as federal chair of the Great Lakes Regional Commission.[20]

27

The Fight to Ban DDT

JANET LEE, Nelson's sister, was visiting the governor's mansion, in the small Madison enclave of Maple Bluff, on a day when the village was aggressively spraying and fogging with DDT to kill mosquitoes. "If it's going to kill mosquitoes," Janet asked, "how many other things is it going to kill?" Nelson, who would become a leading voice for pesticide control and the first member of Congress to propose a ban on DDT, always credited Janet with raising his awareness of the issue.[1]

By the early 1960s, Janet was not the only one questioning the widespread use of DDT. Rachel Carson's groundbreaking *Silent Spring*, published in 1962, eloquently examined, in simple language, the effect of chemical pesticides on songbirds. Carson's widely read book touched off a national debate and helped launch the modern environmental movement.

The insecticide DDT had been hailed as nothing short of miraculous when it was introduced during World War II. The "miracle bug killer," sprayed from airplanes, had killed 85 to 95 percent of the mosquitoes, flies, and other disease-bearing insects on Saipan within hours of the landing by American troops in 1944. Top army specialists in preventive medicine compared the development of DDT to the discovery of penicillin or antiseptics. Although not then available to civilians and "still dangerous to man unless properly used," an Associated Press story said the chemical "may open up an era of better living in the postwar world." Saipan was the first time it was sprayed from airplanes, but DDT was being widely used in other ways by the armed forces. Soldiers were dusting their underwear with it as an antilouse powder. Civilians

273

and GIs alike were sprayed with dusting guns, the nozzles stuck up their sleeves and inside trouser waistbands. Periodically, "delousing spray" was used on troops after their showers, to kill lice and eggs.[2]

When DDT became available to the general public in 1945, it was widely used by farmers and householders alike to kill flies, mosquitoes, bedbugs, fleas, and other insects. A one-pound pressurized DDT "bomb" sold for four dollars, and it cost as little as seventy-five cents a pound when purchased to use as a powder or spray. One application could keep a barn free of flies for a whole season, a University of Wisconsin entomologist said. In the future, homes and barns painted with paint containing DDT might remain insect-free for years, he said. The city of Rockford, Illinois, hit by a polio epidemic, was sprayed with DDT from an army plane to kill flies, believed to be spreading the disease. Eagle River, a resort area in northern Wisconsin, paid for aerial spraying to give tourists a bug-free summer.[3]

There were early warnings that the miraculous chemical could cause harm. In 1945 an Interior Department scientist said that excessive use of DDT could kill birds, fish, turtles, and frogs. DDT "will kill a lot of things we don't want killed," Dr. Clarence Cottam warned. "It kills beneficial insects as well as obnoxious insects. Therefore, it should be used with understanding, intelligence and caution. If used in excess, it will be like scalping to cure dandruff." A congressional committee was told that DDT showed up in the meat, milk, and butter of cows fed on crops dusted with DDT. A proposal to spray the shoreline of Wisconsin's huge Lake Winnebago, where millions of lake flies hatched each year, was abandoned in 1947 when the United States Public Health Service said it could harm beneficial insects, fish, and wildlife. Even so, Swiss chemist Dr. Paul Mueller won the 1948 Nobel Prize in medicine for his discovery of the insect-killing properties of DDT, credited with increasing the world's food supply and suppressing insect-borne diseases. Twenty years later, in the face of mounting evidence that DDT was killing birds and causing other environmental damage, scientists continued to defend its use.[4]

The first regulation of DDT and other pesticides was intended to prevent excessive use. Wisconsin passed a law in 1947 making it illegal to use insecticides in amounts that might be dangerous to humans or animals, although it was not clear what a "safe" level was. The state

Conservation Department then issued "drastic new rules" requiring seven-day notification of any planned use of DDT in forest and non-crop areas. The action came in response to complaints from property owners on northern Wisconsin lakes, who believed DDT spraying was killing fish. Milk and dairy products contaminated with DDT would be banned from interstate commerce, a Food and Drug Administration official told a Milwaukee convention of entomologists in 1949. DDT had been found to have a "chronic toxic effect on animals," he said, and to have a cumulative effect passed on from a dairy cow to someone who drinks the milk. A week later, the U.S. Department of Agriculture issued a statement saying: "There is no justification for public alarm as to the safety of the milk supply from the standpoint of DDT contamination." However, the department issued new warnings against using DDT in dairy barns, on dairy cattle, or on crops fed to dairy cattle.[5]

With some restrictions and cautions, DDT use continued unabated. Including its chemical derivatives, DDT was the world's most widely used insecticide for more than twenty years. In the 1950s, communities began to spray with DDT to fight Dutch elm disease, a fungus spread by the elm bark beetle, which killed hundreds of thousands of American elms and left some cities and neighborhoods virtually treeless. In Wisconsin, a debate raged about whether DDT's use to save trees was justified when there was evidence the chemical also was killing songbirds. The state entomologist said DDT was the only insecticide that would be effective, which justified its use. Bird lovers asked for more regulations or a total end to spraying. Some communities did cut back or quit spraying DDT for mosquitoes or Dutch elm disease, or used a less toxic chemical.

In 1959 the Milwaukee suburb of Shorewood nearly experienced the silent spring Rachel Carson's book would describe a few years later. A study by University of Wisconsin wildlife biologists found that the number of robins nesting in DDT-sprayed areas was substantially lower than in nonsprayed areas. Their songbird census found differences of 69 to 98 percent between sprayed and nonsprayed areas. Shorewood, which had sprayed more liberally than other municipalities, had 2 percent as many robins as the unsprayed control areas, and only 10 percent as many birds of all species. The state entomologist criticized the study as unscientific, and the Janesville city forester, while admitting that DDT affected songbirds, said the choice was "between using it or losing our trees." He did not mention the other option: losing the birds. By 1962 the city of Milwaukee and many other local governments had voluntarily stopped using DDT, citing the harmful effects on bird life.[6]

Evidence continued to mount that DDT was having serious, long-term consequences. Most bald eagle carcasses examined in North America had traces of DDT residue. Worse yet, DDT was discovered in fish and penguins in Antarctica, an uninhabited continent where no pesticides had ever been used. Researchers found high DDT levels in fish and gulls in Door County, the scenic peninsula between the waters of Green Bay and Lake Michigan in northeastern Wisconsin. The Conservation Department found DDT residue in all of the hundreds of fish it collected from thirty lakes across the state, with higher levels in commercial species in Lake Michigan.

Nelson had heard enough. He announced in January 1966 that he would introduce a bill to ban DDT. In the meantime, he urged the Department of Agriculture to stop recommending DDT use by farmers and gardeners. Despite "overwhelming evidence of damage to the environment and the dangers of DDT contamination of feed and food," Nelson said, a department publication included 363 recommended uses of DDT. On 12 July 1966 he introduced the bill to ban the sale of DDT. "The long range biological effects of this global contamination, which is building up every day that use of DDT continues, are not yet known, but the potential is present for a national calamity," Nelson said. "Indeed, the damage already done is colossal." He could not find a single House member to introduce a companion bill. The legislation was sent to committee and not even scheduled for a hearing. Nelson continued to introduce it every session.[7]

In 1968 DDT went on trial in Wisconsin. The Environmental Defense Fund (EDF), representing two citizen groups, filed a petition with the Wisconsin Department of Natural Resources (DNR), charging that DDT was a pollutant of Wisconsin's waters. That required the DNR to hold a formal administrative hearing on the question. A finding that DDT was a pollutant could allow it to be banned in Wisconsin. The implications were broad, as the case won national attention and media coverage. EDF, a national organization, handled the legal case on behalf of the Citizens Natural Resources Association and the Izaak Walton League.

When the hearing began in the ornate assembly chambers of Wisconsin's capitol, Nelson was the lead witness for the environmentalists. He was not a scientist or expert witness, as were many who testified later. But his history of advocacy and knowledge of the issue made him a logical choice to frame the question in a larger context and "to lend stature, importance and publicity to the hearing that followed."[8]

Nelson, in a presentation that was "quintessential political environmentalism," said that damage done by DDT far outweighed its benefits. He catalogued cases from around the world where DDT had been found in high levels in birds, fish, and wildlife, and even in human fat tissue. "In only one generation," he said, pesticides such as DDT "have contaminated the atmosphere, the seas, the lakes and the streams and infiltrated the tissues of most of the world's creatures, from reindeer in Alaska to penguins in the Antarctic, including man himself." Lake Michigan, he said, "had the highest concentrations of pesticides of any of the Great Lakes, and was swiftly approaching the lethal stage." Wisconsin's action to ban DDT, he said, "will represent the first ray of hope on the horizon for endangered species and perhaps man for many generations to come."[9]

The hearing continued intermittently for several months, with both sides presenting expert witnesses. Industry witnesses denied DDT was a significant pollutant and said it had been valuable for disease control and crop production. But DDT use had already dropped sharply in the United States as other pesticides began to replace it. The peak year for DDT production was 1963, as *Silent Spring* gained notice. The president of the nation's largest DDT manufacturer testified that U.S. production in 1963 was 183 million pounds, but had dropped to 103 million pounds by 1967, of which 70 percent was exported, mostly to countries which used it to fight malaria.[10]

Environmentalists felt they had won a victory, exposing DDT as harmful to the environment, putting the pesticide industry on the defensive, and raising the issue in the national spotlight and even the network television news. The hearing ended in May 1969, and hearing examiner Maurice Van Sustern took the matter under advisement. By the time he declared a year later that DDT was, indeed, a pollutant of Wisconsin waters, the pesticide already had been banned in Wisconsin, Michigan, and elsewhere, in large part due to evidence produced at the hearing. Pressure was mounting for federal action, and although a federal ban was still three years away, some federal agencies moved to restrict DDT's use. The tide clearly had turned.[11]

Wisconsin's legislature enacted a ban on distribution, sale, and use of DDT in January 1970 and Governor Warren Knowles signed it into law the next month. The ban—similar to the federal ban Nelson could not find a cosponsor for in 1966—sailed through the assembly unanimously and passed the state senate on a voice vote.[12]

Federal action was slower. Nelson and a growing army of environmentalists kept the pressure on. The Department of Agriculture announced in late 1969 it was "canceling" the use of DDT in residential areas, and the resulting publicity convinced many Americans that the chemical had been banned. In fact, the order was appealed by chemical companies, beginning a lengthy legal review process that might last several years, with no restrictions on DDT in the meantime. The ban was "virtually nonexistent," Nelson complained, while the public had been misled into thinking the government had enacted a ban. "No single use of DDT in the United States has been stopped," he said. He urged the chairman of the newly created Environmental Quality Council to declare DDT "an imminent hazard to the public" and order a stop to its manufacture and use. Several environmental groups filed a lawsuit against the secretary of agriculture asking for an outright ban on DDT, but Secretary Clifford Hardin said it did not meet the "imminent hazard" standard. "DDT has been shown to be a carcinogen and an environmental hazard," an EDF biologist said. "If that doesn't constitute an imminent hazard to the public, what does?"[13]

The new Environmental Protection Agency (EPA), created in late 1970, took over responsibility for pesticide regulation. Within six weeks, the EPA had begun the process that would lead to a ban on DDT. A lawsuit by EDF resulted in a court order for a sixty-day review to see whether DDT use should be banned immediately. Environmentalists were disappointed when the EPA concluded that DDT should not be immediately suspended, allowing use of the product while court appeals from manufacturers dragged on.

On 14 June 1972, EPA administrator William Ruckelshaus announced the final cancellation of virtually all remaining uses for DDT in the United States. The ban was effective 31 December 1972 to allow time for a phase-out. Both manufacturers and environmentalists quickly challenged it in court, the industry seeking to nullify the order and the EDF asking for an immediate ban. On 13 December 1973, a federal appeals court upheld the EPA ban, ending the long struggle.[14]

A Broader Focus

Nelson hailed the EPA's action, calling it "a significant environmental decision that will have world-wide repercussions." DDT, he said, had been "irrationally and excessively sprayed and dusted and has spread its killing qualities throughout the entire world-wide ecosystem." Nelson already had broadened his focus to include a far wider range of pesticides. The day after Ruckelshaus's announcement, Nelson told a Senate committee that "the single strategy of chemical pest control has been an economic, environmental, agricultural and public health failure." Nelson was testifying on the proposed Federal Environmental Pesticide Control Act, of which he was a sponsor. The new law, the first major revision in pesticide regulation since 1947, took effect in late 1972. It required all pesticides to be registered with the EPA, which had authority to determine if they posed a high risk to humans or the environment, and severely restricted or prohibited their use.[15]

One reporter, writing about Nelson's battle against DDT, said Nelson had "a bug's viewpoint . . . he hates the stuff."[16] That was true of pesticides in general. Nelson introduced legislation in 1970 to ban the toxic pesticides aldrin and dieldrin, which were ultimately banned by the EPA as cancer-causing agents. He sponsored bills to establish a national pesticide commission, to set uniform standards for pesticides, and to prohibit the sale or shipment of specific toxic chemicals. They did not pass but helped lay the groundwork for pesticide regulation in the 1970s, and many Nelson proposals eventually became law.

He fought a long battle against the use of 2,4,5-T, a toxic herbicide containing dioxin, used in Vietnam as a defoliant and domestically as a weed and brush killer. The EPA halted used of the herbicide (which, combined with 2,4-D, was known as Agent Orange), in Vietnam in April 1970, citing its possible link to birth defects. Nelson subsequently sponsored an amendment to the defense appropriations bill in 1970 to prohibit the use of all defoliants in Vietnam, calling their use "a dangerous kind of environmental warfare that represents a real threat for world-wide disaster." That amendment failed as the Pentagon lobbied heavily that pesticides were needed to protect the troops. But the Defense Department announced a phase-out of the defoliation program the next year.[17]

The EPA order also put an end to home use of the chemical as a weed killer. That did not affect most use of the herbicide for brush and weed control on range, pasture, forest, highway rights-of-way and other nonfarm land. In 1972, when several hundred acres of woodland in southwestern Wisconsin's Grant County were sprayed with 2,4,5-T from a helicopter, Nelson was outraged. "It is hardly believable," he said, "that after the lessons of Vietnam, we would tolerate the same tactics of defoliation to be used in our own backyard." The spraying— paid for by farmers to clear the hillsides for use as pasture for beef cattle—violated both state and federal laws, he charged, which required advance notification and prohibited spraying that would run off into streams and rivers. "It is utter folly . . . to permit the uncontrolled use of this pesticide for a single additional day."[18]

While state agriculture officials, chemical companies, scientists, and farmers defended the chemical and the property owners' right to use it, Nelson wrote the EPA to ask for an outright ban on 2,4,5-T. "The continued widespread use of this agent is clearly a dangerous gamble," Nelson wrote EPA's Ruckelshaus. The ban on DDT came only after "worldwide permanent environmental damage had been done," Nelson said. "Certainly it should not be necessary to travel the same disastrous route with 2,4,5-T that we traveled with DDT." Nelson called dioxin, contained in the herbicide, "the most toxic substance ever synthetically produced. . . . About a drop in a medicine dropper can kill an estimated 1,200 men." There had been no adequate studies on the safety of 2,4,5-T, Nelson said, asking that its use be banned unless it was proven safe.[19]

One of the defenders of the pesticide, a University of Wisconsin agronomist, invited Nelson to attend the 1973 Wisconsin Pest Control Conference with Industry, which included a session on the controversial Grant County spraying. It was "a convention of pesticide defenders," and Nelson agreed to speak and face his harshest critics. He stunned the audience of four hundred when he announced that the EPA had told him it was preparing to cancel its approval of the use of 2,4,5-T on range land, which would ban the kind of spraying done in Grant County. A lawsuit delayed the EPA action, but in April 1973 a federal appeals court ruled in EPA's favor and a cancellation order was issued. Nelson continued to push for a total ban and fought unsuccessfully in 1974 to stop use of the chemical in national forests. It was 1979 before the EPA finally issued an order suspending about 75 percent of the uses of 2,4,5-T. A total ban came in 1985, when Dow Chemical, the manufacturer, withdrew its opposition and the EPA cancelled its registration.[20]

Declaring attempts to control insects with chemicals a failure, Nelson introduced a bill calling for integrated pest control, an environmentally sensitive program that minimizes the use of pesticides and focuses instead on natural and biological solutions. The bill authorized a $2 million federal pilot program to do field research in nonchemical pest control and provided grants to researchers. The chemical program was doomed from the start, Nelson said, because insects developed resistance to pesticides. "Some would have us believe that we either use pesticides or starve," he said. In fact, "[i]f we continue to rely on broad spectrum chemicals, we may very well imperil our abilities to continue to produce an adequate supply of food and fiber."[21] His bill passed the Senate in 1972 but died in the House. Years later, reflecting on his career, Nelson said the failure to win approval of integrated pest management was his biggest disappointment.

On the other hand, the long battle to ban DDT had paid huge dividends. Twenty-five years after the ban took effect, there were ten times as many bald eagles in the United States as there had been in 1972. DDT, which the birds took in through fish they ate, weakened the shells of the eagles' eggs so that they broke during incubation. From a low of fewer than five hundred nesting pairs of eagles in the 1960s, the population soared to more than five thousand pairs in 1997.[22] By the year 2000, bald eagles were off the endangered species list. Peregrine falcons, ospreys, and brown pelicans—all in danger of extinction—also rebounded after the DDT ban.

28

Vietnam

NELSON KNEW almost from the start that the Vietnam War was a mistake. He tried to prevent large-scale U.S. involvement in Vietnam before it began. When that failed, he took an early, politically risky stance against the war.

Nelson was not the first senator to question U.S. involvement. A 1962 visit to Vietnam had convinced Senate majority leader Mike Mansfield that the United States had already wasted $2 billion and should extricate itself. Ernest Gruening of Alaska and Wayne Morse of Oregon were expressing serious doubts, if not outright opposition to U.S. involvement. Although the 16,500 U.S. servicemen in Vietnam at the beginning of 1964 were there in an "advisory" or supporting role, not as combat troops, 118 had died in Southeast Asia in 1963. But the critics and skeptics—especially among elected officials—were still few in number when Nelson went on the record.[1]

Lyndon Johnson, whose visit to Vietnam as vice president in 1961 led him to encourage President Kennedy to defend Southeast Asia from communism, was now commander in chief. Vietnam policy loomed as an issue in the 1964 presidential election, with Johnson facing conservative Senator Barry Goldwater of Arizona. Goldwater wanted stronger, swifter action to end the conflict. In May 1964 Goldwater suggested using low-yield, tactical nuclear weapons to defoliate enemy supply lines and forests along the border in Vietnam.[2]

Goldwater's comments and the furor they caused were probably what prompted a reporter in Wausau, Wisconsin, to ask Nelson about Vietnam the next day. Nelson, in town for a dinner honoring Wisconsin

Congressman David Obey, pulled no punches. The United States should reexamine its commitment and "set some timetable for withdrawal from the situation," he said in an interview. "If the government cannot become viable, independent, and successfully defend itself, then the United States is going to have to make an orderly withdrawal. I don't think that additional men and materials and economic aid . . . is going to solve the problem in South Vietnam." France had given up and pulled out of Vietnam in 1954, losing despite having three hundred thousand troops in the country, Nelson said. There was a lesson there, he suggested.[3]

In an interview with a Wausau television reporter, Obey recalled, "Gaylord said the war was a terrible mistake, and if the country doesn't reverse itself we will end up with five hundred thousand troops in Vietnam. The interviewer stopped the camera and said, 'I think you misspoke. I'll ask the question again.' Gaylord said that was what he meant to say, and the TV person said, 'Well, it's your funeral.'" Leaving the station, Nelson said to Obey, "Maybe I've beat myself."[4]

The White House strategy was to minimize Vietnam as an issue in the 1964 presidential campaign. "Keep Vietnam quiet. . . . Make it a functional, factual issue, send more aid, more weapons, a few more men to Saigon" in the words of author and historian David Halberstam. At about the time Nelson was asking questions in Wausau, former Secretary of State Dean Acheson was warning the White House that things were not going well in Vietnam. LBJ's inner circle talked about getting Congress to pass a resolution, to protect the president on the issue and neutralize Goldwater. A vague resolution was drafted, but none was introduced.[5]

The Tonkin Gulf incident changed everything. It gave Johnson the congressional stamp of approval he wanted. Despite assurances to the contrary, the resolution passed by Congress in response to the incident would later be cited as the authority for massive expansion of the U.S. role in Southeast Asia, deployment of a half million troops, bombing of North Vietnam, and even an invasion of Cambodia. No further vote to declare or expand the war was ever taken by the Congress.

What really happened in the Gulf of Tonkin in August 1964 was murky at the time and remains so, despite a number of books and inquiries into the naval skirmish off the coast of North Vietnam. It is clear there was an attack by North Vietnamese torpedo boats, known as PT boats, on 2 August 1964 against the destroyer USS *Maddox,* but not that it was an unprovoked attack against an American ship on routine patrol, as it was portrayed. The ship was on an intelligence mission and at times within the twelve-mile offshore limit North Vietnam claimed as its boundary. The *Maddox* fired back and sank one of the PT boats. Two days later the Pentagon reported another deliberate and unprovoked attack on two U.S. destroyers, the *Maddox* and the *C. Turner Joy,* operating in the same area. Whether there was such an attack, or whether the American warships were spooked into firing at phantom attackers, is still debated. On the basis of Pentagon reports, Johnson ordered U.S. air strikes against the North Vietnam bases of the PT boats and an oil depot.

Late that night, the president told the American public that he had ordered retaliation after "renewed hostile actions" against U.S. ships. The American response would be "limited and fitting," he declared. "We still seek no wider war." He was sending a resolution to the Congress, he said, where leaders of both parties already had assured him of their support.[6]

Tonkin Gulf Resolution

"As I have repeatedly made clear, the United States intends no rashness and seeks no wider war," Johnson said in a message to Congress the next day. His resolution, which became known as the Gulf of Tonkin resolution, was simple: "That the Congress approves and supports the determination of the President, as Commander in Chief, to take all necessary measures to repel any armed attack against the forces of the United States and to prevent further aggression." A second section said the peace and security of Southeast Asia were vital to the U.S. national interest.[7]

Nelson wanted to know what that meant. Was the Congress being asked to write the president a blank check? He asked J. William Fulbright, chairman of the Foreign Relations Committee and floor manager for the resolution, on the Senate floor. "Am I to understand that it is the sense of Congress that we are saying to the executive branch, 'If it becomes necessary to prevent further aggression, we agree now, in advance, that you may land as many divisions as deemed necessary, and engage in a direct military assault on North Vietnam, if it becomes the judgment of the Executive, the Commander in Chief, that this is the only way to prevent further aggression?'"8

That would be "a grave decision on the part of our country," Fulbright said. "I personally feel it would be very unwise under any circumstances to put a large land army on the Asian continent. It has been a sort of article of faith since I have been in the Senate, that we should not be bogged down." But, he admitted, "I do not know what the limits are" on what action the president could take. "I do not know how to answer the Senator's question and give him an absolute assurance that large numbers of troops would not be put ashore. I would deplore it. And I hope the conditions do not justify it now."9

Nelson said he intended to vote for the resolution. "I do not think, however, that Congress should leave the impression that it consents to a radical change in our mission or objective in South Vietnam," he said. That mission was to help establish "a viable, independent regime, which can manage its own affairs, so that ultimately we can withdraw from South Vietnam." Fulbright agreed, and said the resolution was "quite consistent with our existing mission and what has been our understanding of what we have been doing in South Vietnam for the last ten years."

Nelson was still uneasy enough that when he walked into the Senate with Senator George McGovern the next morning, for the final debate on the resolution, he had an amendment in his hand. It said: "The Congress also approves and supports the efforts of the President to bring the problem of peace in Southeast Asia to the Security Council of the United Nations, and the President's declaration that the United States, seeking no extension of the present military conflict, will respond to provocation in a way that is 'limited and fitting.' Our continuing policy is to limit our role to the provision of aid, training assistance, and military advice, and it is the sense of Congress that, except when provoked to a greater response, we should continue to avoid a direct military involvement in the Southeast Asian conflict."10

McGovern and Nelson had talked intensely about the issue and agreed that neither could support the resolution if, McGovern said, it meant "an open-ended endorsement of a larger American role in Vietnam." McGovern said he would support Nelson's amendment. Soon after the debate began, the pair walked up to Fulbright in the front row of the Senate, and Nelson said he wanted to introduce the amendment. "Don't do it," Fulbright said. "We want this mainly to show bipartisan support and to undercut Goldwater. We'd like to see it pass unanimously. The campaign is coming up and Goldwater is going to hit him for not using our full power." Procedurally, a Senate amendment would send the issue to a conference committee with the House, which could be a drawn-out affair. Johnson had privately told Fulbright he wanted no amendments, "not even the Ten Commandments." The administration wanted strong bipartisan action now, Fulbright said. The president did now want to expand the war, Fulbright said, and he would say so again on the Senate floor.[11]

Nelson rose to say he was disturbed that every senator who spoke seemed to have his own interpretation of what the resolution meant. To clarify the matter, he offered his amendment and asked Fulbright to accept it. "I do not object to it as a statement of policy," Fulbright said. "I believe it is an accurate reflection of what I believe is the President's policy, judging from his own statements." But accepting the amendment would confuse matters, require a conference committee, and delay action, he said. Nelson, a freshman, was "no foreign policy expert" and had "a great deal of respect" for Fulbright, who was certainly "not a war monger," he said. So he deferred to Fulbright and did not press the amendment or request a roll call. Nelson and McGovern voted with the majority when the resolution passed 88–2. Only Morse and Gruening voted no. The House vote was unanimous.[12]

For the record, Nelson took the floor the next day to say he had based his vote for the resolution on Fulbright's assurance that it meant "no change in our basic mission in Vietnam. That mission is one of providing material support and advice. It is not to substitute our armed forces for those of the South Vietnamese government, nor to join them in a land war, nor to fight their war for them."[13]

President Johnson, running as the voice of reason against the hawkish Goldwater, echoed Nelson's remarks, pledging in October that he was "not about to send American boys nine or ten thousand miles away from home to do what Asian boys ought to be doing for themselves." Johnson's stance was to maintain the U.S. commitment in Vietnam, not to escalate or expand American involvement. Compared with Goldwater, who complained of a "no-win" policy and called for bombing North Vietnam, Johnson sounded like the peace candidate. But there were signs that some in the administration wanted to widen the war and that the Tonkin Gulf resolution might be used to justify it. When Nelson read *New York Times* articles suggesting the United States might provoke an attack to justify attacking North Vietnam, he wrote a letter to the editor, recounting the resolution's history. The resolution "in no way approved in advance or gave Congressional endorsement to the expansion of the war," Nelson wrote. The legislative history, he said "defines, limits, and interprets the sense of Congress in approving the resolution."[14]

Rapid Escalation

Not long after Johnson's landslide victory, both the political instability of the Saigon government and the military pressure from the Viet Cong increased. Without warning or debate, escalation came quickly. In February 1965, the Viet Cong attacked U.S. bases, killing eight American soldiers at Pleiku, and Johnson ordered retaliatory air strikes. On 2 March, Operation Rolling Thunder was launched, sending American bombers to North Vietnam in the first air raids that were not direct responses to attacks. On 8 March, the first combat troops, thirty-five hundred Marines, landed at Da Nang to defend the air base. Two weeks later, the first campus teach-in on Vietnam took place at the University of Michigan. The battle, at home and in Southeast Asia, was beginning to take shape.

Nelson opposed escalation, telling constituents who wrote him that if Vietnam did not stabilize, he favored "an orderly disengagement" rather than risk being drawn into "another Korea." In mid-February, his friend Hubert Humphrey, now vice president, invited Nelson and four other liberal senators—Frank Church of Idaho, Eugene McCarthy of Minnesota, Stephen Young of Ohio, and McGovern—to his private office to discuss Vietnam. The "discussion" consisted mostly of a lecture by Johnson advisor McGeorge Bundy "on the need for unified support for the president's Vietnam policies," while Humphrey sat silently. "It was a very strange thing and irritated us all," Nelson said. Bundy said the senators' speeches and criticism could undermine U.S. efforts and give North Vietnam the impression the country was not unified behind the president. Did Bundy want them to "give up the freedom of speech in this country because some dictator doesn't understand it?" Nelson asked. Bundy said no, but the senators thought Bundy was indeed trying to stifle their dissent.[15]

In fact, there was an effort to silence critics, and the attacks came from both sides of the aisle. Russell Long, the Democratic whip, lashed out at "modern day appeasers and isolationists" who were undermining the president, and Republican Everett Dirksen of Illinois sounded a similar theme. Wisconsin Congressman Melvin Laird tried to stop federal grants to a Pennsylvania professor who had criticized Vietnam policy, drawing a sharp rebuke from Robert Kastenmeier, the liberal congressman from Madison. "We are witnessing an assault on free speech and public debate such as we have not seen since the days of McCarthy," the *Capital Times* editorialized. Nelson was quiet on Vietnam in the early months of 1965, and one national peace leader charged he had been silenced by White House pressure. Nelson and his staff dismissed the claim. But a *Capital Times* column in early May noted that Nelson had not spoken up as Johnson escalated the war.[16]

Public statements aside, Vietnam was very much on the minds of Nelson and his Senate colleagues. "We talked about it daily," recalled Walter Mondale, who said "the biggest mistake I ever made" was his support of the war for four years. "It is difficult to recreate the heartache, the sadness, the bitterness, the disarray that was growing in American life that pinned us all down. And while we did a lot of other things, there was no escaping the centrality of that issue." While he and Nelson disagreed, "Gaylord was very respectful of me. Gaylord would make his case and do it with dignity. He would not be offensive or confrontational." Mondale said later that he was poorly informed. "The one thing I would like to redo in my public life is to redo those years, and see the facts, change my mind, and have been helpful to try to end that war."[17]

Johnson believed the Tonkin Gulf resolution was all the authorization he needed for escalation. "He carried that thing around in his pocket," Nelson said. "I was at a meeting with him at the White House when he pulled it out and said, 'You guys authorized this.'" Although he was confident what he called the "504 to 2" resolution backed his action and "had plenty of unspent funds in other programs" that he could have used, Johnson pressed for another vote on a $700 million appropriation "to meet mounting military costs in Vietnam." He asked for action at "the earliest possible moment" and said every member of Congress who voted for the appropriation "is also voting to persist in our effort to halt Communist aggression in South Vietnam. Each is saying that the President and the Congress stand united before the world" to defend South Vietnam's independence. "I do not ask complete approval for every phrase and action of your government. I do ask for prompt support of our basic course: resistance to aggression, moderation in the use of power, and a constant search for peace," his message said.[18]

"I Need My Conscience"

Kastenmeier called Nelson the afternoon of 5 May 1965 to tell him the House had passed the appropriation 408–7 and it was coming to the Senate the next day. "What are you going to do?" asked Kastenmeier, who had voted for the appropriation. "I'm going to write a statement," Nelson said, "and if I can write one that will stand on its merits and politically, I will vote against it." He started that afternoon in his office, took it home, and worked it over until 3 A.M. He rose a few hours later to do some more revising and put some finishing touches on it when he got to his office at 7:30 A.M. "I was satisfied that it was good on the merits and was politically defensible," he said. "It was one typewritten page. I spent about an hour per line."[19]

Nelson already had prepared another, longer statement on the war, entitled "The Underlying Consensus on Vietnam," which he entered into the record. That consensus was "that we do not want another Korea, that the problems of Vietnam should be settled by negotiations, and that ultimately, unless the people of that country can settle their own problems, we will not be able to do the job for them." He warned that "war hawks" wanted the United States to fight a land war and wanted critics to keep quiet. Nelson said he supported a continued U.S. role in Vietnam "as long as there is some possibility of accomplishing our original mission," but warned it would be a tragic mistake to "take on the task of fighting their war for them as well as running their government."[20]

Then he turned to the statement on which he had labored through the night. His "cardinal principle" was "not to engage American troops in a land war in South Vietnam," Nelson said. Disagreement on tactics should not be mistaken for lack of support for the president. "The issue before us is not whether we are unified in our purpose. We certainly are." The issue, he said, was "the wisdom of acting within hours" on the appropriation, which was probably necessary but not urgent, just to demonstrate support for the president. "My objection does not run to the merits of this appropriation," Nelson said. "No matter what the variances of viewpoint, we all know this money will be needed in the future and will be spent." His objection was that the hasty action, without a full discussion, might be seen as support for "a substantial expansion of our role in Vietnam, if not a fundamental change in our mission there," although that was not the intent. "I decline to lend my name in any way to that kind of misinterpretation." Indeed, the action "was designed to show the world that Congress and the country emphatically supported President Johnson's policies of firmness and strength in dealing with Communist aggression," the *New York Times* said.[21]

"Members of the Senate, known as the world's greatest deliberative body, are stumbling over each other to see who can say 'yea' the quickest and the loudest," Nelson said. "I regret it, and I think that someday we shall all regret it." No one had explained to him "the grave necessity for instant action," and there had not even been a caucus to explain the urgency, he said. "Thus, reluctantly, I express my opposition to our procedure here by voting 'nay.' The support in the Congress for this measure is clearly overwhelming. Obviously, you need my vote less than I need my conscience." The vote was 87–3, with Morse and Gruening the other "nay" votes.[22]

Throughout the rest of Nelson's career, the vote would be cited as the day he took a courageous stand against a U.S. land war in Vietnam, far ahead of his colleagues and public opinion. After that, according to Wisconsin political lore, he opposed the war and voted against every Vietnam appropriation. In fact, Nelson tacked a bit before settling on a course. It was 1967 when he cast a vote that was probably more courageous and politically risky, but in the retelling of the story over time his votes and statements have almost been compressed into a single incident.

After Nelson's 1965 vote, Madison's *Capital Times* praised him as acting in the tradition of Fighting Bob La Follette, who risked his career by opposing the U.S. entry into World War I. But news coverage made it clear that Nelson had voted as much against the hasty decision making as against the appropriation. "Nelson Raps Haste on Arms Fund Vote," the *Milwaukee Journal* headline said, and the story quoted Nelson as saying his vote was not on the merits. The *Milwaukee Sentinel* said, "Nelson made it clear that he was not disputing the appropriation sought by President Johnson, but the manner in which it was rammed through Congress." The *Capital Times* said Nelson's vote came because "there was no legitimate need for such hasty action."[23]

Even with the qualifying language, it was a risky vote for a senator still trying to find his footing on the issue. "In my neck of the woods," David Obey said, "Johnson was seen as dragging his feet on getting into the war. We had people saying we ought to nuke 'em, send in more troops." Several outspoken Senate doves voted yes, rather than join Nelson in opposing the appropriation, even on procedural grounds. The vote was subject to criticism and to misrepresentation. Nelson did oppose further U.S. intervention, but not abandonment of South Vietnam or an immediate pullout. He was not comfortable being lumped in with Morse and Gruening, much harsher critics of LBJ and his policy, and did not even like it when the Associated Press took his photo with them after the vote. He felt strongly that the country was rushing blindly ahead, without adequate discussion and debate about alternatives. And he resented Johnson's attempt to stampede the Congress into supporting his actions. "Here was this tough Texan pointing his gun at my feet and saying 'Dance' and I was damned if I'd do it," he said in a line repeated by columnist Stewart Alsop in the *Saturday Evening Post*.[24]

After that vote, Nelson took a low profile again, making no official statements despite Johnson's decision to send fifty thousand more troops and double the size of the draft. Kastenmeier held high-profile public hearings on Vietnam in Madison, but Nelson did not participate. Even in liberal Madison the issue was highly divisive. At the urging of the police chief, Kastenmeier was denied use of the City-County Building for the hearings. While others made it a crusade, Nelson did not beat the antiwar drum every day. "I don't think there's any more to say," Nelson said, defending his silence in August 1965. "How many times do you say it?"[25]

He said it directly to the president when he had an opportunity. Nelson, in Austin to speak at the University of Texas, was invited to join the Johnsons at the LBJ Ranch and take part in a memorial service for

John F. Kennedy in nearby Fredericksburg marking the second anniversary of JFK's death. In the car, Nelson asked, "Can't we get the bombing stopped?" Johnson replied that he had told the Soviet Union, "'I'll stop my air force from bombing if you can get [Hanoi] to stop sending troops into the South,' but they said they had no control over North Vietnam."[26]

Nelson spoke up strongly in January 1966, after President Johnson said in his State of the Union address that the loss of Vietnam would lead to the loss of much of Asia to the Communists. The so-called domino theory was "completely fraudulent," Nelson said, and top administration officials had told him so privately. For more than a year, he had "considered each step of the escalation of the war in Vietnam as a tragic mistake," he said. There were no easy answers, but the best course was to "continue with great patience to seek a negotiated settlement while firmly refusing to escalate the conflict further. Our top military leaders agree that it would be insanity for the United States to become involved in a large Asian land war," he said. Even if a million American troops were sent to Vietnam, "we would leave behind us only a charred, desolate country with little hope that it could maintain its independence one moment beyond the time we left." [27]

Nelson's comments drew praise from Dane County Democrats but sharp criticism from Senator William Proxmire and Milwaukee Congressman Clement Zablocki. Proxmire defended higher troop levels, saying, "We aren't winning now but we have stopped losing." Zablocki defended the domino theory, saying Laos, Cambodia, and Thailand all would be in danger of falling to communism if Vietnam fell. Nelson, on a Milwaukee television interview program, said either side could be proven right. "I might be wrong. Anybody might be wrong in this situation," he said. Nelson backed Johnson's peace initiatives and bombing halt, he said, but would vote against an upcoming appropriation request if it clearly was to escalate the ground war.[28]

Supporting the Troops

In fact, Nelson voted for a $4.8 billion appropriation on 1 March 1966 and another $13.1 billion on 22 March 1966. The government had sent

American troops to Vietnam, and "so long as our men fight there we must have the best equipment and support we are able to give them as a nation," Nelson said. "Although there were differences of opinion and vigorous debate over sending our troops there, that decision was made. In my judgment it is not in our national interest to withdraw that commitment. Nor is it in our national interest to broaden that commitment." The Senate debated for eleven days before approving the first appropriation 94-2 and defeating, 92-5, an attempt by Wayne Morse to repeal the Gulf of Tonkin resolution. Gruening and Morse were the only Senate votes against the two appropriations. Fulbright, McCarthy, and Young joined them in backing Morse's Tonkin Gulf repeal.[29]

During the debate, Fulbright repeated what he had said in an earlier exchange with Secretary of State Dean Rusk. "I believe one of the most serious mistakes I have made as chairman was in not accepting or urging the Senate to accept the amendment offered by [Nelson] in August 1964. . . . I believe it was a mistake and I commend the Senator from Wisconsin for having more foresight than I had at that time . . . as to the possible significance of that resolution." The Nelson amendment was "very sensible" and should have been debated, Fulbright conceded, in an apology he was to repeat a number of times over the course of the war.[30]

The Nelson Doctrine

When Johnson sent American bombers to hit oil storage depots near Hanoi and Haiphong in North Vietnam in late June 1966, hoping to force the Hanoi government to the negotiating table, Nelson called for an end to the bombing. "The administration has tested escalation without success. Now is the time for a comprehensive reappraisal," he said, in what the *Milwaukee Journal* described as "by far the strongest [comment] he has made on the subject of American involvement in Vietnam." He called for "a careful and orderly de-escalation. Our bombing of the north should stop, and our aggressive search for enemy contact should be limited to necessary defensive moves. . . . Our objective should be to see that orderly elections are held, that a South Vietnamese army is created that can pacify the south and defend the government." That could take several years and might not succeed, he said. "But if, with the umbrella of our protection they cannot create a government with public support and an army willing and able to defend the south, nothing we can do will save them."[31]

That became the Nelson doctrine. He had defined his position and set his course. But there remained the nagging questions of how vocal to be, and how to vote on appropriations to support troops already in the field. "Nelson has consistently opposed his own Democratic administration's Vietnam policy, but he has maintained long periods of silence on the sensitive issue for fear his position might be misinterpreted," the *Milwaukee Journal* reported. Nelson, meeting with a group of peace-seeking Wisconsin clergymen, said his vote against the 1965 appropriation had taught him that "there's no way to get your position to the people. The American Legion adopts resolutions against you and the newspapers crank out editorials." Unwilling to commit his vote on an upcoming appropriations bill, Nelson told the clergy he would oppose funds for escalating the war but would vote for funds to support troops already in Vietnam.[32]

When the vote came on 1 March 1967, Nelson gave up on trying to make the fine distinctions about how much went for which purpose. This time he drew the line once and for all. "I am voting against the supplemental authorization in order to express my opposition to past escalation of the conflict and the future escalation that is certain to follow," Nelson said. He also wanted to show his "deep regret that we have failed to adequately explore the possibility of reaching the negotiating table by the cessation of bombing for a sufficient time to test the real intent of Hanoi." Only Morse joined him in voting against a $4.5 billion appropriation. Kastenmeier was one of thirteen nay's in the House. Nelson told the Milwaukee Press Club that he would have voted for the appropriation if there were any danger that it would not pass. On 21 March 1967, he joined Morse and Gruening in voting against a $12.5 billion appropriation, again saying, "[I]f there were any question about the adequacy of supplies or equipment for our troops, I would vote for whatever appropriations were necessary to remedy it." He said that "from a purely political point of view" it would have been easier to vote "aye," but that "would not be honest with myself or my constituents."[33]

Nelson was trying to support the troops while opposing the war, a stand that carried some political risk. Even Wisconsin Democrats were divided. Nelson's mail supported him whenever he took an antiwar stand, but those who wrote were far from a representative sample of the public. In 1966 the state Democratic convention passed a strong resolution, sponsored by Kastenmeier, calling for a cease-fire, bombing halt, and negotiations. But in 1967, although "delegates cheered Nelson when he denounced the war and called for a halt to the bombing and a cease-fire," the next day they narrowly defeated a Nelson-backed resolution calling for a halt to the bombing of North Vietnam. Opposition to the war was growing, Nelson said, predicting that "within six months there won't be any hawks."[34]

People in Wisconsin still generally supported the president, and John Schmitt, Wisconsin AFL-CIO president and a friend since Nelson's army days, was among those who let Nelson know that "our boys don't like what you're saying worth a damn," Nelson recalled. At a union conference in September 1967, Nelson "went through the whole thing," telling the delegates that escalation was "a catastrophic mistake," but he believed Johnson "will do everything he can to reach a settlement." Many Johnson critics had supported intervention and escalation earlier, he said. "Because they knew I was a friend of labor, I got a polite reception but not an enthusiastic one," Nelson said. "If I had been running then it would have been a serious handicap, but I was convinced it was such a serious blunder that it would be totally exposed by the time I ran in 1968. I'm not sure I would have had the guts to vote against that stuff if I had been up the next year. I don't know; I never had to face it. I was satisfied in my own mind the public would turn against it by the time I ran."[35]

The Tet Offensive

Public sentiment did change by the spring of 1968, in the wake of the Tet offensive, which saw Communist troops capture the city of Hue and even seize part of the U.S. embassy in Saigon. The offensive was a military defeat but a psychological victory for the Viet Cong and Hanoi. It shocked many Americans who believed the United States was "winning" the war with its military presence and pacification programs. President Johnson, meanwhile, was facing a growing challenge from doves within his own party. Nelson said in late September, while calling again for a bombing halt, that he would support LBJ if he ran for reelection in 1968. "I think the war's a great mistake, but I think he's a great man," he said.[36] Two months later, when Senator Eugene McCarthy said he would challenge Johnson as an antiwar candidate in Wisconsin's presidential primary, Nelson said he would remain neutral.

With one-half million American troops in Vietnam, rumors of a further troop buildup ignited a far-ranging Senate debate on 7 March 1968. More troops would accomplish nothing, Nelson said. "So to what avail are we pouring in troops and troops and killing and killing in that place, where you cannot have a conventional military victory? I believe it is a tragic situation; and I say that we are worse off now, with 500,000 troops there, than when we did not have any troops on the ground there at all. And we would be worse off with 700,000 or one million troops than we are now."[37]

A week later, McCarthy got 40 percent of the vote in the New Hampshire presidential primary, seriously embarrassing Johnson. A few days later, Senator Robert Kennedy entered the race for president. The Wisconsin primary on 2 April was next, and the outlook was bleak for the president. A Democratic National Committee memo to the White House had warned in December that Wisconsin was "a state fraught with problems for the Administration. . . . . We are faced with limited pro-Johnson loyalties in a land where Kennedys made great friendships and where the Vice President's [Humphrey's] friends of 1960 seem to be in good numbers anti-Vietnam in 1967," the memo warned. "It is a state where our message has not been told. The facts and our side of Vietnam have just not penetrated." A Wisconsin poll a week before the primary indicated Johnson was likely to get less than half the vote. A national Gallup poll showed only a 36 percent job approval rating for Johnson and 26 percent approval for his handling of Vietnam.[38]

On 31 March 1968, Johnson stunned the nation with an announcement that he would not seek reelection, after a speech in which he announced a halt to air raids and naval shelling of North Vietnam and invited Hanoi to negotiate a settlement. Thirty-six hours later, the polls opened in Wisconsin, with McCarthy and Richard Nixon the only active candidates on the ballot. That ended predictions of a record turnout and a huge Republican crossover to vote against Johnson. Voters gave McCarthy 56.2 percent of the vote to Johnson's 34.6. Write-ins gave Kennedy 6.3 percent. Two days later, Dr. Martin Luther King Jr. was assassinated, and months of tumult followed: urban riots over Dr. King's death, growing student protests, the assassination of Robert Kennedy, a Poor People's encampment in Washington, and the emergence of the Yippies, who promised a wild reception for national convention delegates. On 10 May, peace talks opened in Paris but soon deadlocked over Hanoi's insistence on a bombing halt. Nelson proposed a total, mutual cease-fire, followed by free elections and phased withdrawal of both U.S. and North Vietnamese troops, one province at a time.[39]

Nelson continued to vote against Vietnam appropriations. In 1968 he voted six times against military procurement, construction, and supplemental appropriations for the war, usually with one or two others. In one case he was the only nay vote.

It pained him to see his friend Vice President Humphrey portrayed as a hawk and forced to toe the Johnson administration line. He recalled Humphrey telling him, as they rode home together from a White House briefing early in the war, that "some people in the Pentagon and the State Department want to send in three hundred thousand troops. The president will never get sucked into that." Nelson argued against any platform plank that defended past policies on Vietnam. "I for one would feel morally bound to repudiate that plank in the platform and campaign against it," he told the Democratic Platform Committee. Nelson attended the national convention, but was not a delegate since he had been neutral in the primary. "I knew it was a disaster from every aspect," Nelson said, with students mobilized to take a stand in Chicago. Wisconsin's delegation was for McCarthy, and its chairman, Donald O. Peterson, was an antiwar activist who had been part of the Dump Johnson movement launched in 1967. On nomination night, as police and protesters battled in the streets in what was later termed a "police riot," Peterson, at the microphone to cast Wisconsin's votes, told delegates what was happening and asked that the convention be moved from Chicago. When the convention ended, Nelson went back to Washington rather than to Wisconsin and "waited until it blew over. I didn't want to be involved with that disaster."[40]

Winning Reelection

Vietnam did not dominate Nelson's reelection campaign, although it was an issue. His opponent, state senator Jerris Leonard, supported continued bombing and called Nelson's antiwar stand "a meaningless protest." He said Nelson's position "would have delivered millions of people in Southeast Asia into the hands of the communists." He said Nelson had been inconsistent, voting once to support the troops, then against an appropriation, "for the Tonkin Gulf resolution but against support for it." Nelson said his record was consistent—against escalation and money to send more troops, but for support of troops already there. The core of Eugene McCarthy's campaign in Madison, a hotbed of antiwar activity, enlisted in the Nelson and Kastenmeier reelection efforts. Nelson, during a whistlestop train tour with Attorney General Bronson La Follette, the Democratic candidate for governor, said, "[T]here is no decision that I have made in my life that I am more proud of than that vote in 1965" against the appropriations bill. "Whether you agree with me or not, I voted my conscience," Nelson said in a final debate five days before the election.[41]

Nelson won in a ticket-splitting landslide, with 62 percent of the vote. Republicans won every other statewide office. Nelson won by 375,000 votes while Republican Governor Warren P. Knowles won reelection by 100,000 votes. Richard Nixon carried Wisconsin with 48 percent of the vote, Humphrey getting 44.3 percent and independent George Wallace 7.6 percent. Although he had campaigned hard on his record on consumer and environmental issues, Nelson singled out Vietnam in an election night interview. "I think my stand in opposition to going into the war [in Vietnam] helped me substantially," he said. And "he felt the way he 'stood up' for his position brought him even the admiration of those who basically were against his dovish attitude."[42]

"Vietnamization"

Nixon's plan to "Vietnamize" the war, gradually reducing American troop levels while continuing air strikes, fueled more widespread political opposition and the growing antiwar movement. Nelson joined other Democrats calling for a speedier withdrawal timetable, continued to press for a total cease-fire, and issued a statement in support of the 15 October 1969 Moratorium Day. But now Nelson, who considered his antiwar credentials impeccable, found himself being criticized for not being active or vocal enough. When he declined to join Wisconsin marchers in a 15 November 1969 Moratorium March in Washington, the protesters were disappointed. Nelson told the delegation that he supported the march but Senate business had to be his priority. "I very much appreciate the leadership the Senator has offered in the past, but I feel like he has let us down in the last two weeks, and certainly today," an Oshkosh campus minister said. "We feel your first priority ought to be with us," he told Nelson. "There is a point at which you put your body in the street." But Nelson had just announced plans for the environmental teach-in that was to become Earth Day and felt he was continuing to do his share to stop the war. "My son said to me, 'You should be on the Senate floor filibustering against the war every day,'" Nelson said in a 1975 interview. "It was a fair criticism. I clearly could have said more than I did."[43]

In May 1970, Nelson quietly joined demonstrators on the Ellipse near the White House in a protest against the U.S. invasion of Cambodia and a memorial for four Kent State University students killed by National Guardsmen during a campus protest. The day before, he had been challenged by a group of young antiwar activists, including Jim Doyle, the son of his longtime personal friend James E. Doyle, who had become a federal judge. (The younger Doyle, then a Harvard Law School student, was elected governor of Wisconsin in 2002.) Doyle and the others were "not impressed with his excellent credentials as an early opponent of the Vietnam war," and unhappy with his account of his long record on the issue. That history was well and good, they said, but what was he going to do about the war this weekend? The next week, at the University of Wisconsin in Madison, Nelson faced a raucous crowd that heckled, debated, interrupted, and sometimes applauded him as he argued for nonviolence and the election of peace candidates to end the war.[44]

While antiwar sentiment grew, impatient opponents of the war continued to suffer setbacks in the Senate. The McGovern-Hatfield amendment, calling for withdrawal of all U.S. troops by the end of 1971, failed in the fall of 1970. Nelson, who had pressed for an end to the military draft since 1964, lost on an attempt to end the involuntary use of draftees in Vietnam. The Cooper-Church amendment, to cut off funding for the war, fell three votes short in October 1971. Nelson supported every attempt to end the war.

He tried unsuccessfully in 1970 to ban the use of defoliants in

Vietnam, warning that the chemicals could damage the ecology of the entire region. In January 1972, introducing a bill requiring a full-scale study of ecological damage, Nelson was eloquent. He catalogued the damage: an area the size of Rhode Island flattened and scraped bare of foliage; prime forest acreage the size of Massachusetts, destroyed by a hundred million pounds of poisonous herbicides; twenty-three million huge craters, forty feet across and twenty-six feet deep, created by five-hundred-pound bombs, with tonnage amounting to three pounds for every person on earth—eight billion pounds; destruction of 80 percent of timber forests and 10 percent of all cultivated land in the nation. Calling it a "monumental catastrophe," Nelson said:

> That is what we have done to our ally, South Vietnam. . . . The huge areas destroyed, pockmarked, scorched and bulldozed resemble the moon and are no more productive. . . . Quite frankly, I am unable adequately to describe the horror of what we have done there. . . . There is nothing in the history of warfare to compare with it. A "scorched earth" policy has been a tactic of warfare throughout history, but never before has a land been so massively altered and mutilated that vast areas can never be used again or even inhabited by man or animal. This is impersonal, automated and mechanistic warfare brought to its logical conclusion—utter, permanent, total destruction. . . . The cold, hard and cruel irony of it all is that South Vietnam would have been better off losing to Hanoi than winning with us.[45]

When Nixon ordered the mining of Haiphong Harbor and intensive bombing of military targets in North Vietnam in May 1972, Nelson said Congress should "simply cut off appropriations and terminate our involvement in Vietnam." In June, after Defense Secretary Laird said that the administration might need another $5 billion appropriation for Vietnam, Nelson said he would not vote for "one more cent in this investment in political bankruptcy" and joined Proxmire in a sharp attack on Laird. Despite their political differences, Nelson had a longstanding friendship with Laird which began in the state senate, continued when Laird was in the House, and even survived when he joined the Nixon cabinet. (One night, after a party and drinks with some Wisconsin friends, Nelson and Laird had gotten into an alcohol-fueled dispute over the location of the hot line to the Soviet Union. Laird's driver took the pair on a 2 A.M. trip to the Pentagon, where Laird triumphantly

showed Nelson the hot line telephone in his office.) It was unusual for
Nelson to directly attack Laird, but Nelson's patience had run out. He
was appalled that Laird could claim the Vietnamization had been a success while saying the war could last four or five more years. "If that is
successful Vietnamization, I wonder what they consider unsuccessful
Vietnamization," Nelson said. "Obviously this war has gone on too long
and has cost too much." Nelson by that time was officially backing
McGovern for president. Laird, who was to play a role in Nixon's reelection, said McGovern's program would cost a billion dollars for
white flags of surrender.[46]

The American role in Vietnam ended with a peace agreement
signed in January 1973 in Paris, after a final round of bombing of North
Vietnam over the Christmas holidays. The last U.S. combat ground
troops had left the previous August, and twenty-seven thousand American troops in the country at the time of the cease-fire were withdrawn
by March 1973. "Let us hope that our political leaders in both political
parties have learned a lesson from this mistaken enterprise and will not
involve this country again in a civil war where the vital interests of this
country are not at stake," Nelson said.[47]

Senate majority leader Mike Mansfield, recalling in 1975 Nelson's
questions on the Tonkin Gulf resolution eleven years earlier, said: "History may have taken a different turn if the Senate had done what was
right rather than what was expedient, and had followed the advice of
[Nelson]."[48]

29

Earth Day

NELSON HAD LONG SOUGHT to elevate environmental issues to the top of the nation's political agenda. He sensed a growing environmental awareness among Americans and looked for a way to channel their energy into political change. "In speaking around the country about the issue, I was satisfied that the public was interested and concerned. Everybody in every community, almost, was seeing the deterioration of the environment around them. I knew there was a great public interest in the issue of the environment," he said. The challenge was how to mobilize that interest and convert it to action.[1]

The idea came to him during a speaking tour in California in the summer of 1969. After speaking at a water quality conference in Santa Barbara, Nelson viewed the residue of a disastrous oil spill nearby. On a flight to Berkeley for his next speech, he read an article about teach-ins on Vietnam being conducted on college campuses. "It popped into my head. That's it!" Nelson said. "Why not have an environmental teach-in and get everyone involved?"[2]

Upon his return to Washington, D.C., he began to lay the groundwork. He formed a nonprofit organization, Environmental Teach-In, Inc., and persuaded Paul "Pete" McCloskey, a moderate California Republican congressman, to join him as cochair, ensuring that the group would be nonpartisan. Nelson recruited Sydney Howe, president of the Conservation Foundation, as a board member. Howe, a well-known and highly regarded conservationist, would be acceptable to a wide spectrum of other groups.

Nelson also raised some seed money. Larry Rockefeller, then a young environmental lawyer, wrote a check for the first one thousand dollars. Nelson called United Auto Workers President Walter Reuther for a two thousand dollar donation, which he used to leverage a matching contribution from George Meany, AFL-CIO president. Meany was less enthusiastic, but would not be outdone by the more liberal Reuther. The Conservation Foundation contributed twenty thousand dollars, and Nelson donated all of the honoraria he received for his environmental speeches, totaling eighteen thousand dollars by Earth Day. The total budget was less than two hundred thousand dollars, much of it from small contributions.[3]

Nelson went public with his plan on 20 September 1969 in a speech in Seattle to the Washington Environmental Council. He called for a national teach-in on "The Crisis of the Environment" on every college campus in the nation the next spring, all on the same day. Nelson said he would take the lead in organizing the event, for students, faculty, scientists, and public leaders to discuss "the threat to the ecology of the world."

"I am convinced that the same concern the youth of this nation took in changing this nation's priorities on the war in Vietnam and on civil rights can be shown for the problems of the environment," Nelson said. Young people could take the leadership away from the "indifferent, venal men who are concerned with progress and profit for the sake of progress and profit alone and consider the environment the problem of the birdwatchers and butterfly chasers," he said.[4]

His announcement prompted a short national wire service story, and suddenly "it simply took off like gangbusters" with calls and mail flooding his Senate office from people who wanted to get involved. Two of his Senate staff members, John Heritage and Linda Billings, handled the requests, with Nelson frequently called off the Senate floor to field telephone calls from reporters and campus organizers across the country.[5]

A month later, when Nelson spoke at a national student conference at Airlie House in Warrenton, Virginia, he talked about opening and staffing a national office. The one hundred student activists from across the country were enthusiastic. The next day several of them showed up at Nelson's Senate office to say they had met, chosen a chairman, and formed a committee to run the teach-ins. "Not so fast. I'm gonna choose and run it," Nelson told them, adding that they were welcome to participate or do something else on their own.[6]

A group of "campus militants . . . saw this as another opportunity and springboard to militantly bring to the attention of the country all the ills and negatives associated with capitalism and an unresponsive democratic system," said Bud Jordahl. "They were giving [John] Heritage a fit, visiting the office every day, wanting to run the whole thing." Nelson asked Jordahl, then on the University of Wisconsin faculty, to come to Washington to help get things on track. "These were bright, young, energetic, highly motivated students," Jordahl recalled. "They were not anarchists, but they wanted a militant Earth Day. Gaylord wanted a peaceful national teach-in." Jordahl finally laid it out for the students at a meeting: The senator wants a committee with some members of national stature. He wants to raise some money to get the idea off the ground, and wants an event different from the one you envision. "We didn't want to alienate them," Jordahl said. "We just wanted them to go away," and they did.[7]

When it came time to hire someone to coordinate Earth Day events, an experienced campus activist got the job. Denis Hayes, a Harvard graduate student, read about the planned teach-in and made an appointment with Nelson and Heritage. He left with "a charter to kick up as much dust as possible around Harvard and surrounding educational institutions." Hayes, as student body president of Stanford University the previous year, had been involved in organizing against the Vietnam War, the invasion of Czechoslovakia, and classified military research on campus. Nelson checked Hayes out with McCloskey and others, had Heritage do a thorough background check, and then asked Hayes to head up the teach-in office. Hayes left school to do it full-time.[8]

The headquarters soon outgrew its first office, which John Gardner of Common Cause had donated. A grungy, chaotic office above a Chinese restaurant on P Street became the national nerve center, staffed by energetic and idealistic young people, a mixture of volunteers and full-time staff members who worked day and night for minimal or no pay. Hayes recruited activists from around the country. "We saw ourselves at a pivotal point in history," he said. While drawing on veterans of political protest movements, the Earth Day cadre set out to win widespread support. The environmental movement had the potential to reach across and unify all segments of the population. That was Nelson's vision, and it was the goal of the young people he enlisted in his crusade.[9]

"We consciously set out to build a movement to bring America back together, and let everyone under the umbrella with a shared set of values," Hayes said. "We tapped into something that resonated very strongly with the American people. Gaylord recognized the potential to merge old conservation values with new energy conservation issues. But no one knew how gigantic it would be."[10]

Nelson would insist, in later years, that no one could have organized Earth Day. What made it work, he said, was that it organized itself. "Earth Day worked because of the spontaneous response at the grassroots level. We had neither the time nor the resources to organize twenty million demonstrators and the thousands of schools and local communities that participated. That was the remarkable thing about Earth Day. It organized itself," Nelson said.[11]

By the time the office opened in January and regional coordinators began work, there were signs that something big was in the wind. The *New York Times*, in a front-page story by environmental reporter Gladwin Hill, said that growing concern about the environment "is sweeping this nation's campuses with an intensity that may be on its way to eclipsing student discontent over the war in Vietnam." Campus environmental groups across the country—in Tennessee, Wisconsin, Massachusetts, Illinois, California, Connecticut, Minnesota, Maine, Colorado, and Hawaii—were already active and looking forward to "the first D-Day of the movement, next April 22," Hill reported. "Given the present-rising pitch of interest, some supporters think, it could be a bigger and more meaningful event than the antiwar demonstrations." That story ran on 30 November 1969, before Earth Day efforts were really off the ground, and before Earth Day had its name. The activities described offered a small preview of Earth Day. A University of Minnesota group picked up twenty-six thousand empty cans and tried unsuccessfully to return them to the manufacturer to be recycled. University of Illinois students removed six tons of refuse from a nearby creek and convinced local officials to adopt a plan to beautify it. University of Washington students conducted a learn-in. Others picketed, petitioned, confronted polluters, and began legal action. The issue was bringing together "former antiwar activists, young Democrats, crew-cut fraternity members, and so-called hippies," *Newsweek* said. "Indeed, the strength and promise of the burgeoning interest in the integrity of the American landscape is its appeal to students of all political leanings."[12] Environmental awareness was simmering on the nation's campuses. Earth Day would bring it to a boil, and it would spill over well beyond the campuses.

The Environmental Teach-In office in Washington served as a clearinghouse for information, and requests poured in by the thousands, even before the doors were open. Nelson had sent an early mailing to every governor and two hundred mayors, asking them to issue proclamations. His office had sent articles to college newspapers and *Scholastic* magazine, read by teachers across the country. The Washington office added mailings to conservation groups, teachers, garden clubs, ministers, and others. Those who contacted the office received four pages of information, stressing that the teach-in would be a day of national action but planned and organized locally. It offered a list of activities being planned by colleges, high schools, and communities, ranging from seminars and speeches to mass phone calls to polluters, displays of dead fish, and literally turning a spotlight on a polluting smokestack. Other conservation organizations helped spread the word. *The Environmental Handbook,* published by newly formed Friends of the Earth specifically for the Earth Day teach-ins, quickly sold out its first printing. The national office organized its incoming mail by ZIP code and put people in touch with each other. Eventually, the mailing list reached sixty thousand.[13]

Introducing "Earth Day"

A full-page advertisement in the Sunday *New York Times* on 18 January 1970, with a bold headline, introduced "Earth Day" to the vocabulary. The ad said:

> A disease has infected our country. It has brought smog to Yosemite, dumped garbage in the Hudson, sprayed DDT in our food, and left our cities in decay. Its carrier is man.
>
> Earth Day is a commitment to make life better, not just bigger and faster; to provide real rather than rhetorical solutions. It is a day

to re-examine the ethic of individual progress at mankind's expense. It is a day to challenge the corporate and governmental leaders who promise change, but who shortchange the necessary programs. It is a day for looking beyond tomorrow. April 22 seeks a future worth living. April 22 seeks a future.

The advertisement asked for responses and contributions, and both poured in. The ad had been prepared, pro bono, by a top New York advertising agency, which presented several mock-ups to the Environmental Teach-In staff. There were a half dozen choices for a name on the sample advertisements, such as Ecology Day and Environment Day. Earth Day won hands down. Nelson said he really didn't care what it was called, and did not think the name was a critical component of the event's success. Nelson himself continued to call it the environmental teach-in, but by 22 April the media were calling it Earth Day.

The national office encouraged local governments to sanction the events. John Lindsay, New York's mayor, was the most cooperative, allowing the use of Central Park, closing Fifth Avenue, and making his political operatives and the police force available. His blessing and active participation helped put Earth Day in the spotlight in the world's biggest media center.

By late February the potential enormity of Earth Day began to dawn on the national office. It was becoming clear that events and activities were being planned on a scale that no one could have predicted. The early contacts were with campus groups. But as the idea spread, many of those who organized community events were in their mid to late thirties, often college educated, many of them women at home raising children. They had missed out on much of the civil rights and antiwar movement of the 1960s, but now they decided in huge numbers to become involved in saving the environment.

In the two weeks leading up to Earth Day, Nelson traveled the country on a seventeen-stop speaking tour that took him to schools, labor unions, and state legislatures. He called for a campaign to elect an "ecology congress" in a speech to the Pennsylvania legislature. "People from coast to coast are disgusted and angry at the accelerating destruction of our environment and the quality of life," he said. To really clean up pollution would require an investment of $25 billion a year or more, he said on CBS Television's *Face the Nation*. "No administration has understood the size of the issue," he said. "It is much more important than space, weapons systems, or the money we're wasting in Vietnam." When a Yale University student challenged him on how he would cut the space program to pay for the cleanup, Nelson said, "I wouldn't revise the space program. I'd terminate it," and the audience broke into applause. "The moon is going to be there for a long time. It will be just as dead 30 years from now as it is today. The only purpose of getting to the moon that I know of is to see what this country will look like if we don't stop doing what we're doing." If spiraling population growth, the world's biggest problem, continued unchecked, "we might as well forget finding solutions to any of our social and environmental problems," he told another college audience in New Haven, Connecticut. Even if the country made environmental cleanup its top priority, "we would fail unless we could find a reasonable check on the nation's population growth," he said.[14]

On 21 April, Nelson told the United Auto Workers convention in Atlantic City, New Jersey, that the automobile was becoming the symbol of the environmental crisis. "The heart of the problem is the internal combustion engine, which has powered America into unparalleled affluence, but now may drive it to unprecedented environmental disaster," Nelson said, calling for development of a pollution-free auto engine. President Walter Reuther had told his members the day before that "the auto industry is one of the worst culprits and it has failed to meet its public responsibility," and called for the industry to join government in developing a modern mass transportation system. The convention passed a resolution declaring that the UAW would raise the pollution issue in its contract negotiations, since the workers had a stake in helping society solve the problem, and in keeping their own jobs in the face of threats that polluting engines would be banned.[15]

On the eve of Earth Day, Nelson arrived home in Madison to learn that the permit for a planned Earth Day parade had been canceled. The city council was worried that the parade of nonpolluting vehicles, sponsored by the campus Engineers and Scientists for Professional Responsibility, might somehow spawn the kind of violent, window-breaking spree the city had experienced the previous weekend when a peace rally was disrupted by radicals. A small group bicycled and marched up State Street on Earth Day anyway, picking up litter along the way and collecting cigarette butts from the capitol lawn. That night, thousands of students at the University of Wisconsin Stock Pavilion cheered when Nelson told them that "the hope of mankind is that the Red Army and the Pentagon will become obsolete." A peaceful American-Soviet agreement could allow money to be spent on improving the environment instead of on weapons, he said. Without a cutback in military spending the United States could not spend the $25 billion needed annually to clean up pollution, Nelson said. Both sides had enough weapons to kill everyone in the world once, Nelson said. "Why do we need to do it twice?"[16]

Later that night, at a Milwaukee teach-in, his standard comment that unchecked population growth was the biggest threat to the environment touched off a debate with author and cities critic Jane Jacobs, who was also on the program. "By any standard, the United States is overpopulated now," Nelson said. "[I]f the population of the world goes from three billion to seven billion in the next thirty-five years, it will be impossible to maintain a quality environment in this country or any country in the world." Jacobs said the environmental movement was "laboring under the delusion that population and affluence are causing environmental deterioration." The prospect of any government population control program frightened her, Jacobs said. "As things stand, we are not a fit society to possess public powers for population control."[17]

On Earth Day itself, at Indiana University, at a massive teach-in in Denver, and at the University of California in Berkeley, Nelson gave what had become his standard, passionate call for an unprecedented battle against pollution. He finished the tour on 23 April at the University of Southern California in Los Angeles. He was warmly received everywhere he went, although twenty young women on the Indiana campus dressed in witch costumes, danced, tossed birth control pills at the crowd, and chanted, "Free our bodies, free our minds." A Senate subcommittee chaired by Nelson had been investigating the safety of birth control pills, which had prompted similar protests at the hearings.[18]

By the time Earth Day arrived, "Conservatives were for it. Liberals were for it. Democrats, Republicans and Independents were for it. So were the ins, the outs, the executive and legislative branches of government," the *New York Times* reported. "It was Earth Day, and, like Mother's Day, no man in public office could be against it." Indeed, while Senator Edward Kennedy spoke at Yale, Senator Barry Goldwater was at Adelphi University in Garden City, Long Island, and elected officials of all stripes were taking part in events.[19]

Critics Left and Right

But Earth Day was not without its detractors. Criticism came from both sides of the political spectrum, for very different reasons.

The right-wing John Birch Society did not like the date Nelson had chosen because 22 April was the hundredth anniversary of the birth of Vladimir Lenin, and Earth Day was nothing but an ill-disguised attempt to honor the revolutionary Communist leader, they claimed. "Subversive elements plan to make American children live in an environment that is good for them," a Mississippi delegate to a Daughters of the American Revolution convention warned. Nelson had chosen the date as the one that could maximize participation on college campuses. He determined that the week of 19–25 April was the best bet. It did not fall during exams or spring breaks, did not conflict with religious holidays such as Easter or Passover, and was late enough in spring to have decent weather. More students were likely to be in class, and there would be less competition with other events midweek, so he chose Wednesday, 22 April.[20]

Nelson had no idea it was Lenin's birthday, but he did some research and had a response ready when the question came up, as it did with some frequency. With only 365 days a year and 3.7 billion people in the world, every day was the birthday of 10 million living people, Nelson explained. "On any given day, a lot of both good and bad people were born," he said. "A person many consider the world's first environmentalist, Saint Francis of Assisi, was born on April 22. So was Queen Isabella. More importantly, so was my Aunt Tillie." His humor defused the question, but some took it seriously. The Los Angeles City Council passed an Earth Day resolution on 20 April 1970, but only after sharp debate, and voting 8–6 for an amendment expressing "concern" about the date and a hope that it would be changed in future years.[21]

On the political left, Earth Day drew fire for taking attention and energy from issues like racism, poverty, and the Vietnam War. "The nation's concern with the environment has done what George Wallace was unable to do: Distract the nation from the human problems of the black and brown Americans, living in just as much misery as ever," Mayor Richard Hatcher of Gary, Indiana, said. Journalist I. F. Stone, speaking at the rally at the Washington Monument, called Earth Day a "beautiful snow job" designed to distract attention from government military and spending policies. "We here tonight are being conned," Stone said. "The country is slipping into a wider war in Southeast Asia and we're sitting here talking about litter bugs." A Philadelphia group, the Young Great Society, boycotted the local observance. "What about the pollution of the mind, the pollution of the houses, the pollution of the dirty, uncared-for systems left to the poor," the group's leader, Herman Wrice, asked. "Can we really accomplish anything with a big outdoor rally? How many weekends are those college kids going to go out in their boats and fish for trash? Meanwhile, we've still got sewers stopped up with rats."[22]

On Earth Day, protesters waving Viet Cong flags stormed the stage and disrupted a speech by Governor William Milliken at Michigan State University, and Senator Henry Jackson was heckled while speaking in Seattle. But protest from radical groups was almost nonexistent. If anything, like the Young Greats in Philadelphia, they simply stayed away. The FBI, however, sent agents to monitor events in Washington and three other cities, at the request of Nixon aide John Ehrlichman, looking for "the involvement of radical groups in the ecology movement," according to a memo in Nelson's FBI files.[23]

Environment, Broadly Defined

In his speech at the University of Wisconsin in Madison on the eve of Earth Day, Nelson made it clear he saw the movement as broadly focused. He said:

Our goal is not to forget about the worst environments in America—in the ghettos, in Appalachia and elsewhere. Our goal is an environment of decency, quality and mutual respect for all human beings and all other living creatures—an environment without ugliness, without ghettoes, without poverty, without discrimination, without hunger and without war. Our goal is a decent environment in its deepest and broadest sense.

The battle to restore a proper relationship between man and his environment, between man and other living creatures, will require a long, sustained, political, moral, ethical and financial commitment far beyond any commitment ever made by any society in the history of man. Are we able? Yes. Are we willing? That's the unanswered question.[24]

In Denver, Nelson said the broad support for Earth Day could be the beginning of "a new national coalition whose objective is to put quality of human life on a par with Gross National Product as an aim of this society. [Earth Day is] dramatic evidence of a broad new American concern that cuts across generations and ideologies. Yet some are saying it is a 'cop out' from the Vietnam war issue and a 'cop out' by the middle class from facing the problems of the black ghetto. Just because it looks like a consensus, don't drop out yet. The fact that so many Americans can agree on a problem could be the best news in decades. Earth Day may be symbolic of new perspectives on the still pressing problems of the last decade—of race, of war, of poverty, of the relevancy of modern-day institutions."[25]

Weather and events cooperated, and the media gave the day widespread positive coverage. If Manhattan's event had been rained out, or if the United States had invaded Cambodia on 22 April, millions still would have participated in Earth Day. But it may not have had either the immediate impact or the permanent imprint it made on the national consciousness. As it was, Earth Day changed everything.

"It did exactly what I was aiming for," Nelson said. "It was a big enough demonstration to get the attention of the political establishment and force the issue on to the political agenda. The public was already there, ahead of the politicians. When the people demonstrated their interest, the politicians responded. All through the 1970s and into the 1980s we passed a tremendous amount of environmental legislation because the politicians were responding."[26]

30

Immune to Presidential Fever

THE "URGENT" TELEPHONE MESSAGE from George McGovern on 13 July 1972 was a surprise. Nelson thought he had put the issue to rest a week earlier. During a two-hour lunch at the Monocle, a restaurant and bar near the Senate office building, the two close friends and Senate seatmates had discussed possible candidates for vice president, including Nelson himself. Nelson had made it clear he did not want the nomination. "I'd seriously consider it only if you could guarantee that I wouldn't win," he said. But that was a hypothetical "what if" question — Would you be interested?[1]

Now McGovern was asking him again: "I'd like to have you join me on the ticket and run for vice-president." This time the question was not hypothetical. McGovern was calling from Miami, where he had been nominated the night before as his party's candidate for president.[2]

In the ten-minute conversation, McGovern reminded Nelson that their views on most issues were similar and said he had no doubt Nelson had the ability to assume the presidency "if the job were to come your way." Nelson, doodling on a piece of paper on his desk, just listened while McGovern made his case. There was a moment when Nelson "thought I might be stampeded into doing something I'd regret. I hated to say no because I really wanted to help George with a very difficult problem."[3]

But Nelson's answer was the same as it had been a week earlier. "George, I don't want that damn job. If I had to serve as vice-president to anybody, you'd be the guy I would do it for. But I feel that serving as vice-president would be the end of my political career." It would be the end of his political independence to speak his own mind on policy, Nelson said, and he was not willing to give that up. He also suggested it could be trouble at home, because he and Carrie Lee had agreed he would not run. In fact, the Nelsons had not decided anything. Carrie Lee could never remember being consulted about Nelson's plans in his entire career. He made his own decisions. "When I told George no, I exaggerated a little. I said my wife would leave me," Nelson said later. "Hell, I needed some excuse." In the McGovern campaign chronicles, the several books written by staff members, Nelson's "inviolable pact" with Carrie Lee was always cited as one reason he declined.[4]

Nelson said he would not run under any circumstances. McGovern was not surprised and did not argue or pressure him. They discussed other candidates, and Nelson recommended another close friend: "The guy who wants it is Tom Eagleton and he's the guy I'd pick if I were in your shoes." Senator Eagleton, of Missouri, was on McGovern's short list of potential candidates. Senators Walter Mondale and Edward Kennedy had spoken well of Eagleton, but McGovern had skipped over him because he did not know him personally. Nelson, Eagleton, and their wives had become good social and political friends since Eagleton's arrival in the Senate in 1968, and spent a lot of time together. Nelson reassured McGovern: "I know Tom well. He's very intelligent, high quality, high integrity, well informed, a good speaker, very presentable, a first rate person. By any measure I'd rank him high in any situation."[5]

McGovern hung up the phone in his suite at the Doral Hotel, told his staff that "Nelson and his wife" had agreed Nelson would not accept the nomination. "Well, I guess it's Eagleton," he said, placing the call that would derail his long-shot presidential candidacy. Eagleton had publicly said he wanted the nomination and did not hesitate when the call came. "George, before you change your mind, I hasten to accept," he said immediately.[6]

Nelson had not been McGovern's first choice for a running mate, or even his second. Politically, Kennedy offered the biggest lift, despite the shadow of the 1969 Chappaquiddick tragedy. When reelected, Kennedy had pledged to serve his full Senate term, which ran until 1976. Kennedy had told McGovern in an earlier meeting that family responsibilities made it difficult to think about running, but McGovern thought he had left the door open a crack. McGovern continued to hope, right up until the convention, that he could persuade Kennedy to run.[7]

His backup was to be Senator Abraham Ribicoff of Connecticut, a Kennedy ally who had been a governor and cabinet member. But in June Ribicoff told McGovern he didn't want to be considered because he was too old (sixty-two) and wanted to remain in the Senate. McGovern had talked to Leonard Woodcock, United Auto Workers president, but other labor leaders were unenthusiastic and Woodcock's name was dropped. Governor Reuben Askew of Florida, also high on the list, said he could not leave his governorship after only two years. As the convention began there was no clear second choice after Kennedy.[8]

The night he won the nomination, McGovern called Kennedy in Hyannisport, Massachusetts, and tried once more to persuade him to join the ticket. Kennedy said he would sleep on it, but told reporters the next morning he had turned it down. McGovern asked his staff and advisors for a list of possible choices, and more than twenty people assembled the next morning. The first brainstorm session produced a list of about twenty people that included television news anchor Walter Cronkite. Several more rounds of discussion and votes narrowed it to seven: Mondale of Minnesota; Eagleton; Governor Patrick Lucey of Wisconsin; Ribicoff; Sargent Shriver, a Kennedy in-law who had been director of the Peace Corps and ambassador to France; Boston Mayor Kevin White; and Lawrence O'Brien, chairman of the Democratic National Committee. McGovern knew Ribicoff was a nonstarter. He assumed that Mondale, up for reelection, would not run either, which he confirmed. Shriver was in Moscow. Lucey wanted the nomination but was eliminated because he was a McGovern loyalist who would be seen as too much "in the family."[9]

McGovern called Mayor White, who said he would accept, but McGovern did not make the formal offer and close the deal. He called Kennedy to get his sign-off, and was surprised when Kennedy was cool to White's candidacy and said he might even rethink his own availability. John Kenneth Galbraith, the Harvard economist who was a friend and advisor to both McGovern and Kennedy, ended White's candidacy when he said the Massachusetts delegation would walk out if White were nominated, because of his strong opposition to them during the state's primary. Kennedy called back and said no again to running himself and—apparently unaware of Galbraith's position—gave lukewarm approval to White.[10]

An hour before the convention deadline for nominating a vice presidential candidate, only Eagleton and O'Brien remained on the list. McGovern was not comfortable with either. "I'm going to ask Gaylord Nelson," he told his advisors. "He's a trusted friend. I've sat next to him in the Senate for ten years. I know his strengths and his weaknesses and he knows mine." Their views were compatible, Nelson was articulate and persuasive, and he had good ties to labor, environmental, and farm groups. "I had total confidence in him as a person of the most absolute integrity. I had heard Lyndon Johnson say, 'Pick a vice president you can absolutely trust,' and I had that feeling about Gaylord."[11]

Although a close friend and ally, Nelson did not have Lucey's problem of being identified as a McGovernite. With his friends Hubert Humphrey and Edmund Muskie also on the ballot, Nelson had remained neutral in the Wisconsin primary, where McGovern had won his first victory. But Nelson helped "behind the scenes" and gave McGovern an issue besides Vietnam that would resonate with Wisconsin voters. A month before the primary, Nelson introduced the Tax Reform Act of 1972, to close loopholes of $16 billion and provide property tax relief. Through a plan to give federal income tax credits for property tax payments, Nelson claimed it would reduce Wisconsin property taxes by 30 percent. At Nelson's urging, McGovern "jumped on it immediately, and it was one of the most helpful suggestions anyone made to me on the way to the nomination." Calling it the Nelson-McGovern property tax relief act, he "discussed it night and day in Wisconsin, second only to hammering against the continued war in Vietnam and the waste in excessive military spending."[12]

Nelson had turned down an invitation to chair the convention's platform committee. But Nelson had spoken to the convention, at McGovern's request, in a credentials battle over California's delegates. McGovern had won the winner-take-all California primary in June. Nelson had broken his personal tradition and endorsed McGovern before that primary, denouncing those who called McGovern irresponsible and radical, defending him as "a level-headed, practical, decent man."[13] The convention's Credentials Committee, controlled by stop-McGovern forces, had ruled that the 271 California delegates must be split according to vote totals, which would take away 150 delegates—and perhaps the nomination—from McGovern. The issue was to be decided by the full convention.

Nelson told the delegates the question was: "Can we rule ourselves by law, or will power be our only guideline?" A party reform commission, chaired by McGovern, had made the rules for delegate selection. Nothing prohibited a winner-take-all system and everyone understood that was the rule in California. "Everyone played by those rules. Nobody questioned their validity until somebody won and somebody lost," Nelson said. "The question before us is fundamental. We are being asked to surrender party reform to political expediency . . . to throw out the window this party's commitment to law over force." What was at stake, he concluded, was "the heart and soul of the Democratic Party. What do we stand for if we don't stand for simple justice? What do we care about if we don't care about basic fairness? What are we about if we are not about the rule of law?" It was a strong speech but had little to do with the convention's vote to overturn the Credentials Committee and seat McGovern's delegates. The vote was a show of strength by McGovern forces, augmented by a small number of other delegates whose consciences were offended by the power play—among them the leader of Wisconsin's Humphrey delegation.[14] The outcome virtually assured McGovern's first ballot nomination. Nelson flew back to Washington on Tuesday. On Wednesday night, McGovern was nominated. On Thursday afternoon, he called Nelson.

Nelson's polite refusal did not surprise McGovern. He hoped Nelson might say yes, but understood why he didn't. Nelson loved the Senate, was comfortable and influential in his role there, and was finally beginning to see real progress on environmental issues. He knew McGovern's campaign against Nixon was a long shot, and a losing effort could damage his own reelection campaign for the Senate in 1974. Finally, "he had seen enough of the vice presidency that he didn't want the job. Hubert Humphrey had told everybody who would listen that it was a lousy job," McGovern said.[15]

"I would do anything for George McGovern except run for vice president," Nelson told a reporter. That included pleading McGovern's case with organized labor, which was cool to his candidacy. Nelson, whose rapport with the unions was excellent, agreed to help. Nelson called Steelworkers President I. W. Abel, whom he considered a "good, intelligent, thoughtful labor leader," and made a pitch for a McGovern endorsement, saying, "he's got as good a record as I do." Abel snapped back, "Don't demean yourself." Abel and his AFL-CIO brethren were upset with McGovern on three counts—his early opposition to the Vietnam War, which many unions, especially the building trades, supported; a vote he had cast against the AFL-CIO six years earlier on an antiunion provision of the Taft-Hartley Act; and the fact that the reform commission he headed had replaced many union delegates to the national convention with bearded hippies, women's libbers, and kooks, in the hard hats' view. Nelson and other Democrats with good labor credentials could not budge the AFL-CIO, which remained neutral.[16]

Nelson said he would actively campaign for the ticket. But the McGovern-Eagleton ticket remained intact for only eighteen days. Nelson, who was instrumental in bringing the two candidates together, also played a key role in their separation.

The Eagleton Problem

The disclosure, ten days after the convention, that Eagleton had been hospitalized three times for depression and twice had received electroshock treatment, had stopped the McGovern campaign in its tracks. In the glare of the national media spotlight, McGovern responded erratically, declaring he was behind Eagleton "1,000 percent" one day and beginning the process of getting him off the ticket the next. The campaign was paralyzed for nearly a week, as the political and public pressure mounted and McGovern agonized about whether to ask Eagleton to leave the ticket.

McGovern's first inclination was to stand by Eagleton, and Nelson initially agreed. But the tide of public opinion, expressed publicly in newspaper editorials and privately by Democratic donors, was turning against Eagleton—and against McGovern's handling of his selection. Two days after the disclosure, McGovern called Nelson for advice. Nelson, in Washington himself, offered to take an informal sounding in Wisconsin, where Sherman Stock, his top staff member in the state, was making several appearances on Nelson's behalf that day. Wherever he went, Stock sought out Democrats he knew to ask for their appraisal of the situation, talking "very pointedly" with them. Every person he spoke to was "edgy" about keeping Eagleton; not one spoke up strongly in favor of keeping him on the ticket. Stock told Nelson, who relayed the information to McGovern. Nelson told McGovern he had changed his own mind and believed "a reconsideration was required" of Eagleton's candidacy.[17]

McGovern already had signaled the news media, within forty-eight hours of his "1,000 percent" support, that he was reconsidering. Theodore White, who chronicled the campaign, later called the 1,000 percent statement "possibly the most damaging single faux pas ever made by a Presidential candidate." McGovern now felt he had no choice but to ask Eagleton to leave the ticket. On Sunday, 30 July, McGovern and Eagleton met privately. Eagleton made his case for staying on the ticket and McGovern gave the counterarguments. They agreed to sleep on it.[18]

The next morning, McGovern was aboard *Air Force Two*, with a delegation of senators en route to New Orleans for the funeral of Senator Allen Ellender. Nelson was still at home shaving when McGovern called him from the plane. "If Tom hasn't announced his withdrawal by 10 A.M., would you go over and tell him I called and would like him to announce it?" McGovern asked.[19]

"I sure as hell don't want to, but I will convey what you have told me and let him make up his own mind," Nelson replied. "The last thing in the world I wanted to do was convey that message to my friend Tom," Nelson recalled. About 10:10, having heard nothing about an Eagleton decision, Nelson reluctantly made his way to Eagleton's Senate office, which was staked out by photographers. Eagleton was on the telephone when he came in, and Nelson could hear the conversation while he waited. Eagleton seemed in good spirits and told whoever was on the telephone that he had decided to withdraw. "That was the end of that. I never did have to tell him George called me," Nelson recalled. When he hung up, the two discussed the issue, and although Nelson downplayed his role and said he did nothing to influence the decision, Eagleton and his staff credited Nelson for the help he gave his friend in thinking it through. "Senator Nelson is a very wise and intuitive person about the ways of politics, and he was of great assistance to us in this decision," Eagleton said. Eagleton "values Senator Nelson's advice and counsel probably more than any other member of the Senate," an Eagleton aide said. "It was clear when Nelson left, Eagleton knew what his decision would be."[20] Nelson would say Eagleton's mind was made up before their conversation, but Eagleton clearly relied on him for support and advice even after the fact.

Nelson participated in one more painful meeting upon McGovern's return to Washington. He and Eagleton met in the Marble Room, the private, senators-only room off the Senate floor, next to the Democratic cloakroom. The national press corps crowded into the nearby Senate Caucus Room to await an announcement. Nelson, whom both Mc-Govern and Eagleton would describe as their closest friend in the Senate, was the only other person present. McGovern had invited him "on the assumption that the presence of a mutual friend respected by both Eagleton and me would be helpful in reaching a final understanding." Nelson asked Eagleton, who said he, too, would like to have him present. The decision on Eagleton's fate had been made, but he and McGovern once more went through the pros and cons. Eagleton said he was resigned to leaving the ticket, provided that his physical or mental health was not the reason given.[21]

Eagleton and McGovern went into the next room. Eagleton got two of his doctors on the telephone and put McGovern on the line, returning to sit with Nelson while McGovern spoke to the doctors. After-ward, they agreed on the statements they would make to the news media a short time later. "I didn't have to do anything. I was just there," Nelson said, insisting he was a passive observer, not an active partici-pant. Nelson had "very little to say," Eagleton said. McGovern said Nelson "was in on the crucial conversation just before we went out to meet the press." In any event, as Theodore White put it, when the con-versation ended, "the McGovern-Eagleton ticket was over."[22]

Any hope for McGovern's long-shot candidacy was over as well. McGovern went through the list of potential running mates again, and Kennedy, Ribicoff, Humphrey, Askew, and Muskie all declined before Sargent Shriver agreed to join the ticket. He knew better than to ask Nelson again. Even if Nelson had a change of heart—a highly unlikely development—he could never agree to replace his friend Tom Eagleton.

Nelson for President

The 1972 campaign was not the first or last time Nelson's name was touted for national office, although it was the only time he had to decline a proffered nomination. He was frequently mentioned as a potential candidate for president or vice president, but his answer was always no. Nelson was a rarity—an attractive candidate who was immune to the fever that inflames politicians' desire for higher office, who had never been bitten by the presidential bug. That did not preclude others from promoting his candidacy.

The 1976 presidential nomination was wide open on the Democratic side, after McGovern's crushing defeat and Richard Nixon's midterm resignation. Gerald Ford, who had succeeded to the presidency, faced a challenge from Ronald Reagan. By 1974 many Democrats were beginning to jockey for position—Representative Morris Udall of Arizona; Senators Fred Harris of Oklahoma, Scoop Jackson of Washington, and Lloyd Bentsen of Texas; and Governor George Wallace of Alabama. Walter Mondale had already gotten in and out of the race. Democrats had scheduled an unprecedented midterm convention in Kansas City, to adopt a new party charter, look over the crop of would-be 1976 candidates, and assess what had to be done to rebuild the party after its 1972 presidential disaster, in which the McGovern-Shriver ticket had carried only Massachusetts.

On the eve of the convention, a banner headline in Madison's *Capital Times* announced a Nelson for president effort, spearheaded by a group of Wisconsin Democrats—David Carley, a longtime Nelson ally who had become a successful businessman; John Schmitt, Wisconsin AFL-CIO president; Attorney General Bronson La Follette, grandson of Fighting Bob; and state representative Marjorie "Midge" Miller, a Madison activist in liberal and feminist causes. Senator J. William Fulbright of Arkansas and Leonard Woodcock also were named as members, but Woodcock quickly said he and the UAW were not supporting anyone yet. "We need somebody who can look down the road and see where we are going," Miller said. "Nelson is that kind of a person. He's tried and tested on the environmental issues and the war issues. He's a man of perception. I think he is a man of honor when honor is a thing that is hard to come by." Nelson had just been reelected to a third term in the Senate with 62 percent of the vote.[23]

Reporter John Patrick Hunter highlighted the problem for Nelson boosters in his third paragraph: "Nelson has been consulted several times but has refused to give the go-ahead signal" or authorize the official formation of a campaign committee. "I didn't respond in any positive way to it," Nelson said later. He simply had no interest. That did not stop the Nelson enthusiasts in Kansas City, who distributed the *Capital Times* story and talked up a Nelson candidacy with national political reporters and other delegates. They hoped a groundswell of support might persuade Nelson to at least look seriously at the race. Governor Patrick Lucey said at convention that he would give his "full and enthusiastic support" to Nelson, with a big qualifier—if Nelson "could be persuaded to make a full and active campaign." Lucey knew as well as anyone how unlikely that was to happen. "It doesn't look like we're going to talk Gaylord into it," one supporter said. "We couldn't even get him to come to Kansas City."[24]

Even after the convention, Carley and the *Capital Times* continued to talk excitedly about the enthusiasm Nelson's candidacy was generating. Carley said it would not be a "favorite son" effort, that there was growing national enthusiasm, and that "we will not quit easily the fight to persuade Nelson" to join the race. In Nelson's long career, this was the first attempt at a genuine draft. While Carley, Miller, and others maintained their public optimism, John Wyngaard, the insightful columnist, captured the truth. Acknowledging Nelson's appeal and ability, Wyngaard reeled off the reasons he would say no to the effort: wear and tear on his family, an unwillingness to make the kind of "financial arrangements that make good men flinch," his age (sixty in 1976), and lack of the fire in the belly, which his friend Mondale had acknowledged when he dropped out of the race. But the overriding reason, the column concluded, was how much Nelson loved the Senate and his role as an insider who was "quite satisfied with his career as it has evolved."[25]

Morris Rubin, publisher of *The Progressive* magazine and a longtime Nelson friend, had offered much the same observation when former Senator Ernest Gruening of Alaska urged him in early 1974 to promote Nelson as a presidential candidate. Gruening, one of Nelson's two allies in voting against Vietnam War appropriations, cited Nelson's "impeccable and enlightened public record" and suggested that he be drafted, even if he did not want the job. Rubin's letter in reply called Nelson "the ablest, most creative, most progressive and most forward-looking leader in sight. The trouble, as you accurately note, is that he does not want to be President." Rubin, who had just spent a week fishing with Nelson and two other friends in the Gulf of Mexico, said he was "convinced down to my toe-tips that no amount of cajoling, blandishments, or pressure will move him—and that goes for Carrie Lee as well—perhaps even more so."[26]

Nelson said much the same thing years later. "I never had any presidential bug or idea at all. The idea of taking two or three years to organize a national campaign was not appealing to me." He was quite content in the Senate. He liked his lifestyle, his wide circle of friends, the give-and-take at dinner parties—the whole scene. He was well respected, wielded some power, could get things done. He never said he would not like to be president—but he didn't want to run for the job and that was the Faustian bargain required. "I can't imagine any circumstances in which I would be involved in a presidential race," he said. "If someone would appoint me, I'd take it."[27]

The *Mayaguez* Incident

Whether caused by the Wisconsin committee, dissatisfaction with the Democratic presidential field, or Nelson's courageous stand on another controversial issue—the seizure of an American merchant ship, the *Mayaguez*—the subject of Nelson and the presidency intrigued some Washington political pundits during 1975. In a political insider column for the liberal *New Times* magazine, Robert Sam Anson, a newsman who had written McGovern's biography, asked where liberals would turn if Udall's candidacy fizzled. Nelson was a logical choice, but needed a draft to get him in the race, he said. McGovern would be likely to support Nelson, who had a sense of humor and the courage of his convictions, he reported. One ex-McGovern staffer said: "Gaylord Nelson is George McGovern with hair on his chest."[28]

Historian Arthur Schlesinger Jr. wrote in the *Wall Street Journal* that Nelson, "a wise and effective Senator," would immediately "command wide support throughout the party" if he ran, "but he remains obstinately resistant." Nelson was "one of the least likely to run, and at the same time the man regarded by many as the most suited for the job," a *Washington Monthly* article said. The article bemoaned the fact that the race for the Democratic nomination would be won "not by the swiftest but by the most driven." Nelson said that if he talked about the issues he cared about—world resource management, excessive military spending, the dangers of giantism—"I'd get run right out of the ballpark."[29]

In May 1975, Nelson stood alone in the Senate to question U.S. military action to free the *Mayaguez*, which had been captured by Cambodia's Khmer Rouge army. President Ford called it piracy and acted quickly, without consulting Congress, to order military action. The ship and its crew were freed, and reaction from the public and the Congress was nearly unanimous in support of Ford's action. Nelson strongly dissented:

> What vital national interest was at stake to justify such a precipitate and violent response? Did we need to sacrifice any of the lives of our soldiers, endanger the ship's crew, and bomb a Cambodian airport in order to settle this dispute? The answer, I think, is no. We did not even bother to give the negotiation process a fair trial. . . . The test of the strength and maturity of a superpower is better measured by its restraint in minor incidents rather than a demonstration of the power the world already knows we have at our command. I dissent from the conventional wisdom that tells us we must prove our virility and maintain our credibility by responding with violence wherever and whenever we may be challenged, however minor the insult.[30]

Nelson's stand won praise from columnists and editorial writers. While the presidential field played it safe, Nelson had the courage to emulate Adlai Stevenson and "talk sense to the American public," Tom Braden wrote in the *Washington Post*. Anthony Lewis of the *New York Times* called Nelson "the outstanding voice of reason and proportion." Braden quoted from some of Nelson's mail: "Go live in Cambodia." "Drop dead, you yellow-bellied traitor." "You are despicable and disgusting." "Let's give America back its pride." The mail was not all from Wisconsin, and it was not all negative or vicious. As time passed, more people wondered about the decision, especially upon learning more details of the operation. Marines who stormed aboard the container ship had found it empty, and Cambodia had sent a message indicating it would return the ship before the raid took place. The crew already had been released before the marines landed on a nearby island. Forty-one American servicemen lost their lives in the operation, and fifty more were wounded in trying to rescue the thirty-nine crew members who already had been released.[31]

As was often the case, Nelson was ahead of the curve—which may have its political rewards in hindsight but is a dangerous place for a mainstream presidential candidate. But Nelson was not a presidential candidate; he was a senator from Wisconsin with five years remaining in his term, free to speak his mind. Nor was his statement a calculated effort to get national attention. In fact, he simply responded to news media inquiries about the issue. With the exception of Earth Day and his crusade to focus attention on environmental issues, he never sought the national spotlight. In 1973 he turned down a chance to serve on the Senate Watergate Committee, which brought widespread media exposure to its members, especially chairman Sam Ervin. "Sam wants you," Senate majority leader Mike Mansfield told Nelson, but Nelson was up for reelection in 1974 and thought the committee would be meeting right through the election and making some enemies. "I didn't go and I don't regret it," he said later.[32] He might have added that it would be an enormous amount of work and a major time commitment, which he was not anxious to make.

Nelson wasn't afraid of a fight, of taking an unpopular stand, of conflict and controversy. His early stance on Vietnam and espousal of an environmental agenda that included banning the internal combustion engine were evidence of that. In 1971 he cast the only Senate vote against a new, widely promoted and heavily lobbied federal Conquest of Cancer agency, causing some constituents to ask why he had voted "in favor of cancer." He was vindicated when his position—that the cancer fight should remain in the National Institutes of Health, not be waged by an agency reporting directly to the president—prevailed in the House and in the final bill. He cast a hard vote in 1970 against the Newspaper Preservation Act, which would benefit the *Capital Times,* outraging Editor Miles McMillin, one of his best friends. He was among a handful of senators voting against confirmation of Henry Kissinger, Gerald Ford, Nelson Rockefeller, Clement Haynsworth, and other presidential appointees he felt did not measure up. But he wanted to pick his fights and did not feel obligated to get into every one that came along. For example, he talked about abortion only when cornered, not even responding to constituent letters on the emotional issue. Although he considered himself pro-choice, he saw no need to publicize that or to debate an issue on which there was no room for compromise. He had little to say about gun control, either. "Not an instinctive fighter" was how Ralph Nader's Congress Project put it, but added that "Nelson, when he has to fight, is successful."[33]

His response to the *Mayaguez* incident endeared him to those seeking a different kind of candidate, since all of the active and likely candidates had played it safe. They all wanted to be president too badly to take any risky, unpopular, or principled stands, the refrain went. Ambition was suspect. The *Washington Monthly* called it the "Mondale Paradox: anyone who is willing to run for president is temperamentally unsuited for the job." Udall underscored that in a comment to Meg Greenfield in *Newsweek*. For years, Udall said, the press and public had complained about the choice of candidates and wondered, where are the Jimmy Carters, the Walter Mondales, the Morris Udalls? "It is interesting that as soon as you announce, they take your name off the list," Udall said. "They want to know where are the Frank Churches— *where is Gaylord Nelson?*"[34]

Gaylord Nelson was in the U.S. Senate and quite content there, thank you. He hoped Udall would be the nominee and thought that he would be a good president and had "the bottom line qualification to be president: He had a sense of humor and he could laugh at himself."[35] As was his custom, Nelson kept that to himself and did not make any endorsement. Without his encouragement, the Nelson for president talk quietly evaporated. If there was a year that Nelson might have made a successful run, it was 1976. The unheralded and unknown Jimmy Carter proved that. But Carter wanted the job. Nelson did not.

31

The Environmental Decade

EARTH DAY INTRODUCED the Environmental Decade, an unparalleled period of legislative and grassroots activity to protect the nation's environment. More significant environmental legislation was signed into law during the eleven-year "decade" (1970-80) than during the 170-year period prior to Earth Day. Congress passed twenty-eight major environmental laws and hundreds of other public lands bills to protect and conserve natural resources.

"After Earth Day, nothing was the same," environmental writer Philip Shabecoff said. Earth Day brought revolutionary change and "touched off a great burst of activism that profoundly affected the nation's laws, its economy, its corporations, its farms, its politics, science, education, religion, and journalism." It achieved Nelson's long-sought goal of putting the environment onto the nation's political agenda. "Most important, the social forces unleashed after Earth Day changed, probably forever, the way Americans think about the environment."[1]

The turbulent 1960s had laid the groundwork, with the civil rights movement and the Great Society bringing major social change. Environmental awareness and pressure to clean up the environment had been building. Rachel Carson's *Silent Spring* and Paul Ehrlich's *The Population Bomb* had dramatized the issues and sparked national debate. The Wilderness Act, early versions of clean air and clean water acts, and the National Environmental Policy Act all became law in the 1960s. Earth Day took the movement to another, higher level.

President Nixon was "totally unprepared for the tidal wave of public opinion" on the issue when he took office in 1969, an aide said. A year later, in his 1970 State of the Union address, Nixon said that next to the desire for peace, the environment "may well become the major concern of the American people in the decade of the '70s." Some Democrats called Nixon a "Johnny come lately" on the issue, but Nelson welcomed Nixon's awakening. "The prestige of the President is a crucial factor in bringing this nation to realize that it must clean up the environment," Nelson said.[2]

Nelson had laid out his own ambitious and comprehensive environmental agenda for the 1970s in a Senate speech three days earlier. The 1960s had brought great prosperity, he said, but at a great price. "America has bought environmental disaster on the installment plan: Buy affluence now and let future generations pay the price. Trading away the future is a high price to pay for an electric swizzle stick—or a car with greater horsepower." He called for a new set of values, a new ecological ethic that considered the well-being of present and future generations, "where bigger is not necessarily better—where slower can be faster—and where less can be more." The key, he said, was "to put gross national quality above gross national product."[3]

Nelson's list included clean automobile engines, phosphorus-free detergents, a ban on eight toxic pesticides, elimination of all nonreturnable bottles and cans, antipollution devices on jet aircraft engines, creation of a federal environmental advocacy agency, a ban on dumping waste into the oceans and Great Lakes, tough federal controls on strip mining, a halt to oil drilling in the ocean, an environmental education program, a public transportation program, a national land use policy, and more. A commitment of $20 to $25 billion a year would be needed "just to begin the fight," Nelson said.[4]

Nelson also proposed a constitutional amendment, simply stating: *"Every person has the right to a decent environment. The United States and every state shall guarantee this right."* The amendment, he said, would give recourse to any citizen "to protect the sensitivities and well-being of himself, his family or his community from environmental assault." Several senators hailed the idea or signed on as cosponsors, but Nelson never took the amendment seriously. "It was a totally unmanageable proposition; it wouldn't work," he said decades later. "I never expected it to go." It got attention and was a useful educational tool to discuss the issues, but "I knew if I went before the Judiciary Committee they would eat me alive." The amendment went nowhere and died a quiet death in committee.[5]

Much of Nelson's legislative package fared better, and many major provisions became law during his last decade in office. The Environmental Decade began on 1 January 1970 when President Nixon signed the National Environmental Policy Act, including creation of a White House Council on Environmental Quality, which Nelson had proposed. In the flurry of post-Earth Day activity, half of the twenty bills on Nelson's environmental agenda had been passed, incorporated into other legislation, or had hearings completed by July 1970.[6] In some cases, like strip mining and pesticide control, action took most of the decade to complete.

Cleaning Up Auto Emissions

A blanket of smog choked the Atlantic seaboard from Maine to Florida during one hot week in late July of 1970. A cloud of pollution hovered over the nation's capital, where the Senate was working on a new clean air bill, the biggest piece of environmental legislation since Earth Day. Nelson seized the moment as a dramatic opportunity to move against the nation's biggest air polluter. He introduced an amendment to the Clean Air Act to ban the internal combustion engine after 1 January 1975. The gasoline-burning, exhaust-spewing engines, Nelson said, were the source of 60 percent of the nation's air pollution and as much as 90 percent in some metropolitan areas. A "disaster of colossal proportions" was in the offing, Nelson warned, painting a picture of a future day when entire metropolitan regions would be shut down repeatedly because of health hazards. He also called for a three-year moratorium on styling changes in new models and for the estimated $2 billion a year being spent on "fashion, frills, and fins" to be used instead to develop a clean, nonpolluting engine.[7]

The industry, predictably, said Nelson was badly informed, the proposal premature, and the deadline impossible. The president of American Motors, the smallest automaker and at the time Wisconsin's largest private employer, led the charge. He said the industry was not "callously indifferent and totally unresponsive" but the problem was difficult to solve. Nelson, he said, has "little or no knowledge of automobile design or manufacturing and apparently hasn't taken the trouble to find out." Henry Ford II, president of the company his grandfather started, warned that Nelson's bill could mean the end of auto manufacturing by 1975.[8]

The Senate adopted Nelson amendments to require a 90 percent reduction in auto emissions by 1975. The final conference committee bill that became law was not as tough but included Nelson's major provisions for emission control standards to reduce hydrocarbons, nitrous oxides, and carbon monoxide. Congress later delayed the deadline, but catalytic converters and unleaded gasoline were introduced by 1975 in response to the standards. Congress set the first fuel economy goals in 1974, as the nation experienced its first real energy crisis. By 1981 most new cars featured sophisticated catalytic converters, oxygen sensors, and computers and met Clean Air Act standards for the first time. Nelson had "raised the right issue" and forced the industry to change.[9]

More Victories

Nelson's Environmental Quality Education Act, to expand programs and courses from preschool through college and adult education, was signed by President Nixon on 30 October 1970. The program was funded only through 1975, however, and was repealed in 1981 by President Ronald Reagan. With or without federal programs or funding, environmental studies grew rapidly at all levels of education, and schools continued to be the backbone of Earth Day observances into the twenty-first century. To help institutionalize Earth Day, Nelson sponsored and organized Earth Week in 1971, 1972, and 1973, suggesting themes and encouraging schools to participate. He was prescient in choosing energy conservation as the theme of Earth Week 1973, three weeks before the oil embargo caused a national energy crisis. Wisconsin was the first state to mandate environmental education in elementary and high schools, and other states followed suit.[10]

Nelson won a battle to protect Everglades National Park in Florida from a nearby airport project that threatened the water supply for the Everglades, sometimes described as "a river of grass." The huge jet airport would have wiped out part of a large swamp that furnishes the Everglades with much of its surface water, without which the fragile ecosystem would be destroyed. In 1970 Nelson won approval of a provision to guarantee an adequate flow of water to the park. The airport project was eventually dropped after an outcry by ecologists and conservationists who opposed it.[11]

Nelson's Wisconsin colleague, William Proxmire, who had waged a long and sometimes lonely battle to cut off funding for development of a supersonic transport plane (SST), won his first Senate vote in December 1970 after switching tactics and focusing on environmental rather than economic arguments against the SST. The vote "demonstrates that the environmental issue has come of age," said Nelson, who had also been an early opponent of the SST, saying it could damage the stratosphere, foul the atmosphere, and perhaps even affect the world's weather. The SST was killed permanently the next spring.[12]

The Environmental Protection Agency, the federal environmental watchdog, was created without congressional action on 2 December 1970, and Nixon named William Ruckelshaus to head the new agency. Ruckelshaus issued the order to ban DDT in 1972, acting administratively to accomplish what Nelson had been trying to do legislatively since 1966.[13]

The Clean Air Act was the major piece of legislation enacted in 1970. While Nelson had an important role in shaping it, Edmund Muskie of Maine was the main author. As chairman of the Public Works Committee's environmental subcommittee, Muskie played the leading role in passage of key environmental legislation during the decade. If Nelson was the visionary, Muskie was the legislative craftsman. Nelson played the "bad cop" role, one Senate staff member said, allowing Muskie to win approval of "moderately progressive" policies to ward off something stronger from Nelson. In closed-door mark-up sessions on bills, Muskie would use the threat of a Nelson floor fight to leverage passage of his bills. "Muskie used Senator Nelson's commitment to radical change to propel radical change," said the staffer. Nelson's proposal to ban the internal combustion engine, for example, helped Muskie win the Clean Air Act requirements of 90 percent reduction in auto emissions. Scoop Jackson of Washington, the Interior chairman, also authored and guided a number of bills to passage. Nelson's decision in 1971 to give up his Interior seat to join the Senate Finance Committee reduced his hands-on influence on environmental bills. "I've gotten all the parks I can get for Wisconsin for the next twenty years," Nelson said, and he would be in a powerful position to pursue broader environmental interests on Finance. He continued to be a major force, the Senate's "resident national philosopher on ecology, though his critics would prefer that to read gadfly," *The New Republic* said.[14]

Although he had to work from outside of the relevant committees, a 1972 Ralph Nader report said Nelson "seeks to articulate environmental issues and educate his colleagues" in his floor speeches. He poked, pushed, prodded, and cajoled senators, many of whom looked to him for guidance on environmental issues. Nelson had demonstrated "foresight and confident leadership . . . along with a skillful ability to generate and pass important legislation when dealing with environmental and conservation issues," the Nader report said. "Environmental quality is a gut issue for Nelson. His heart is really in the battle." Nelson "would talk to anybody who would listen about the environment, about rivers, about forests, about the land and the wildlife," George McGovern said. "He was a genuine lover of beauty and nature."[15]

An Environmental Agenda

To Nelson, the accomplishments of 1970 were just a start—a down payment on what the nation owed the environment for its years of neglect. In January 1971 Nelson unveiled an environmental protection package of twenty-four bills and resolutions. His package included many familiar items but also broke some new ground with proposals to prohibit all commercial supersonic transport flights in the United States, require testing of new food additives, tax throwaway packaging, revise the mineral leasing law, halt poisoning of predators by federal agents, prohibit hunting from aircraft, allow states to use highway money for public transportation, declare a moratorium on offshore oil drilling, and protect and restore lake shorelines. "In years past, it would have been futile to think that Congress would consider, much less pass, any really tough environmental measures," Nelson said. "Now it is reasonable to hope that many of these . . . will be enacted into law."[16]

A number of Nelson proposals became law during the 1971–72 session. The Clean Water Act of 1972, with Muskie taking a lead role, was the first comprehensive national legislation to deal with water pollution.

One of its key components was the authorization for massive federal aid to help build municipal sewage treatment plants. Nelson had proposed, as early as 1966, that the federal government pay up to 90 percent of the cost of the plants, putting water cleanup at the same level as interstate highways. The Clean Water Act did not go all the way, but it did provide for 75 percent federal funding. It also included a Nelson amendment authorizing $800 million in long-term, low interest federal loans to small businesses for water pollution control and his proposal to ban dumping in the Great Lakes without permits. The Clean Water Act passed resoundingly over a Nixon veto. An ocean dumping ban Nelson had proposed also passed as part of a bigger measure, the Marine Protection, Research, and Sanctuaries Act.[17]

A comprehensive reform of pesticide control, similar in many respects to proposals Nelson had introduced, passed in 1972 as the Federal Environmental Pesticide Control Act. While it did not ban outright some of the toxic pesticides Nelson had targeted, it greatly broadened federal enforcement authority and set up a pesticide registry system. Bills similar to Nelson proposals to protect wild mustangs and to ban hunting from airplanes—designed primarily to save western timber wolves—both became law, and the president issued an executive order to ban the use of poisons in the federal predator control program, as Nelson had proposed. The Marine Mammal Protection Act, of which he was a cosponsor, was passed to stop the slaughter of seals and protect other ocean mammals. Finally, his bill to protect the lower Saint Croix River was signed into law.[18]

The League of Conservation Voters, formed in 1970 as the political arm of the environmental movement, gave Nelson a perfect score for his voting record during the Ninety-second Congress—the only member of Congress to achieve 100 percent. The list of roll call votes included Nelson's unsuccessful attempts to withhold funding for five major Corps of Engineer dam projects—including the massive Tennessee-Tombigbee Waterway in the South—until they complied with the National Environmental Policy Act. Nelson's amendment to withhold funds for Project Sanguine, which proposed building a huge antenna and radio transmission system in northern Wisconsin to allow communication with submarines, also made the list.[19] The massive size of the project threatened the scenic beauty and natural environment of the north woods, opponents said, and the extremely low frequency radiation posed potential health hazards. Nelson successfully limited expenditures to feasibility and environmental impact studies for the project, which would undergo two name changes and years of controversy before it eventually would be built in the 1980s as Project ELF.

Energy Crisis

Nelson had long warned of the dangers of wasting natural resources and the depletion of cheap and plentiful supplies of energy and raw materials. Having chosen energy conservation as the theme for Earth Week 1973, he gave a major speech at a candlelight dinner in Burlington, Wisconsin, whose residents had demonstrated ways to save energy. In the speech Nelson called for a $2.5-billion-a-year federal program to research and find ways to conserve energy, a national energy council appointed by the president to head the program, and a national energy conservation program. The nation's energy policy was "anarchy," he said, because of "our belief as a people that nature would provide an endless bounty and that technology would solve any problem." Kicking off Earth Week, he predicted in an interview on the *Today* television show that American gasoline prices—then at about thirty cents a gallon—would soon rise to as much as one dollar a gallon and challenged the auto industry to develop lighter vehicles to save gasoline.[20]

His words were prophetic. Arab oil producing countries, angry at the United States for aiding Israel in the Yom Kippur War, cut off oil exports to the United States in October 1973. Fuel prices skyrocketed, long lines formed at gas stations, and the nation reduced the speed limit to fifty-five miles per hour and took other actions to conserve energy— even turning off the lights on the national Christmas tree. The federal government established price, production, allocation, and marketing controls, and the nation began to look seriously at alternative sources of energy and ways to become more independent of foreign supplies. The embargo ended in March 1974, but American dependence on oil and its vulnerability to shortages had been demonstrated, and energy conservation was now a mainstream concern. "We are witnessing nothing less than the end of a national era," Nelson said. "The age of easy resource answers and reckless waste is finished."[21]

The energy crisis helped to justify the veto of a bill to establish federal regulations on strip mining. In 1965 Nelson had introduced the first bill to control strip mining and make mine operators responsible for land reclamation. At that point, more than three million acres had been dug up by strip mines, leaving behind huge stretches of blighted landscape that had been ripped, gouged, and abandoned. "Strip mining . . . destroys the land surface, increases erosion, pollutes rivers and streams, destroys natural beauty, and threatens public safety," Nelson's bill declared. The mining industry argued strongly for state regulation, which often was weak or nonexistent. Nelson introduced a bill in four straight sessions but got no action. But in 1973 the Senate passed several tough Nelson amendments to another strip mining bill. They required mining companies to restore mined areas to their original contours, banned dumping downslope from mining cuts, and authorized an excise tax to pay for reclamation from past mining operations. The United Mine Workers, environmental groups, and the President's Council on Environmental Quality all supported his amendments and the bill. But the coal companies, claiming the environmental provisions would increase utility bills at a time when rates were already soaring, successfully lobbied President Gerald Ford to veto the bill in December 1974.[22] An effective strip mining bill sponsored by House Interior Committee chairman Morris Udall of Arizona, supported by Nelson and environmentalists, finally became law in 1977.

Lame-Duck Legislation

The environmental decade ended when Ronald Reagan became president and installed James Watt as secretary of Interior. But it did not end with Reagan's election. Between election day in November 1980 and inauguration day in January 1981, the lame-duck Congress enacted two major environmental laws, the Alaska lands bill and Superfund, and lame-duck President Jimmy Carter signed them into law.

The effort to pass the Alaska lands bill spanned three administrations and five sessions of Congress. The idea had been on environmentalists' wish list since the passage of the Wilderness Act in 1964, and the legislation had been nine years in the making by the time it passed. The Alaska congressional delegation, led by Senator Ted Stevens, had always prevented passage. After a 1978 attempt at passage again ended in deadlock, Nelson joined Interior Secretary Cecil Andrus in urging President Carter to use his executive power to provide interim protection to the lands. Carter and Andrus did that with orders protecting more than one hundred million acres of land. The bill finally cleared Congress in the summer of 1980, but a Senate-House conference committee did not reach an agreement until after the November election. It was signed into law on 2 December 1980 as the Alaska National Interest Lands Conservation Act. "It was clear to anybody that if it didn't pass before 1980, Reagan would come in and you wouldn't ever set aside nearly as much wilderness and park lands," Nelson said. The bill protected 104.3 million acres, including twelve new parks, fifty-six million acres of wilderness, twenty-five wild and scenic rivers, and eleven new national wildlife refuges. "You'll never adopt anything like that again," Nelson said.[23]

Congress passed Superfund legislation nine days after President Carter signed the Alaska lands act. Love Canal, the disastrous hazardous waste dump at Niagara Falls, New York, came to light in 1978 and dramatized the need for a national cleanup program. Thousands of abandoned, leaking waste sites across the country posed threats to public health and the environment. Superfund—officially the Comprehensive Environmental Response, Compensation, and Liability Act—gave the EPA authority to identify hazardous sites, clean up the worst of them, and require the responsible party to pay for the cleanup. Superfund also established a trust fund to pay for cleanup in emergency situations.[24]

Nelson was a lame duck, too, one of several liberal senators who were victims of the 1980 Reagan landslide. Fittingly, in his final days on the Senate floor, he won passage of one more Wisconsin conservation bill, to prevent an estate on the upper Saint Croix River from being developed. The bill authorized the National Park Service to acquire the land, using condemnation if necessary, to add it to the Saint Croix Scenic Riverway. Nelson said the bill would "protect 1,380 acres of unspoiled scenic beauty, virgin timber, trout streams and lakes, nature trails and quiet, forest-covered hillsides and valleys." It was the last of

Nelson's bills still pending. His longtime ally, the *Capital Times,* noted its passage in an editorial and commented that Nelson's successor, Robert Kasten, had claimed during the campaign that Nelson was not "relevant" for the 1980s. "Nothing could be further from the truth," the newspaper said. "Nelson's final contribution to Wisconsin and the country is graphic proof of the falsity of that claim."[25]

32

A Lasting Legacy

NELSON'S LOSS of his Senate seat in 1980 stunned many Wisconsin citizens, political insiders, and Nelson friends. From all appearances, Nelson started his reelection campaign in a strong position. He had won five statewide elections and was reelected to the Senate twice by huge margins. In 1974 he had easily defeated Thomas Petri, a young Republican state senator, winning 63 percent of the vote. Nelson was never really challenged in that race against Petri, whom he described as "an able, honest, talented, fair-minded, perceptive man of commitment and perception and dedication." He added, with a laugh, "How often do you find two people like that in the same race?"[1]

But 1980 was different. While election night was a shock, in retrospect the loss was not as surprising as it seemed. Many Nelson friends and supporters—with the benefit of hindsight—claimed to have at least been uneasy about the race, even if they had not expected or predicted defeat. There were signs that all was not well. Nelson was a somewhat reluctant, or at least ambivalent, candidate, some said. His campaign was beset by problems and never really engaged until too late. His opponent ran an aggressive, sophisticated, hard-hitting campaign. President Jimmy Carter's reelection bid was in serious trouble, plagued by double-digit inflation and an ongoing hostage crisis in Iran. An organized conservative effort targeted a group of liberal Democratic senators for defeat and swept all but one of them out of office.

The times were different, but so was the candidate's profile and focus. Nelson, the unabashed liberal, now resisted the label, calling himself "a compassionate pragmatist" as the campaign began. Already a

member of the Senate Finance Committee, Nelson had become chairman of the Small Business Committee in 1975. He was talking about tax
policy, the need to eliminate red tape, stop inflation, curb wasteful
spending, and support a strong national defense. "So—is there a new
Nelson?" asked one reporter. The answer was no, not really. Nelson was
still fighting for a federal manpower bill, for environmental programs,
and to protect civil liberties. He had saved Social Security from bankruptcy, putting together bipartisan support to push through a $277 bil-
lion tax increase over ten years. He was still winning high ratings from
the AFL-CIO, Americans for Democratic Action, and other liberal
groups. But there was "a new emphasis, coinciding with his reelection
campaign." Public opinion had shifted to the right two years earlier,
Congressman Les Aspin's campaign manager said afterward, and Nelson waited too long to try to catch the wave.[2]

Republican voters nominated Robert Kasten, a former congressman, who won a four-way September primary with only 37 percent of
the vote. Kasten declared on election night that he would "hit hard on
the "Nelson gap—the difference between what he's been saying in Wisconsin and his votes in Washington." Kasten had suffered what many
saw as a career-ending upset defeat in the GOP primary for governor in
1978. He was "a clear underdog" against Nelson, with only eight weeks
between the primary and general elections, one analyst said, but that
could change, "especially if Nelson fulfills a lifelong tendency to loaf or
joke his way through the campaign."[3]

The Republican Senate Campaign Committee targeted Wisconsin
as one of eight states to receive maximum financial help, and Kasten
immediately went on the offensive. He attacked Nelson's small business
record as the worst in the Senate, citing ratings from a national organization, "a perfect example of the Nelson gap." Nelson protested that
he had a good record as Small Business Committee chairman, and that
the group had chosen votes that were minor or irrelevant.[4]

The campaign themes were clearly laid out in the first Nelson-
Kasten debate in late September. It was a slugfest. Kasten accused Nelson of saying one thing and doing another, of taking credit for things he
hadn't done, of flip-flopping on issues on the eve of the campaign. He
ripped Nelson for voting against defense budgets and for his small business record. Kasten, thirty-eight, said Nelson, sixty-four, had ideas that

were "worn out" and not appropriate for the 1980s. Nelson said Kasten had never passed a bill during four years in Congress. Nelson registered "probably the clearest knockdown of the evening" in his closing remarks, when he said Kasten had collected his full salary during his last year in Congress but showed up to vote only half the time. Kasten had a 53 percent House attendance record in 1978, when he was in Wisconsin campaigning for governor. Nelson had the last word in the debate, and "Kasten's face and scalp turned crimson," as he listened with no chance to defend himself.[5]

Meanwhile, the Nelson campaign was floundering, without clear direction, with a split between Washington and Wisconsin staff. The internal tensions finally resulted in campaign manager Louis Hanson, Nelson's longtime friend, associate, and aide-de-camp, leaving the campaign and returning to his northern Wisconsin home to recuperate. Kevin Gottlieb, Nelson's executive assistant in the Senate, came to Wisconsin two weeks after the September primary and took charge. In early October, when Kasten released a poll showing Kasten and Nelson in a dead heat, Nelson did not argue. Kasten, by virtue of having to win a primary, was "much better organized," Nelson said. "We're late. There's no question about it."[6]

Once Congress adjourned in October, Nelson hit the campaign trail hard. "Gaylord is busting his ass," a staff member said. Nelson "doesn't like campaigning, but does it to a fare-thee-well once he gets started," a *Washington Post* writer found. But there were signs that he was not connecting with voters the way he had in past campaigns, and Nelson was uncharacteristically cranky and irritable at times. "This was a different Nelson on the campaign trail," said a *Capital Times* reporter who had covered him for years. At a state bricklayers convention, "many members . . . gave Nelson a standing ovation—but not all of them. Many of the younger members clapped politely, but there was not the enthusiasm that the older members had for this man they had known for years," a reporter noted. To a new generation of voters Nelson was simply "a name in the news" whose accomplishments were ancient history, not an old friend who had fought for the issues they cared about. A debate sponsored by a Milwaukee Jewish congregation, long a Nelson stronghold, was pronounced a draw by the rabbi. When Vice President Walter Mondale campaigned with Nelson, Mondale "felt he wasn't campaigning well, wasn't at his best. I don't know what it was, but the spark and charm wasn't quite there . . . I could tell it wasn't clicking." A columnist warned Nelson, in print, "Most people have forgotten who Gaylord Nelson is or what he's like, and your more frequent appearances in the state during the last six months haven't sufficiently reestablished your personal presence."[7]

Nelson's campaign hit Kasten hard in television commercials, portraying him as a do-nothing congressman who had never passed a bill and didn't show up for work half of the time. The negative ads were a sharp departure from Nelson's previous nice-guy, issue-based campaigns. His aggressive campaigning and advertising appeared to have turned the tide, when Milwaukee newspaper polls in the final three weeks showed Nelson with leads of 20 percent or more. The mid-October polls suggested the race was over, but there was still "an anti-incumbent, anti-spending, anti-liberal tide running in this state," a columnist said, and Ronald Reagan's candidacy could help Kasten tap that sentiment. After listening to Reagan debate President Carter, Nelson turned off the car radio and told Gottlieb, "It's over." Did he think Reagan would win, Gottlieb asked. "Yes, but that's not what I'm talking about," Nelson said. "Ronald Reagan proved to the American people tonight that he is not a crazy man, not someone to be feared. If he wins it will bring out people who normally don't vote. That means I'm done."[8]

Kasten, who had a reputation for last-minute attacks and brass-knuckle tactics, counterpunched in the final weeks, with a television commercial in which a photo of a smiling Kasten was plastered with mud, thrown from off camera, presumably by Nelson. Kasten charged that Nelson had missed 63 percent of the hearings of the Small Business Committee he chaired, and that only 2 percent of the bills Nelson sponsored had become law. He claimed Nelson had used Senate funds to buy voter lists and pay for a newspaper clipping service for his campaign, which outraged Nelson.

A few days before the election, a Kasten surrogate said Nelson did not even own or rent a home in Wisconsin—one charge which was true. Nelson lived in Maryland and used his friend John Lawton's Madison home as a voting address, a common practice. Petri had tried to raise the issue in the 1974 race, calling Nelson a "Marylander," but it didn't stick. In 1980 it may have hit closer to the mark. Nelson's love for Wisconsin had not waned, and he certainly considered himself a Wisconsinite, but it had been eighteen years since he lived in the state, and his legislative focus was more on national issues. He was "starting to bridle at the tremendous demands" of traveling back to the state, he said after leaving office, recalling a time when he had flown to Wisconsin four times in seven days.[9] His heart was still in Wisconsin, but his center of gravity was Washington, D.C. Nelson and his staff insisted he was in Wisconsin at every opportunity, but perception often is reality in politics, and some observers, reporters, and voters suggested he may have lost touch.

The election was a disaster for Democrats, as a Reagan landslide swept Republicans into office across the nation. Although the Nelson-Kasten race was so close it would not be decided until 3 A.M., Nelson had an early indication, based on his Milwaukee County margin, that he would lose. As the night dragged on, he watched as his Senate colleagues and liberal soulmates, one after another, went down to defeat— George McGovern in South Dakota, Birch Bayh in Indiana, Frank Church in Idaho, John Culver in Iowa. Republicans gained twelve seats and took control of the Senate. Wisconsin was the last race decided. Kasten's final margin of victory was a razor thin 40,000 of 2.2 million votes cast. Reagan beat Carter in the state by 107,000 votes while independent John B. Anderson and running mate Patrick Lucey, former Wisconsin governor, polled 160,000 votes. A postelection poll showed that a surge to the GOP by undecided voters and vote-switching by others in the final days had given Reagan and Kasten their victories.

"No Tears"

Nelson was philosophical in defeat. When Tom Eagleton, who had won his own race, called Nelson, "all choked, bordering on crying," about Nelson's defeat, it was Nelson who consoled him. "His voice was almost chipper," Eagleton said. "There were no tears in this family," Carrie Lee said proudly the next morning as the Nelsons and their three children left for a Door County getaway that had been planned win or lose. "The state of Wisconsin got thirty good years out of Gaylord. They were good for him, too," she said. The rare family time together was a chance, Nelson said, "for the kids to see it didn't crush the old man. They could tell after four days together that I wasn't going to die or anything like that." Returning to the Capitol for a lame duck session of Congress, Nelson was more concerned about whether his staff would find jobs than what might happen to him. He admitted to being disappointed, but that was the extent of it. "I've known all my life that in this game you live and die by the sword. I've tried to steel myself for the day this would come. If I'm licked, I'm licked. This is no game for crybabies." Then he laughed. "If there's one thing I've learned, it's to compromise with the inevitable."[10]

"You know how these self-contained Norwegians are," Carrie Lee said. "He's the most well-balanced human being I know. He's in charge of his life." In all their years together, she said, "I've never heard him bitch much about anything. He just seems to take things in stride." Despite the Scandinavian stoicism they shared, Mondale said, "I think the defeat in 1980 hurt him. I'm an expert on politicians. That kind of hurt, there's no medicine for it, only time, and I wonder if you ever get over it." On the other hand, he said, "Something inside [Nelson] wasn't so sure he wanted it. Sometimes what people think they want is not what they want. It's harder to decide when to quit than when to start, I believe. Gaylord had been at it for three decades, was now in his mid-sixties, didn't have the ego that demanded it, and may have laid back against the oars—if it works out OK, but if not that's OK, too."[11]

Maybe he could have "done more, campaigned harder, spent a little more time at it," Nelson said. "But politics is such an all-consuming business that you must set some limits on how much you're going to do. Your constituents will be your family and you'll just be at it all day and all night, Saturdays and Sundays. But if that's the case, I say to hell with it." As it was, he said, his "only regret was that I didn't have more time with my kids as they were growing up." Carrie Lee would second that, telling a reporter the morning after the election, "As a politician, my husband was on the road for thirty years, and more often than not I was running a single-parent home." She was proud that she could do it and be "the one constant" in the children's lives, as the reporter put it. The children were grown, but Nelson said Carrie Lee had been going to the theater without him for eighteen years, and he was going to rectify that.[12]

The Perfect Job

But what next? Nelson was only months from his sixty-fifth birthday, but was clearly not ready to slow down, let alone retire. He had some options. John Lawton would welcome him back at his Madison law firm, but the Nelsons had been rooted in the Washington area for eighteen years, making that unlikely. Nelson clearly could have taken the path of many former members of Congress and made a substantial amount of money by adding his name to a firm's letterhead and lobbying his former colleagues. There were offers, or at least feelers, from some major Washington law firms with six-figure salaries attached. For doing little more than making an occasional well-placed telephone call to an old friend in the Senate, Nelson could have done well financially. But, as his friends knew well, that was not his style. Money had never been a motivating factor in his career, and thirty-two years of public life had not enriched him. His net worth was perhaps $150,000 when he left the Senate. The Nelsons lived comfortably, but modestly, in the Kensington, Maryland, home they had purchased in 1971, and he would draw a $30,000 annual Senate pension. Nelson wanted to remain active, and he also wanted to make a contribution, to do something he considered worthwhile. Bernie Koteen, a communications attorney and close Nelson friend, did some exploring and engineered an opportunity that was the perfect fit.

Nelson became chairman of the Wilderness Society, a Washington-based national organization devoted to preserving America's public lands and keeping them wild. Nelson, delighted, said he had never imagined there was such a job. In fact, there had not been such a job. The position he was offered—at perhaps half the salary he could have pulled down in the private sector—had been created to take advantage of his availability, society president William Turnage said, calling Nelson "Mr. Environment." As chairman, Nelson would be the group's chief spokesman and make speeches to colleges and organizations across the nation. It was an ideal job for Nelson, perhaps the nation's most prominent spokesperson on environmental issues. It was a position with no specific portfolio, freeing him to set his own agenda. He later assumed the title of counselor, a sort of "utility infielder or designated hitter" who spoke out and testified on national issues, advised the Wilderness Society on policy, and served as a resource for staff members who could learn from his experience and knowledge.[13]

Nelson's affiliation with the Wilderness Society closed the circle and proved again the ecologists' mantra that "everything is connected." Wisconsin wildlife ecologist Aldo Leopold, whose espousal of a "land ethic" in his classic environmental book, *A Sand County Almanac,* greatly influenced Nelson's thinking, was one of the founders of the Wilderness Society in 1935. Another was Benton MacKaye, the father of the Appalachian Trail, which Nelson-sponsored legislation had preserved.

Histories of the American environmental movement generally divide it into three parts, or waves. The first wave—the conservation movement—began in the early twentieth century with President Theodore Roosevelt, his chief forester, Gifford Pinchot, and naturalist John Muir, who spent his formative years in Wisconsin. The second wave was the environmental activism—some would say revolution—which emerged full-blown from the ferment of the 1960s on the first Earth Day. That "golden age" of the movement, the Environmental Decade, ended with Reagan's election. The "third wave" was launched in the 1980s, with a broader, global focus and new strategies and techniques. The movement became more mature and "in many ways more pragmatic and professional," wrote Philip Shabecoff. Environmentalism adapted to meet the growing threats and sophisticated opposition it faced from a hostile government and corporations whose bottom lines were threatened. The "third wave" was more likely to fight for the environment in the Capitol, in the courtroom, in the media, and on the Internet than in the streets. However, there remained a fringe element of hard-core, radical environmental activists and militants who favored direct action.[14]

Nelson was one of the few who bridged all three waves of the movement. As a legislator and governor of Wisconsin in the 1950s, the final decade of the first wave, he was a leading voice for conservation of natural resources. He was a key player in launching the second wave, pressing issues in the Senate in the 1960s and founding Earth Day. Now, at the Wilderness Society, he was an active participant in the third wave. When Nelson joined the organization it had forty-two thousand members, but Reagan's Interior Secretary James Watt and his antienvironmental policies actually were a boon to membership and fund-raising. By 1990 the Wilderness Society had grown to three hundred thousand members, opened regional offices, and hired a professional staff.

In the 1990s Nelson focused on population control, a cause he had espoused for a quarter century or more. Planet Earth, he warned, had a limited carrying capacity and could not support an unlimited population. He took the risky position of proposing drastically reduced immigration quotas for the United States, opening himself to charges of racism and insensitivity to global needs. Those who said the country could not solve the world's problem alone were accepting the "Global Pothole Theory," he said, suggesting that if you couldn't fill all of the potholes in the world, there was no point in filling the one in front of your own house. His prominence as Earth Day founder brought more speaking invitations than he could ever fulfill, and he traveled extensively to preach the environmental gospel. He had made a one-year commitment to the Wilderness Society when he took the job. He asked to be taken off the payroll twenty years later—but kept his office, continued to work every day, and traveled frequently, at age eighty-five, to speak on environmental topics. Every summer he returned to Wisconsin, with his family, for a vacation that always included time in Door County, a stay at Martin Hanson's northern retreat, and time in his beloved Clear Lake.

His message for Earth Day 2000 encapsulated his views as a new century began:

> Forging and maintaining a sustainable society is The Challenge for this and all generations to come. At this point in history, no nation has managed to evolve into a sustainable society. We are all pursuing a self-destructive course of fueling our economies by drawing down our natural capital—that is to say, by degrading and depleting our resource base—and counting it on the income side of the ledger. This, obviously, is not a sustainable situation over the long term. . . .
>
> We have finally come to understand that the real wealth of a nation is its air, water, soil, forests, rivers, lakes, oceans, scenic beauty, wildlife habitats, and biodiversity. Take this resource away, and all that is left is a wasteland. That's the whole economy. That is where all the economic activity and all the jobs come from. These biological systems contain the sustaining wealth of the world. . . . As we continue to degrade them, we are consuming our capital. And in the process, we erode our living standards and compromise the quality of our habitat. We are veering down a dangerous path. We are not just toying with nature; we are compromising the capacity of natural systems to do what they need to do to preserve a livable world.[15]

"We need a generation imbued with an environmental ethic," Nelson said repeatedly over the years, "which causes society to always ask the question: 'If we intrude on this work of nature, what will the consequences be?'" Such an ethic would recognize "the bonds that unite the species man with the natural systems of the planet" and would affirm humans' stewardship role on the planet, he said. The message and goal had not changed in the half-century since Aldo Leopold wrote, in *A Sand County Almanac,* of the need for what he called a land ethic: "A land ethic, then, reflects the existence of an ecological conscience, and this in turn reflects a conviction of individual responsibility for the health of the land." The land ethic "changes the role of Homo Sapiens from conqueror of the land-community to a plain member and citizen of it."[16] That, in a few sentences, was what the environmental movement was all about. Nelson's environmentalism was a direct descendant of Leopold's conservation.

"A new environmental ethic is evolving," Nelson said twenty-five years after the first Earth Day. In his visits to grade schools in the 1990s, he found young people well informed on environmental issues. He told of one young girl who proudly told him that when her mother came home with a can of tuna that did not have a "dolphin-safe" symbol, she insisted they drive back to the grocery store and exchange it. "This is the evolution of an ethic," he said. It is due in large part to Earth Day, Earth Week, and the ongoing environmental education the movement spawned in the nation's classrooms. "That's the heart of the matter," he said.[17]

Nurturing the new post-Earth Day ethic were environmental reporters, publications, lawyers, and environmental institutes at most major universities—all virtually nonexistent before Earth Day. The movement "wrought profound changes in American life—to its landscape, its institutions, and its people," one environmental writer said. "[Environmentalism] has changed the way most Americans look at the world and the way we live our daily lives." A majority of Americans consider themselves to be environmentalists, and "most of us now think of a healthy environment as a basic human right."[18]

Nelson's substantial legacy to Wisconsin and the nation was recognized with a large number of awards and honors, including the nation's highest civilian award, the Presidential Medal of Freedom, which he received in 1995. President William Clinton noted Nelson's career as "marked by integrity, civility, and vision. His legacy is inscribed in legislation, including the National Environmental Education Act and the 1964 Wilderness Act. As the father of Earth Day, he is the grandfather of all that grew out of that event." When the *Milwaukee Journal Sentinel* asked a panel of historians and other experts to name the most significant people in Wisconsin in the twentieth century, Nelson ranked fourth—behind Fighting Bob La Follette, Aldo Leopold, and Frank Lloyd Wright. The same panel ranked Nelson's establishment of the Outdoor Recreation Act Program in 1961 as the sixth most significant event of the century in Wisconsin.[19] A state park near Madison bears his name. The United Nations awarded him an Environmental Leadership Medal and Only One World Award. The University of Wisconsin named him its Centennial Alumnus, friends and admirers endowed a chair in his name at the university's Institute for Environmental Studies, and in 2002 the legislature and governor named the institute for him.

"I've loved every minute of it," Nelson said as he prepared to leave the Senate. "I thought about being a Senator when I was still a young boy. I was Mr. Mitty before it was even written. How can I complain?"[20] That was before he knew the opportunity that awaited him to spend the next two decades-plus with the Wilderness Society, promoting the issue closest to his heart.

"The maximum ambition I ever had, I lucked out and achieved," he said. "I got to be governor and U.S. senator and spend my life involved in politics, which is what I wanted to do."[21]

Not bad for a guy from Clear Lake.

Notes

Bibliography

Index

Notes

Abbreviations

AP	Associated Press
CLN	Carrie Lee Nelson
CQA	*Congressional Quarterly Almanac*
CT	*Capital Times*
GAN	Gaylord A. Nelson
MJ	*Milwaukee Journal*
MS	*Milwaukee Sentinel*
NYT	*New York Times*
UPI	United Press International
WP	*Washington Post*
WSJ	*Wisconsin State Journal*

The archives of the Wisconsin Historical Society in Madison is the depository for a large collection of materials from the political and personal life of Gaylord Nelson. It includes the Gaylord A. Nelson Papers, 1958–63, official papers from his term as governor of Wisconsin, which are catalogued and indexed. In the notes that follow, I refer to such items as "Nelson Papers" and identify their location by box number. The collection also includes papers from his term as U.S. senator, 1963–81; these materials are largely unprocessed, and I refer to such items as "Nelson Senate Papers." In addition, there is unprocessed family memorabilia that I refer to as "Nelson Family Papers." Film, videotape, and photographs are in the Society's visual materials archives.

Citations to interviews by Jim Cavanaugh in these notes refer to tape recordings from the Wisconsin Democratic Party Oral History Project, which is housed in the Wisconsin Historical Society Archives.

Prologue

1. Gladwin Hill, "Activity Ranges from Oratory to Legislation," *NYT*, 23 April 1970.

2. "A Giant Step—Or a Springtime Skip?" *Newsweek*, 4 May 1970, 27; Casey Burko, "Scott to Sue Milwaukee over Dumping and Polluting Lake," *Chicago Tribune*, 23 April 1970.

3. Richard Harwood, "Earth Day Stirs Nation," *WP*, 23 April 1970; "Area Holds Cleanup with Rally," *WP*, 23 April 1970.

4. Hill, "Activity Ranges."

5. Robert B. Semple Jr., "Nixon, Stressing Quality of Life, Asks in State of Union Message for Battle to Save Environment," *NYT,* 23 January 1970.

6. Hill, "Activity Ranges."

7. "Students in Earth Week Demonstration," *Clear Lake Star,* 30 April 1970.

8. Joseph Lelyveld, "Mood Is Joyful As City Gives Its Support," *NYT,* 23 April 1970; Harwood, "Earth Day"; "Earth Day Used by Firms for Vowing to Be Cleaner, Telling of Steps Taken," *Wall Street Journal,* 23 April 1970.

9. Harwood, "Earth Day."

10. "The Dawning of Earth Day," *Time,* 27 April 1970, 46; "Giant Step"; "The Good Earth," *NYT,* 23 April 1970.

11. GAN, Earth Day speech, University of Wisconsin, Madison, 21 April 1970, videotape, visual materials archive, Wisconsin Historical Society.

12. "Dawning of Earth Day."

13. Philip Shabecoff, *A Fierce Green Fire* (New York: Hill and Wang, 1993), 113; John Steele Gordon, "The American Environment," *American Heritage,* October 1993, 32.

14. GAN, "Earth Day—Where Do We Go from Here?" (speech at Catalyst Conference, University of Illinois, Urbana–Champaign, 6 October 1990), cited in *San Diego Earth Times* on-line.

15. Ibid.

16. W. O. Turnage, "Annual Report 1980, The Wilderness Society," *Living Wilderness* (Wilderness Society), spring 1981, 34.

17. Gaylord Nelson, "The Genesis of Earth Day," *Wisconsin Academy Review* 44 (fall 1998): 47.

Chapter 1. The Nelsons of Clear Lake

1. GAN, remarks, Janet Lee memorial service, 8 May 1999.

2. What the locals call Little Clear Lake is officially named Ice House Lake. Mud Lake was partially drained to build a road, and only a marsh remains.

3. Much of the material about early Clear Lake is from a book published by the community, *Clear Lake Centennial, 1875–1975.*

4. *1925 Wisconsin Blue Book* (Madison: Legislative Reference Library), 689.

5. Ruth Bunker Christiansen, comp., *Polk County Place Names and Fact Book* (Frederic, Wis., 1975), 1; "Will Phillips Remembers Clear Lake in the Year 1888," in *Clear Lake Centennial,* 13.

6. *Clear Lake Centennial,* 11–13.

7. Paul W. Glad, *The History of Wisconsin,* vol. 5, *War, a New Era, and Depression 1914–1940* (Madison: State Historical Society of Wisconsin, 1990), 212.

8. H. Russell Austin, *The Wisconsin Story,* rev. ed. (Milwaukee: Milwaukee Journal Co., 1973), 275.

9. John D. Buenker, *The History of Wisconsin,* vol. 4, *The Progressive Era, 1893–1914* (Madison: State Historical Society of Wisconsin, 1998), 491.

10. Robert S. Maxwell, *La Follette and the Rise of the Progressives in Wisconsin* (Madison: State Historical Society of Wisconsin, 1956), 192–93.

11. Unless otherwise noted, descriptions, recollections, and observations of family life and of life in Clear Lake during Nelson's childhood are from interviews by the author of Gaylord A. Nelson and his siblings Stannard Nelson and Janet Lee.

12. GAN, interview by author, 11 January 1993; Mary B. Nelson, speech text, Nelson Family Papers, Wisconsin Historical Society.

13. Postcards in Nelson Family Papers.

14. Andriessen/Bradt family tree from Janet Lee and GAN.

15. "Bradt Family News," vol. 1, no. 3, July 1990; John M. Ware, ed., *A Standard History of Waupaca County, Wisconsin* (Chicago: Lewis Publishing, 1917), 2:611–12.

16. "Bradt Family News"; John Patrick Hunter, "Nelson Grandfather Carved Proud Record in Civil War As Boy of 16," *CT,* 16 December 1958.

17. Ware, *History of Waupaca County,* 2:611–12.

18. The O'Brien immigration is recounted in a typewritten document among GAN's personal papers; Ware, *History of Waupaca County,* 2:612.

19. The Nilsson/Nelson family history is largely from an unpublished manuscript by Gertrude C. Nelson, sister of Anton Nelson, "The Honorable Governor Gaylord A. Nelson," in the possession of the author.

20. Nelson Family Papers.

21. GAN to Mary B. Nelson, 15 April 1930, Nelson Family Papers.

22. Charles T. Clark, interview by author, 2 July 1993.

23. Mrs. Harry Repp to Anton and Mary Nelson, 8 July 1956, Nelson Family Papers.

24. Glad, *History of Wisconsin,* 5:371, map.

Chapter 2. Happy

1. This chapter is based on interviews by the author with Gaylord Nelson, siblings Stannard Nelson and Janet Lee, and Clear Lake friends Erland Hanna, R. L. (Rusty) Peirson, C. Allan Benson, Tom Nilssen Jr., Fred Booth, William Barthman, Helen Holmes Hinds, Roger Jones, and Charles T. Clark. Nelson's sister Margaret (Peggy) died in March 1994 after a long illness in Portland, Oregon, where she had lived most of her adult life. Janet Lee died in October 1998.

Chapter 3. Into the World

1. Unless otherwise noted, most material in this chapter is from a series of interviews of GAN by the author.

2. GAN, speech text, fiftieth anniversary, Class of 1939, San Jose State University, California.

3. GAN, speech text, Wisconsin Law Alumni Association, 31 March 2000.

Chapter 4. General Nelson

1. Unless otherwise noted, material in this chapter is from a series of interviews with Gaylord and Carrie Lee Nelson by the author and from Nelson's military records.
2. GAN, interview by Jim Cavanaugh, 25 March 1985; E. Frederic Morrow, *Forty Years a Guinea Pig* (New York: Pilgrim Press, 1980), 48.
3. Wolfgang Saxon, "Harold Curtis Fleming Dies at 70; Tirelessly Fought for Civil Rights," *NYT,* 6 September 1992.
4. Morrow, *Forty Years,* 50.
5. Myra MacPherson, *The Power Lovers* (New York: G. P. Putnam, 1975), excerpted in *MJ,* 3 October 1975.
6. Helen Holmes Hinds, interview by author, 1 July 1993.
7. William R. Bechtel, "Will New Governor Be Able to Wrestle?" *MJ,* 5 November 1958.

Chapter 5. Losing with La Follette

1. Austin, *Wisconsin Story,* 313–14.
2. William F. Thompson, *The History of Wisconsin,* vol. 6, *Continuity and Change, 1940–1965* (Madison: State Historical Society of Wisconsin, 1988), 425–26, 446; Roger T. Johnson, *Robert M. La Follette Jr.* (Madison: State Historical Society of Wisconsin, 1964), 94–95, 103.
3. GAN, interview by Jim Cavanaugh, 25 March 1985.
4. Johnson, *La Follette,* 105–6; Thompson, *History of Wisconsin,* 6:438–41.
5. William A. Norris, "Progressives Now Back in GOP Fold," *MS,* 18 March 1946.
6. Laurence C. Eklund, "GOP Merger Approved at Portage Meet," *MJ,* 18 March 1946.
7. Thompson, *History of Wisconsin,* 6:450.
8. "Gaylord Nelson to Run for Assembly," *Clear Lake Star,* 16 May 1946.
9. "Local Candidate Expresses Views," *Clear Lake Star,* 8 August 1946.
10. Austin, *Wisconsin Story,* 354; Thompson, *History of Wisconsin,* 6:457.
11. GAN, interview by author, 3 July 1993.
12. Walter Shapiro, "Gaylord Nelson and the Myth of the White Knight," *Washington Monthly,* July–August 1975.
13. CLN, interview by author, 25 March 1999.
14. Thompson, *History of Wisconsin,* 6:566.
15. CLN, interview by author, 1 March 1993.
16. Ibid.

Chapter 6. Building a Party

1. Richard C. Haney, *A History of the Democratic Party of Wisconsin, 1949–1989* (Madison: Democratic Party of Wisconsin, 1989), 4-5.

2. Laurence C. Eklund, "GOP Merger Approved at Portage Meet," *MJ*, 18 March 1946.

3. GAN, interview by author, 3 July 1993.

4. Ibid.

5. "Gaylord Nelson Seeks Senate Seat on Democratic Ticket," *WSJ*, 23 July 1948.

6. Fred A. Risser, letter to author, 22 October 1999.

7. *1950 Wisconsin Blue Book* (Madison: Wisconsin Legislative Reference Library, 1950).

8. Ibid.; GAN, interview by author, 3 July 1993.

9. GAN, remarks at twenty-fifth anniversary celebration of Lawton and Cates, S.C., Madison, 22 March 1985; Thompson, *History of Wisconsin*, 6: 570-71.

10. Nelson's bill was SB-205; the Republican bill was AB-490. *Index to the Journals of the 69th Session of the Wisconsin Legislature, 1949* (Madison: Wisconsin Legislature, 1949); GAN, interview by author, 14 January 1993.

11. *1950 Wisconsin Blue Book*, 34; Edwin R. Bayley, interview by author, 15 July 1993.

12. Laird quote from "Gaylord Nelson: A Profile," Wisconsin Public Television, 22 April 1990; GAN, interview by Jim Cavanaugh, 28 March 1985.

13. GAN and CLN, interviews by author, 25 March 1999.

14. Haney, *History of the Democratic Party*, 7.

15. Jim Doyle, interview by Jim Cavanaugh, 23 January 1985.

16. Haney, *History of the Democratic Party*, 7; GAN, interview by author, 18 July 1993.

17. Interviews by Jim Cavanaugh of GAN, 25 March 1985, and Jim Doyle, 30 January 1985; Thompson, *History of Wisconsin*, 6:573.

18. "Nelson Named Co-Chairman of State DOC," *CT*, 29 August 1949.

19. Haney, *History of the Democratic Party*, 6-7.

20. GAN, interview by Jim Cavanaugh, 25 March 1985.

21. *Index to the Journals of the 70th Session of the Wisconsin Legislature, 1951* (Madison: Wisconsin Legislature, 1951). Nelson's bill was SB-558.

Chapter 7. Taking on McCarthy

1. Michael O'Brien, *McCarthy and McCarthyism in Wisconsin* (Columbia: University of Missouri Press, 1980), 84-88.

2. Ibid., 92-97; William T. Evjue, "A Reply to Mr. Johnson," *CT*, 14 March 1941; "CIO at Gisholt Assails Evjue As 'Dictator,'" *CT*, 13 March 1941.

3. Thomas C. Reeves, *The Life and Times of Joe McCarthy* (New York: Stein and Day, 1982), 195.

4. Joseph McCarthy, Remarks, *Congressional Record*, 81st Cong., 2d sess., 96, pt. 2:1952–54.

5. Reeves, *Life and Times*, 304, 364.

6. "Asks Hearings in Wisconsin on McCarthy," *CT*, 9 November 1951; Miles McMillin, "Nelson Gives Probers New Affidavits on Sen. McCarthy," *CT*, 27 February 1952.

7. Doyle, interview by Jim Cavanaugh, 30 January 1985.

8. GAN, interview by Jim Cavanaugh, 25 March 1985; Thompson, *History of Wisconsin*, 6:588–90.

9. GAN, interview by author, 18 July 1993.

10. Ibid.

11. Fairchild, interview by Jim Cavanaugh, 12 March 1985; Thompson, *History of Wisconsin*, 6:592–93; O'Brien, *McCarthy and McCarthyism*, 140; Haney, *History of the Democratic Party*, 8.

12. O'Brien, *McCarthy and McCarthyism*, 114–15.

13. GAN, interview by author, 18 July 1993; Edwin R. Bayley, *Joe McCarthy and the Press* (Madison: University of Wisconsin Press, 1981), 130.

14. GAN, interview by author, 18 July 1993.

15. GAN, interview by author, 14 January 1993; GAN, remarks, Lawton and Cates anniversary, 22 March 1985.

16. *1954 Wisconsin Blue Book* (Madison: Legislative Reference Library, 1954).

17. Doyle, interview by Jim Cavanaugh, 30 January 1985; O'Brien, *McCarthy and McCarthyism*, 145–46; AP, "Sen. McCarthy Defeats Fairchild," *CT*, 5 November 1952.

Chapter 8. Getting Ready to Run

1. Haney, *History of the Democratic Party*, 4; Thompson, *History of Wisconsin*, 6:596–97.

2. "Draft Nelson for Congress, Local AFL Union Urges," *CT*, 16 December 1953; "Labor Federation Backs Draft of Sen. Nelson As Congress Candidate," *CT*, 22 December 1953.

3. "Charges Dane GOP Has Deserted Ike in Favor of McCarthy," *CT*, 15 February 1954.

4. "Nelson Jabs at McCarthy," *MJ*, 15 February 1954.

5. "Farmers Urge Sen. Nelson to Run against Rep. Davis," *CT*, 10 March 1954; "Nelson to Seek Seat in Congress," *CT*, 20 May 1954.

6. GAN, interview by author, 18 July 1993.

7. CLN, interview by author, 25 March 1999.

8. Ibid.; William Korbel, interview by author, 16 July 1993.

9. "Nelson Challenges Davis to Sue or Withdraw Threat," *CT,* 23 August 1954.

10. Miles McMillin, "Sparks Fly As Davis and Nelson Clash over Tidelands Oil," *CT,* 20 September 1954.

11. Ibid.

12. Austin, *Wisconsin Story,* 352.

13. Thompson, *History of Wisconsin,* 6:597–99.

14. O'Brien, *McCarthy and McCarthyism,* 160; W. H. Lawrence, "Welch Assails M'Carthy's 'Cruelty' and 'Recklessness' in Attack on Aide; Senator, on Stand, Tells of Red Hunt," *NYT,* 10 June 1954; "McCarthy's Worst Enemy," *WSJ,* 11 June 1954.

15. O'Brien, *McCarthy and McCarthyism,* 158, 168–75.

16. GAN, interview by Jim Cavanaugh, 28 March 1985; CLN, interview by author, 25 March 1999.

17. William Robbins, "Nelson, Thompson and Bruner Appear As Legislative Winners," *WSJ,* 7 November 1956; *Wisconsin Blue Book, 1950–58.*

18. Jay G. Sykes, *Proxmire* (Washington: Robert B. Luce, 1972), 88; GAN, interview by author, 18 July 1993.

19. O'Brien, *McCarthy and McCarthyism,* 208; Henry Maier, interview by Jim Cavanaugh, 25 April 1985; GAN, interview by author, 18 July 1993.

20. "Nelson Pulls Out; Proxmire Issues Challenge to Reuss," *CT,* 10 May 1957; GAN, interview by author, 18 July 1993; Thompson, *History of Wisconsin,* 6:559–60.

21. J. Sykes, *Proxmire,* 90–92.

22. GAN, interview by author, 18 July 1993.

Chapter 9. Nelson for Governor

1. "'Nelson for Governor' Draft Is Launched at Janesville," *CT,* 5 September 1957; "Nelson Eyes Governor Race in '58," *CT,* 10 September 1957; AP, "Urge Reuss and Nelson Both to Run," *CT,* 12 September 1957; "262 Sign Petition to Draft Nelson to Run for Governor," *CT,* 14 September 1957.

2. GAN, interview by author, 18 July 1993; Reuss, interview by author, 22 June 1999.

3. Aldric Revell, "Nelson Runs for Governor," *CT,* 16 September 1957.

4. "No Need for a Sales Tax, Nelson Says," *CT,* 17 September 1957.

5. The *Capital Times* reported each appearance, apparently from Nelson press releases.

6. Aldric Revell, "Proxmire, Nelson Lash GOP on Stump," *CT,* 10 March 1958; Haney, *History of the Democratic Party,* 12.

7. "Says 'You and Me' Hurt Most by Republican Tax Gimmicks," *Wisconsin CIO News,* 22 March 1957.

8. GAN, interview by author, 18 July 1993.

358 • Notes to pages 83–90

9. Lew Roberts, "Nelson Works Hard at Getting Public to Know and Hear Him," *WSJ*, 22 October 1958.

10. Miles McMillin, "Hometown Gives Nelson Warm Campaign Send-off," *CT*, 9 December 1957.

11. Carl Eifert, "GOP Must Overcome Gov. Nelson's Charm," *MJ*, 8 August 1960.

12. Ibid.

13. GAN, interview by author, 18 July 1993; Shapiro, "Nelson and the Myth."

14. Eifert, "GOP Must Overcome"; Roberts, "Nelson Works Hard."

15. Elliott Maraniss, "Meet Wisconsin's New First Family," *CT*, 5 November 1958.

16. James D. Selk, "Loner Nelson Quips Along, Sure of Victory," *WSJ*, 27 October 1968.

17. Eifert, "GOP Must Overcome."

18. Aldric Revell, "Nelson Says GOP Sweeps Problems 'Under the Rug,'" *CT*, 14 January 1958; "Nelson Calls for New Leadership," *CT*, 26 February 1958; "Nelson Hits Secrecy in State Rule," *CT*, 17 April 1958; Aldric Revell, "Nelson Hailed As Liberal Trailblazer," *CT*, 21 April 1958.

19. Aldric Revell, "20 Years of GOP Too Long: Nelson," *CT*, 8 July 1958.

20. Haney, *History of the Democratic Party*, 12.

21. William R. Bechtel, "Lyndon Johnson Called Inadequate by Nelson," *MJ*, 21 April 1958; Edwin R. Bayley, "Some Think Nelson 'Rocks Boat,'" *MJ*, 8 May 1958.

22. Thompson, *History of Wisconsin*, 6:669–73.

23. GAN, interview by author, 18 July 1993.

24. Leon D. Epstein, *Politics in Wisconsin* (Madison: University of Wisconsin Press, 1958), 128; Edwin R. Bayley, "500 Excited Democrats Flock to Dinner That Drew 60 in '57," *MJ*, 10 March 1958.

25. Edwin R. Bayley, "Nelson Stresses Need to Revise State Taxes," *MJ*, 15 June 1958; Cyrus F. Rice, "Dems Cheer 'Pinch' Talk by Nelson," *MS*, 15 June 1958.

26. Bayley, "Nelson Stresses Need."

27. Edwin R. Bayley, "State's Democrats Retreat from Sales Tax Opposition," *MJ*, 16 June 1958; "Dems Demand Study of Taxes Paid in State," *MS*, 16 June 1958.

28. "Dems Demand Study."

29. Kenneth R. Fry, "Mrs. Phillips Wins Election to Democratic Party Post," *MJ*, 15 June 1958; Bayley, "Democrats Retreat."

30. GAN, interview by author, 23 March 1999.

Chapter 10. A Two-Party State

1. Thompson, *History of Wisconsin*, 6:671.

2. "Nelson Says Debt Hidden by Thomson," *CT*, 4 August 1958; Aldric

Revell, "Nelson Charges Thomson Hoax," *CT,* 13 August 1958; Austin, *Wisconsin Story,* 371.

3. "Gov. Thomson, Nelson Trade New Punches," *WSJ,* 9 August 1958; "Governor Hit on Sales Tax," *MJ,* 12 August 1958; William R. Bechtel, "Both Candidates Shun Top Issue—Sales Tax," *MJ,* 28 April 1958.

4. "Nelson Hits Thomson, Sees Road Fund Lag," *MJ,* 28 August 1958; "Nelson Cites Articles to Back Road 'Flop' Charge," *CT,* 2 September 1958; "Nelson 'Congratulates' Thomson on 7-Mile Road," *CT,* 5 September 1958; GAN, interview by author, 23 March 1999.

5. "Nelson Holds Foe Responsible for School Debt Rise," *CT,* 25 September 1958.

6. "Thomson Blasts Nelson 'Confusion,'" *WSJ,* 8 August 1958; "Thomson Charges Nelson with 'Corrupt Campaigning,'" *CT,* 14 August 1958; "Nelson Cites Articles"; "Nelson Blasts Building Cost," *MJ,* 7 August 1958.

7. Edwin R. Bayley, "Waukesha Democrats Hear a 'New' Nelson," *MJ,* 10 August 1958.

8. "Nelson Raps 'Dry Rot' in GOP Rule," *CT,* 19 September 1958.

9. Ibid.; GAN, interview by author, 18 July 1993.

10. "Thomson Given Good Margin in Farm Poll," *WSJ,* 20 September 1958; "Draws Close to Thomson," *CT,* 29 October 1958; "Proxmire Sure Nelson Will Win," *CT,* 2 August 1958; UPI, "Farm Chief Sees Sweep for Nelson," *CT,* 12 September 1958; "Carl Thompson Sees Victory for Nelson in Governor Race," *CT,* 25 October 1958.

11. Aldric Revell, "Nelson Hailed by Thousands in 24-Hour Drive in Milwaukee," *CT,* 28 October 1958; Loren H. Osman, "Nelson Stalks Votes on a Sleepless Night," *MJ,* 27 October 1958; GAN, interview by author, 18 July 1993.

12. GAN, interview by author, 18 July 1993.

13. "Nelson Has Set Fine Example Talking Issues in the Campaign," *MJ,* 2 November 1958.

14. Elliott Maraniss, "Nelson Last to Believe His Victory," *CT,* 5 November 1958.

15. *1960 Wisconsin Blue Book* (Madison: Wisconsin Legislative Reference Library, 1960).

Chapter 11. An Ambitious Agenda

1. CLN, interview by author, 25 March 1999.

2. "The Governor," *Let's See* (Milwaukee), 6–19 February 1959.

3. Lew Roberts, "Nelson Drives at Reorganizing State Agencies," *WSJ,* 25 November 1958; "Hush-Hush about State Debt," *Waukesha Freeman,* 26 November 1958; William C. Robbins, "Nelson to Use 'Microscope' on Fund Pleas," *WSJ,* 3 December 1958.

4. "Party's Party and Everyone Busy As Bee," *WSJ,* 4 January 1959; Colleen Dishon, "Inaugural Ball Is Held, Ends Day of Activities," *MJ,* 6 January 1959;

John Patrick Hunter "Nelson Plans to Meet Department Heads Each Week," *CT*, 6 January 1959.

5. "No Governor for 11 Minutes Today," *CT*, 5 January 1959.

6. Aldric Revell, "Nelson Pledges Return to 'Old Bob' Philosophy," *CT*, 5 January 1959.

7. GAN, inaugural address, reprinted in *CT*, 5 January 1959.

8. Ibid.

9. Ibid.

10. Kenneth Fry, "Governor Tells Taxpayers to Prepare to Pay More," *MJ*, 6 January 1959; Aldric Revell, "Nelson Warns of Tax Hike," *CT*, 6 January 1959.

11. Thompson, *History of Wisconsin*, 6:677.

12. GAN, interview by author, 3 May 1995.

13. Thompson, *History of Wisconsin*, 6:678.

14. Lew Roberts, "No. 1 Nelson Plan Economic Growth," *WSJ*, 23 January 1959.

15. GAN, interview by author, 3 May 1995.

16. Ibid.

17. Ibid.

18. "Nelson Names College Regents," *MJ*, 27 April 1959; GAN, interview by author, 3 May 1995; "Gov. Nelson Reappoints 2 Administrative Aides," *La Crosse Tribune*, 23 June 1960.

19. "Gov. Nelson Figures That He Batted .500," *MJ*, 26 July 1959; "Nelson Notes Bills' Success," *MJ*, 27 July 1959; "Nelson Claims 'Substantial Success' for His Program," *CT*, 27 July 1959.

20. Aldric Revell, "Skirmishes in '59 Legislature Set '60 Campaign Issues," *CT*, 27 July 1959.

21. Aldric Revell, "Nelson for State Withholding Tax," *CT*, 2 March 1959; UPI, "Pay-As-Go Tax Urged by Nelson," *WSJ*, 15 March 1959.

22. Aldric Revell, "'Bare Bones' for 1 Year," *CT*, 4 February 1959; Aldric Revell, "Budget Accord Nearer," *CT*, 3 June 1959; "Budget Bill to Governor," *CT*, 23 June 1959.

23. John Patrick Hunter, "800 Crowd Hearing Hall," *CT*, 22 April 1959; John Wyngaard, "Nelson Shows New Side in Fight for Tax," *Green Bay Press Gazette*, 22 April 1959.

24. Hunter, "800 Crowd."

25. Aldric Revell, "Tax Study Group Named by Nelson," *CT*, 11 June 1959; Aldric Revell, "Nelson Asks Tax Recommendations before Sept. 15," *CT*, 25 June 1959.

26. GAN, interview by author, 3 May 1995.

27. Aldric Revell, "Nelson Ducks on Sales Tax," *CT*, 18 September 1959.

28. William T. Evjue, "A Platform Pledge Is Sacred Covenant with the People," *CT*, 22 September 1959.

29. Aldric Revell, "No Sales Tax Now, Nelson Pledges," *CT*, 20 October

1959; William R. Bechtel, "Nelson Asks Withholding Tax, Rise in Bank and Cigaret Levies," *MJ*, 11 November 1959; Aldric Revell, "State Faces Financial Deadlock," *CT*, 12 November 1959.

30. Kenneth Ray, "GOP Sets Battle Line on Nelson's Tax Plan," *MJ*, 12 November 1959; Aldric Revell, "Nelson Will Campaign on Taxes," *CT*, 23 November 1959.

31. Aldric Revell, "Over 50 Speak on Two Bills," *CT*, 12 December 1959.

32. Kenneth Fry, "Recess Demanded by Angry Nelson," *MJ*, 14 January 1960.

33. "Nelson Yields, with a Rebuke," *WSJ*, 15 January 1960; Aldric Revell, "Senate Kills Budget Bill," *CT*, 15 January 1960; "Purely Partisan Struggle That Created Legislative Stalemate," *MJ*, 15 January 1960.

34. William R. Bechtel, "Nelson Sees No Need to Raise Tax," *MJ*, 17 May 1960; "Republicans Show Who They Represent," *CT*, 30 May 1960; Thompson, *History of Wisconsin*, 6:679.

Chapter 12. Family Fights

1. Theodore H. White, *The Making of the President 1960* (New York: Atheneum Publishers, 1962), 80.

2. John Reynolds, interview by Jim Cavanaugh, 11 April 1985.

3. William R. Bechtel, "Lyndon Johnson Called Inadequate by Nelson," *MJ*, 21 April 1958; Patrick J. Lucey, interview by Jim Cavanaugh, 18 April 1985; White, *Making of the President 1960*, 82.

4. GAN, interview by author, 15 July 1993.

5. John O'Donnell, "Capitol Stuff," *New York Daily News*, 15 June 1969; Marquis W. Childs, "Wisconsin Battle Lines Are Drawn for Kind of Fight Democrats Dread," *St. Louis Post-Dispatch*, 19 July 1959.

6. GAN, interview by author, 15 July 1993.

7. "'Unfounded' Charges Hit," *CT*, 8 February 1960.

8. William C. Robbins, "Nelson Raps Humphrey Blast at Kennedy Vote," *WSJ*, 23 March 1960.

9. "Not Criticizing Humphrey Personally, Nelson Says," *CT*, 25 March 1960; GAN, conversation with author.

10. Thompson, *History of Wisconsin*, 6:687–93.

11. James E. Doyle, interview by Charles T. Morrissey, transcript, 15 January 1966, Oral History Interviews, John Fitzgerald Kennedy Library, Boston.

12. Lucey, interview by Jim Cavanaugh; Proxmire, interview by Jim Cavanaugh, 27 March 1985; Frank Nikolay, conversation with author.

13. Lucey, interview by Jim Cavanaugh; Haney, *History of Democratic Party*, 12.

14. Lucey, interview by Jim Cavanaugh; GAN, interview by Jim Cavanaugh, 28 March 1985; GAN, interview by author, 28 September 1997.

15. "Foes Meet, Avoid Strife," *MJ,* 29 May 1958; Lucey, interview by Jim Cavanaugh.

16. Haney, *History of Democratic Party,* 12; GAN, interview by author, 28 September 1997; GAN, interview by Jim Cavanaugh, 28 March 1985.

Chapter 13. Still the Underdogs

1. "Nelson Is Candidate for Second Term as Governor," *CT,* 7 June 1960; John Wyngaard, "Nelson's Personality May Be Best Appeal to Voters," *Green Bay Press Gazette,* 15 June 1960; Ira Kapenstein, "November Is Test, Nelson Tells Party," *MJ,* 26 June 1960.

2. Thompson, *History of Wisconsin,* 6:560, 6:694.

3. *1962 Wisconsin Blue Book* (Madison: Wisconsin Legislative Reference Library, 1962), 722, 743–44; Kapenstein, "November Is Test."

4. "Gov. Nelson to Make Film for Presidential Campaign," *MJ,* 21 June 1960.

5. Ira Kapenstein, "Gov. Nelson Strongly Considered for Vice-Presidential Nomination," *MJ,* 11 July 1960; John Wyngaard, "Gov. Nelson Maintains His Neutral Stand," *Green Bay Press Gazette,* 9 July 1960.

6. GAN, interview by author, 15 July 1993.

7. Ibid.; William R. Bechtel, "Nelson Not Consulted on Johnson, He Says," *MJ,* 18 July 1960.

8. Carl Eifert, "Governor's Vacation Just Didn't Work Out," *MJ,* 1 August 1960.

9. Monica Bayley, interview by author, 16 July 1993.

10. Lucy Colbert, "Come Along for a Visit with Mrs. Gaylord Nelson," *Racine Journal-Times,* 18 December 1960.

11. CLN, interview, 25 March 1999; "Not Dedicated to Politics, Wife of Governor Asserts," *MJ,* 9 November 1960.

12. John Wyngaard, "Nelson Shows New Side in Fight for Tax," *Green Bay Press Gazette,* 22 April 1959; Kenneth E. Fry, "Gaylord Nelson Has Changed since Serving in Top State Job," *MJ,* 25 October 1960.

13. "Nelson's Humor Seen As an Asset Politically," *MJ,* 9 November 1960.

14. David W. Adamany, "1960 Election in Wisconsin" (master's thesis, University of Wisconsin, 1963), 88.

15. Ira Kapenstein, "Kuehn-Nelson Debate Is Political Milestone," *MJ,* 20 September 1960; "Nelson-Kuehn Debate Too Much like Alphonse and Gaston," *CT,* 26 September 1960.

16. Aldric Revell, "Nelson and Kuehn Emphasize 2 Issues," *CT,* 20 September 1960.

17. Kenneth Fry, "Nelson Sees Gains in Fox Valley," *MJ,* 14 October 1960; Aldric Revell, "Nelson Hails Dem Rise in GOP Areas," *CT,* 14 October 1960.

18. "Kuehn Cites Need of Tax Uniformity," *MS,* 3 November 1960; Aldric Revell, "Kuehn Urges '61 Sales Tax," *CT,* 3 November 1960.

19. AP, "Agriculturist Poll Shows Nelson Far Out in Front," *CT,* 1 November 1960; Harvey Breuscher, AP, "Nelson 'Smashing Favorite' to Win a Second Term," *CT,* 4 November 1960; "Attempt to Label Nash Communist Fails," *CT,* 5 November 1960; Adamany, "1960 Election," 93; William R. Bechtel, "Nelson Advisors Aim at Biggest Victory Yet," *MJ,* 22 August 1960.

20. John Patrick Hunter, "Governor Takes Off from Returns to See Ill Friend," *CT,* 9 November 1960; Adamany, "1960 Election," 95.

21. Thompson, *History of Wisconsin,* 6:697.

22. Aldric Revell, "Nelson Program Chances Crushed by GOP Surge," *CT,* 10 November 1960; John Patrick Hunter, "Nelson Pledges Fight for 'Best Program I Know,'" *CT,* 10 November 1960; John Patrick Hunter, "Nelson Vows to Fight Hard for His Plans," *MJ,* 10 November 1960.

23. "Nelson Won't Accept Kennedy Cabinet Job," *MJ,* 21 November 1960; William R. Bechtel, "Nelson Hits Hard in Inaugural Talk," *MJ,* 3 January 1961.

24. Llewellyn G. Roberts, "Nelson Offers 40 Proposals," *WSJ,* 19 January 1961.

Chapter 14. The Conservation Governor

1. Two important sources, used extensively for this chapter, are Thomas R. Huffman's *Protectors of the Land and Water* (Chapel Hill: University of North Carolina Press, 1994), and Richard A. Conover, "Wisconsin's Conservation Land Acquisition Program: A Study of Natural Resources Policy-Making" (Ph.D. dissertation, Colorado State University, 1974).

2. "Governor Signs Conservation and Recreation Budget," *CT,* 16 October 1959.

3. I. V. Fine and E. E. Werner, "Wisconsin's Share of the Chicago Vacation-Recreation Market," *Wisconsin Vacation-Recreation Papers,* February 1960, cited in Huffman, *Protectors,* 25.

4. Huffman, *Protectors,* 25; Walter Scott, address at Wisconsin chapter, Soil Conservation Association of America, 23 July 1959, cited in Conover, "Wisconsin's Conservation," 71; "Nelson Tours State Parks, Talks of Adding Campsites," *CT,* 30 August 1960.

5. "Nelson on Resources," *CT,* 14 October 1958; "Nelson Raps Politics in Fisheries," *CT,* 17 October 1958.

6. Aldric Revell, "Nelson Asks New Resource Bureau," *CT,* 23 April 1959; Harold C. Jordahl, notes to author, 11 April 2002.

7. Conover, "Wisconsin's Conservation," 76–77.

8. GAN, interview by author, 3 May 1995.

9. Conover, "Wisconsin's Conservation," 80, 87–88.

10. John Wyngaard, "Governor Readies 'Crash' Program to Expand Recreational Resources," *Green Bay Press Gazette,* 14 February 1961.

11. GAN, text of resource development message, *MJ,* 15 March 1965.

12. Dan Satran, "Nelson's Crash Plans for Recreation Win Wide Support in Resort Areas," *CT,* 27 March 1961.

13. Richard Bradee, "Conservation Dept. Sets Own Terms for Nelson Plan," *CT*, 15 April 1961.

14. "Resource Plan Given by Nelson," *CT*, 30 May 1961; AP, "Nelson Lists Projects for Southwest Region," *MJ*, 30 May 1961; "30 New Lakes for Southwest in Nelson Plan," *MS*, 30 May 1961.

15. "We Like It," *Cadott Sentinel*, 4 May 1961; "Lauds Nelson Program for Conservation," *Wisconsin Rapids Tribune*, 1 May 1961; UPI, "Game Congress Endorses Nelson's 'Crash' Program," *Shawano Evening Leader*, 19 May 1961; John Wyngaard, "Conservation Doing Better Than Expected," *Appleton Post Crescent*, 30 May 1961.

16. Nelson Papers, box 24.

17. Huffman, *Protectors*, 39; "Resource Plan Supported Strongly," *MJ*, 25 May 1961; AP, "Nelson Urges Approval for Outdoor Plan," *Fond du Lac Commonwealth Reporter*, 25 May 1961.

18. Conover, "Wisconsin's Conservation," 97–98; "Land Acquisition Brings Protests," *Appleton Post Crescent*, 29 May 1961.

19. Conover, "Wisconsin's Conservation," 98–101; John Wyngaard, "Nelson's Conservation Plan Passes Assembly," *La Crosse Tribune*, 13 July 1961.

20. GAN, interview by author, 3 May 1995.

21. AP, "Senate OKs $50 Million Outdoor Bill," *Oshkosh Northwestern*, 11 August 1961; "Outdoor Plan Is Approved," *MJ*, 11 August 1961.

22. John Wyngaard, "Legislature Passes Nelson Outdoor Bill," *Appleton Post Crescent*, 11 August 1961; John Brogan, interview by author, 17 July 1993. Although there is agreement on the events, the identity of the Republican businessman is in dispute. Brogan says it was Fred Burrall of Green Bay. Conover, citing a letter from columnist John Wyngaard, says it was A. C. "Snick" Gross.

23. Brogan, interview by author; GAN, interview by author, 3 May 1995; Aldric Revell, "$50 Million Resources Plan Passed," *CT*, 11 August 1961.

24. Huffman, *Protectors*, 41; "Signs Conservation Bill," photo, *CT*, 2 September 1961; "Nelson Signs Resource Bill," *MJ*, 28 August 1961; "Recreation Race Is Seen for U.S. Space," *MJ*, 23 September 1961; John Wyngaard, "Recreational Lands Bill Political Coup," *Appleton Post Crescent*, 17 August 1961.

25. Huffman, *Protectors*, 44, 32.

26. "State Resource Gains Outlined by Governor," *MJ*, 20 September 1962.

27. Thompson, *History of Wisconsin*, 6:297–98.

28. Ibid.

Chapter 15. The Great Tax Debate

1. "Governor Declines Comment on Blue Ribbon Tax Package," *WSJ*, 15 December 1960.

2. "Door Is Closed Gently on Sales Tax Proposal," *MJ*, 15 February 1961.

3. William R. Bechtel, "Surprise Tax Plan Gets Nelson Off Hook," *MJ*, 16 February 1961; Llewellyn G. Roberts, "Nelson Seeks 1% Tax Boost," *WSJ*, 16 February 1961.

4. Aldric Revell, "Nelson Lashes Out at Do-Nothing GOP Legislature," *CT*, 24 April 1961.

5. "All Democrats Vote against Sales Tax," *CT*, 30 March 1961; William R. Bechtel, "Action Irks Legislators at Convention," *MJ*, 11 June 1961; Llewellyn G. Roberts, "Legislature May Recess without Tax Bill Voting," *WSJ*, 1 July 1961; "GOP Convention Action Imperils State Tax Bill," *MJ*, 12 June 1961.

6. Aldric Revell, "Nelson Vetoes Sales Tax, Opens Door to Compromise," *CT*, 30 August 1961; "GOP Rips Nelson for His Action," *WSJ*, 31 August 1961.

7. Llewellyn G. Roberts, "'No Sale' Yet on Sales Tax," *WSJ*, 6 October 1961.

8. GAN, interview by Jim Cavanaugh, 28 March 1985; UPI, "Democrats Buzz over Disclosure Nelson Asked Lucey to Step Down," *WSJ*, 16 September 1961; William R. Bechtel, "Nelson Backs Nikolay in Challenge to Lucey," *MJ*, 30 August 1961; Aldric Revell, "Governor Makes Peace Offer to Pro-Lucey Dems," *CT*, 20 September 1961.

9. Edwin R. Bayley, interview by author, 15 July 1993; John Patrick Hunter, "Nelson and Lucey Reach Peace Pact," *CT*, 21 September 1961.

10. Roberts, "'No Sale'"; GAN, interview by author, 3 May 1995.

11. "Sales Tax Splits Nelson and Party," *CT*, 16 October 1961; GAN, interview by author, 3 May 1995; William C. Robbins, "Nelson Unconcerned by Slap from Party," *WSJ*, 17 October 1961.

12. William R. Bechtel, "Nelson Raps Convention Tax Decision," *MJ*, 16 October 1961.

13. William R. Bechtel, "Letters Hail Governor on Convention Speech," *MJ*, 23 October 1961;
William R. Bechtel, "Nelson Broke Ranks in Sales Tax Dispute," *MJ*, 16 October 1961.

14. Richard Bradee, "3% Luxury Sales Tax Proposed by Nelson," *CT*, 23 October 1961.

15. GAN, speech text, reprinted in *CT*, 31 October 1961; John Wyngaard, "Evolution of Thinking by Governor Shown in Speech," *Green Bay Press Gazette*, 4 November 1961.

16. GAN, interview by author, 3 May 1995.

17. Aldric Revell, "Many Foes at Hearing," *CT*, 9 November 1961.

18. "Nelson in Plea to Assembly," *CT*, 4 December 1961.

19. Llewellyn G. Roberts, "It's Compromise or Chaos, Nelson Warns Legislators," *WSJ*, 12 December 1961; Richard Bradee, "Nelson's Tax Bill Passed," *CT*, 13 December 1961; Thompson, *History of Wisconsin*, 6:705.

20. GAN, interview by author, 3 May 1995.

21. Richard Bradee, "Nelson's Tax Bill Passes!" *CT*, 23 December 1961; Carl Eifert, "Nelson Signs Tax Revision Bill into Law," *MJ*, 28 December 1961;

Aldric Revell, "Governor Signs Tax Bill; Lashes Bank Loophole," *CT,* 28 December 1961.

22. Revell, "Governor Signs."

23. Thompson, *History of Wisconsin,* 6:700, 6:703; Austin, *Wisconsin Story,* 376.

24. Harold C. Jordahl Jr., "Gaylord Nelson: An Extraordinary Environmental Leader," nomination of GAN for Tyler Prize for Environmental Achievement, 1998; GAN, "The Legend and the Legacy" (paper presented at colloquium, "The Wisconsin Idea: A Tribute to Carlisle P. Runge," University of Wisconsin–Madison, 28 March 1981); Jordahl, note to author, 11 April 2002.

25. Austin, *Wisconsin Story,* 371; John Patrick Hunter, "Governor's Sister Joins Vigil of Capitol 'Liberty Lobbyists,'" *CT,* 2 August 1961; Janet Lee, interview by author, 24 February 1993.

26. Austin, *Wisconsin Story,* 375; Thompson, *History of Wisconsin,* 6:700.

Chapter 16. On to the Senate

1. GAN, interview by author, 3 May 1995.

2. Aldric Revell, "How Nelson-Wiley Senate Race Shapes Up," *CT,* 23 April 1962.

3. Aldric Revell, "No 3rd Term, Nelson Says," *CT,* 12 March 1962; CLN, conversation with author.

4. "Nelson in U.S. Senate Race," *CT,* 28 May 1962; Harvey Breuscher, AP, "Nelson Launches Campaign," *CT,* 12 June 1962.

5. "Luceys Claim Insult, Quit Nelson Dinner," *MJ,* 25 October 1967.

6. GAN, interview by Cavanaugh, 28 March 1985.

7. John W. Kole, "Democrats' Tax View Solidifies No. 1 Issue," MJ, 7 June 1962; Aldric Revell, "Governor Backs Dem Tax Plank," *CT,* 6 June 1962; William C. Robbins, "Gov. Nelson in Serious Trouble, He Says, Because of Sales Tax," *WSJ,* 23 June 1962.

8. Aldric Revell, "Voters Mad at Tax: Nelson," *CT,* 23 June 1962.

9. Ibid.

10. William R. Bechtel, "Nelson's Frank Talk Bared Real Troubles," *MJ,* 9 July 1962; William R. Bechtel, "Nelson Was Spurred by Poor Poll Showing," *MJ,* 14 November 1962.

11. "Kefauver Lashes Wiley's Drug Role," *CT,* 31 October 1962.

12. UPI, "Wiley Attacks Nelson for 'Empty Chair' Campaigning," *CT,* 21 September 1962.

13. "Quizzed on Medicare, Wiley Becomes Angry," *MJ,* 9 October 1962; "Medicare Bill Letter 'Mistake,' Wiley Says," *MJ,* 21 October 1962.

14. Doris Fleeson, "A Look at the Wisconsin Campaign," *CT,* 20 October 1962.

15. Robert S. Allen and Paul Scott, "Nelson Gets Cold Shoulder from

Dems," *CT,* 17 August 1962; "Nelson Given Kennedy Aid," *MJ,* 29 October 1962.

16. Gerald S. and Deborah H. Strober, *Let Us Begin Anew* (New York: HarperCollins, 1993), 377; Robert F. Kennedy, *Thirteen Days* (New York: W. W. Norton, 1969), 37; GAN, interview by author, 6 October 1999.

17. Strober and Strober, *Let Us Begin Anew,* 386.

18. Ira Kapenstein, "Politicians Give Edge to Nelson Over Wiley," *MJ,* 28 October 1962; Ivan Kaye, "Kennedy's Call to Wiley Is Blow to Nelson's Hopes," *CT,* 23 October 1962.

19. Theodore C. Sorensen, *Kennedy* (New York: Harper and Row, 1965), 724.

20. "'No Talk' Race by Wiley Hit," *CT,* 30 October 1962; "Nelson Urges Wiley to Resume Campaign," *MJ,* 26 October 1962; "Wiley Blasts Nelson, Says He Is 'Stupid'," *MJ,* 27 October 1962.

21. Ira Kapenstein, "Affected by Emotion, Wiley Ends Speech," *MJ,* 2 November 1962; Ira Kapenstein, "Wiley Covers Small Towns in His Homestretch Drive," *MJ,* 3 November 1962.

22. "Nelson Sheds Woes in His Biggest Night," *MJ,* 7 November 1962; Robert W. Wells, "Kuehn 'Won' Early, Awoke to His Defeat," *MJ,* 7 November 1962.

23. John Wyngaard, "Wiley's Campaign Fell Far Short of Earlier Attempts," *Green Bay Press Gazette,* 19 November 1962.

Chapter 17. The First Shall Be Last

1. AP, "Family Watches As Nelson Takes Oath," *CT,* 9 January 1963.

2. Godfrey Sperling Jr., "The State of Government," *Christian Science Monitor,* 3 January 1963.

3. "Nelson Takes Office in Senate Ceremony, *MJ,* 27 January 1963; Ira Kapenstein, "Washington's Ways Trip Up the Nelsons," *MJ,* 27 January 1963.

4. "Nelson Back in Madison, Rents Home in Washington," *MS,* 19 November 1962; CLN, interview by author, 25 March 1999; "Nelson Buys Own Home in Chevy Chase," *MJ,* 31 January 1963.

5. "Nelson Buys Own Home"; Richard Bradee, "17 Years in Senate Brought Changes for Nelson, His Campaign," *MS,* 30 October 1980.

6. Robert C. Bjorklund, "New Senator Ponders Position," *WSJ,* 27 January 1963.

7. J. Sykes, *Proxmire.*

8. Richard O. Powers, AP, "In Exercise, Gaylord Has a Half Nelson on Proxmire," *WSJ,* 31 May 1963.

9. GAN, interview by author, 23 March 1999.

10. John Wyngaard, "Proxmire's Place in New Democratic Setup Is Eyed," *Green Bay Press Gazette,* 20 November 1962; Harry McPherson, *A Political Education* (Boston: Houghton Mifflin, 1988), 38.

11. "Details of Nelson's Anti-Dixie Stand," *CT,* 21 January 1963; "Nelson Raps Johnson Stand on Filibuster," *MS,* 1 February 1963; Richard S. Vonier, "Wit, Reputation Work for Nelson," *MJ,* 6 November 1968.

12. "Balk Proxmire, Give Nelson Posts Asked," *MS,* 15 February 1963.

13. "Nelson Gives First Speech," *MJ,* 25 March 1963.

14. GAN, interview by author, 9 January 1993.

15. GAN, interview by author, 19 July 1993; Wayne Aspinall, interview by Charles T. Morrissey, transcript, 10 November 1965, Oral History Interviews, JFK Library; Henry Reuss, interview by author, 22 June 1999.

16. Michael Frome, "Rate Your Candidate," *Field and Stream,* September 1968.

Chapter 18. Enlisting the President

1. GAN, interview by Edwin Bayley, transcript, 1 July 1964, Oral History Interviews, JFK Library.

2. Ibid.

3. Lee White, quoted in Gerald and Deborah Strober, *Let Us Begin Anew,* 151; Mike Manatos to Larry O'Brien, 11 March 1963, Office Files of White House Aides—Manatos, Lyndon Baines Johnson Library, Austin, Tex.

4. "Kennedy Will Make Inspection Tour of Conservation Areas in Fall," *MJ,* 26 May 1963; AP, "Nelson Hails Recreation Tour," *MS,* 28 May 1963; Ira Kapenstein, "Kennedy Plans Tour of Conservation Areas," *MJ,* 17 July 1963.

5. John Fitzgerald Kennedy to GAN, 16 May 1963. The original letter is displayed at Clear Lake Area Historical Museum, Clear Lake, Wis.

6. GAN to John Fitzgerald Kennedy, 29 August 1963, Name File, White House Central Files, LBJ Library.

7. Ibid.

8. Ibid.

9. Ibid.

10. "President Won't Stop in State on His Tour," *MJ,* 1 September 1963.

11. Edwin R. Bayley, interview by Larry Hackman, 10 October 1968, Oral History Interviews, JFK Library; GAN, interview by author, 15 July 1993.

12. GAN, interview by Bayley; "Nelson Wooed," *MS,* 13 September 1963.

13. Ira Kapenstein, "Nelson's Anger Spurs Action at White House," *MJ,* 15 September 1963; "Nelson Says JFK May Visit State," *MS,* 10 September 1963; William R. Bechtel, interview by author, 11 June 1993.

14. GAN, interview by author, 15 July 1993.

15. Ibid.; Milo Mason, "Interview: Gaylord Nelson," *Natural Resources and Environment* (ABA), summer 1995.

16. "President Gets Good Look at Islands' Bald Eagles," *MS,* 25 September 1963; Martin Hanson, interview by author, 4 July 1993.

17. "Nelson Newsletter," September 1963.

18. Tom Wicker, "President Seeks Midwest Support for His Program," *NYT,* 25 September 1963; Cy Rice, "6,000 Jam Ashland Airport," *MS,* 25 September 1963.

19. Rice, "6,000 Jam Ashland Airport."

20. Wicker, "President Seeks"; Sander Vanocur, "Kennedy's Voyage of Discovery," *Harper's,* April 1964.

21. Tom Wicker, "President Tours Three States in West," *NYT,* 26 September 1963; Julius Duscha, "President Adds Political Touch to Tour," *WP,* 26 September 1963.

22. AP, "Kennedy Lauds Role in Resource Projects," *MJ,* 26 September 1963; Vancour, "Kennedy's Voyage"; Wicker, "President Tours"; Alan L. Otten, "Kennedy's Theme Is Muted on Trip," *Wall Street Journal,* 30 September 1963.

23. Julius Duscha, "Kennedy's Western Trip a Vast Educational Effort," *WP,* 29 September 1963; Vanocur, "Kennedy's Voyage"; Peter Lisagor, "Kennedy Politicking As He Travels," *Chicago Daily News,* 25 September 1963.

24. AP, "JFK Rips Isolation of Past," *MS,* 27 September 1963; Tom Wicker, "Kennedy Attacks Goldwater Line," *NYT,* 27 September 1963; AP, "Kennedy Finds Peril in Conservative Ideas," *MJ,* 27 September 1963.

25. UPI, "Kennedy Samples Rustic Life," *MS,* 28 September 1963.

26. Tom Wicker, "Kennedy Predicts Cut in Work Week," *NYT,* 29 September 1963.

27. "'64 Warm-Up," *NYT,* 29 September 1963.

28. Duscha, "Kennedy's Western Trip"; Duscha, "President Adds"; "Conservation Stressed in JFK's Visit to Dam," *WP,* 29 September 1963; Julius Duscha, "JFK Holds to Conservation Vow," *WP,* 30 September 1963.

29. "On the 'Conservation' Trail," *NYT,* 29 September 1963.

30. Mason, "Interview."

Chapter 19. Joining the Club

1. George McGovern, interview by author, 11 June 1993.

2. GAN, interview by author, 28 September 1997.

3. Ibid.; GAN, interviews by author, 24 June 1999, and 2 June 2000; Walter Mondale, interview by author, 9 September 1993.

4. McGovern, interview by author.

5. Thomas Eagleton, interview by author, 11 August 2000.

6. GAN, interviews by author, 2 June 2000, 24 June 1999, and 9 January 1993.

7. "Russell Billiu Long," *Biographical Directory of the United States Congress,* http://bioguide.congress.gov; Robert Mann, *Legacy to Power: Senator Russell Long of Louisiana* (New York: Paragon House, 1992), 104.

8. GAN, interview by author, 24 June 1999.

9. John W. Kole, "Nelson Builds Respect, Bright Future," *MJ,* 26 November 1965; Alfred Maund, "Proxmire Asks End to Postal 'Spoils,'" *CT,* 18 January 1965.

10. Richard Sykes, "Gaylord Nelson Report," in Ralph Nader Congress Project, *Citizens Look at Congress* (Washington, D.C.: Grossman, 1972), [9]: 12; Dave Zweifel, "Nelson's Reported Backing of Long Draws Criticism," *CT,* 3 January 1969; "Sen. Nelson Explains His Vote for Long," WSJ, 3 February 1969.

11. CLN, interview by author, 25 March 1999; GAN, interview by author, 28 September 1997.

12. Eagleton, interview by author.

13. Kevin Gottlieb, interview by author, 26 February 1993.

14. Mann, *Legacy to Power,* 287; Gottlieb, interview by author.

15. "Nelson Lashes 'Arrogant' Letter from Union Chiefs," *CT,* 7 October 1965; Kenneth Scheibel, "Energetic Nelson Keeps Adding to Ambitious List of Endeavors," *La Crosse Tribune,* 20 June 1965; Robert Kastenmeier, interview by author, 1 March 1993.

16. GAN, interviews by author, 28 September 1997 and 9 January 1993.

17. John W. Kole, "Nelson to Oppose Davis Judgeship," *MJ,* 14 February 1974; GAN, interview by author, 9 January 1993; Richard Bradee, "Nelson Attitude Blamed by Davis," *MS,* 5 April 1974.

18. "AMC Tax Refund Pushed by Nelson," *CT,* 10 November 1967.

19. GAN, interview by author, 23 March 1999.

20. Joe Miller, "A Reluctant Darkhorse for 1972," Nelson Senate Papers.

21. GAN, interview by author, 16 July 1993.

22. CLN, interview by author, 25 March 1999.

23. Joe Miller, interview by author, telephone, 22 September 2001; CLN, interviews by author, 29 March 1999, and telephone, 21 September 2001.

24. CLN, interview by author, 25 March 1999.

25. Ibid.

26. Bernie Koteen, interview by author, 2 March 1993.

27. Eagleton, interview by author.

28. Marilyn Gardner, "Nelsons Host Pre-Inaugural Dinner," *MJ,* 18 January 1965.

29. CLN, interview by author, 25 March 1999.

30. Miller, interview by author.

31. GAN, interviews by author, 24 June 1999 and 28 September 1997; CLN, interview by author, 25 March 1999.

Chapter 20. Defending the Constitution

1. "Nelson Shuns Debate Plea," *MJ,* 7 February 1961; Esther Kaplan, interview by author, telephone, 16 November 2001.

2. "Walter Charges Foes with Communist Ties," *MJ,* 29 January 1961; GAN, interview by author, 3 May 1995.

3. "Nelson Attacks Committee on Un-American Activities," *CT,* 31 January 1961.

4. Laurence C. Eklund, "House OK's Funds for Walter Probers," *MJ,* 2 March 1961.

5. Assembly Joint Resolution 30, 1961 session, Nelson Papers, box 21; "3 Dems Whipped into Line; Censure Nelson on HUAC," *CT,* 9 March 1961.

6. "State Legion Hears Call for Defense of Minority Rights," *CT,* 15 July 1961; Jack Sullivan, "State Legion Champions HUAC," *MS,* 16 July 1961; "State Legion Asks for Law to Curb Reds," *MJ,* 15 July 1961.

7. "GOP Attacks Nelson, Lucey Blasts 'Smear,'" *MJ,* 4 November 1962.

8. "Loyalty Oath Letter Arouses Nelson Ire," *MJ,* 16 March 1965; "Loophole on Oaths Applied for Nelson," *MS,* 18 March 1965; John W. Kole, "Nelson Critics Assail Refusal to Take Oaths," *MJ,* 10 May 1965.

9. "Sens. Nelson, Proxmire Should Stand Up for the University," *CT,* 27 June 1966; GAN to William T. Evjue, 30 June 1966, Nelson Senate Papers; "Nelson Rips into Dodd Committee Smear of U.W.," *CT,* 4 July 1966.

10. GAN to Evjue, 30 June 1966; "Nelson Rips into Dodd Committee."

11. Erwin Knoll, "Will They Investigate the Investigators?" *CT,* 19 April 1971.

12. Memo, T. J. Smith to E. S. Miller, FBI File HQ 94-57932.

13. Memo, M. A. Jones to C. DeLoach, FBI File HQ 94-57932.

14. GAN, *Congressional Record* (15 April 1971), 92d Cong., 1st sess., 117, pt. 8:10491-96.

15. GAN, *Congressional Record* (10 December 1971), 92d Cong., 1st sess., 117, pt. 35:46159-64.

16. *CQA* 1974, 273; Andrew H. Malcolm, "Violent Drug Raids against the Innocent Found Widespread," *NYT,* 24 June 1974; *Congressional Record,* 93d Cong., 2d sess., 120, pt. 17:22822, 22989.

17. GAN, interview by author, 2 June 2000.

18. GAN, Letter to the Editor, *WP,* 30 June 1997.

19. Ibid.; "Ruling on Nixon Tapes Was Victory for Nelson," *MJ,* 30 June 1977; Department of Justice, "Government Announces Settlement over Nixon Presidential Papers," press release, 12 June 2000.

20. John H. Averill, "Senate Adopts Ethics Code Despite Some Unhappiness," *Los Angeles Times,* 2 April 1977; Martin Tolchin, "Senate Votes Limit of $8,625 a Member on Outside Earnings," *NYT,* 23 March 1977; Michael Lynn, "Gaylord Nelson's 'His Own Man,'" *Green Bay Press Gazette,* 13 February 1977; *Congressional Quarterly Weekly Report,* 26 February 1977, 344.

21. GAN, interview by author, 23 March 1999; William T. Evjue, *A Fighting Editor* (Madison, Wis.: Capital Times, 1968), 668.

22. Sherman Stock, letter to author, 1 December 1999.

23. "Nelson Gave Third of Extra Pay Away," *MJ,* 14 May 1971; "Nelson

Discloses Worth," *MJ,* 21 April 1974; "Proxmire Big Earner for Speeches," *MJ,* 16 May 1975; "Disclosure Form Hides Senate Wealth," *MJ,* 22 May 1980.

24. Stuart Levitan, "Old Friends Wage War on Senate Floor," *CT,* 21 March 1977.

25. Tolchin, "Senate Votes Limit"; Ernest B. Fergurson, "One Ethics Standard for Senate, Another for Everyone Else," *Los Angeles Times,* 27 March 1977; Stuart Levitan, "Nelson, Ethics Code Survive Muskie," *CT,* 23 March 1977; Levitan, "Old Friends."

26. New York Times Service, "Senate Passes Code of Ethics," *WSJ,* 2 April 1977; Stuart Levitan, "A Victory for Ethics," *CT,* 2 April 1977; Levitan, "Nelson, Ethics Code."

Chapter 21. Saving the Appalachian Trail

1. GAN, foreword to *Appalachian Adventure* (Atlanta: Longstreet Press, 1995); Donald Dale Jackson, "The Long Way Round," *Wilderness,* summer 1998.

2. Ibid.; GAN, interview by Ronald J. Tipton and Edward B. Garvey, transcript, 12 December 1983, for Legislative History of National Hiking Trails System.

3. Benton MacKaye, "An Appalachian Trail: A Project in Regional Planning," *Journal of the American Institute of Architects,* October 1921.

4. Jackson, "Long Way Round."

5. GAN, *Congressional Record,* 88th Cong., 2d sess., 110, pt. 9:11458–61.

6. GAN, interview by Tipton and Garvey, 12 December 1983; Jackson, "Long Way Round."

7. GAN, *Congressional Record,* 89th Cong., 2d sess., 112, pt. 6:7393–96.

8. Jackson, "Long Way Round."

9. Zillmer quote from Ice Age Park and Trail Foundation Web site; Henry S. Reuss, *When Government Was Good* (Madison: University of Wisconsin Press, 1999), 78–80; UPI, "Ice Age Bill Is Approved by Senate," *CT,* 2 October 1964.

Chapter 22. The Hard Detergent Battle

1. "Conservation Needs Listed," *MJ,* 19 May 1962; "Detergent Bar Needed—Nelson," *MS,* 7 August 1962; "Nelson Asks State Ban on Detergents," *CT,* 15 December 1962.

2. GAN, *Congressional Record,* 92d Cong., 1st sess., 117, pt. 31:40303–10; AP, "Plan Soft Solution to Suds Problem," *MS,* 23 April 1963; "Governor Signs Detergent Bill," *MJ,* 19 December 1963; *Laws of Wisconsin,* 1963–1964, Vol. II, Chapter 434.

3. "Sen. Nelson Unmoved by 'Soft' Soap," *MS,* 22 May 1965; Laurence C. Eklund, "Nelson Isn't Satisfied with Detergent Pledge," *MJ,* 21 May 1965; Thomas McIntyre, *Congressional Record,* 92d Cong., 1st sess., 117, pt. 31:40303–10.

4. P. Re Velle and C. Re Velle, *The Environment: Issues and Choices for Society*, 3d ed. (Boston: Jones and Barlett, 1988), cited in Chris Knud-Hansen, "Historical Perspective of the Phosphate Detergent Conflict" (Working Paper 94-54, Conflict Resolution Consortium, University of Colorado, February 1994); House Committee on Government Operations, *Phosphates in Detergents and the Eutrophication of America's Waters*, 91st Cong., 2d sess., H. Rept. 91-1004, 14 April 1970, cited in Knud-Hansen, "Historical Perspective"; Knud-Hansen, "Historical Perspective."

5. GAN, *Congressional Record*, 92d Cong., 1st sess., 117, 31:4030310.

6. Ibid.; "Why Wait to Label Detergents," *Minneapolis Tribune*, 1 May 1971; "Strange Stance on Detergents," *MJ*, 8 May 1971.

7. Knud-Hansen, "Historical Perspective"; Peter Vanderpoel, "Washington's Poor Advice," *Minneapolis Tribune*, 7 October 1971; "Whitewash for Phosphates," *NYT*, 22 September 1971; "Ring around the Government's Collar," *WP*, 2 October 1971; R. V. Percival, "Checks without Balance: Executive Office Oversight of the Environmental Protection Agency," *Law and Contemporary Problems* 54 (autumn 1991): 127, cited in Knud-Hansen, "Historical Perspective."

8. GAN, testimony to the Senate Committee on Commerce, Subcommittee on the Environment, 15 October 1971, *Congressional Record*, 92d Cong., 1st sess., 117, 31:40303-10.

9. House Committee on Government Operations, *Phosphates in Detergents: Government Action and Public Confusion*, 92d Cong., 2d sess., H. Rept. 92-918, 15 March 1972, cited in Knud-Hansen, "Historical Perspective."

10. Washington Post News Service, "EPA Ready to Back Phosphate Ban," *CT*, 20 July 1977; Paul G. Hayes, "Battle over Phosphates in Detergents Resumes," *MJ*, 14 August 1977.

11. David W. Litke, "Review of Phosphorous Control Measures in the United States and Their Effects on Water Quality," (Denver, Colo.: U.S. Geological Survey, 1999), Water-Resources Investigations Report 99-4007:1.

Chapter 23. The Great Society

1. Thompson, *History of Wisconsin*, 6:338-39.

2. Sorensen, *Kennedy*, 495-96.

3. GAN, interview by author, 15 July 1993.

4. AP, "Sen. Nelson Bids for Fast Action," *CT*, 28 November 1963.

5. "Nelson Raps State CC for Using Racist Propaganda," *CT*, 30 March 1964; "Nelson Accuses State CC of False Rights Bill Attack," *CT*, 24 February 1964; "Sen. Nelson Assails Rights Bill Hysteria," *CT*, 25 March 1964; "Nelson Lashes Wallace on 'Police State' Course," *CT*, 26 March 1964.

6. Thompson, *History of Wisconsin*, 6:730-31; correspondence files, Nelson Senate Papers.

7. Correspondence files, Nelson Senate Papers.

8. Ibid.

9. GAN, interview by author, 15 July 1993.

10. Press release 65-43, Nelson Senate Papers.

11. Thompson, *History of Wisconsin,* 6:384–90; GAN to Paul Poberezny, 29 September 1967, Nelson Senate Papers.

12. Thompson, *History of Wisconsin,* 6:394–95.

13. *Congressional Record,* 88th Cong., 2d sess., 110, pt. 1:1111–17.

14. "The Face of America's Poor," *CT,* 2 September 1963.

15. *Congressional Record,* 88th Cong., 2d sess., 110, pt. 1:1111–17; "5-Cent Rise Asked in Cigarette Tax," *NYT,* 28 January 1964.

16. Alfred Maund, "Nelson Spurs Poverty War," *CT,* 10 August 1964.

17. Nelson legislative memo, 20 April 1967, Nelson Senate Papers; "Movie on Nelson Program," *CT,* 6 June 1966; "Expand Nelson's Anti-Poverty Plan," *CT,* 1 September 1967.

18. Press release 65-30, Nelson Senate Papers; GAN, "Speech on 10th Anniversary of the Teacher Corps," Nelson Senate Papers; GAN, interview by author, 2 June 2000.

19. Matt Pommer, "Teacher Corps Nelson's Idea," *CT,* 9 August 1965; "Teacher Corps: Odyssey of Cliff-Hangers," *Southern Education Report,* December 1966; Jonathan Fox, "Gore Corps, a Good Old Idea for Education," *New Republic,* 2 February 2000.

20. James G. Wieghart, "Nelson Hits Poverty Rumors," *MS,* 1 February 1967; "Nelson Hits Backers of Great Society Cuts," *MJ,* 1 February 1967.

21. "Nelson Pleads for OEO," *CT,* 17 February 1969; Richard Critchfield, "Keep OEO, Nixon Asks; Plans but Few Changes," *Washington Star,* 19 February 1969.

22. 1974 *CQA,* 495, 497, 501.

23. Ibid., 489, 491; "Legal Aid Nears Crisis," *CT,* 21 February 1974.

24. Jerry Voorhis, *The Strange Case of Richard Milhous Nixon* (New York: Paul S. Eriksson, 1972), 67–68; 1970 *CQA,* 658, 662, 665; 1971 *CQA,* 186, 189; Voorhis, *Strange Case,* 69–70.

25. 1973 *CQA,* 346–49; Paul C. Light, "Government's Greatest Achievements of the Past Half Century," Brookings Institution, Reform Watch Brief No. 2, November 2000.

Chapter 24. Islands and Rivers

1. GAN, *America's Last Chance* (Waukesha, Wis.: Country Beautiful, 1970), 22.

2. Harold C. Jordahl Jr., *A Unique Collection of Islands* (Madison: University of Wisconsin Extension, 1994).

3. Hanson, interview by author.

4. Jordahl, *Unique Collection,* 221, 264, 266.

5. John O. Holzheuter, *Madeline Island and the Chequamegon Region* (Madison: State Historical Society of Wisconsin, 1974), 48–49, cited in Jordahl, *Unique Collection,* 15; Jordahl, *Unique Collection,* 229–33; UPI, "Ask Shoreline Recreation Area," *CT,* 23 May 1962.

6. Jordahl, *Unique Collection,* 234.

7. Ibid., 236–38.

8. John Patrick Hunter, "Udall Hails Nelson Conservation Plan," *CT,* 10 October 1962; "Nelson Asks State Ban on Detergents," *CT,* 15 December 1962; Harold C. Jordahl Jr., "Gaylord Nelson: An Extraordinary Environmental Leader," nomination of GAN for Tyler Prize for Environmental Achievement, 1998.

9. *Public Papers of the Presidents of the United States: John F. Kennedy* (Washington, D.C.: U.S. Government Printing Office, 1964), 707–9, cited in Jordahl, *Unique Collection,* 253; "The Nelson Newsletter," September 1963, Nelson Senate Papers; GAN, interview by Kathleen Lidfors, 4 March 1985, cited in Jordahl, *Unique Collection,* 251.

10. Jordahl, *Unique Collection,* 241, 437, 609, 820–21.

11. Ibid., 465–69; John Patrick Hunter, "Film on Apostles Steals Show from Nelson, Udall," *CT,* 3 April 1964.

12. Jordahl, *Unique Collection,* 293, 311, 505, 510, 511, 725.

13. "Apostle Island Plan Told," *CT,* 30 August 1965; GAN, legislative memo, 29 August 1965, Nelson Senate Papers.

14. Jordahl, *Unique Collection,* 406, 408, 419, 420.

15. Ibid., 420–24; William R. Bechtel to Joseph A. Califano Jr., 6 September 1967, LE/PA 3, LBJ Library; Phillip S. Hughes to Larry Levinson, 30 September 1967, LE/PA 3, LBJ Library.

16. "Another Apostle Islands Try," *CT,* 27 January 1969; UPI, "Sen. Nelson Scores Hickel's Views," *WP,* 3 January 1969; Erwin Knoll, "Report from Washington," *CT,* 27 January 1969; "Senate Passes Apostle Isles Lakeshore Bill," *MS,* 27 June 1969; Jordahl, *Unique Collection,* 710.

17. Jordahl, *Unique Collection,* 549–58, 575.

18. Ibid., 560; "Apostle Islands Lakeshore Voted," *CT,* 11 September 1970; GAN, legislative memo; "Nelson Newsletter," November 1970, Nelson Senate Papers.

19. Nelson for Senate Committee, "A Report on Senator Gaylord Nelson, a Man and His Record," supplement to *WSJ,* 20 October 1974; AP, "Senate Prevents Cutting of York Island Trees," *CT,* 23 May 1974; Jordahl, *Unique Collection,* 707–8; GAN, interview by Lidfors, cited in Jordahl, *Unique Collection,* 707.

20. Theodore J. Karamanski, *Saving the Saint Croix* (National Park Service, Midwest Region), 1, 22.

21. Ibid., 47, 50–51; Sigurd Olson, testimony at hearings of the Special Subcommittee of the Committee on Public Works, cited in Karamanski, *Saving the Saint Croix,* 65–66.

22. GAN, "Statement before a Joint Hearing by the Minnesota Conservation Commissioner, Wayne Olson, and the Minnesota Water Pollution Control Commission in Stillwater, Minnesota," 14 January 1965, Nelson Senate Papers.

23. Ibid.; Mondale, interview by author.

24. Karamanski, *Saving the Saint Croix,* 54, 85.

25. Ibid., 76, 79–80; GAN, interview by author, 24 June 1999.

26. Karamanski, *Saving the Saint Croix,* 86, 92, 98–99; Huffman, *Protectors of the Land and Water,* 86–87; Tim Palmer, *Endangered Rivers and the Conservation Movement* (Berkeley: University of California Press, 1986), cited in Karamanski, *Saving the Saint Croix,* 72.

27. "Two Nelson Bills Signed by Johnson," *CT,* 3 October 1968; "Nelson Newsletter," September 1968, Nelson Senate Papers.

28. AP, "Nelson Gets Enthusiastic Endorsement of Lombardi," *CT,* 4 October 1968; Charlie House, "Udall, Nelson Ride Wolf River Rapids," *MJ,* 4 October 1968; David Maraniss, *When Pride Still Mattered* (New York: Simon & Schuster, 1999), 438–39, 447; AP, "Udall Lauds Nelson as Conservationist at St. Croix Fete," *CT,* 5 October 1968.

29. Karamanski, *Saving the Saint Croix,* 166; Mondale quote from "Gaylord Nelson: A Profile," Wisconsin Public Television, 22 April 1990.

Chapter 25. Protecting Consumers

1. GAN, interview by author, 17 March 2001; "Nelson Urges U.S. Tire Safety Rules," *CT,* 13 January 1965; AP, "May Order Hazards of Tires Bared," *CT,* 25 March 1965.

2. UPI, "Nelson Bills Call for Auto Safety," *CT,* 23 February 1965; David R. Jones, "Senate Bill Backs Car Safety Drive," *NYT,* 24 February 1965; GAN, interview by author, 3 May 1995.

3. David Bollier, Citizen Action and Other Big Ideas: A History of Ralph Nader and the Modern Consumer Movement (Washington: Center for Study of Responsive Law, 1989); press release 66–28, Nelson Senate Papers; GAN statement, 10 March 1966, Nelson Senate Papers; Harry Kelly, AP, "GM Apologies End Hearings into Gumshoe Caper," *Green Bay Press-Gazette,* 23 March 1966.

4. AP, "Nelson Likens Auto Safety to Pearl Harbor," *CT,* 4 February 1966; Charlie House, "Road Safety Effort a Scandal, Nelson Tells Car, Tire Experts," *MJ,* 4 February 1966.

5. "Nelson Hails Traffic Safety Act," *CT,* 2 September 1966; AP, "Nelson Cites Tire Firm's 'Brushoff,'" *CT,* 26 August 1967; AP, "Nelson backs Defective Tire Recall Measure," *CT,* 9 November 1967.

6. Jack Anderson, "Tire Industry Raises Slush Fund to Fight Nelson, Nader," *CT,* 13 December 1969; Robert F. Buckhorn, *Nader: The People's Lawyer* (Englewood Cliffs, N.J.: Prentice-Hall, 1972), cited in Frank Aukofer,

"Anti-Nelson Scheme Traced to Tire Industry," *MJ*, 2 April 1972; Erwin Knoll, "The Tire Industry Sought to Discredit Nelson, Nader," *CT*, 27 March 1972.

7. Laurence C. Eklund, "Nelson's Initial Target May Be Drug Firms," *MJ*, 19 June 1966; "Sen. Nelson Says Drug Companies 'Shortchange' Public," *CT*, 26 April 1967; Douglas W. Cray, "Nelson Committee to Open Hearings on Drug Prices," *NYT*, 15 May 1967.

8. Patrick H. Sloyan, UPI, "Nelson Probe Cites Drug Profiteering," *CT*, 15 May 1967; "Nelson Asks Why Drug Costs Vary," *CT*, 22 May 1967; "MD Raps Brand Name Use in Drafting Prescriptions," *CT*, 8 June 1967.

9. Drew Pearson, "Drug Industry Invades State, Attacks Nelson," *CT*, 7 July 1967; Benjamin Gordon, interview by author, 3 March 1993.

10. Joe Pecor, "Drug Firms Hit for 'Intimidation'," *MS*, 22 August 1967; UPI, "Nelson and Drug Firm Head Clash on Medicine Price," *CT*, 14 September 1967; "Sen. Nelson's Monopoly Probe Reveals High Price of Drugs," *CT*, 18 September 1967; "Post Office Slaps 'Hidden' Drug Ad," *CT*, 6 December 1967.

11. "The Dangers of Chloromycetin," *Time*, 16 February 1968, 74; GAN to Dr. Austin Smith, 15 August 1968, Nelson Senate Papers; GAN, interview by author, 2 June 2000.

12. U.S. Senate Select Committee on Small Business, *Competitive Problems in the Drug Industry*, hearings before the Subcommittee on Monopoly. 90th Cong., 1st and 2d sess., pt. 6, 29 November 1967; 6, 8, 27, 28, 29 February 1968, 2222–23.

13. Ibid.

14 Ibid., 2204; Patrick J. Sloyan, UPI, "FDA Crackdown on Death-Causing Drug Announced," *CT*, 29 February 1968.

15. *Competitive Problems in the Drug Industry*, 2646–47, 2651.

16. Morton Mintz, "Hearings Curtailed Use of Dangerous Drug—Nelson," *CT*, 31 July 1968.

17. Harold M. Schmeck Jr., "Drug Salesmen Scored in Senate," *NYT*, 18 September 1968; "The Drug Peddlers," *New Republic*, 21 September 1968, 16.

18. "Nelson Newsletter," October 1968, Nelson Senate Papers; "Regulating the Drug Industry," *WP*, 23 September 1968; "The Price of Drugs," *NYT*, 23 September 1968.

19. "Nelson Target of Drug Firms," *Kenosha Labor*, 26 September 1968; Erwin Knoll, "Report from Washington," *CT*, 23 September 1968; John Patrick Hunter, "Nelson Lets Go a Blast As Train Chugs through State," *CT*, 27 September, 1968; Rosemary Kendrick, "Nelson Scores Smashing Win over Jerris Leonard," *CT*, 6 November 1968.

20. William B. Mead, UPI, "Doctor Says AMA Helped Drug Firms Push the Pill," *CT*, 15 January 1970; H. L. Schwartz III, AP, "Women Should Get Clear, Concise Data about the Pill," *CT*, 16 January 1970; AP, "Testimony on the Pill Shocks Many Women," *WSJ*, 18 January 1970; "Poll on the Pill," *Newsweek*, 9 February 1970.

21. "Nelson Probe Causing Panic," *CT,* 26 February 1970; UPI, "Nelson Attacked for Pill Scare," *WSJ,* 4 March 1970; AP, "Friend, Foes of the Pill Clash," *WSJ,* 25 February 1970.

22. Schwartz, "Women Should"; "Testimony," CT; "Poll," *Newsweek;* "Nelson Attacked," *WSJ.*

23. UPI, "FDA Will Require Warning in Packages of Birth Pills," *CT,* 4 March 1970; Mike Feinsilber, UPI, "Nelson Takes Credit for Birth Control Pill Warning," *CT,* 5 March 1970; Betti Logan, *Newsday,* "After the Scare, It's Back to Pill," *CT,* 25 November 1971.

24. Tamar Nordenberg, "Protecting against Unintended Pregnancy: A Guide to Contraceptive Choices," *FDA Consumer,* April 1997, revised June 2000.

25. Erwin Knoll, "Nelson Learns about 'Dandy Drug'—Caffeine, Sugar," *CT,* 31 May 1971; Richard Bradee, "Doctor Nelson Has Own Cold Remedy," *MS,* 25 December 1971; Erwin Knoll, "Weight Drugs 'Quackery,' Nelson Declares at Probe," *CT,* 13 December 1972.

26. Morton Mintz, "HEW Plan Seeks to Cut Cost of Medicare, Medicaid Drugs," *WP,* 19 December 1973; Tim Wyngaard, "Nelson's and Kennedy's Staffs Jab at Each Other," *CT,* 8 November 1973; Gordon, interview by author; Theo Lippman Jr., *Senator Ted Kennedy* (New York: W. W. Norton, 1976), 233–34.

Chapter 26. The Great Lakes

1. Web sites of Great Lakes Information Network (http://www.great-lakes.net) and Environmental Protection Agency's Great Lakes National Program (http://www.epa.gov/glnpo).

2. GAN, "America's Last Chance," remarks to midwinter meeting, State Bar of Wisconsin, Milwaukee, 19 February 1965, Nelson Senate Papers.

3. Ibid.

4. GAN, "America's Last Chance," remarks to National Wildlife Federation, Washington, D.C., 5 March 1965, Nelson Senate Papers.

5. Ibid.

6. John W. Kole, "Conservation Plan Asks All-Out Effort," *MJ,* 8 February 1965; GAN, "America's Last Chance," 19 February 1965.

7. "Nelson Set to Fight Pollution on Lakes," *MS,* 10 February 1965; GAN, "America's Last Chance," 5 March 1965.

8. "The Threat to Our Waters," *MJ,* 31 October–4 November 1965; GAN, "America's Last Chance," 5 March 1965.

9. GAN, "Remarks on Introduction of Waste Management Research Bill," 17 February 1966, Nelson Senate Papers.

10. John W. Kole, "Nelson Maps Massive Drive to Clean Up Lakes, Streams," *MJ,* 3 February 1966; Laurence C. Eklund, "Bill for 'Clean Waters' Introduced by Nelson," *MJ,* 16 May 1966; Drew Pearson, "Grim Facts behind

Nelson's Fight to Cut Pollution," *CT,* 12 July 1966; "Nelson Proposes Aid to Cut Industrial Waste," *MJ,* 15 October 1966; "Senator Gaylord Nelson's Comprehensive Water Pollution Control Legislative Program," n.d., Nelson Senate Papers; "Nelson to Push Pollution Battle," *MS,* 4 February 1966.

11. "Johnson Pollution Bill Termed Only a Start," *MJ,* 24 February 1966.

12. "Clean Water Bill Passed Despite Nixon Veto Threat," *MJ,* 5 October 1972; Shabecoff, *Fierce Green Fire,* 268.

13. "Nelson Asks Pollution Meetings," *MJ,* 17 March 1966; "Pollution Survey Pledged by U.S.," *MJ,* 24 March 1966; "Knowles Rejects Nelson's Pollution Plan," *MJ,* 26 March 1966; James G. Wieghart, "State Can Bar U.S. Pollution Control," *MS,* 1 April 1966.

14. "Knowles Playing with Dynamite in Stand on Pollution, Nelson Says," *MJ,* 21 May 1966; "Curious Cover-up of Pollution Data Needs Thorough Probe," *CT,* 24 May 1966; AP, "Nelson Raps Knowles on Pollution," *CT,* 16 September 1966.

15. Alfred Maund, "Nelson Gives Up on Knowles," *CT,* 26 September 1966; "Nelson Asks 4-State Conference," *CT,* 13 March 1967.

16. Laurence C. Eklund, "Nelson Raps Inaction on Great Lakes Pollution," *MJ,* 21 September 1967; James G. Wieghart, "Governors Fear Polluters—Nelson," *MS,* 21 September 1967.

17. "Nelson Scores Victory on Pollution," *CT,* 1 December 1967; "Nelson Hits Foes of Pollution Parley," *CT,* 26 December 1967; "Don't Pass the Buck, Lake Parley Urged," *MS,* 6 February 1968; "State Pollution Efforts Lag, Nelson Charges," *MJ,* 6 February 1968; paper, "Great Lakes Pollution Conferences," n.d., Nelson Senate Papers.

18. "Nelson Asks Lake Superior Pollution Talks," *MJ,* 11 April 1968.

19. GAN, interview by Ed Edwin, transcript of tape recording, 21 December 1981, Columbia University Oral History Project; GAN, note to author, 30 April 2002.

20. William R. Bechtel, "Gaylord Nelson and an Environmental Vision Which Changed and Shaped the Nation," with letter to Dr. Jerome B. Walker, 29 July 1998, in author's possession.

Chapter 27. The Fight to Ban DDT

1. Richard Bradee, "Environmental Bug First Bit Nelson in Madison in 1959," *MS,* 16 April 1990.

2. Frank Carey, AP, "Miracle Bug Killer Used by Americans," *MJ,* 26 November 1944.

3. "DDT 'Sends' Its Victims into Insect Dance of Death," *MJ,* 7 January 1945; "Army Plane Sprays DDT over Polio Infested City," *MJ,* 20 August 1945.

4. William S. Conway, AP, "Care Is Urged in DDT's Use," *MJ,* 20 August 1945; AP, "DDT Put on Crops Shows Up in Milk," *Tampa Daily*

Times, 24 May 1947; "Winnebago Lake Flies Safe; DDT Use Is Hit," *MJ*, 3 June 1947.

5. "State Will Regulate Insecticide Spraying," *MJ*, 7 March 1948; "DDT in Milk Faces Ban as Health Peril," *MJ*, 24 March 1949; Robert L. Geiger, AP, "New Insecticides Safe When Properly Used," *MJ*, 8 May 1949.

6. "Bird Mortality Boosted by DDT, Study Shows," *MJ*, 14 December 1959; "State, Municipal Officials Split over Report on Bird-DDT Link," *MJ*, 16 December 1959.

7. UPI, "Drop DDT from Pesticide Lists, Nelson Urges," *MS*, 20 June 1966; GAN, *Congressional Record*, 89th Cong., 2d sess., 112, pt. 12:15195204; James Spaulding, "Scientists Oppose Ban on DDT, Assert Danger Is Exaggerated," *MJ*, 23 July 1966.

8. Marion Lane Rogers, *Acorn Days* (New York: Environmental Defense Fund, 1990), 183.

9. Huffman, *Protectors of the Land and Water*, 177; Quincy Dadisman, "Sen. Nelson Proposes Ban on DDT Use," *MS*, 3 December 1968; Whitney Gould, "Nelson Urges Ban on Use of DDT," *CT*, 2 December 1968; Robert Franzmann, "Bleak Future Feared without Ban on DDT," *WSJ*, 3 December 1968.

10. Quincy Dadisman, "'Silent Spring' Hurt Sales, DDT Maker Tells Hearing," *MS*, 15 May 1969.

11. Quincy Dadisman, "Hearings in State Led to DDT Bans," *MS*, 15 June 1972.

12. James W. McCulla, "DDT Ban OK'd, Sent to Knowles," *MJ*, 9 January 1970.

13. "Use of DDT Drops in U.S. but Not because of Laws," *NYT*, 2 August 1970; "Nelson Says Ban on DDT Nonexistent," *MS*, 2 March 1970; "No Single Use of DDT Halted, Nelson Charges," *CT*, 2 March 1970; "Country Misled on DDT—Nelson," *MJ*, 2 March 1970.

14. *DDT Regulatory History: A Brief Survey (to 1975)*, EPA Report, July 1975; UPI, "U.S. Bans DDT Use, Cites Harm to Man," *MJ*, 14 June 1972.

15. GAN, press release 72–85, Nelson Senate Papers; John W. Kole, "Nelson Hails DDT Ban, Sets Sights on New Target, *MJ*, 15 June 1972; EPA, press release, 8 November 1972.

16. Marguerite Davis, UPI, "Nelson Shares Bug's View of DDT—They Hate It," *MS*, 6 June 1967.

17. NYT Service "Herbicide 2,4,5-T Partially Banned," *MJ*, 16 April 1970; Erwin Knoll, "Report from Washington," *CT*, 24 August 1970, 31 August 1970.

18. Erwin Knoll, "Grant County Scarred by Killer Defoliant—Nelson," *CT*, 11 August 1972; "Killer Spray Used with State's OK," *CT*, 18 August 1972.

19. UPI, "Nelson Asks Ban on Herbicide," WSJ, 12 September 1972.

20. Whitney Gould, "Nelson Stuns Pesticide Men with Defoliant Ban Report," *CT*, 17 January 1973; UPI, "Court Upholds EPA Ban on Weedkiller," *CT*, 21 April 1973; AP and UPI, "2,4,5-T Herbicide Banned by EPA," MJ, 2 March

1979; Environmental Defense, "EPA Suspends Some Uses of 2,4,5-T," newsletter, March 1979.

21. "Chemical Insect War a Flop, Nelson Says," *MJ*, 2 October 1971.

22. Environmental Defense, "25 Years after DDT Ban, Bald Eagle, Osprey Numbers Soar," news release, 13 June 1997; Daryl Kelly, "Pelican Well Again?" *Los Angeles Times*, 14 May 1997; James Gerstenzang, "Bald Eagle May Fly Its Protective Coop," *Los Angeles Times*, 6 May 1998.

Chapter 28. Vietnam

1. Nelson recalled that he spoke out publicly against the war as early as late 1962, after his election to the Senate, in an interview in Wausau, but the earliest documentation that the author could find was in May 1964, also in Wausau.

2. "Goldwater Poses New Asian Tactic," *NYT*, 25 May 1964.

3. "Nelson Asks Timetable for Vietnam," *MJ*, 27 May 1964.

4. David Obey, interview by author, telephone, 22 January 2002.

5. David Halberstam, *The Best and the Brightest* (New York: Random House, 1969), 402–4.

6. "The President's Address," *NYT*, 4 August 1961.

7. U.S. Department of State, *Bulletin*, 24 August 1964.

8. *Congressional Record*, 88th Cong., 2nd sess., 110, pt. 14:18406.

9. Ibid., 14:18406–07.

10. *Congressional Record*, 88th Cong., 2d sess., 110, pt.14:18459.

11. McGovern, interview by author; Anthony Austin, *The President's War* (New York: J. B. Lippincott, 1971), 103.

12. *Congressional Record*, 88th Cong., 2d sess., 110, pt. 14:18459; GAN, interview by author, 16 July 1993.

13. *Congressional Record*, 88th Cong., 2d sess., 110, pt. 14:18672.

14. Brian VanDeMark, *Into the Quagmire* (New York: Oxford University Press, 1991), 18–19; "Senator Nelson Denies Congress Approved Expansion of War," *NYT*, 6 October 1964.

15. Alfred Maund, "We Mustn't Let Vietnam Become 'Another Korea,'" *CT*, 4 January 1965; Albert Eisele, *Almost to the Presidency* (Blue Earth, Minn.: Piper Co., 1972), 234–35.

16. "Stifle Debate on Vietnam," *MS*, 12 May 1965; "Nelson's Vietnam Vote Is in Tradition of La Follette," *CT*, 7 May 1965; "Official Pressure Denied by Nelson," *MJ*, 19 March 1965; "Nelson Now Is Silent," *CT*, 3 May 1965.

17. Mondale, interview by author.

18. GAN, interview by author, 16 July 1993; Austin, *President's War*, 117; *Congressional Record*, 89th Cong., 1st sess., 111, pt. 7:9492–93.

19. GAN, interview by author, 16 July 1993.

20. *Congressional Record*, 89th Cong., 1st sess., 111, pt. 7:9754–58.

21. Ibid.; John D. Morris, "Senate, 88-3, Votes Vietnam War Fund," *NYT,* 7 May 1965.

22. *Congressional Record,* 89th Cong., 1st sess., 111, pt. 7:9759.

23. "Nelson Upholds Tradition of La Follette in Senate," *CT,* 7 May 1965; John W. Kole, "Nelson Raps Haste on Arms Fund Vote," *MJ,* 6 May 1995; "Nelson Rips Haste in War Fund Bill," *MS,* 7 May 1965; Alfred Maund, "Nelson Criticizes Rush to Endorse Viet War Policy," *CT,* 7 May 1965.

24. Obey, interview by author; "U.S. Course in Vietnam Disturbs Nelson," *MS,* 25 August 1965; Stewart Alsop, "The Anti-Johnson Underground," *Saturday Evening Post,* 14 August 1965.

25. "The Original Doves," *CT,* 25 January 1973; "U.S. Course in Vietnam."

26. White House Diaries, 22 November 1965, LBJ Library; GAN, interview by author, 19 July 1993.

27. John W. Kole, "Escalation of War Tragic, Nelson Says," *MJ,* 16 January 1966.

28. John W. Kole, "Nelson's View Lashed," *MJ,* 21 January 1966; "Nelson Backs Johnson on Recent War Policy," *MJ,* 24 January 1966.

29. "Nelson Explains Vote on Viet Spending Bill," *CT,* 2 March 1966; "Funds for Vietnam OK'd, Slap at Johnson Beaten," *MJ,* 2 March 1966; E. W. Kenworthy, "Rusk Says Peace of World Is Issue in Vietnam War," *NYT,* 19 February 1966.

30. "Fulbright Sorry He Balked at Nelson's Move on Viet," *CT,* 21 February 1966; *Congressional Record,* 89th Cong., 2d sess., 122, pt. 4:4378.

31. Laurence C. Eklund, "Nelson Calls for End to Bombing in North," *MJ,* 2 July 1966.

32. Ibid.; Alfred Maund, "Peace-Seeking Clergymen and Their Washington Trip," *CT,* 6 February 1967.

33. John W. Kole, "Only Nelson, Morse Oppose War Funds," *MJ,* 2 March 1967; "Nelson Defends Vote on War Bill," *MJ,* 11 March 1967; "Nelson Opposes Bill to Add to War Appropriation," *CT,* 21 March 1967.

34. John Patrick Hunter, "Dem Split on War Mirrors U.S. Feeling," *CT,* 12 June 1967.

35. Leon Hughes, "Nelson Says Johnson Is Trying to End War," *MJ,* 16 September 1967; GAN, interview by author, 16 July 1993.

36. John Gruber, "Sen. Nelson Again Asks Shift in Vietnam Policy," *WSJ,* 25 September 1967.

37. *Congressional Record,* 90th Cong., 2d sess., 114, pt. 5:5652.

38. Memo, John Criswell to Marvin Watson, 11 December 1967, Ex PR16, White House Central Files, box 76, LBJ Library; memo, Fred Panzer to Marvin Watson, 28 March 1968, Ex PR16, White House Central Files, box 76, LBJ Library; Tom Wicker, "Johnson Says He Won't Run," *NYT,* 1 April 1968.

39. Wicker, "Johnson Says"; Donald Janson, "Wisconsin Weighs Impact on Voting," *NYT,* 1 April 1968; "Nelson Proposes Plan to End Vietnam War," *MJ,* 20 May 1968.

40. Press release 68-143, Nelson Senate Papers; GAN, interview by author, 16 July 1993.

41. "Nelson, Leonard Debate War Issue," *CT,* 16 September 1968; Richard S. Vonier, "Nelson Faces Strong Leonard Attack," *MJ,* 30 October 1968; John Patrick Hunter, "Nelson Cheered by 400 As He Cites Anti-War Record," *CT,* 28 September 1968; AP, "Nelson Holds Firm in Debate with Leonard," *CT,* 1 November 1968.

42. Ken Zimmerman, "Leonard Suffers GOP Crossover," *MS,* 6 November 1968.

43. "Nelson Refusal to Take Part in March Disappoints Callers," *WSJ,* 15 November 1969; Shapiro, "Nelson and the Myth."

44. "What Have You Done Lately?" *CT,* 13 May 1970; Joseph McBride, "Nelson Meets Communications Gap," *WSJ,* 16 May 1970.

45. *Congressional Record,,* 92d Cong., 2d sess., 118, pt. 2:1634–35.

46. "Democrats Blast Blockade," *MS,* 10 May 1972; Erwin Knoll, "Will Vote against War Funds: Nelson," *CT,* 7 June 1972; Melvin Laird to GAN, 29 May 2001; GAN, interview by author, 24 June 1999; John W. Kole, "Nelson, Proxmire Team Up, Rip Laird," *MJ,* 8 June 1972.

47. Richard Bradee, "Skepticism Tempers Lawmaker Joy," *MS,* 24 January 1973.

48. *Congressional Record,* 94th Cong., 1st sess., 121, pt. 25:32679.

Chapter 29. Earth Day

1. GAN, interview by author, 9 January 1993.

2. Ibid.

3. GAN, interview by author, 2 June 2000; GAN, "History of Earth Day," Wilderness Society flyer.

4. Charles Russell, "College Teach-ins on Environment Crisis Proposed," *Seattle Post-Intelligencer,* 21 September 1969.

5. GAN, interview by author, 9 January 1993.

6. GAN, interview by author, 22 July 2000.

7. Harold C. Jordahl, interview by author, telephone, 1 August 2001.

8. Denis Hayes, interview by author, telephone, 28 June 2001; Harold C. Jordahl, notes to author, 11 April 2002.

9. Hayes, interview by author.

10. Ibid.

11. "History of Earth Day."

12. Gladwin Hill, "Environment May Eclipse Vietnam as College Issue," *NYT,* 30 November 1969; Philip W. Semas, "Students Make Environment a Major Issue," *Chronicle of Higher Education,* 5 January 1970; "New Bag on Campus," *Newsweek,* 22 December 1969.

13. Hayes, interview by author.

14. John W. Kole, "Nelson Urges Vote for Ecology Congress," *MJ,* 14 April

1970; AP, "Nelson Sees Pollution Cost of $25 Billion," *MS*, 20 April 1970; John W. Kole, "Nelson Matches Wits with Students on Environment," *MJ*, 16 April 1970; "Nelson Sees Population as No. 1 Problem," *MS*, 17 April 1970.

15. Walter P. Reuther, "Two-Ton Gadgets," speech at UAW convention, Atlantic City, N.J., 20 April 1970; GAN, press release 70-57, Nelson Senate Papers.

16. "Madison Protestors Rampage," *MJ*, 19 April 1970; Quincy Dadisman, "Nelson: Peace Is Mankind's Hope," *MS*, 22 April 1970.

17. Paul G. Hayes, "Population Concepts Collide in Earth Week Events," *MJ*, 22 April 1970.

18. Richard Harwood, "Earth Day Stirs Nation," *WP*, 23 April 1970.

19. Nan Robertson, "Earth Day, like Mother's, Pulls Capital Together," *NYT*, 23 April 1970.

20. "A Memento Mori to the Earth, *Time*, 4 May 1970, 16.

21. "City Council Gives Reluctant Backing to April 22 Earth Day," *Los Angeles Times*, 21 April 1970.

22. Jack Rosenthal, "Some Troubled by Environmental Drive," *NYT*, 22 April 1970; "Area Holds Cleanup with Rally," *WP*, 23 April 1970.

23. Memo, E. S. Miller to T. J. Smith, 2 July 1973, FBI File HQ 94-57932.

24. GAN, speech at University of Wisconsin, 21 April 1970, visual materials archives, Wisconsin Historical Society.

25. GAN, press release 70-62, Nelson Senate Papers.

26. GAN, interview by author, 9 January 1993.

Chapter 30. Immune to Presidential Fever

1. Erwin Knoll, "Nelson Had Last VP Refusal, Pushed Eagleton," *CT*, 15 July 1972.

2. Ibid.

3. Ibid.; "Nelson Says He Rejected No. 2 Job," *MJ*, 15 July 1972; John W. Kole, "Nelson Not Pressured to Accept Ticket Offer," *MJ*, 23 July 1972.

4. Knoll, "Nelson Had Last VP Refusal"; GAN, conversation with author; Richard Dougherty, *Goodbye, Mr. Christian* (Garden City, N.Y.: Doubleday, 1973), 156.

5. GAN, interview by author, 16 July 1993.

6. Gordon L. Weil, *The Long Shot* (New York: W.W. Norton, 1973.), 168-69.

7. Ibid., 157.

8. Ibid., 158-59; George McGovern, *Grassroots* (New York: Random House, 1977), 194.

9. Gary W. Hart, *Right from the Start* (New York: Quadrangle, 1973), 239-40; Dougherty, *Goodbye*, 151-52.

10. McGovern, *Grassroots*, 197-98.

11. Ibid., 198; McGovern, interview by author.

12. McGovern, interview by author; McGovern, *Grassroots*, 181.

13. "Nelson Backs McGovern; Suggests Humphrey Quit," *CT,* 3 June 1972.

14. "Nelson's Speech on California Delegates Challenge," *CT,* 11 July 1972; James D. Selk, "Good Blocks by Lucey, Nelson," *WSJ,* 11 July 1972.

15. McGovern, interview by author.

16. Knoll, "Nelson Had Last VP Refusal"; GAN, interview by author, 16 July 1993.

17. McGovern, *Grassroots*, 209–10; Sherman Stock, interview by author, telephone, 20 August 2000.

18. Theodore H. White, *The Making of the President 1972* (New York: Atheneum, 1973), 213, 216–17.

19. GAN, interview by author, 16 July 1993.

20. Ibid.; Erwin Knoll, "Muskie Is Nelson's VP Preference," *CT,* 1 August 1972; Al Eisele, "Eagleton Got Advice from Nelson," *St. Paul Dispatch,* 31 July 1972.

21. McGovern, *Grassroots*, 214.

22. GAN, interview by author, 16 July 1993; Eisele, "Eagleton Got"; McGovern, interview by author; White, *Making of the President 1972,* 217.

23. John Patrick Hunter, "Nelson Presidential Bid Pushed," *CT,* 4 December 1974.

24. Ibid.; GAN, interview by author, 19 July 1993; "Lucey Would Back Active Nelson Drive," *CT,* 6 December 1974; John W. Kole, "Accent on the News," *MJ,* 30 December 1974.

25. John Patrick Hunter, "Drive for Nelson Gathering Steam," *CT,* 11 December 1974; David Carley, "Carley Extols Nelson Qualities," *CT,* 12 December 1974; John Wyngaard, "Nelson Boom Will Fade," *Green Bay Press Gazette,* 20 December 1974.

26. Ernest Gruening to Morris H. Rubin, 15 January 1974, and Rubin to Gruening, 5 February 1974, Nelson Senate Papers.

27. GAN, interview by author, 19 July 1993; Kole, "Accent on the News."

28. Sam Anson, "If Not Mo, What about Gaylord?" *New Times,* 27 December 1974, 13.

29. Arthur Schlesinger Jr., "And in This Corner," *Wall Street Journal,* 28 January 1975; Shapiro, "Nelson and the Myth."

30. GAN, *Congressional Record,* 94th Cong., 1st sess., 121, pt. 11:14651.

31. Tom Braden, "One Man and a Crowd," *WP,* 31 May 1975; Anthony Lewis, "An Instructive Ordeal?" *NYT,* 29 December 1975.

32. GAN, interview by author, 2 June 2000.

33. R. Sykes, "Nelson Report."

34. Shapiro, "Nelson and the Myth"; Meg Greenfield, "Mrs. Snow and the Democrats," *Newsweek,* 7 July 1975.

35. GAN, interview by the author, 24 June 1993.

Chapter 31. The Environmental Decade

1. Shabecoff, *Fierce Green Fire*, 114.

2. John C. Whitaker, "Earth Day Recollections: What It Was Like When the Movement Took Off," *EPA Journal*, July/August 1988; John W. Kole, "Nelson Welcomes New Ally in Nixon," *MJ*, 23 January 1970; "Nelson, Proxmire Praise President's Pollution Fight," *MS*, 23 January 1970.

3. GAN, *Congressional Record*, 91st Cong., 2d sess., 116, pt. 1:82.

4. Ibid., 82–85; Laurence C. Eklund, "Nelson Maps Pollution War," *MJ*, 17 January 1970.

5. GAN, *Congressional Record*, 91st Cong., 2d sess., 116, pt. 1:82–87; GAN, interview by author, 24 June 1999.

6. Peter C. Stuart, "Congress Toys with Nixon Legislation," *Christian Science Monitor*, 29 July 1970.

7. Helen Kahn, "Gas-Engine Ban by '75 Is Sought," *Automotive News*, 10 August 1970; Warren Weaver Jr., "Nelson Asks Ban on Gas Engines by 1975 as Air Pollution Curb," *NYT*, 4 August 1970.

8. "Senator Nelson Zeroes in on Polluter Number One: The Internal Combustion Engine," WITI-TV editorial no. 2396, 24 August 1970, Nelson Senate Papers; AP, "Nelson Plan for Low Polluting Auto Engine Called Premature," *Merrill (Wis.) Daily Herald*, 6 August 1970; "Clearing the Air," *The Paper* (Oshkosh, Wis.), 15–16 August 1970; Henry Ford II, "Five Who Care," *Look*, 21 April 1970.

9. "Milestones in Auto Emissions Control," EPA Fact Sheet OMS-12, August 1994; GAN, interview by author, 24 June 1999.

10. "National Environmental Education Act of 1990," http://www.sierra club.org; GAN, interview by author, 9 January 1993.

11. Nelson Environmental Record, Nelson Senate Papers; *Encyclopedia Britannica*, http://www.britannica.com, s.v. "Ecology."

12. J. Sykes, *Proxmire*, 218–25; Erwin Knoll, "Report from Washington," *CT*, 7 December 1970; GAN interview by author, 24 June 1999.

13. EPA, History Office, Timeline 1970–79; Shabecoff, *Fierce Green Fire*, 130; EPA, press release, 31 December 1972.

14. R. Sykes, "Nelson Report"; Leon G. Billings, remarks at "A Gala for Gaylord," Washington, D.C., 13 April 2000; John W. Kole, "Still Too Many Tax Dodges: Nelson," *MJ*, 31 January 1971; "Pollution Politics," *New Republic*, 31 October 1970.

15. R. Sykes, "Nelson Report"; McGovern, interview by author.

16. *Congressional Record*, 92d Cong., 1st sess., 117, pt. 1:535–38.

17. "Legislative Memo, 92d Congress, Nelson Environment Record," Nelson Senate Papers.

18. Ibid.; UPI, "Senate Accepts Nelson's 'Weather War' Ban," *CT*, 29 July 1972.

19. "Nelson 'Perfect' on Ecology," *CT,* 21 October 1972.

20. AP, "Town Puts Energy into Saving It," *CT,* 11 April 1973; AP, "Nelson Sees Future Gasoline Price Raise," *WSJ,* 11 April 1973; UPI, "Nelson Urges National Council to Spur Energy Conservation," *WSJ,* 12 April 1973.

21. AP, "Nelson Sees End of Era As Energy Crisis Grows," *CT,* 12 November 1973; "Energy Crisis Paradoxes," *CT,* 13 November 1973.

22. Harry Ernst, "U.S. Strip Mining Control Sought," *Charleston (W.Va.) Gazette,* 27 October 1965; Nelson press release, 10 September 1973, Nelson Senate Papers; "Strip Mine Compromise," *CT,* 5 December 1974.

23. Rocky Barker, "Cecil Andrus Knew How to Take a Stand," *High Country News,* 20 February 1995.

24. *The Superfund Progress Report,* EPA 540-R-98-044, October 1998.

25. AP, "House Approves Nelson's Bill to Protect St. Croix," *CT,* 11 December 1980; "Nelson Climaxes Great Record," *CT,* 12 December 1980.

Chapter 32. A Lasting Legacy

1. AP, "A Nice Guy Like Me," *WSJ,* 16 June 1974.

2. Donald Pfarrer, "Nelson Aiming at Pragmatist Image," *MJ,* 25 May 1980; Richard Bradee, "Nelson Had Sensed 'Something Wrong,'" *MS,* 6 November 1980.

3. Donald Pfarrer, "Kasten's Bid for Senate to Focus on 'Nelson Gap,'" *MJ,* 10 September 1980; Kenneth R. Lamke, "Kasten Needs to Boost Support from Outstate to Defeat Nelson," *MS,* 11 September 1980.

4. Daniel P. Hanley Jr., "Nelson Is No Friend of Business, Kasten Says," *MJ,* 21 September 1980; "Nelson Record Embroiled in Tiff," *MJ,* 23 September 1980.

5. Donald Pfarrer, "Kasten, Nelson Toss Harsh Words in Debate on Their Performance," *MJ,* 27 September 1980; AP, "Kasten Says Nelson's Ideas Are 'Worn Out,'" *WSJ,* 28 September 1970.

6. Kenneth R. Lamke, "Nelson Preparing for Hard Fight at Polls," *MS,* 4 October 1980.

7. Ward Sinclair, "Energized Nelson Runs Harder for Re-election Than Ever Before," *WP,* reprinted in *CT,* 20 October 1980; Phil Haslanger, "Nelson-Kasten Race Is Now a Shootout," *CT,* 6 October 1980; John Patrick Hunter, "Nelson: A Giant Falls," *CT,* 10 November 1980; Mondale, interview by author; Kenneth R. Lamke, "Candidates Given Advice," *MS,* 20 October 1980.

8. Donald Pfarrer, "Nelson Hard to Get Mad At," *MJ,* 23 October 1980; Gottlieb, interview by author.

9. Paul Fanlund, "Nelson Enjoys Life on Sidelines," *WSJ,* 2 March 1986.

10. Eagleton quote from "Gaylord Nelson: A Profile," Wisconsin Public Television, 22 April 1990; Dorothy Austin, "Mrs. Nelson Calm in Defeat," *MS,* 6 November 1980; John Patrick Hunter, "Nelson Family Finds Loss Didn't

Crush the 'Old Man,'" *CT*, 15 November 1980; Tony Kornheiser, "18 Years Led Friend, Foe to Admire Nelson," *WP*, reprinted in *MJ*, 16 November 1980.

11. Frank A. Aukofer, "Nelson 'in Debt' to Kasten," *MJ*, 7 July 1985; Mondale, interview by author.

12. GAN, "A Veteran Senator Comes to Terms with His Gravest Fear: Defeat at the Polls," *People*, 6 April 1981; Austin, "Mrs. Nelson."

13. Tom Fischer-Smith, "Nelson Content on Sidelines," *Appleton Post-Crescent*, 21 April 1988.

14. Shabecoff, *Fierce Green Fire*, 257. Another Shabecoff book, *Earth Rising* (Washington, D.C.: Island Press, 2000), traces the history of the environmental movement and describes the challenge to the movement in the twenty-first century.

15. GAN, "The Environmental Future: How Do We Get There from Here?" 22 April 2000, essay issued for Earth Day, posted on Negative Population Growth Web site, http://www.npg.org/forums/forum_enviro.htm.

16. GAN, interview by author, 2 June 2000; GAN, preface, *A New Ethic for a New Earth*, ed. Glenn C. Stone (Andover, Conn.: Faith-Man-Nature Group, National Council of Churches, 1971); Aldo Leopold, *A Sand County Almanac* (New York: Ballantine Books, 1970), 258, 240.

17. Mason, "Interview."

18. Shabecoff, *Earth Rising*, 9.

19. "Remarks by the President in Presentation of the Presidential Medal of Freedom," White House, 29 September 1995; "Milestones" and "Leaders," *Milwaukee Journal Sentinel*, 30 December 1999.

20. Kornheiser, "18 Years."

21. GAN, interview by author, 19 July 1993.

Bibliography

Adamany, David W. "1960 Election in Wisconsin." Master's thesis, University of Wisconsin, 1963.

Anson, Robert Sam. *McGovern: A Biography*. New York: Holt, Rinehart & Winston, 1972.

Austin, Anthony. *The President's War: The Story of the Tonkin Gulf Resolution and How the Nation Was Trapped in Vietnam*. New York: Lippincott, 1971.

Austin, H. Russell. *The Wisconsin Story: The Building of a Vanguard State*. Rev. ed. Milwaukee: Milwaukee Journal Co., 1973.

Bayley, Edwin R. *Joe McCarthy and the Press*. Madison: University of Wisconsin Press, 1981.

Berman, William C. *William Fulbright and the Vietnam War: The Dissent of a Political Realist*. Kent, Ohio: Kent State University Press, 1988.

Brokaw, Tom. *The Greatest Generation*. New York: Random House, 1998.

Buenker, John D. *The History of Wisconsin*. Vol. 4, *The Progressive Era, 1893–1914*. Madison: State Historical Society of Wisconsin, 1998.

Carson, Rachel. *Silent Spring*. New York : Houghton Mifflin, 1962.

Christiansen, Ruth Bunker, comp. *Polk County Place Names and Fact Book*. Frederic, Wis.: [Christiansen], 1975.

Conover, Richard A. "Wisconsin's Conservation Land Acquisition Program: A Study of Natural Resource Policy-Making." Ph.D. diss., Colorado State University, Fort Collins, 1974.

Dougherty, Richard. *Goodbye, Mr. Christian: A Personal Account of McGovern's Rise and Fall*. Garden City, N.Y.: Doubleday, 1973.

Ehrlich, Paul R. *The Population Bomb*. New York: Ballantine, 1968.

Eisele, Albert. *Almost to the Presidency*. Blue Earth, Minn.: Piper Co., 1972.

Epstein, Leon D. *Politics in Wisconsin*. Madison: University of Wisconsin Press, 1958.

Evjue, William T. *A Fighting Editor*. Madison: Capital Times, 1968.

Glad, Paul. W. *The History of Wisconsin*. Vol. 5, *War, a New Era, and Depression, 1914–1940*. Madison: State Historical Society of Wisconsin, 1990.

Halberstam, David. *The Best and the Brightest*. New York: Random House, 1969.

Haney, Richard C. *A History of the Democratic Party of Wisconsin, 1949–1989*. Madison: Democratic Party of Wisconsin, 1989.

Hart, Gary. *Right from the Start: A Chronicle of the McGovern Campaign*. New York: Quadrangle, 1973.

Huffman, Thomas R. *Protectors of the Land and Water: Environmentalism in Wisconsin, 1961–1968.* Chapel Hill: University of North Carolina Press, 1994.

Johnson, Roger T. *Robert M. La Follette Jr. and the Decline of the Progressive Party in Wisconsin.* Madison: State Historical Society of Wisconsin, 1964.

Jordahl, Harold C., Jr. *County Forests in Transition: An Account of the Wisconsin County Forest Crop Revolt, 1960–1963.* Madison: University of Wisconsin–Extension, 1984.

———. *A Unique Collection of Islands: The Influence of History, Politics, Policy and Planning on the Establishment of the Apostle Islands National Lakeshore.* Madison: Department of Urban and Regional Planning, University of Wisconsin–Extension, 1994.

Karamanski, Theodore J. *Saving the Saint Croix: An Administrative History of the Saint Croix National Scenic Riverway.* National Park Service, Midwest Region, 1993.

Kennedy, Robert F. *Thirteen Days: A Memoir of the Cuban Missile Crisis.* New York: W. W. Norton, 1969.

La Follette, Robert M. *La Follette's Autobiography : A Personal Narrative of Political Experiences.* Madison: University of Wisconsin Press, 1982.

Leopold, Aldo. *A Sand County Almanac: With Essays on Conservation from "Round River."* New York: Ballantine, 1970.

Lippman, Theo, Jr. *Senator Ted Kennedy: The Career behind the Image.* New York: W. W. Norton, 1976.

MacPherson, Myra. *The Power Lovers: An Intimate Look at Politics and Marriage.* New York: G. P. Putnam, 1975.

Maney, Patrick J. *"Young Bob" La Follette: A Biography of Robert M. La Follette, Jr., 1895–1953.* Columbia: University of Missouri Press, 1978.

Mann, Robert. *Legacy to Power: Senator Russell Long of Louisiana.* New York: Paragon House, 1992.

Maxwell, Robert S. *La Follette and the Rise of the Progressives in Wisconsin.* Madison: State Historical Society of Wisconsin, 1956.

McGovern, George. *Grassroots: The Autobiography of George McGovern.* New York: Random House, 1977.

McPherson, Harry. *A Political Education.* Boston: Houghton Mifflin, 1988.

Morrow, E. Frederic. *Forty Years a Guinea Pig.* New York: Pilgrim Press, 1980.

Nelson, Gaylord A. *America's Last Chance.* Waukesha, Wis.: Country Beautiful, 1970.

Nelson, Gaylord A., with Susan Campbell and Paul Wozniak. *Beyond Earth Day: Fulfilling the Promise.* Madison: University of Wisconsin Press, 2002.

Nesbit, James. *Wisconsin: A History.* Madison: University of Wisconsin Press, 1973.

O'Brien, Michael. *McCarthy and McCarthyism in Wisconsin.* Columbia: University of Missouri Press, 1980.

Reedy, George. *Lyndon B. Johnson: A Memoir.* New York: Andrews and McMeel, 1982.

Reeves, Thomas C. *The Life and Times of Joe McCarthy: A Biography.* New York: Stein and Day, 1982.

Reuss, Henry S. *When Government Was Good: Memories of a Life in Politics.* Madison: University of Wisconsin Press, 1999.

Rogers, Marion Lane. *Acorn Days: The Environmental Defense Fund and How It Grew.* New York: Environmental Defense Fund, 1990.

Shabecoff, Philip. *A Fierce Green Fire: The American Environmental Movement.* New York: Hill and Wang, 1993.

———. *Earth Rising: American Environmentalism in the Twenty-First Century.* Washington, D.C.: Island Press, 2000.

Shulman, Jeffrey, and Teresa Rogers. *Gaylord Nelson: A Day for the Earth.* Frederick, Md.: Twenty-First Century Books, 1992.

Sorensen, Theodore C. *Kennedy.* New York: Harper and Row, 1965.

Strober, Gerald S., and Deborah H. Strober. *Let Us Begin Anew: An Oral History of the Kennedy Presidency.* New York: HarperCollins, 1993.

Sykes, Jay G. *Proxmire.* Washington, D.C.: Robert B. Luce, 1972.

Sykes, Richard. "Gaylord Nelson Report." In Ralph Nader Congress Project, *Citizens Look at Congress,* vol. 9. Washington, D.C.: Grossman, 1972.

Thompson, William F. *The History of Wisconsin.* Vol. 6, *Continuity and Change, 1940–1965.* Madison: State Historical Society of Wisconsin, 1988.

Tuchman, Barbara. *The March of Folly: From Troy to Vietnam.* New York: Ballantine, 1984.

VanDeMark, Brian. *Into the Quagmire: Lyndon Johnson and the Escalation of the Vietnam War.* New York: Oxford University Press, 1991.

Voorhis, Jerry. *The Strange Case of Richard Milhous Nixon.* New York: Paul S. Eriksson, 1972.

Vukelich, George. *North Country Notebook.* Madison, Wis.: North Country Press, 1987.

Ware, John M., ed. *A Standard History of Waupaca County, Wisconsin: An Authentic Narrative of the Past, with Particular Attention to the Modern Era in the Commercial, Industrial, Educational, Civic and Social Development.* 2 vols. Chicago: Lewis Publishing, 1917.

Weil, Gordon L. *The Long Shot: George McGovern Runs for President.* New York: W. W. Norton, 1973.

White, Theodore H. *The Making of the President 1960.* New York: Atheneum, 1962.

———. *The Making of the President 1972.* New York: Atheneum, 1973.

Windchy, Eugene G. *Tonkin Gulf.* Garden City, N.Y.: Doubleday, 1971.

Wisconsin Citizens' Committee on McCarthy's Record. *The McCarthy Record.* Morris H. Rubin, ed. Madison: 1952.

Wisconsin Legislative Reference Bureau, comp. *Wisconsin Blue Book*. Madison: 1964- .

Wisconsin Legislative Reference Library, comp. *Wisconsin Blue Book*. Madison: 1862-1963.

Writers' Program of the Work Projects Administration in Wisconsin. *Wisconsin: A Guide to the Badger State*. New York: Duell, Sloan and Pierce, 1941.

Index